Women, Music, Culture

Women, Music, Culture: An Introduction is an undergraduate textbook on the contributions of women in music. Covering the major historical art-music periods as well as a number of popular and world music styles, it uses a wide variety of musical examples to bring biographical and historical information to life. Students are challenged to actively engage with the material, and to think critically about the power of perspective in historical narrative. Guided Listening Experiences teach students how to listen and analyze numerous styles and genres, from the sonata form of a Fanny Mendelssohn Hensel trio to the interplay of musician, space, and reverberation in Pauline Oliveros' "Lear," or the cyclical harmonic progression of a Bessie Smith blues song. Critical Thinking questions throughout the textbook reinforce main points and actively engage readers in considering issues such as gender and control in music, how spiritual tradition is intertwined with music, and how women in music are perceived cross-culturally.

Women, Music, Culture: An Introduction examines a community of women involved in the world of music, including composers, producers, consumers, performers, technicians, mothers, educators, and listeners.

Features

- **Focus** sections explain genres and compositional processes
- Over fifty **Guided Listening Experiences** provide analytical and formal references
- Audio CD with select musical examples
- Includes **Questions for Critical Thinking and Discussion**, **Ideas for Further Research**, and a running glossary
- Companion website with interactive quizzes for students, links to audio and video materials, flashcards, PowerPoint® slides, bonus listening guides, and a test bank for instructors

Julie C. Dunbar teaches music history, music appreciation, and instrumental music education at Edgewood College in Madison, Wisconsin, where she also conducts instrumental ensembles. Her research and past publications focus on music in sociocultural contexts as well as historical issues in music education.

Women, Music, Culture

An Introduction

Julie C. Dunbar

Edgewood College

NEW YORK AND LONDON

First published 2011
by Routledge
711 Third Avenue, 8th Floor, New York, NY 10017

Simultaneously published in the UK
by Routledge
2 Park Square, Milton Park, Abingdon, Oxon OX14 4RN

Routledge is an imprint of the Taylor & Francis Group, an informa business

Typeset in Stone Serif by
Florence Production Ltd, Stoodleigh, Devon, UK
Printed and bound in the United States of America on acid-free paper by
Edwards Brothers, Inc.

Library of Congress Cataloging in Publication Data
Dunbar, Julie C.
Women, music, culture: an introduction/Julie C. Dunbar.
p. cm.
Includes index.
1. Women musicians—Textbooks. 2. Feminism and music—Textbooks. 3. Gender identity in music—Textbooks. 4. Women composers—Textbooks. 5. Music—Social aspects—Textbooks.
I. Title.
ML82.D86 2011
780.82—dc22 2010027315

ISBN13: 978–0–415–87562–2 (hbk)
ISBN13: 978–0–415–87563–9 (pbk)
ISBN13: 978–0–203–83477–0 (ebk)

To Ron, Katie, Jacob, and Michaela,
to the Schaaf and Dunbar families,
and to God

Contents

Guided Listening Experiences Summary

Focus Topics Summary

Preface

WHY WAS THIS BOOK WRITTEN?

Interest in a topic often comes from personal experience. As a former trumpet player and as a conductor of collegiate instrumental ensembles, I have lived in a minority world as a woman. Despite this, I spent the early years of my teaching career handing down a musical story that greatly ignored the achievements of women *and* the historical issues that impacted (and often limited) their work. My excuse might seem weak, but it was practical. There were no materials on the undergraduate market that provided the kinds of engaging experiences that were available in traditional musicology and music appreciation textbooks. Like many professors who eventually opted to write a separate course on "women in music," I leaned heavily on research that had been produced since the 1980s. As much as that work enriched my teaching, I still faced the challenge of finding supporting materials that my *students* could grasp. I tried giving them research excerpts, but most of the material was written at a graduate level and contained sophisticated musical analyses that proved inaccessible. On top of that, the material was scattered throughout scholarly journals and books, and it took a lot of time to pull together recordings of the works that were referenced. Along with having to figure out how to provide student access to listening examples, I had to piece together a reading packet. I kept wishing that *someone* would write an undergraduate textbook. In the end, I decided that such a book was long overdue, and began my work. Standing on the shoulders of a community of scholars who had produced the best research in the field, I created an engaging, referenced textbook that undergraduates, including non-music majors, could use.

Women, Music, Culture: An Introduction asks students to think deeply and differently about their personal musical experiences as well as the musical world that is typically documented in undergraduate materials. This textbook encourages critical thinking skills by challenging students to question and assess material as they develop an increasingly sophisticated musical vocabulary. Unlike many "prepackaged" courses that lean heavily on rote memorization of dry facts, the ancillary materials also reflect my desire to make students grapple with important issues that impact their lives. Essay questions and reflection opportunities are interspersed with the more typical multiple-choice questions and electronic flashcards in the hope that students succeed in building lifelong skills and the ability to formulate well-informed perspectives.

ORGANIZATION

The organization of *Women, Music, Culture: An Introduction* changed several times throughout the review process. Some reviewers desired a chronological approach, but the majority encouraged me to create a thematic organization. You will note, at first glance, that the table of contents does reveal a topical design. Thematic design allows students to consider big-picture issues that span time and place, but also challenges them to question the separation of art and popular music in traditional musicology. At the same time, excellent instructors find a variety of effective ways to design course delivery. Beneath the surface, you will find opportunities to use alternative approaches. Instructors who prefer to present art music and popular separately, for example, can easily scramble the order of the major sections. Similarly, the components of a chronologically-based course are in place, and can be assembled as desired. Several possible course configurations are suggested in the instructor manual for those who seek ideas, as well as pedagogical pros and cons to each approach.

KEY FEATURES

In many ways, a good textbook is like a good teacher—flexible and responsive to the needs of the student. Here are ways in which *Women, Music, Culture: An Introduction* delivers a dynamic, interactive learning experience.

- **A complete listening experience**—A music textbook needs to include ample musical examples, not just biographical detail. This textbook resembles other collegiate music textbooks on today's market in its use of ancillary materials and listening guides. It is an important step forward in the scholarly history of women in music. A much more diverse student population can now access the subject matter, and instructors who wish to open courses to non-music majors have workable material with which to work.
- **Listening guides**—Over fifty in-text listening experiences interconnect with topical materials, with additional listening guides available on the course website. The listening guides are designed with the non-

music reader in mind, but also provide music majors access to more extensive analyses via bibliographic references.

- **Flexible organization**—Each major section is topically focused to encourage students to make links between historical periods and intercultural situations. Instructors who prefer a sequential walk through history can easily create a chronological path of their own design without disrupting the flow of the material.
- **Pedagogical design**
  - — Introductory segments set the stage for each chapter.
  - — Closing summaries serve as a review, and additionally help students make connections to current music and issues of immediate relevance to them.
  - — Critical thinking exercises have been carefully developed in both prose sections and in end-of-chapter sections.
  - — Guided research projects further encourage students to question material, wrestle with issues, consider multiple perspectives, and apply their knowledge to new material.
  - — A "running glossary" places important terms in multiple chapters both to reinforce concepts and to allow professors and students to use the book flexibly. Placement of vocabulary definitions in the margins encourages immediate application of key terms.
  - — "Focus" sections explain genres and compositional processes for readers with limited musical knowledge, allowing students to use or omit those sections according to their various musical backgrounds.
  - — For students who read music, scores for several of the guided listening experiences are available in two anthologies edited by James Briscoe. These include the *Contemporary Anthology of Music by Women* (Indiana University Press, 1997) and the *New Historical Anthology of Music by Women* (Indiana University Press, 2004).

ANCILLARIES

- A CD packaged with the book contains a sampling of musical material presented throughout the text. The eleven tracks on the disc include field recordings as well as works that are difficult for students to access by other means. Because it is so critical that students listen to the music and not just read about it, I wanted to be sure that they could access these works.

- An i-Tunes playlist includes an additional 40 tracks that can be conveniently accessed on the companion website. Students may already have access to certain popular music tracks, and instructors usually pick and choose from listening lists. The option to choose what is needed offers the most flexibility in the overall price of the book and recordings. It also negates the necessity of permission costs that would have greatly increased the price of the textbook.
- The companion website is located at: www.routledge.com/textbooks/9780415875639. This is an excellent resource, and includes the following features:
  - Links to interactive websites and music video clips to bring the performed art of music to life.
  - Flashcards with definitions to help with exam preparation.
  - PowerPoint slides for each chapter to introduce materials and help with review.
  - An iTunes playlist to conveniently direct students to recordings for guided listening experiences beyond those contained on the CD.
  - Supplementary guided listening experience charts to download for even more listening exercises.
  - Practice quizzes to help students with exam preparation.
  - An instructor test bank that includes both multiple choice and essay questions.

TO THE INSTRUCTOR

Many instructors have been waiting a long time for a textbook on women in music, and some may be expecting inclusion of all women they consider to be "major" composers. It is important to note that this textbook is not intended to be an encyclopedic collection of composers and works. Indeed, many professors of "women in music" courses decry the "great composer" approach for good reason, as there is much more to the musical world than the commitment of notes to a page. Instead, readers will find a textbook that challenges students to consider a broader view, including discussion of women as performers, conductors, listeners, producers, and teachers, as well as composers. Representative composers and works were carefully selected for pedagogical reasons, with guided listening experiences intended to address a wide variety of genres, music fundamentals, and forms. The selected works lend themselves well to critical thinking exercises and application to other music that students may encounter. When students are prepared in this manner, professors can easily enhance the experience with additional listening examples that reflect their unique interests.

While it was not possible to extensively cover world music topics, numerous references to intercultural gender roles in music remind readers to look beyond the Western canon. With a focused chapter on world music to set the stage, other examples include an extensive comparison between the Japanese geisha tradition and Renaissance court culture; parallel examinations of traditional instrumental ensembles such as the gamelan, West African drumming ensembles, and Western orchestras; the blending of Eastern and Western traditions in the work of such composers as Chen Yi; the blending of vernacular sources with traditional art music sources.

The guided listening experiences were carefully created to ensure understanding of music fundamentals and to ensure a balance of forms and genres. By the end of the text, students will have encountered major forms such as sonata, rondo, theme, and variations, as well as popular music forms such as 12-bar blues and 32-bar song form, among others. Most major genres covered in collegiate art music courses are included. A running timeline on the side of each art music and jazz chart indicates important formal events in minutes and seconds, but also provides aural guideposts for less-experienced musicians. Students are given specific listening tasks in each listening experience, as well as a big-picture sense of form, as appropriate.

My original dream was to include a multiple CD set with the text, but because of student budgets and the high cost of permission to use copyrighted music, it just was not realistic. Much of the work of women in art music rests in the post-1950 period, making it especially challenging to attain rights at an affordable level. Similarly, popular music permissions are extremely expensive. Instead, I placed less-accessible material on the CD for convenience, and created a digital playlist for selections that are readily available on iTunes. Additional guided listening experiences beyond the fifty included in the textbook are available on the website for those who wish to do more listening. It is my sincere hope that handling the recorded selections in this manner will make the textbook and recordings affordable while still delivering excellent content.

A SPECIAL NOTE TO STUDENTS

Women, Music, Culture: An Introduction allows you to examine assumptions made about music and musicians in culture, and to question the control of music that is preserved, distributed, and held in high regard. I hope the day will come when the work of women in music is adequately integrated into readily available materials, but that day has not yet arrived. Until then, it is my sincere hope that this textbook will allow you to access the world of music with greater vision, and to be in control of the knowledge needed to address issues of gender-based injustice.

Julie Dunbar, July 2010

Acknowledgments

I am grateful to many people who helped to make this book a reality. First, I thank the editors at Routledge who were willing to shepherd and promote this project, particularly Constance Ditzel and Denny Tek. Even yet, publishing an undergraduate textbook on women in music is a risk that not every publisher is willing to take, but without risk, true progress cannot take place. I am also grateful to the anonymous reviewers who helped to critique the book, as well as several reviewers who offered extensive advice along the way, including Jennifer Post, Music Instrument Museum, Phoenix, Arizona; Jacqueline Warwick, Dalhousie University, Canada; Elizabeth Hinkle-Turner, University of North Texas; and Susan Cook, University of Wisconsin. Your selfless dedication to the field is laudable, and your care made a tremendous difference in the outcome of this project. Thanks also to copy-editor Amanda Crook and project manager Rosie White of Florence Production Ltd for their thorough work and patience. I am also grateful to the students at Edgewood College who helped with photo research, graphic design, and notation work, including Lisa Kaminski, Jessica Kellogg, and Ryan Dolan, and to Jan Mailloux for editing. Certainly, this book would not have happened without the tremendous support of my Music Department colleagues, including administrative assistant Julia Melzer, and the faculty who not only covered a heavy workload in my absence but additionally helped to review material. I owe tremendous gratitude to professors Blake Walter, Beatriz Aguilar, and Albert Pinsonneault, and especially thank Blake Walter for reviewing guided listening charts. Finally, I cannot begin to express the outpouring of love and support that I have received from my family, Ron, Katie, Jacob, and Michaela Dunbar. This was a huge project, and you have helped in every imaginable way. Ron, you are so very humble, selfless, and gifted. Thank you, and I love you.

PART I

Telling Musical Stories

MISSING VOICES IN THE DOCUMENTATION OF MUSICAL TRADITIONS

INTRODUCTION TO PART I

TELLING MUSICAL STORIES

Missing Voices in the Documentation of Musical Traditions

In Western culture, people from the past become part of the present when they are brought to life on the pages of written history. In contrast, those who are not recognized in writing are often forgotten. As such, the focus of Part I is to examine the power of perspective, documentation, and publication in the shaping of cultural beliefs regarding women's roles in music. This segment of the text should provide the reader with a lens through which to view other historical trends, as well as some tools with which to assess gender representation in current written materials.

Along with introducing basic terminology and formats that will be used throughout the text, **Chapter 1** introduces a wide variety of genres in which women have been active participants. Examples taken from the worlds of art music, popular music, and jazz allow useful comparisons between art and popular music construction. The chapter also introduces a culturally based model that explains the role of perspective in determining what is deemed "worthy" of historical preservation.

In **Chapter 2**, the Judeo-Christian roots of historical music documentation are examined, focusing on the development of sacred genres that formed a cornerstone of the Western art music canon. Musicologists' tendency to legitimize music that was preserved via written methods is investigated, along with the inclination of authors to focus on public-sphere rituals that initially excluded women. The trajectory of the canon is followed by examining two twentieth-century works by women that represent opposite aesthetic ends of culturally defined gender spheres.

Chapter 3 reflects on the representation of women in the field of ethnomusicology, and includes an analysis of visual imagery in academic and popular music teaching materials. Although many world music traditions were originally preserved via aural tradition, academics in the "world music" arena replicated several trends in Western musicology that limited the reporting of women's roles, and these filtered into the mass music market. This included a focus on public-sphere rituals performed by men and the use of a presentation style that utilized analytical models. The chapter acknowledges the special issues that have sometimes precluded researchers from accessing the musical work of women, but also suggests some solutions. To help the reader better understand alternative presentation styles, interview data and storytelling narrative are included in this chapter, with a special focus on the often-forgotten musical role of mothers.

CHAPTER 1

Reflections on "Deep Listening" Exploring Music in Context

> *A frame can make or break a picture. So too with music; the "silence" frames the sound.*
> *Give enough time to the silences so that you can hear the message of the sound.*[1]
>
> Nadia Boulanger, Composer, Conductor, Educator

We live in a noisy world. For a quick reminder of your capacity to selectively listen, close your eyes and focus on the sounds that surround you at this moment. Alter your perception by listening intentionally to sounds produced by living things and sounds that are created via electricity; sounds that are musical and sounds that are irritating; sounds that are within you, and sounds that are external.[2] Many of us listen in the manner in which we read—selectively skimming information from an immense field of choices. But if we habitually avoid conscious listening experiences, we risk losing the chance to encounter the present, to connect deeply with ourselves and others, to hear the message of the sound.

Composer Pauline Oliveros' work with music and "deep listening," for which she has named a recording, a book, and even an institute, serves as a wonderful starting point for the task I hope to accomplish in this book. Long known as a leader in the field of experimental and electronic music, Oliveros' venture into the world of "deep listening" has encouraged people to mindfully listen—to perceive, analyze, interact, and connect with sound. For Oliveros, music is sometimes a "welcome by-product" of the deep listening experience. At the same time, perceptive listening can help the listener turn everyday sound into an **aesthetic experience** as well.[3]

AESTHETIC EXPERIENCE emotional and sometimes physiological response elicited by an artistic work

The aesthetic musical experience is powerful in and of itself, and we will explore it quite deeply in this book by listening intently, perceptively, and analytically. But music is also a barometer of culture, and an agent for change.

The aesthetic-cultural connection is forged strongly throughout the pages of this book, as narratives of women and music are discovered, examined, and created.

LISTENING EXPERIENCE: EXCERPT FROM *DEEP LISTENING*

> *Writing about music is like dancing about architecture.*
>
> Anonymous

This is an invitation to become an active participant as you journey through this book. Reading about music without listening to the music being discussed is surface-level skimming, and will not be very interesting. Dive in! This chapter presents four experiential musical exercises that will help you connect music with context. Using a three-step process, you will *listen* and *analyze* the musical experience using a musical vocabulary that will serve as a foundation for later work in the book. After deepening aesthetic understanding, we will turn to a *contextual discussion* to place each piece within a meaningful sociocultural framework. The discussion will not be the only way to contextualize the piece, but will lend insight into some of the ways in which narratives impact perception and receptivity to issues pertaining to women and music.

Listen

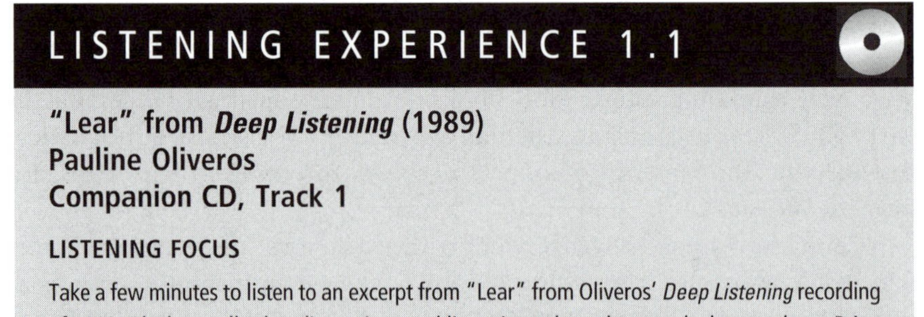

LISTENING EXPERIENCE 1.1

"Lear" from *Deep Listening* (1989)
Pauline Oliveros
Companion CD, Track 1

LISTENING FOCUS

Take a few minutes to listen to an excerpt from "Lear" from Oliveros' *Deep Listening* recording of 1989. Block out all other distractions and listen intently to the sounds that you hear. Bring your mind back to the musical sounds if your attention begins to diminish. After you have listened deeply, continue with the reflections that follow.

How was the experience? Did extraneous sounds interfere or become part of the musical soundscape? Listen one more time and add an analytical layer to the experience; imagine how and where the sounds were created, and then note your response to the excerpt, including your emotional reaction to the overall experience.

Figure 1.1
Pauline Oliveros.
Source: Photo by Pieter Kers, courtesy of Pauline Oliveros

Analyze

Musically, "Lear" is an excellent study in **timbre** and features an absence of strict **form**. Oliveros and two other performer/composers used rope to lower an accordion, sea shells, a trombone, a garden hose, didgeridoos, and themselves into a deep, abandoned cistern in the Seattle, Washington area. In a space that once held two million gallons of water, the three composers began to experiment with the forty-five-second reverberation time of their acoustical chamber, creating sounds that almost seem to be electronically produced. With no alternating current available, the musicians recorded their session using battery-powered equipment. Listening and reacting to one another as the sound interconnected with the space was challenging and rewarding. Not only was the sound amplified, but it continually surrounded the composers and melded into subsequent sounds that the composers produced in response to the reverberated tones. According to Oliveros, the space inside of the cistern was, in effect, "an instrument played simultaneously by all three composers."[4]

TIMBRE
the characteristic quality of sound that distinguishes one voice or musical instrument from another; "tone color"

FORM
the way in which segments are structured in a unified whole; a "blueprint" for the structure of the piece

Contextual Discussion: Was It Music?

Was "Lear" music to you? Trying to define music with words is as elusive as trying to describe the smell of your favorite food or the touch of water; the splendor of the sensory experience is largely found in its ineffability. At the same time, it is helpful to think about why people consider some sound "music" and other sound "noise." Further, it is important to investigate how sound that *is* labeled music is further labeled "good" and "bad," "worthy of study," or "trivial." Only then can one begin to assess how women fit into the broader musical picture.

Music is often defined as humanly organized sound, and although that definition negates the musicality of spontaneous laughter, birdsong, and other natural sounds that many composers embrace, it will initially serve to help us think about *how* and *why* humans organize sound and call it music. The human creator of music initially decides how to balance unity and variety of sound to generate something that is perceived as music versus something that is perceived as noise. Imagine sound encounters along a continuum where extreme unity and extreme variety exist on each end. At some point along that continuum most listeners find a balance that equals a musical experience (see Figure 1.2).

To experiment with this concept, try tapping a pencil on this book using a steady beat for a period of one to two minutes. At what point is this a musical experience, and at what point does it become noise? Now try tapping the pencil really hard once, followed by three soft taps. *Tap* tap tap tap. Continue this pattern for thirty seconds. Did the pencil tapping become music? If you continued, at what point would it become noise again?

The variety end of the spectrum operates in much the same manner as the unity end: too much might be considered noise. Consider a child who sits at a piano and randomly strikes the keys. You can try this without a keyboard by singing a wide variety of pitches with your voice. Only when you begin to formulate repeated rhythmic or melodic patterns is it likely that your "performance" will be perceived as music by a majority of listeners. Think again about "Lear," and try to describe your reaction to it in these terms.

The concept of balancing unity and variety can be applied in a broader sense when one considers how the aesthetic impact of a work is often lost upon repeated hearings. Almost all listeners will have had the experience of

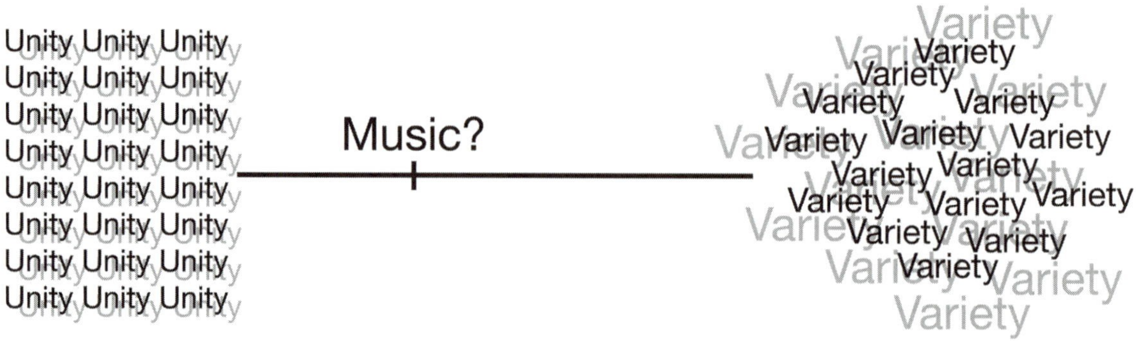

Figure 1.2
Noise music model.

growing to like a Top-40 song that has been repeatedly "plugged" by a disc jockey, only to find it really dull after hearing it a few too many times. The varied shifts in melodic structure, harmony, and rhythm—initially perceived as desirable—eventually become too familiar. At some point the musical work is perceived as a unified whole until it approaches the realm of noise.

Just as individuals vary in their perception of what constitutes music, so they differ in assessing musical value. What is beautiful and powerful to one person may be ugly or trivial to the next. One way in which musicologists have historically debated and assigned musical significance is via separation of art and popular music into spheres deemed "worthy" and "not worthy" of study. Although the line that separates art and popular music is admittedly artificial and often blurred, it will serve as a starting point for examining how music is given relative value. To begin the examination of art and popular music spheres, it is important to understand the framework utilized in this text.

A SOCIOCULTURAL MODEL FOR STUDYING MUSIC

Music is multi-faceted and is studied from a variety of perspectives. The scientist looks to sound waves and acoustics; the mathematician looks at numerical sequences and patterns; the political scientist studies music as a vehicle for protest; the sociologist studies ways in which music reflects and transforms culture. Even musicians differ in their approaches, as some favor a theoretical analysis while others look at overall aesthetic issues, for example. This text utilizes a model that places a music analysis method alongside a sociocultural analysis method to deepen the reader's examination of interactions between music and culture (see Figure 1.3). We will examine and analyze music utilizing musical elements such as **melody**, form, **rhythm**, timbre, and **harmony**, and then, with a deeper understanding of the inner workings of music, we will use the culture side of the model to discover how non-musical issues intersect with music. The model suggests that music and culture have a symbiotic relationship: music reflects and shapes culture; culture reflects and shapes music.

MELODY
a sequence of single tones, usually unified in a system such as a key or mode; the "tune" of a work

RHYTHM
the time-oriented organization of silence and sound

HARMONY
two or more tones sounding simultaneously

To experiment with the model, try a brief exercise pertaining to perceptions and stereotypes about audiences in popular music venues. Borrow from the sociocultural side of the model and consider how *belief systems* might impact the type of live performance one attends, and how non-musical assumptions can become associated with particular genres. To assist with this experiment, use the following list of *sociocultural descriptors* that help shape belief systems, and describe the performers and audience members you envision at a heavy metal concert: *age, gender, educational background, socio-economic status, geographical location, race, ethnicity*. Now apply the list to folk

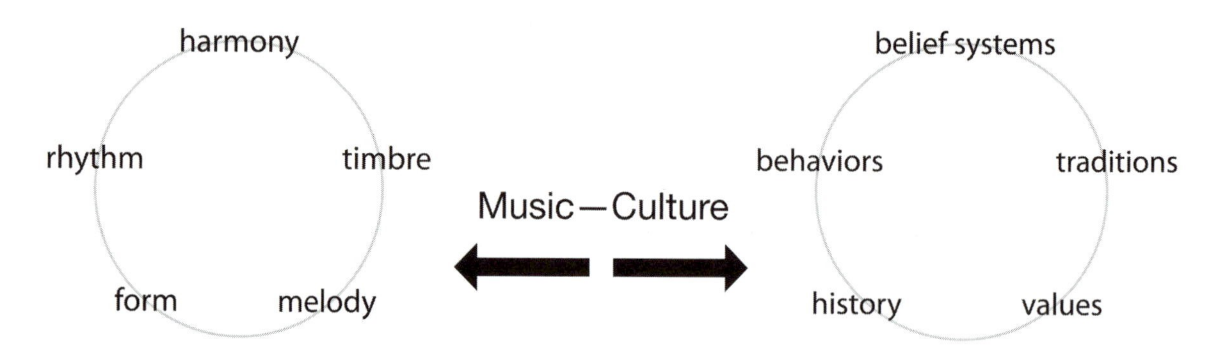

Figure 1.3
Sociocultural model.

music performers and their audience. Did your assumptions differ in the two settings? Finally, go through the list one more time and define *yourself*. In which ways did your own belief system impact your assessment?

Before leaving the model, consider musical elements that might impact non-musical perceptions. What is it about heavy metal *music* that might be associated with the performers and audience that you imagined? And folk music? For example, electrifying a guitar (and subsequently changing the timbre and volume of the instrument) has historically led to significant changes in perception about the guitarist when it comes to gender expectations. As the text progresses, there will be frequent explanations of musical elements as they intersect with non-musical associations.

LISTENING EXPERIENCE: "UNBREAK MY HEART"

Now let's take a former Top-40 hit and analyze it using both sides of the model. Toni Braxton's 1996 single "Unbreak My Heart," written by Diane Warren, is an accessible popular music selection to use for an initial elements-of-music exercise. Musical form is a good starting point for analysis because it represents the "big picture" of a musical creation. It is, in a sense, a blueprint for presenting the musical whole to the listener. The concepts of unity and variety that were previously discussed can also be applied quite easily here.

Listen

See **Listening Experience 1.2.**

Analyze

Verse/chorus form provides a fairly even balance of unity and variety in this song, but you probably noticed a brief section that did not fit the A/B format. Many popular songwriters add a bridge to create a slight variation in the formal structure of the work. If we label the bridge as "C," the form might be labeled as follows:

Introduction A B A B C B Ending

As simple as it is to add a bridge to a popular song, the small element of variety is welcomed by listeners. The bridge also serves as a great set-up for the return of familiar, earlier material at the work's close.

LISTENING EXPERIENCE 1.2

"Unbreak my Heart" (1996)
Written by Diane Warren, performed by Toni Braxton
Playlist

LISTENING FOCUS

Rather than just "hearing" this pop song as you might do while concentrating on a non-musical task, listen perceptively by doing an introductory form exercise. Musicians traditionally label formal sections with letters to indicate areas of musical repetition and contrast. A verse/chorus format would thus be labeled A B A B, depending on the number of verse/chorus repetitions. After listening for the brief introduction in this song, begin to label the form using letters to represent major sections of the work. Every time you hear major segments of new material, use a new letter (C, D, and so on.) After you determine the form, continue with the reflections that follow.

Contextual Discussion: Extra-musical Connotations

Like all popular songs, "Unbreak My Heart" eventually fell off the charts, but it remains the second biggest-selling single by a female artist in Billboard history. We have noted that the form is somewhat simple, and other than the possible interest of Braxton's rich contralto voice (showcased by Warren with an extremely low vocal range in the verses) there appears to be nothing overly remarkable about the song compositionally. What else might have contributed to the song's tremendous popularity? We can borrow from the sociocultural side of the model to examine possible answers.

Many years ago I asked a group of students to demonstrate the importance of context in studying music traditions. A woman stood before the class and asked if her demonstration could be a dance, and as the introduction to "Unbreak My Heart" floated across the room, the forty-something single mother of five children closed her eyes and withdrew into another place as she enacted a slow, sad, powerful story with her face and body. When the music was over she opened her eyes, and the classroom fell into stunned silence. The lyrics were about her life, and the power of the lyrics came alive via the conduit of music. Her personal *history* impacted her reaction to Braxton's performance, and my perception and reaction was altered too.

As an R&B/soul singer whose roots in church music are evident in her vocal sound and expression, Toni Braxton follows a blues *tradition* as well, by effectively expressing the hardships of women via song. The twentieth-century female blues singer had a profound role in communicating social messages to the community-at-large through musical performance. To ignore the lyrics in the blues tradition is to ignore the heart of the genre, for one of the goals of the blues is to express what ethnomusicologist Jeff Titon calls "truth." Truth is not necessarily the autobiography of the singer's life but rather is that "gut level" feeling that the listener gets when a performer delivers a message that resonates with the audience.[5] Braxton may or may not have brought a personal history of hardship into her musical expression on this recording, but what matters is that her message connects with the listener. While this is not a blues song, Braxton is aligned with women blues artists who made themselves famous for their ability to interpret music and convey it effectively to an audience, eliciting emotional response.

Quite a different historical issue that has endured for woman singers is that of constant association with maintaining a visual image. Using the *values* segment of the sociocultural model, let us briefly introduce the topic of non-musical expectations for women performers in the late twentieth century, and then follow with further discussion later in the text.

Like most popular music marketed since the early 1980s, "Unbreak My Heart" was promoted with a video that has been seen by over two million people on YouTube alone, and those viewings began nearly a decade after the song was on the charts. Viewers not only heard Toni Braxton sing her hit song, but also watched her star in a music video that told one specific story that the viewer may or may not have imagined upon only hearing the lyrics sung. Readers can probably find the video fairly easily yet today and, if you do, you will notice that throughout the four-and-a-half-minute song Braxton is shown in dozens of quickly changing scenes in continuous wardrobe change. Shown in revealing black clothing throughout most of the video, Braxton is displayed in everything from lingerie to swimming suits and is eventually shown in a shower scene that runs for over thirty seconds. Like many music videos, it is doubtful that the visual imagery had much to do with the thoughts and emotions that many listeners had prior to seeing the footage. Although the marketing of female singers has long been connected to the visual, the post-music television (MTV) era has been especially demanding for women in terms of presenting an image that meets a visual standard.

This excerpt from Braxton's Billboard biography shows how the marketing of women performers extends beyond the musical:

> Toni Braxton was one of the most popular and commercially successful female R&B singers of the '90s, thanks to her ability to straddle seemingly opposite worlds. Braxton was soulful enough for R&B audiences, but smooth enough for adult contemporary; sophisticated enough for adults, but sultry enough for younger listeners; strong enough in the face of heartbreak to appeal to women, but ravishing enough to nab the fellas.[6]

What are the non-musical values of the American popular music scene that make it difficult for many talented women to survive in the industry? For women in music, the study of music video is an entrance point to examining a variety of answers to that question.

LISTENING EXPERIENCE: "SCHWANENLIED"

Listen

One of our tasks in this section is to investigate similarities and differences between art song and popular **song**, both musically and culturally. The art song featured here is by nineteenth-century German composer Fanny Mendelssohn Hensel. Despite the seemingly trivial fact that listening examples two and three both are songs, it is significant to remember that for art *and* popular music the song **genre** has long rested in the female sphere. Hensel's *deviation* from societal expectations of her time is marked by her foray out of the realm of the private domain—her home—and into the public world of published song. Had this work not been published, Fanny Hensel's "Schwanenlied" most likely would have suffered the fate of many works composed by women in an era that lacked recording technology. (See **Listening Experience 1.3**, p. 12.)

SONG
musical work that is sung and has lyrics

GENRE
a classification or style; in music, could refer to any number of popular or art music styles such as rock, pop, songs, symphonies, opera

Analyze

Romantic-era **art song** typically featured one singer with a piano accompaniment in a duet-like setting in which the piano was no longer limited to strict accompaniment. Like the vocal line, the piano part would often musically depict the text, and the text was a critical third component of the genre. As is the case with blues-related texts, it is vital for listeners to understand art song texts if they are to experience the musical whole. Most poetry selected for art song was written by well-respected poets, and in the case of Romantic-era Germany, writers such as Johann Wolfgang von Göethe and

ART SONG
a song written by a trained composer to convey a specific artistic idea, as in projecting the mood and meaning of a poetic text

LISTENING EXPERIENCE 1.3

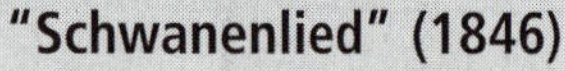

"Schwanenlied" (1846)
Fanny Mendelssohn Hensel
Score available in the *New Historical Anthology of Music by Women*
Playlist

LISTENING FOCUS

This listening experience includes a three-step process.

1. Listen carefully to Hensel's "Swan Song" and attempt to write the big-picture form using letters as you did for the Braxton example.
2. Focus on the singer's voice, and attempt to draw a diagram that shows the general shape of the melody as it rises and falls.
3. Read the analysis section for this work. Then, return to the guided listening chart (below) and listen one more time.

TIMED LISTENING GUIDE

0:00 Brief piano introduction

Verse One (translated from the original German)

0:02 **Phrase** One *A star falls down from its twinkling height,*
initial lulling rhythmic motive; wide-ranging melodic leaps

0:13 Phrase Two *It is the star of love that I see falling there.*
similar rhythmic style, new melodic material

0:25 Phrase Three *So much falls from the apple tree, from the white leaves;*
new melodic material again

0:36 Phrase Four *The teasing breezes come and urge on their game*
new melodic material

0:46 Phrase Four repeated
melodic leap and long melisma to musically depict the idea of "teasing breezes"

1:05 Piano interlude

Verse Two

1:15 Phrase One *The swan sings in the pond, and paddles up and down*
identical to phrase one, verse one

1:26 Phrase Two *And singing more and more gently, he disappears into the depths of the river*
initially identical to phrase two, verse one, but with complete pause in both piano and voice on "Fluthengrab" to musically depict "the depths of the river"; very soft

1:45 Phrase Three *It is so quiet and dark, scattered is leaf and blossom*
identical to phrase three, verse one

1:57 Phrase Four *The star has flickered into dust, the swan song has faded away.*
identical to phrase four, verse one

2:08 Phrase Four repeated *The star has flickered into dust, the swan song has faded away.*
as in verse one, with melodic leap and melisma

Heinrich Heine, were favored by composers such as Hensel. With her piano skills and her gift of lyricism, the art song genre showcased many of Fanny Hensel's greatest abilities.

PHRASE
a short, distinct part or passage; a musical "sentence"

The form featured in Hensel's composition is fairly simple and seems to indicate fewer areas of "big-picture" compositional variety than the Braxton/Warren tune. This song features two verses and no chorus, so if you labeled the form A A you captured it fairly well. Most experienced analysts would indicate A A to reflect the slight musical change in the second verse, a change that is noteworthy in terms of text depiction. Unlike the Braxton tune, "Schwanenlied" features subtle but deliberate rhythmic and melodic alteration to reflect the emotional meaning of the text, a technique known as **word painting**. To better understand this musical technique, look at Hensel's melodic contour and rhythmic text setting. Unlike the initial melodic line in "Unbreak My Heart," which was heavily centered on one pitch, Hensel's melody gently rises and falls against the backdrop of a smoothly rolling piano accompaniment to musically capture Heine's portrait of a swan moving gently on water. Also note how the singer portrays the text "the teasing breezes come and urge on their game" with a lift of the voice and **melismatic** melodic motion. (See Figure 1.4 for melodic comparison.)

WORD PAINTING
in texted works, using musical gestures or elements to reflect movement and emotion in the text

MELISMA
a succession of multiple pitches sung on a single syllable

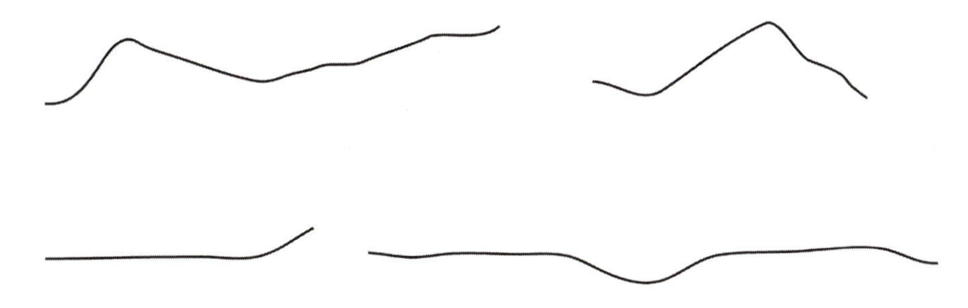

Figure 1.4
The opening melodic contour of Hensel's song, pictured above, compared to the opening measures of "Unbreak my Heart," underneath.

In the altered second verse, the composer places a fermata where the vocal and piano parts pause to represent a serious turn of events: the swan disappears into the depths of the river, still and dark. At the end of the poem, the swan song fades away with a diminuendo of the vocal and piano parts, metaphorically depicting the ancient story of the mute swan that sings one last beautiful song before it dies.[7] For a guided listening experience, return to the "Schwanenlied" listening experience table.

Contextual Discussion: "Specialists" and Their Work

"The art of music has always been the product of specialists,"[8] claimed Hermann Closson in a 1930 article in *Modern Music*, a journal sponsored by the League of Composers. Founded in 1923, the League promoted performances of new and innovative compositions in part because their members were experiencing a narrow following among listeners. Although they created performance settings in numerous intellectual venues such as universities, many of *Modern Music*'s writers did not express interest in expanding their audience beyond a select clientele, and rather bluntly declared the majority of the world unable to create, understand, or appreciate art music.[9] From their elitist standpoint, the group also omitted and dismissed women composers, sometimes quite directly. League member Aaron Copland, who eventually studied with French pedagogue Nadia Boulanger, was initially quite reluctant to do so, and echoed the common thought that women were not able to compose or teach composition: "No one to my knowledge had ever before thought of studying with a woman."[10]

Unlike the League of Composers, music educators of the same era believed that an educational campaign was the key to the general public accessing and appreciating art music. With the advent of the radio in American homes and schools in the 1930s, the educators had a tool for reaching everyone, and as they prepared listening lists and lesson plans on the works of Bach, Beethoven, and Wagner, they wrote enthusiastically about turning America into a nation of art music connoisseurs. In terms of gender inclusivity, though, this group failed as resoundingly as did the League of Composers, and the fact that art music cannot survive on commercial radio today might suggest that the music educators failed in their overall art music campaign as well. The debate between the composers and educators of that era regarding the general public's ability to create and appreciate art music is as alive today as it was then, and deserves our attention here.

The aesthetic experience that can result from listening to music is nearly as difficult to define as the term "music" itself, but for many art music consumers it is a desired outcome. The term aesthetic is often associated with "beauty," but aesthetic meaning is much deeper than that, and is characterized by a reaction to art that is based on perception of artistic elements and a subsequent cognitive-emotional reaction. Artistic works about war, for example, are rarely considered beautiful, but elicit emotionally powerful responses nonetheless. The aesthetic response is as difficult to measure as it is to define, but can range from physiological changes (such as accelerated heart rate and changes in respiration) to loss of attentional control—a feeling of being completely absorbed and emotionally elevated by the artistic experience, temporarily removed beyond the time and space of the performance setting.

What are the technical differences between art and popular music that cause debate regarding the average listener's ability to respond aesthetically to art music? Although the same musical building blocks are used in each sphere, it can be difficult for the beginning art music listener to perceive complex use of musical elements well enough to find satisfaction in the composer's manipulation of them. In terms of the interplay of unity and variety in form, for example, art music's basic use of form is not unlike popular music in many regards. But if popular music is a quick-read novel, art music might be considered an extensive "classic." Popular music themes usually emerge quickly, peak, and fade within three to four minutes, while art music often extends the musical experience, taking time to explore themes and ideas more deeply. Like walking through a house with many rooms (and perhaps a few mirrors), art music can lead the listener on an extended aural journey that includes secondary themes, transitions, and unexpected harmonic shifts. Proponents of aesthetic education claim that few listeners can grasp such complexity without formal instruction.[11]

This overly simple example holds up fairly well when comparing popular song form to large-scale art music forms such as those used in symphonies or concertos, but what about the three-minute art song that we just heard? The art music association of "Schwanenlied" can be viewed both in musical terms and as a product of social construction. Musically, "Schwanenlied" did not display extreme length or complexity of form, but it did present some understated musical detail that loses aesthetic meaning if the listener lacks the ability to understand Hensel's intent to dramatize Heine's text. Whether due to an inability to translate the language or to grasp the complexity of the poetry, the loss of the music-text connection results in only a surface-level aural experience.

It is also important to introduce the concept of social construction as it pertains to art music when we consider that Hensel's song, with performance roots in the domestic music scene of Romantic-era Berlin, now fully resides in the scholarly world of art music. In spite of her outstanding performing and compositional capabilities, an upper-middle-class woman in nineteenth-century Germany had an obligation to uphold family honor by remaining outside of the public domain as a musician. Hensel's usual performance venue was her home, and in that setting she both performed and entertained as per societal expectation. In this sense, she joined the ranks of many women who sang, played keyboard, and presumably wrote music that was not intended for widespread public consumption. How did her work move beyond the private domain?

For Hensel, the privilege of wealth and family connection allowed a private music education that elevated her potential and allowed her to achieve what subsequent generations of women also achieved when they finally had a chance to receive formal instruction: though performed in a domestic setting, Hensel's work was artistically on a par with well-known, musically educated composers of her time, most of whom were male. But the reconstruction of Hensel's work into the product of a specialist required more than ability.

Hensel's social class allowed her to gather a select, socially connected audience who could discuss, and thereby verbally disseminate, her work. This was not the domestic setting of the average Berliner, but rather a salon-series aimed at least in part to showcase Hensel's own ability. When Hensel stepped forward to publish, however, the composer decisively carried her work out of the private domain and into the wider world of preserved Western art music. If music from this era was to be known, revered, and perceived as the work of a specialist, publication was critical. "Schwanenlied" no longer resonates at Sunday afternoon domestic gatherings, but instead lives on in the concert hall, on commercial recordings, and on the pages of textbooks. Its aesthetic purpose has prevailed and its creator is becoming, at last, a "specialist."

LISTENING EXPERIENCE: "SWING SHIFT"

In the previous section we examined the aesthetic side of music: art for the sake of art. But for many listeners, the everyday value and joy of music is found in its "extra-musical" connections. Work, healing, and teaching are just some of the categories that fall under the auspices of **utilitarianism**—a functional "use" for music that is enhanced by the musical experience. Many utilitarian musical functions are strongly associated with women, but we will consider one that was traditionally connected with men when we investigate dance-band music of 1940s America. At the same time, we will consider how labeling this genre as merely utilitarian is a result of social construction connected with racism.

UTILITARIAN
stressing usefulness over aesthetic value

Listen

See **Listening Experience 1.4**.

Analyze

A typical jazz performance features alterations between full ensemble, sections within the ensemble, and soloists who **improvise** upon a melodic and harmonic foundation. In this short excerpt, a solo saxophonist quickly takes over after the ensemble opening and improvises to the accompaniment of a steady-driving bass and embellishments from the brass section. The entire saxophone section prevails next, and engages in a call-and-response dialogue with the brass until the saxophone soloist returns, again with brass accompaniment. The brass section takes the lead one more time, dialoguing with the saxophones once, and then again until the pianist takes over. With a kick of the drums, the saxes battle the brass one more time and end with a final unison scalar rip.

IMPROVISE
to compose, or simultaneously compose and perform, on the spur of the moment

LISTENING EXPERIENCE 1.4

"Swing Shift" (recorded live during Second World War Jubilee Session)
International Sweethearts of Rhythm
Playlist

LISTENING FOCUS

Rather than listening for large formal sections this time, try to imagine the band on stage, and outline a "play by play" description of who is performing. Your goal is to identify shifts between full sections and featured soloists. This recording is less than two minutes long and the section changes come quickly, so you may have to listen several times. Here is an opening statement to get you started:

Full band opens, followed by tenor sax solo break . . .

What an action-packed minute and a half! This recording of "Swing Shift" provides some good material for a speedy introduction to jazz concepts, but the brevity of the recording is perhaps the bigger story in the sense that it aurally represents the lack of press coverage that women jazz instrumentalists had throughout the twentieth century. After a short musical explanation that will be expanded upon in a subsequent chapter, we will briefly investigate the historical context of the recording in more depth, as well as the musicians whose collective story the recording cannot begin to capture.

Part of the general appeal of this selection is found in the fast **tempo**, but there is another rhythmic element of interest here as well. One of the greatest changes to overtake popular music in the twentieth century was the concept of **swing**. Swing literally turned the musical world around with its emphasis on beats two and four—a marked reversal from the emphasis on beat one that was evident in most popular music prior to the 1920s. Whether it is the toe-tapping feel of a John Philip Sousa march or the *oom* pa pa of a Tin Pan Alley hit such as "Take Me out to the Ballgame," an accent on beat one is an important aural reminder of a bygone era in popular music. The popular music world resoundingly embraced the rhythmic notion of swing, and although the **syncopated** elements of the rhythmic line have waxed and waned over time, a two-four **backbeat** remains the "backbone" of popular music across the globe.

TEMPO
the speed at which a work is performed

SWING
a style of jazz; characterized by the use of large bands, fast tempos, and written arrangements for ensemble playing

SYNCOPATE
to accent a note that falls between main beats

BACKBEAT
in popular music, a primary accent on the second and fourth beats of a four-beat measure

Jazz is musically complex and could easily reside in the art music sphere as well as the utilitarian-entertainment world. Imagine trying to rhythmically notate the sounds heard in Listening Experience 1.4. Against the backdrop of melodic and harmonic structures that are far more complex than those used in other popular music forms, the improvisational element of jazz additionally requires the performer to utilize appropriate rhythmic figures while simultaneously comprehending and negotiating chordal changes that impact scale selection and execution. That jazz was not widely accepted as a scholarly genre until the late twentieth century is connected to social construction, and as we briefly investigate one particular story of women in jazz, we must simultaneously recognize the intersection of gender and race that impacts historical documentation of this genre.

Contextual Discussion: Women's Music History Narratives

> *People have always said that I play like a man. When I was a child that was a compliment. Now that I am an adult, it is not. I play like a competent woman.*[12]
>
> Fostina Dixon-Kilgoe, Jazz Saxophonist

To begin a discussion of women in jazz, it is important to consider the value that music historians place on recordings in the modern era, and how racism and sexism might impact opportunities to record. In genres such as jazz in which performances are at least partly improvised, capturing live performance is considered essential to assessing the musical worth of a group or soloist. A fast perusal of available jazz recordings reveals a noticeable absence of performances by women, and that absence results in the erroneous belief that women did not participate in jazz at the professional level.

How did you picture the band in your mind as you listened to the recording? For many people, swing bands elicit thoughts of Second World War-era movies in which men in uniform and women in dresses are skimming across a polished wood dance floor to the music of an all-male big band. But even if you imagined the performers as women, did you envision an integrated group of African-American women, white women, and women of Asian, Hispanic, and Native American descent? The International Sweethearts of Rhythm captivated African-American audiences well before America's involvement in the Second World War and were written about extensively in the black press, an entire world of communication largely unknown to white Americans. The *Chicago Defender* online archives contain over one hundred articles on the International Sweethearts alone, following the band from downtown Chicago to the European warfront. But despite the group's widespread popularity in the black community, this band remained unknown in jazz history materials until a surge of interest in women's bands emerged in feminist studies of the 1980s.

The audience that you hear in the background of Listening Experience 1.4 was a group of African-American soldiers sitting outdoors in Europe in the mid-1940s. Along with separation of the troops for battle, entertainment

Figure 1.5
The International Sweethearts of Rhythm in an RCA recording session, 1946, with Anne Mae Winburn conducting.

Source: Leonard Feather Collection. Used by permission of the University of Idaho

for soldiers during the Second World War was also segregated, and this recording is from a segment of the Armed Forces Radio "Jubilee Sessions," a variety show intended to entertain African-American troops during the war years. It is one of only a few recordings readily available of the International Sweethearts of Rhythm, despite the fact that the band toured and performed extensively.

The emergence of women's big band narratives mirrors the telling of women's music history in general. In both cases, narratives first emerged from the realm of the unknown, and then were subject to critical analysis and retelling. In terms of the big band story, glorified initial accounts provided some elements of truth, but also fabricated the creation of other exclusionary tales. In the following two segments, you will find condensed versions of two common big band narratives. Notice how the omission of details in one account dramatically impacts reader perception.

The First Story to Emerge

Like the factory scene in America during the Second World War, the entertainment industry was profoundly impacted by the longevity of the war and the number of men serving in the armed forces. Two areas of entertainment where women came to the rescue were professional baseball and music. The All-American Girls Professional Baseball League came into widespread American consciousness after the release of Penny Marshall's 1992 movie

A League of Their Own, which was a fictionalized version of the actual women's league that Philip Wrigley started during the war years. Professional ballplayers were required to "play like men" but "look like women." Along with charm-school training and unneeded makeup, they were required to wear above-the-knee skirts that exposed bodies to bruising as well as gawking.[13]

Similar to the women's baseball league was the phenomenon of all-women big bands. Like the professional baseball teams, the ranks of all-male big bands were also depleted during the war years. To keep morale high and to keep the country's popular dance music alive, all-women big bands were formed during this era. "All-girl" band members also endured a dual demand to be talented and glamorous. Women were expected to maintain "red or yellow" hair color and were required to stain their lips with red dye because lipstick would come off when they played their instruments. It was critical to maintain a feminine image on stage.[14] Like the baseball players, women musicians in the war years did their part in the war effort by providing a needed service until male entertainers returned from the warfront. When the war was over, women's bands faded into history as women band members left the music industry and returned home.

Alternative Narrative

Sherrie Tucker's extensive research on women in big bands provides an alternative telling of the big band narrative. Tucker agrees that many famous all-male bands suffered loss of membership during the war years, but Tucker indicates that people believed the bands were *formed* during the war years because of a widespread notion that most women did not work prior to the war. Tucker's narrative reflects an awareness of labor statistics and racism that critically examines the association of women's big bands with the "Rosie the Riveter" image, an image of white women who left home and hearth to fill vacant factory positions. In reality, 75 percent of women who worked during the war years had worked prior to the war. Of this 75 percent, large numbers were African-American women who had worked in domestic positions, laundries, and other lower-paying jobs.[15] In terms of musical employment for African-American women, some of the swing bands were formed well before the war, had performed extensively, and were well known to their audiences. These bands were professional; bands members were unionized and they were paid.[16]

The International Sweethearts of Rhythm, for example, were formed in 1937. Although they had their start as a non-professional touring ensemble of the Piney Woods Country Life School in Tennessee, the group eventually separated from the school, became professional, and began to hire their own arrangers. They also expanded their ranks to become a multi-racial, multi-ethnic ensemble. Using interview material from former band members, Tucker's narrative goes beyond the glamour that often accompanies big band narratives, and explains how band members suffered as they toured the Jim Crow south. White band members darkened their faces to pass as black, since whites and blacks traveling together could be jailed. Tales of discrimination ranged from lack of housing (band members often lodged with black families or slept on the bus while touring because they were not allowed in hotels) and a frightening recollection of a "firebomb" being placed in a dance hall as a warning. The police frequently stood on the sidelines as the group performed.[17]

Just as the Rosie the Riveter image does not apply in terms of the formation and function of these bands, neither did band-women abandon musical careers at the end of the war. All big bands, male and female, were soon replaced by other forms of popular music, notably rock and roll. But former band members found work as musicians in other venues, including studio employment, solo work in nightclubs, and teaching.[18] Many of the women Tucker interviewed for her book remained active as musicians for decades, some of them into the 1990s.

As we turn back to our brief recording one more time, we do so with an expanded view of a musical performance setting that reflects deep cultural issues surrounding gender, race, and the labor market. Although their opinions are somewhat divided by generational differences, many African-American women musicians believe that gender issues are overshadowed by issues of race, as indicated by jazz keyboardist Shirley Scott: "I have not had a problem being a black woman on stage with a group of black males, but I have indeed experienced problems being a black person in American society."[19] African-American women of the swing band era shared the indignities of male African-American band members who suffered discrimination on the road and lack of coverage by the white press in America. Gender aside, the very creation of the swing genre by African-Americans is negated by historical documents that emphasized the work of white band leaders such as Benny Goodman, "the King of Swing."

The story recounted here is almost as brief as the recording, telling the tale of just one "all-girl" band among hundreds that existed, and omitting documentation of the emergence and marketing of all-white bands of the same era. What other stories were left untold?

SUMMARY

Written history is a phenomenon that necessarily limits the telling of stories. While some written history is simply false, often it is the *omission* of stories—about people, issues, and events—that lead to inaccurate beliefs and deeply-held convictions. In cultures that preserve music history via written documents (or recordings), the power of the documentation process is tremendous, for to lack documentation is often to lack a perception of having existed.

Like any historian, I run the risk of misrepresentation by omission, both willful and unintentional. In addition, much revealing work is yet to be done in the field of research on women and music. As such, just as Pauline Oliveros encourages listeners to *interact* deeply with sound, I encourage readers to interact deeply with this book. Read these narratives, question the material, and seek more. *Allow this book to be only the beginning of your journey into the world of women in music.*

QUESTIONS FOR CRITICAL THINKING AND DISCUSSION

1. Find a piece of popular music from your own collection and do a form analysis. How much unity/variety is featured? Will this piece withstand the test of time?
2. Select a music video of your choice and watch it without sound. What do you notice about the visual images when the soundtrack is absent? Pay special attention to depictions of men and women and camera angles.
3. List as many genres as possible and speculate about gender roles in each. Why do you think these particular gender roles exist in each of these genres?
4. Think about informal musical settings in which women have a role in music, such as a church choir or a mother singing a lullaby. Try to speculate about other informal settings and compile a list of private-sphere musical activities that involve women.

IDEAS FOR FURTHER RESEARCH

1. Seek information on "all-girl" bands of the early twentieth century. Do you notice a racial divide in terms of marketing and availability of recordings? Also research the label "all-girl," and attempt to discover varying perspectives regarding that terminology.
2. Write a paper reflecting on this statement:

   In written documents and in the recorded music industry, selection bias has had a powerful role in the perpetuation of stereotypes regarding the "proper" role of women in music.

CHAPTER 2

Medieval Liturgical Roots and the Documentation of the Western Canon

Researchers who focus on women in the arts often divide women's artistic activity into one of two "spheres" of operation, public and private. Of course, women have participated in private sphere musical activities throughout all time. Not only was music-making in private venues such as the home permitted, it was often a social expectation. But until ethnomusicological research became part of the collegiate curriculum, the culturally rich, deep research that explored music in the private sphere was ignored in textbooks and coursework. Music in the private sphere was not deemed worthy of study.

The musical work of women in the public sphere is less easy to find in recorded history. In public venues, women were historically excluded and were frequently barred from attaining the education they needed to create music that was typically performed in formal settings. Women who did attempt to participate professionally often found that their work could not be published. Since Western culture has relied heavily on printed preservation of music as a means of transmitting knowledge to the next generation, the musical work of women often was lost.

The church, like the Jewish synagogue, was a place of gender separation in terms of music education and performance; as such, it might seem the last place to begin a focused study of women in music. Nonetheless, the voices of women religious did find a place in the public sphere when written music was distributed beyond the convent, and when bystanders outside of the cloistered walls "overheard" the music being performed inside. Though women religious were literally hidden from public view, their music escaped the bounds of the convent.[1]

The focus of this chapter is to reveal the historical roots of the "publish or perish" phenomenon in the Western tradition, and also to examine how that lingering presence impacted the scholarly presentation of representative works by twentieth-century women. To begin the journey, we will examine the "usual" start of the Western music story.

A GLANCE AT EARLY JEWISH TRADITIONS

The documentation of Western music in most textbooks begins with short references to ancient Greece and to music in Judaism. Ancient Greek music is included because Greek theoretical and philosophical work impacts everything from Western scale systems to aesthetic debates. It is unfortunate that there is usually relatively little mention of Jewish musical traditions; Jewish musical history is almost erased from the Western music discourse at various junctures.[2] Some narratives do include a look at the music chronicled in the Hebrew Scriptures, including mention of the psalm settings of David and lesser-known composers, but women are almost always absent in the narrative. There is ample evidence in the Hebrew Scriptures that women participated in musical rituals that included singing lamentations and praise songs, dancing, and playing instruments. Among them are Miriam, Deborah, and Hannah, as well as Jephtha's unnamed daughter in the book of *Judges*.[3]

LITURGY
ritual for public worship; usually has a prescribed format

KOLISHA
"the voice of woman"; a belief in Orthodox Judaism that women must not sing in the presence of men due to the potential to distract men in prayer

Biblical references to Jewish **liturgical** music, however, reveal an absence of musical roles for women. Liturgical music was a vocally based phenomenon, and the eventual banning of women's voices from Jewish liturgical worship, referred to in Hebrew as **kolisha**, was intended to protect men from potential distraction. Musical-liturgical roles of cantor, prayer leader, scriptural reader-chanter, and choir member were strictly reserved for males.[4] Women also were physically separated during services by a curtain or wall, or were sometimes placed in a separate physical location entirely, such as a balcony.

Women continued to be active in non-liturgical music roles by performing in the home as well as at such events as burials and weddings. Still, it was liturgical music—and the work of men who created and performed it—that was documented. The domestic musical involvement of Jewish women in the private sphere remained a relatively untold story until the late twentieth century, and although there is greater involvement of Jewish women in liturgical roles in twenty-first-century Reform and Conservative Judaism, Orthodox Jews still practice the concept of kolisha today.[5]

CHRISTIAN LITURGICAL ROOTS

Musical traditions of the Jewish liturgy strongly impacted early Christian liturgical practice. From the musical repetition of texts, to psalm-singing procedures, to the banning of instruments and women's voices, there were many similarities between the two traditions. Although the early church was a place of gender separation in terms of music education and performance, Christian women in vowed religious orders had an unusual opportunity both to receive an education and to compose and perform music. The majority of women religious remain nameless on the pages of recorded history, but there is one who represents their largely untold story: Hildegard von Bingen.

By the dawn of the twenty-first century, Hildegard von Bingen's name had become inextricably linked to medieval church music. Despite the fact that there are more musical works attributed to Hildegard than to any other composer of her era, however, widely read texts such as Donald Grout's *History of Western Music*, and highly regarded source materials such as the *Oxford Dictionary of Medieval Music* completely failed to mention her in editions as recent as the 1980s. Although Hildegard is a unique case because she was published and known in her day, exploring Hildegard's musical world allows us to investigate the historical underpinnings of women's exclusion from the annals of Western music history.

THE CHURCH AS A PRIMARY SOURCE OF EDUCATION

The church was a powerful educational force in the middle ages. Church-sponsored schools for boys focused on teaching the seven liberal arts, one of which was music. Cathedral schools provided secondary education, and some of these schools developed into major learning centers and universities that are still in existence today. Girls were excluded from church-sponsored schools, and if they learned to read and write at all, their education took place at home. Because women who entered religious orders received formal education, the convent provided a rare educational avenue. As such, there was a clear delineation in educational attainment between women religious and women who were not associated with the convent.

As with general education, systemic church-sponsored music education excluded girls and women. In the fifth century, the church established the **schola cantorum**, or singing school, which initially focused on the teaching and practice of ecclesiastical chant, but eventually also included the study of manuscripts. The church's goal was to prepare trained musicians to carry out musical functions so that clergy could focus their attention on other liturgical areas. Pope Gregory the Great (540–604) solidified the schola, and it spread beyond Italy to other countries, notably France and England. In monasteries, the schola education focused on selected monks who were trained to chant the more elaborate portions of liturgical music.[6]

SCHOLA CANTORUM
"singing school"; church-sponsored school for the teaching of ecclesiastical chant

Although women religious had better access to music education than did other women, they were denied access to the church's prescribed educational approach. As such, even vowed religious had few formal opportunities to study music. Women in convents learned about church music informally and aurally by attending liturgical functions, and women religious in double monasteries (religious houses comprising communities of both men and women) had even more exposure to this type of informal learning because of their shared facilities.

Semi-formally, women within the convent taught new community members what they had previously learned from their predecessors. This system improved over time as convents accepted an increasing number of formally trained musicians who had been sent to them by wealthy families. Women from these families studied with accomplished musicians, and were usually afforded the same education as their male siblings. Religious communities sometimes delayed accepting these known musicians on the premise that additional musical training received at home would make these women even greater musical assets once they entered the convent.[7]

THE CHURCH AS PRESERVER OF MUSIC

Along with having a crucial role in music education, the church was a primary preserver of music. Church leaders believed that music was a tool that could help centralize and unify the geographically expanding church, and Latin was adopted as a universal liturgical language prior to AD 400. With the creation and subsequent development of written notation from the tenth century onward, the vast body of liturgical chant that had been created and distributed aurally was further codified and preserved, creating a cohesive liturgical/musical experience throughout the church world.[8]

Prior to the invention of the European printing press in 1440, musicians gathered around a limited number of hand-copied manuscripts. The preservation of these documents often fell to vowed religious who spent many hours copying music in the **scriptoria**, or writing rooms. In this manner, monks and nuns laboriously preserved not only musical works but literary works as well. Protected somewhat from the ravages of war, churches became reliable and vast storehouses of musical, artistic, and literary materials, much of which was sacred.[9] These chosen artifacts represent a significant portion of the foundation upon which Western education was built.

SCRIPTORIA
a writing room used for copying manuscripts, writing, and studying, usually in a convent or monastery; associated with the preservation of musical manuscripts

LITURGICAL GENRES

A liturgy is an official public-worship ceremony, as opposed to a private devotion. By the time written notation was created, two major types of liturgy had developed: the Mass and the Office. Musically, both liturgies featured chanted text settings that were sung in Latin. **Chant** was **monophonic**, rhythmically free, and featured patterns of repetition that matched text. In terms of function, the two liturgies were significantly different. The Mass was divided into two parts, the first of which focused on teaching via scripture readings, and the second of which focused on the celebration of communion. Both portions occurred in a liturgy that took place at one set time during the day. The **Office** (also known as the divine office or office hours) was a daily devotion in which there was recitation of sung prayers at eight designated hours throughout the day and night. The musical roles for women in the two liturgies were distinctly different.

CHANT
a monophonic, liturgical song; sometimes referred to as "Gregorian" chant or plainsong

MONOPHONIC
music having a single melody without accompaniment or harmonizing parts, as in chant

OFFICE
liturgy of eight prayer services in which psalms, readings, and prayers are recited or sung at specified hours

MASS
Roman church liturgy; also a musical genre or setting for certain parts of this liturgy

ORDINARY
Mass texts that remain the same on most days of the year; musical settings may change

PROPER
Mass texts that change according to specific days of the church calendar

The Mass

By the time written notation was developed, it had become standard practice to set a significant portion of **Mass** text settings to music. These settings were divided into two types, the **Ordinary** and the **Proper**. The Ordinary featured texts that remained stable throughout the church year, while the Proper texts changed to reflect feast days (see Focus Topic 2.1). Although the Mass in the medieval period was strictly liturgical, the musical traditions associated with this liturgy led composers to eventually write masses that were not intended for liturgical use at all. As such, the Mass earned an historical dual-role as both liturgical music and concert genre.

While men and women attended Mass throughout the medieval period, only men presided at the service, and only men performed the accompanying musical functions. Although women had participated musically in the Mass as singers during the early centuries of the Christian church, Constantine banned women from singing in church after the legalization of Christianity in 313. In some monasteries, women religious were even restricted from watching the Mass, only being permitted to see the elevation of the host through a grilled window that was opened during that portion of the liturgy. As such, it is understandable that women composers infrequently wrote music for the Mass.[10]

The Office

While women were musically excluded from the Mass, they wrote and performed music for the Office. The Office was influenced by the Jewish tradition of sung prayer throughout the day, and included a daily schedule of psalm singing, scripture readings, and short accounts of the lives of the saints. Canon Law permitted women to sing in their own religious communities, and since the Office did not forbid them from performing necessary liturgical functions, many women religious performed the Office daily.

The Office was strictly codified by the Rule of St. Benedict, an AD 530 document that provided monastic communities with rules for a prescribed balance of prayer and work. Psalms, antiphons, and responsories were significant musical components of the Office. **Antiphons** were sung before and after psalms, while the **responsory** was a musical response to an intoned reading or lesson. In the medieval period it was not uncommon for members of religious communities to rise during the night to perform the Office at designated hours. In later years, however, much more flexibility was allowed.

ANTIPHON
type of chant sung before or after the recitation of a psalm in the Office; also associated with psalmody in the Mass

RESPONSORY
a verse or set of verses used in the Office; often performed with soloist alternating with group

FOCUS TOPIC 2.1

Genre Focus: The Mass and the Office

The Mass and the Office are two major liturgies of the Roman Catholic Church. They have also been set to music for centuries, and are often performed as concert works that are not intended for worship. The terms are capitalized when referred to liturgically, and are not capitalized when referenced as musical genres.

THE MASS

The Mass is a liturgical celebration of Christ's Last Supper. In today's practice, the readings and prayers are usually spoken, but for centuries Mass texts were primarily sung. Parts of the Mass are divided into the Ordinary and the Proper. Ordinary text settings remain constant throughout the church year, whether a feast day or not. They include the Kyrie, Gloria, Credo, Sanctus, and Agnus Dei.

Proper text settings change to reflect feast days and specific Sundays in the church calendar. Therefore, sung texts such as the Introit, Gradual, Alleluia, Offertory, and Communion feature varied texts depending on the day of the year.

Although the Mass is still a primary liturgy of the Church today, it also became a non-liturgical musical genre. Many of the world's most famous composers have written masses that were never intended for liturgical use, but that nonetheless utilize traditional text settings.

THE OFFICE

In the medieval period the eight office hours were literally performed around the clock. Listed below is one version of the hours and the times at which they were performed. In today's practice, the Office is performed with a much more flexible schedule.

Matins, during the night	Terce, 9 a.m.	Vespers, sunset
Lauds, at dawn	Sext, noon	Compline, bedtime
Prime, 6 a.m.	None, 3 p.m.	

Figure 2.1
Hildegard von Bingen with her scribe, Volmar, who helped record her visions. This illustration appeared in a written record of Hildegard's visions known as the *Scivias*.
Source: Public domain

HILDEGARD VON BINGEN

> *Underneath all the texts, all the sacred psalms and canticles, these watery varieties of sounds and silences . . . must somehow be felt in the pulse, ebb, and flow of the music that sings in me. My new song must float like a feather on the breath of God.*
>
> Hildegard von Bingen

Hildegard von Bingen (1098–1179) was a German Benedictine nun who was known not only as a musician but also as a poet, mystic, artist, scientist, and theologian. Hildegard was the tenth child in her family, and was thus tithed to the Church by her parents. Hildegard left home at the age of seven or eight, and for many years lived in a small anchorage, or cell, that was physically attached to the church of the Benedictine monastery of Disibodenberg. She received her education from the abbess Jutta of Spanheim, and was taught to read and to sing Latin psalms. It is believed that Hildegard was not taught to write; thus she relayed her revelations and writings to a monk named Volmar who acted as her scribe. At Jutta's death in 1136, Hildegard became superior of the monastery, and eventually moved her community of sisters to St. Rupertsburg, near Bingen, on the Rhine River.[11]

Since research on Hildegard's music is continually evolving, there remains debate on the nature of her music education. Some resources indicate that Hildegard simply broke compositional rules because she did not have proper training. More recent research indicates that Hildegard's music incorporated mathematical patterns that suggest a familiarity with the theories of Boethius, Guido of Arezzo, Hucbold, and other music theorists.[12] Some researchers posit that Hildegard denied having access to such materials because of the gender politics of her time; she did not want to acknowledge human instruction.[13] In her own words, Hildegard indicated that her work was marked by the inspiration of God to "give musical forms to divine mysteries."[14]

Hildegard received many visions and revelations from God that she recreated in poetry and music. One of her major works, the *Scivias* (*Know the Ways of the Lord*), presents twenty-six of those revelations, and was written as a response to a divine command to record her visions. Sometimes seen as a rebel in her time for getting her work published, Hildegard in fact obeyed the rules of the Church and sought permission of church officials to publish because she felt commanded by God to do so. As a result, Hildegard's musical and theological works were published in her name in an era when most such work, whether created by men or women, was not credited to a known author or composer.

Hildegard's musical output consisted of a large body of chant, almost certainly the largest of any known composer of her era. Although she wrote parts of the Mass, sometimes by commission, she wrote more often for the Office, the liturgy in which she and her community were permitted to musically participate. In addition, she is credited with writing the first "morality play," a non-liturgical work based on sacred text and dramatized.

WORD PAINTING
in texted works, using musical gestures or elements to reflect movement and emotion in the text

MELISMA
a succession of multiple pitches sung on a single syllable

Musically, Hildegard's chant differed in several significant ways from that of her male contemporaries. Hildegard's intense, symbolic poems lent themselves to musical elaboration, with free verse that suggested irregular, continuous lines rather than shorter strophes. She brought forth the meaning of the text by **word painting**, using musical gestures to reflect movement and emotion in the text. Her work was also marked by the use of extended **melismas**, in which there were as many as fifty notes per syllable of text. Like most liturgical music of her time, Hildegard's work was monophonic, but while most liturgical chant covered a modest one-octave range, Hildegard's chant spanned two to three octaves.[15] It is believed that she wrote in this manner to explore the beauty of the extended upper range of the female voice, to reflect the capabilities of the women in her community, and to metaphorically allow the voices of her performers to address the "female voice" in creation. Many of Hildegard's texts address the Virgin Mary, St. Ursula, and other women.

Listening to a Kyrie Setting by Hildegard

Hildegard's musical settings can be easily distinguished from traditional chant both visually and aurally. Hildegard frequently extends the vocal range beyond an octave, and is also known for utilizing extended melismas, both of which are evident in Listening Experience 2.1. Although Kyrie settings often feature a simple A B A form to follow the three-part text setting (Kyrie eleison, Christe eleison, Kyrie eleison) Hildegard does not repeat the melody on the second Kyrie, but instead uses more extensive melismas on the final statement.

Hildegard's compositional innovation becomes even more apparent in compositions not connected with the Mass. In her *Symphonia armonie celestium revelationum* or *Symphony of the Harmony of the Heavenly Relations*, she created a collection of chants in a cycle, and specifically addressed the life-giving role of women. Hildegard's extended range is featured in free verse that unfolds over time. This **through-composed** technique allows musical flexibility and variation rather than the strict repetition found when stanzas of text are re-set to the same melody. The connection between women, nature, and creation is evident in Hildegard's original poetry, and the musical setting brings forth its free-flowing beauty.

THROUGH-COMPOSED
works in which new music is used for each section, as opposed to forms in which segments recur

The *Ordo Virtutum*

Along with her numerous liturgical compositions, Hildegard von Bingen is credited with creating the first **morality play**, a medieval drama in which moral attributes are personified and dramatized. Her *Ordo Virtutum*, or *Play of the Virtues* (c.1150), is the story of the Anima, or soul, and its struggle to resist evil. All parts of the *Ordo* were sung by women representing the Virtues, allowing women to play the role of leading the faithful to God—a most unusual gender portrayal at that time. The devil is represented by the lone male voice in the play, and the fact that he speaks rather than sings is further depiction of a lack of connection to God. As you listen to Selection 2.2, note the changing vocal timbres as characters dialogue back and forth as they would in a spoken play. In this segment, the characters include the unhappy or unfortunate soul (Infelix Anima), the Virtues, the Knowledge of God (Scientia Dei), and the "Loud Voice of the Devil" (Strepitus diaboli). Notice that it is the devil's loud, spoken voice that opens the excerpt.

MORALITY PLAY
allegorical drama in which the characters personify abstractions, such as vice, virtue, and charity

LISTENING EXPERIENCE 2.1

"Kyrie"
Hildegard von Bingen
Score available in the *New Historical Anthology of Music by Women*
Playlist

LISTENING FOCUS

Listen for three segments that follow the three-part text. Notice an increasing expansion of vocal range and increasingly long melismas.

TEXT

Kyrie eleison (Lord, have mercy); Christe eleison (Christ, have mercy); Kyrie eleison (Lord, have mercy).

FORM AT A GLANCE

A B A

TIMED LISTENING GUIDE

A Section: Kyrie eleison

0:00	first Kyrie statement
0:25	Kyrie statement repeated
0:52	Kyrie statement repeated

B Section: Christe eleison

1:15	first Christe statement; notice the wide vocal range and long melismas
1:41	Christe statement repeated
2:05	Christe statement repeated

A Section: Kyrie eleison

2:32	alteration of opening Kyrie statement, with more extensive melismas
3:04	altered Kyrie statement repeated
3:40	altered Kyrie statement repeated again with an additional melisma on final "eleison"

LISTENING EXPERIENCE 2.2

"The Soul Fights the Devil" from *Ordo Virtutum* (1150)
Hildegard von Bingen
Playlist

LISTENING FOCUS

Ordo Virtutum is a morality play that personifies virtues such as humility, hope, and innocence as they assist the soul in her fight against the devil. The virtues and the soul sing their parts, while the devil can only speak. The work is performed in Latin. The author has paraphrased the content (below) in English. Modern performers musically interpret the play in a variety of ways. Note the intentional use of instruments and vocal harmony in this interpretation.

0:00	**Devil**: ". . . You were in my embrace, I led you out. Yet now you are going back, defying me—but I shall fight you and bring you down!"
0:23	**Penitent Soul**: "I recognized that my ways were wicked, so I fled you . . . Now, I will fight you face to face."
0:51	the soul's tone changes as she addresses humility: "Queen Humility, give me aid!"
1:24	**Humility**: "Victory, you who once conquered this creature in the heavens, run now . . . bind this fiend!"
1:55	**Victory**: "Bravest and most glorious warriors, come, help me to vanquish this deceitful one!"
2:23	**Virtues**: "Oh sweetest warrior . . . how gladly we'll fight against that deceiver, at your side!"
2:56	**Humility**: "Bind him, then, you shining Virtues!"
3:15	**Virtues**: "Queen of us all, we obey you—we shall carry out your orders."
3:39	**Victory**: "Rejoice, the ancient serpent snake is bound."
4:03	**Virtues**: "Praise be to you, Christ, King of the angels!" (in harmony)
4:23	**Chastity**: "In the mind of the Highest, Satan, I trod on your head, and in a virgin form I nurtured a sweet miracle when the Son of God came into the world . . ."
6:00	**Devil**: "You don't know what you are nurturing, for your belly is devoid of the beautiful form that woman receives from man . . ."
6:25	**Chastity**: "How can what you say affect me? Even your suggestion smirches it with foulness . . ."
7:23	**Virtues**: "Who are you God, who held such great counsel in yourself, a counsel that destroyed the draught of hell . . . Praise to you, King, for this."
8:41	**Virtues** continue: "*Almighty Father, from you flowed a fountain in fiery love . . .* " (italicized words in harmony)
8:56	**Virtues** continue: "guide your children into a fair wind . . . steer them in this way *into the heavenly Jerusalem.*" (final words in harmony)

The play continues with a processional.

Both the *Symphonia armonie celestium revelationum* and the *Ordo Virtutum* showcase Hildegard's ability to connect her spirituality with her musical aesthetic. Her view of women as co-creators and source of life links with her textural descriptions of the fruitfulness of nature. The vivid poetry is set to music that is flowing, ornamented, and intended to showcase the female voice. It was music that stood in sharp contrast to liturgical chant that was created by male composers educated by the medieval church.

Banned From Performing Music

Although apparently compliant with the church throughout her lifetime in terms of musical composition and publishing activities, Hildegard suffered a very difficult year in which the church banished her community from performing music in their convent. The church interdict took place in 1178, just one year before her death, after Hildegard refused to obey an order to exhume the body of a young person who was buried in the convent's cemetery. Hildegard's response to the church's ban on musical performance in her community aptly summarizes her thinking about the power of music:

> It is fitting that the body simultaneously with the soul repeatedly sing praises to God through the voice . . . Therefore, those of the Church who have imposed silence on the singing of the chants for the praise of God without well-considered weight of reason so that they have unjustly stripped God of the grace and comeliness of His own praise, unless they will have freed themselves from their errors here on earth, will be without the company of the angelic songs of praise in heaven.[16]

Like Hildegard von Bingen, many women religious composed and performed music for liturgical functions in their convents. Most of their names will never be known, however, because they were not connected to the publishing/preservation function of the church. Despite being the known creator of a significant number of musical works, Hildegard, too, was omitted from the annals of music history until the very end of the twentieth century.

TRACING THE CANONICAL ROOTS INTO THE TWENTIETH CENTURY: GENDERED PATHS

What do we know of women's sacred musical work after Hildegard? In short, relatively little. Silenced by lack of access to education, and prohibited from public worship spaces, the sacred voices of women remained largely silent on paper. In a canon that revered published works, the spiritual performances of everyday life were largely ignored. It was almost as if women did not express their spirituality via music at all.

The twentieth century brought significant change, however. Women's access to education and admittance into public-sphere ritual changed the face of the sacred music story, albeit slowly. In the early years of the century, the Catholic church officially removed the ban on women's singing in the Mass. In the 1960s, the Jewish Reform and Conservative movements allowed women to study for the cantorate and, in that same decade, the Second Vatican Council of the Catholic church permitted increased liturgical roles for women. With participatory access to liturgies, as well as access to education, the twentieth century marked a new era for women in Western sacred music history. As a result, the vast majority of women's written compositional work rests in just one century, as is also the case in the secular music tradition.

To reflect the importance of the twentieth century on women's art music history, an entire segment of this text is devoted to sacred and secular work of that era. Still, it seems important here to specifically address some twentieth-century sacred works by women, particularly in regard to how women's sacred works began to emerge in standard written materials.

Missa Gaia: A Mass for the Concert Hall

Libby Larsen's *Missa Gaia* (Mass for the Earth) is a good example of a late twentieth-century mass that bows to the traditional canon, but displays an inclusive spirituality reflective of its historical time period. Other than traditional Latin titles from the Mass (with movements entitled Introit, Kyrie, Gloria, Credo, Agnus Dei/Sanctus, Benediction) the remaining text, in English, avoids traditional liturgical language entirely. Larsen takes her lyrics from a variety of sources, including works of Dominican mystic Meister Eckhart, Jesuit priest Gerard Manley Hopkins, and Native American poet Joy Harjo, as well as texts from the Bible, and the Chinook Psalter.

All of the movements in *Mass for the Earth* are textually unified, as they focus on the relationship between individuals and the earth. Like the work as a whole, the Kyrie provides an excellent example of Larsen's tendency to present clear lyrics that are sustained by appealing melodic and harmonic language. The theme of circles is found throughout the piece, alluding at times to the circular rhythms of the life cycle. Larsen highlights this musically via use of the circle of fifths, by **octaves** and by open fifths in the chorus, as well as by melodic movement.[17]

OCTAVE
notes spaced eight tones apart; in Western music, this results in renaming the pitch "at the octave," for example, C-C

The formal plan of the Kyrie utilizes a simplicity that is historically found in the Kyrie of the Mass, with two iterations of unison melodic lines that expand to harmonized sections. Larsen musically reflects on the traditional penitence of the Kyrie as well, featuring a pensive oboe solo in the brief orchestral introduction, and a slow tempo throughout. The first line of the text is clearly discernable in a unison statement by women's voices before the chorus divides into **harmony**, first introducing consonant thirds and later using **dissonance** to depict the words "suffer," and "mock." Much of the remaining harmony is in octaves, fourths, and fifths, giving the sound a twentieth-century flavor, and perhaps also alluding symbolically to the circle (see Listening Experience 2.3 for a full analysis).[18]

HARMONY
two or more pitches sounding simultaneously

DISSONANCE
combination of tones that sounds unstable; sometimes considered harsh, or in need of resolution

LISTENING EXPERIENCE 2.3

"Kyrie" from *Missa Gaia* (1991–1992)
Libby Larsen
Text by M. K. Dean, used by permission
Companion CD Track 2

LISTENING FOCUS

Listen for use of unison passages as well as consonant and dissonant segments that are used for text expression.

TIMED LISTENING GUIDE

0:00	orchestral introduction with oboe solo
0:17	"*Blessed sister, holy mother*" unison women's voices moving to octaves
0:26	*"spirit of the fountains, spirit of the garden"* voices divide into harmony
0:35	*"suffer us not to mock ourselves with falsehood"* dissonance on the words "suffer" and "mock"
0:53	*"Teach us to care and not to care"*
1:02	*"Teach us to sit still, even among these rocks."* moving to open harmony
1:16	*"Our piece in his will"* unison voices
1:23	*"even among these rocks"* division into harmony
1:28	*"Sister, mother"* unison voices
1:37	*"and spirit of the river, spirit of the sea"* voices in harmony
1:47	*"Suffer me not to be separated"* dissonance on "suffer" and "separated," ending with octave separation
1:56	*"and let my cry come unto Thee"* unison voices
2:06	"*let my cry come unto Thee*" voices in harmony.

Figure 2.2
Libby Larsen.

Source: Photograph by Ann Marsden, Courtesy of Libby Larsen

Women's Space in the Twentieth-Century Canon

In many ways, Larsen represents the typical twentieth-century composer. Born in 1950, she is of the generation of composers who received a college education; Larsen has bachelor's, master's, and doctoral degrees from the University of Minnesota. Her work encompasses a wide variety of genres, including chamber music, dance, and opera, as well as works for orchestra and chorus. Although she writes instrumental works, it is Larsen's texted works that receive the most documentation, and that reside particularly well in the Western canon's "feminine" compositional sphere; they feature beautiful melodies, transparent textures, gentle timbres, and formal simplicity. Larsen is sometimes labeled an "accessible modern," and her name and photograph are prominently found in the most conservative and revered Western music materials on the market. Her recordings are easily accessed by the public, and she enjoys great success in the concert hall. Despite her many achievements, Larsen is sometimes subject to criticism by those who consider her music not compositionally complex enough to warrant inclusion in the old canon. In part, this assessment is based on the types of works that are typically showcased by authors. But there is another way to view Larsen's music.

While male and female composers alike struggled to maintain an audience in the late twentieth century, Larsen was atypically successful. In writing music that pleases the ear, Larsen tapped an enormous market, even as she perhaps unintentionally embraced a centuries-old aesthetic that has been labeled "feminine." Larsen clearly feels a connection with texted music, and links her compositional ability with her knowledge of audience needs. As she pondered the emergence of text messaging and music technology, for example, she noted that modern audiences were "hard-wired for narrative." She satisfied that need not by "wedding" words and text, but rather by allowing the text to drive the style as she "created an environment" for easily discernable lyrics.[19]

Well-educated and talented composers such as Larsen are abundant in the modern period, but it takes more than talent to achieve fame. For both men and women who compose, finding and captivating an audience additionally requires networking and marketing skills that allow the composer to break through barriers to wider accessibility. In her work as a composer and a self-promoter, Libby Larsen has succeeded undeniably well. *Missa Gaia* exemplifies work that is simultaneously held as an example of women's composition by traditionalists and widely embraced by concert-goers. In the next example, we will discover a woman whose spiritual-musical expression is radically different, and whose work is less accepted by audiences and authors alike.

THE WRONG PATH?

> *When asked where her inspiration comes from, she gestures skyward. "Heaven," she laughs.*[20]
>
> Sofia Gubaidulina

If Hildegard von Bingen stands as a bookmark on the early end of Western sacred music, her spiritual counterpart in the early twenty-first century might be Sofia Gubaidulina. A Russian composer by birth, she spent much of her life working beneath the Soviet regime, surrounded by the artistic limitations of communism. Not unlike the confines of Hildegard's convent, Gubaidulina's works were developed within a restricted environment that could not contain the expression of her deep spirituality. To the Soviet public, Gubaidulina was a composer of film music, but her innovative work lies in the field of art music, where she expresses spirituality in dissonant harmonic language that is quite the opposite of Larsen's accessible modernism. Despite her use of the innovative language that usually catches the attention of traditional musicologists, Gubaidulina thus far has received limited attention on the pages of documented music history. Her story invites us to contemplate the role of aesthetic gender coding on the modern end of the music history timeline.

Born in 1931, Sofia Gubaidulina studied piano and composition at the Kazan Conservatory and received a graduate composition degree from the Moscow Conservatory. As she prepared to leave the Conservatory after her

Figure 2.3
Sofia Gubaidulina: Moscow, Russia.
Source: © Victor Bazhenov/Lebrecht/The Image Works

final graduate exam there, Russian composer Dmitri Shostakovich encouraged Gubaidulina to continue on her "mistaken path," referring to the harsh criticism that she had endured from Conservatory faculty who deemed her work of high quality but of questionable artistic merit. The young composer had been told that she had chosen "the wrong way," and in the Soviet state, said Gubaidulina, "the artist was defenseless."[21] To the Soviets, extreme dissonance was as aesthetically unacceptable as the religious themes that Gubaidulina favored, but kept hidden from their view. But Gubaidulina's "mistaken path" can be traced after she leaves Russia as well, as we analyze her work according to musical gender roles.

Gubaidulina's compositional style is formally complex and highly symbolic, and she aligns her work with that of J. S. Bach in regard to connecting structure to personal spirituality. In the manner of other musicians, Gubaidulina analyzes Bach's use of mathematical series, proportions, and mirror symmetry, but she mathematically connects Bach to spirituality in a way that is often only alluded to by others. What is not apparent to the listener without close examination of a score is that Gubaidulina's use of mathematical series creates an underlying structural pallet on which simple musical figures expand and build in intensity. Gubaidulina frequently uses the **quarter-tone** as a metaphor of an image and its shadow. In spiritual terms, the metaphor might represent good and evil, life and death, or the human and the divine.

QUARTER-TONE
interval half the size of a half-step; the half-step is traditionally recognized as the smallest interval in Western music, thus the quarter-tone can be perceived as dissonant or even "out of tune" by people accustomed to Western tonal music

Gubaidulina's *Seven Words* (shortened from *Seven Words of Christ from the Cross*) is a work that meditates on the seven final phrases that Christ speaks while dying on the cross. Taken from the four gospels of the New Testament, the phrases include "Father, forgive them, they know not what they do"; "My God, my God, why hast though forsaken me?" and "It is finished." Frequently set by composers in choral settings, Gubaidulina recreates the agony and horror of the crucifixion with instruments alone.

References to the crucifixion are made in a variety of ways throughout the seven-movement work. In the first and last movements, the musical texture expands from a single pitch to over six octaves, and physically forms the shape of a cross in the musical notation. In movement VI, "It is Finished," Gubaidulina's sound palette is created in three layers, including a string orchestra, a cello, and a bayan (Russian button accordion). Along with the metaphor of Christ's struggle between death and life, references to the crucifixion are made via use of noticeable dissonance and less apparent structural devices. The bayan soloist, for example, creates a dissonant sound by performing a glissando with the bellows while holding down neighboring buttons on the instrument, but is also symbolically "crossing" one sound over the other. The cellist alludes to the crucifixion by "crucifying" the string with the bow, and by "cutting through" the texture of the music with **chords**.[22] By the start of the final movement, the cellist gradually moves the bow until

CHORD
three or more pitches sounding simultaneously

LISTENING EXPERIENCE 2.4

"It is Finished," Movement VI from *Seven Words* (1982)
Sofia Gubaidulina
Playlist

LISTENING FOCUS

Listen for three intersecting layers, including bayan (accordion), string orchestra, and solo cello. Without text, the composer depicts Christ's suffering and dying.

TIMED LISTENING GUIDE

0:00	bayan solo opens with low tone cluster
0:19	bayan irregular "breaths" begin to alternate with tone clusters
0:37	strings establish ostinato pattern; bayan interjects with breath sounds
0:54	bayan increasingly agitated, strings expand pattern and increase in volume
0:57	cello heard in low range; bayan expands and contracts as strings reach intense level
2:05	string ostinato ceases
2:16	bayan shivers rapidly in and out, alternating with cello tremolo
2:28	bayan produces final gasp, cello centers on one pitch
2:40	cello string crucified; sound fades away

it rests just under the bridge, symbolizing the transition of Christ out of this world. It does not take too much imagination to hear the bayan symbolizing the breath of the dying Christ as the bellows expand in and out, alternating between agonizing tone clusters, deep intakes of air, and shallow shivering gasps. The cello "crucifies" the low C string one final time as the movement draws to a close (see Listening Experience 2.4). Despite the technicality of her work, the true focus of this composer's work is spiritual.[23]

What is the Wrong Path?

As we summarize the brief introduction to gender spheres and music discussed in this chapter, let us first clarify the difference between gender and sex. If we agree that sex is biological and gender is culturally constructed, then we might also agree that music is a *sexually* neutral activity in terms of what is needed to achieve compositional goals. *Gender*, however, has been connected with aesthetic coding for centuries.[24]

Even in the twenty-first century, music gender roles are attributed to composers such as Libby Larsen and Sofia Gubaidulina. Larsen, as noted previously, is sometimes associated with a feminine compositional discourse. Gubaidulina's work aligns with the male aesthetic in its harsh dissonance, mathematically structured form, and overall complexity. The subject matter of *Seven Words*—terror, death, ugliness—is also historically connoted as male. Women who compose have been cast in both gendered roles, but are often better accepted and better documented if they play the feminine part either via genre selection, via timbre choice (flute and harp versus brass and percussion, for example), or via adherence to simple structural designs and less aggressive rhythms.[25] Men have been assigned gendered roles as well, taking criticism for delving into the "feminine" sphere, and being held to a "macho" image in an art that requires deeply personal emotional connection.[26]

SUMMARY

Western music history is deeply rooted in spiritual traditions that form a strong cornerstone of the art music canon. Spirituality is a central part of the human musical experience, and women have always expressed their spirituality via music. In cultures where written history exists, however, it can appear that the undocumented are either incapable or uninterested. This phenomenon is not limited to the Western tradition; it is found worldwide in the documentation of spiritual rituals that utilize music. "Classical" traditions remain the heart of much musicological and ethnomusicological study, but this tendency is continually challenged by other scholars who have expanded their search for musical meaning to encompass a more inclusive view.

QUESTIONS FOR CRITICAL THINKING AND DISCUSSION

1. In your own words, describe how the medieval convent was both restrictive and liberating at the same time.
2. Using the elements of music (rhythm, melody, form, timbre, harmony), compare and contrast Libby Larsen's Kyrie from *Missa Gaia* with the Kyrie of Hildegard von Bingen. Then compare and contrast the performance settings for each work.
3. Discuss Sofia Gubaidulina and Hildegard von Bingen in regard to their musical expression of spirituality.
4. Why are spiritual traditions so deeply intertwined with music? Is this merely an element of documentation, or are there other reasons?
5. Discuss the suggestion that gendered roles exist in art music. Do you agree or disagree, and why?

IDEAS FOR FURTHER RESEARCH

1. Attend a worship service in a tradition of interest to you. Notice musical gender roles, and then research the history of roles in that tradition.
2. Investigate liturgical and non-liturgical music in Judaism, noting ways in which this tradition impacts Western culture.
3. Your instructor probably has several textbooks that chronicle the history of Western music. As a class, access them, and note how modern women are aesthetically represented in the most recent material included.
4. Find other works by Libby Larsen and Sofia Gubaidulina and compare the overall aesthetic of these works to the recorded selections provided in this chapter.

CHAPTER 3

Women in World Music

Another Picture of Musical Documentation

In Chapter 2 we examined the documentation of women in music in the Western canon. By the end of the twentieth century, another field of study captivated not only academe, but also a growing segment of the popular music marketplace. In this chapter, we turn to the documentation of women in "world music," and address gender balance in teaching materials that are found everywhere from the college bookstore to the online retail outlet. Despite **ethnomusicologists**' embrace of private-sphere settings, women are under-represented in world music materials that reach the wider public. This chapter will discuss why, and will then highlight some fascinating alternative stories from both the public and private-sphere world of women in music.

ETHNOMUSICOLOGY
field of study that uses sociological and musicological research methods to study the world's music

DEFINING WORLD MUSIC

What do you think of when you hear the term "world music?" At its broadest conception, it should include any music that has been created, performed, or consumed anywhere. It is important to acknowledge, however, that a much narrower perception is common. Alternative meanings and labels have existed throughout the evolution of ethnomusicological study, and tracing the lineage of the field will better enable our understanding of how women have been portrayed.

In 1960, world music was usually referred to as "non-Western music," delegating the Western canon as the norm and "world music" as anything that existed on the outside. The focus was on ritual-based music of traditional cultures that existed outside of Europe and English-speaking North America. By the 1980s, the definition expanded to include the study of folk and ethnic music, including that of Europe and the United States. By 2000, the definition increasingly embraced popular as well as traditional styles. Increased

SYNCRETISM
the blending and merging of two or more distinct cultures into a distinctive new culture

globalization and the sharing of music via mass media facilitated a **syncretic** blending, and the transnational result defied geographical boundaries. As such, world music also became a recording-industry label that described ethnic-influenced popular music. Along the way, the marketing of "world" instruments for amateur use became big business, with instruments such as the sitar, djembe, and mbira becoming international symbols of their geographical origins.

FIELDWORK
research situation in which a participant-observer is immersed in the culture being studied

However it was defined, world music research methodology provided an excellent opportunity to study women's musical activities. Ethnomusicology is deeply indebted to sociological research methods, and while researchers utilize some of the same written research methods as musicologists, they additionally gather data from the field. **Fieldwork** requires participant-researcher observation and immersion into the culture being studied. Its purpose is to focus on rich, deep contextual meaning, and to provide the reader with descriptive detail. The methodology embraces the study of the private sphere as equally important to the public venue, and is built on the tradition that researchers document the happenings of everyday life.[1]

It would seem natural to investigate women's musical activities in this type of research, but many early studies focused on public-sphere rituals performed by men. The resultant gender imbalance was brought to the attention of the academic world in the 1980s by a number of feminist scholars. Ellen Koskoff's 1987 *Women and Music in Cross-Cultural Perspective* is an example of work that acknowledged the disparity and showcased studies that focused on women. The first decade of the twenty-first century brought forth a large number of similar studies, almost all completed by women.[2] This body of work was a critical addition to the field, but did not get into the hands of a wide audience. Academic textbooks and mass-marketed "teach-yourself-to-play" materials still had a strong tendency to depict world music as a male endeavor. How did this happen?

A WORLD MUSIC CANON?

CASE STUDY
research method that focuses on collection and presentation of detailed information about a particular person or small group; research using this technique is not intended for generalization

With a topic as enormous as world music, there is no way to create a comprehensive textbook. Authors and editors are careful to point out that they use **case study** methodology, and that readers should not assume that the material represents the cultural whole. Still, given the wide array of possible topics in the world, it is surprising that some topics appeared repeatedly in numerous early textbooks. Three cornerstones of first-generation academic materials were Indonesian gamelan music, Hindustani and Karnataka music of India, and West African drumming.[3] Almost all of the initial studies investigated the role of male participants, and failed to explain the absence of women. Some of these topical roots branched all the way into the commercial marketplace.

Readers may remember seeing some world music cornerstone topics covered in grade-school music textbooks, particularly, perhaps, the music of West Africa. The power of the textbook marketplace solidified the early world music core, eventually resulting in the inclusion of the same content in nationalized examinations for teachers. Standardized testing perpetuated a cycle of curricular reproduction within the academic marketplace, as college-level education courses needed to ensure that prospective teachers could pass licensing examinations.[4] Performing ensembles based on these traditions also emerged in high schools and colleges, and the canon became further embedded into a "world music" consciousness. Finally, internet marketing of global instruments and teaching methods helped to proliferate a strikingly similar "world music" picture. Suddenly anyone could purchase a djembe, along with a teaching method designed by an expert, almost always a man.

In the relatively slow, "trickle down" fashion of curricular change, many of the original topics of interest to ethnomusicologists in the 1950s remained in evidence in educational materials a half-century later. It seems safe to say that early studies had a long-lasting influence on a field that portrayed women as lesser-participants.

WORLD MUSIC TEXTBOOKS AT A GLANCE: ILLUSTRATING THE STORY

In his groundbreaking *Teachers and Texts*, Michael Apple suggested that textbooks significantly impact academic curricula.[5] Many professors build their courses around textbooks, and students usually assume that textbook content is accurate and inclusive. Perceptions about world music were interestingly impacted by early textbooks, as first-generation world music courses at the collegiate level were often taught by non-ethnomusicologists. Many professors literally learned both subject matter and methodology from the textbook.[6] Case study methodology ensured a great level of specific detail regarding the topics covered, but the topics of focus were not gender inclusive.

One way to get a general sense of topical coverage in a book is to look at the photography. Photographs not only highlight concepts and people of importance to the author, they leave the reader with lasting impressions. As such, gender representation in world music textbook photography is an important issue to consider.[7] Figures 3.1 and 3.2 show the results of an exercise to replicate the experience of a reader who glances at photographs while paging through a textbook. While not a quantitative study, it does reveal some definite trends. Seven world music textbooks published between 1967 and 2009 were used to compile the data.

Is it fair to judge a book by its cover? Perhaps not, but a look at photography *inside* the textbooks reveals similar coverage. Even in later-edition texts, women were pictured as a minority, while the vast majority of pictures featured men in public-sphere ensemble settings. Figures 3.3, 3.4, and 3.5 show the results of collecting data from four texts published between 1992 and 2009: Figure 3.3 features data from the 1990s texts; Figure 3.4 shows data from the 2000s texts; Figure 3.5 is a compilation of both sets of data. There were 465 photographs where sex was immediately obvious.

If your eyes were drawn away from the text and toward the graphs in this chapter, you have first-hand experience of the power of illustration. A half-century after the inception of the world music academic market, images that featured men significantly outnumbered images that featured women. As might be expected, the content was deeply associated with the photographic coverage.

Why?

One reason for the lack of reporting on women had to do with the initial balance of men and women who studied world music. Highly regarded ethnomusicologist Ruth Stone indicates that women were underrepresented in the field initially,[8] and at surface level that might suggest gender bias among

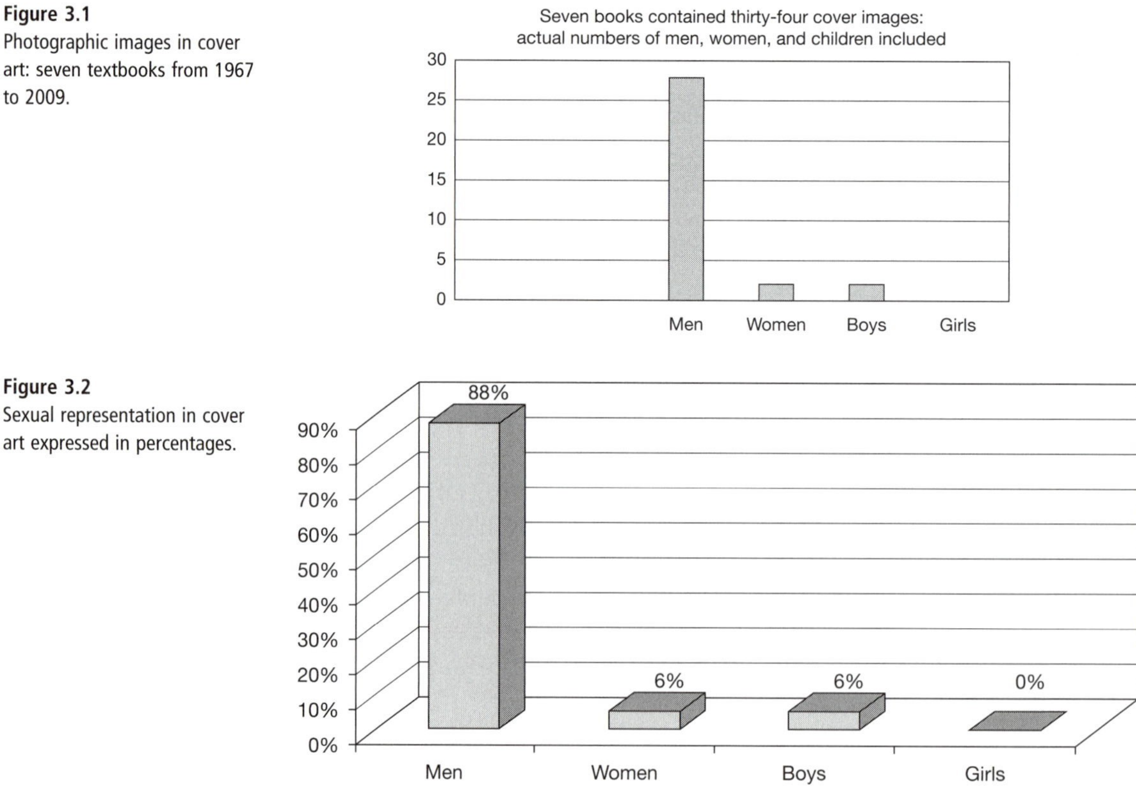

Figure 3.1
Photographic images in cover art: seven textbooks from 1967 to 2009.

Figure 3.2
Sexual representation in cover art expressed in percentages.

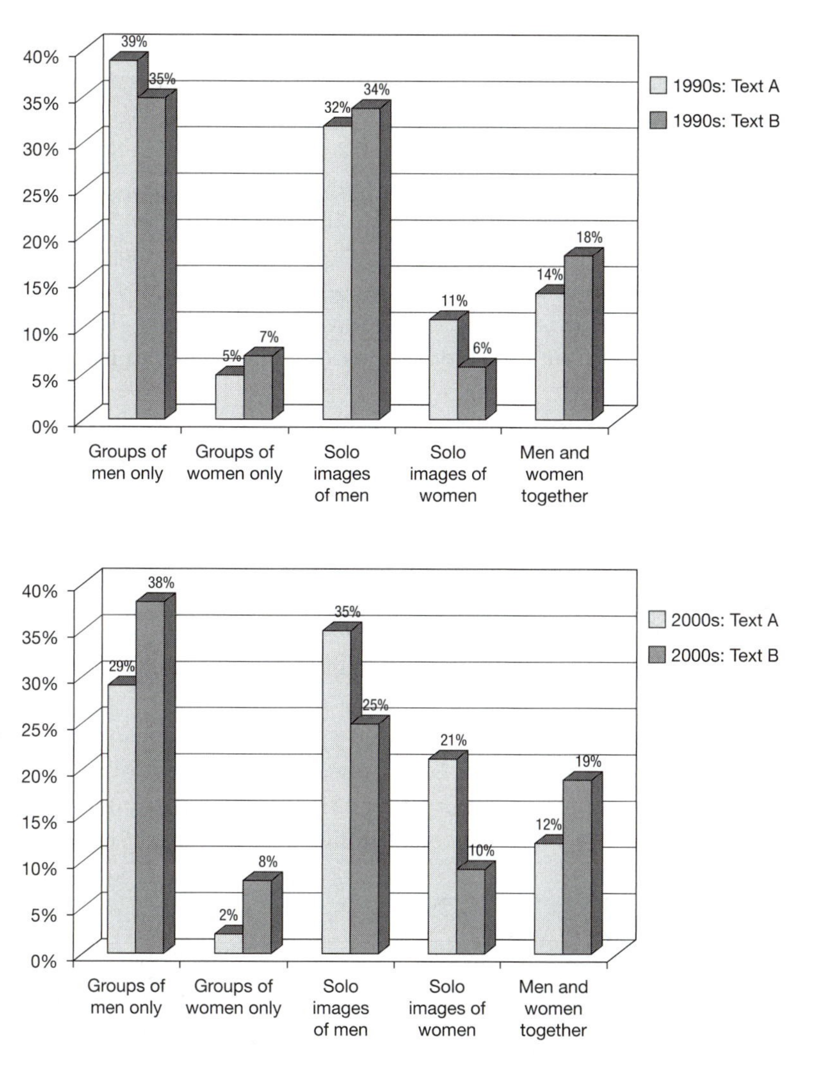

Figure 3.3
Comparing in-text photography: two textbooks from the 1990s.

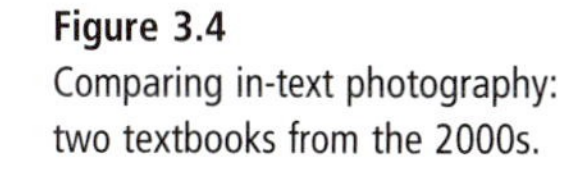

Figure 3.4
Comparing in-text photography: two textbooks from the 2000s.

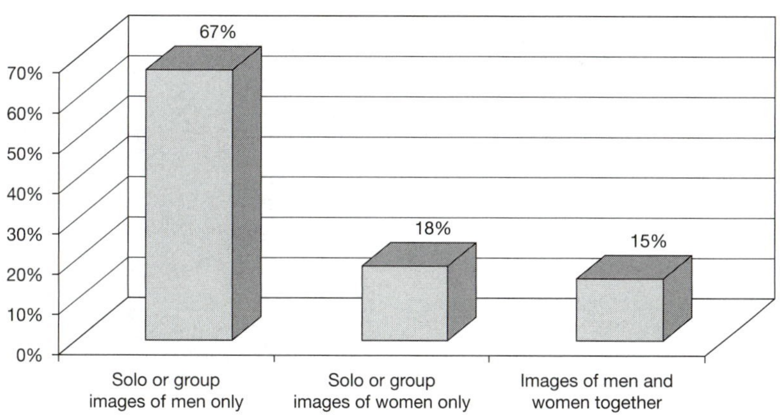

Figure 3.5
Total percentages of men and women in four textbooks: analysis of 465 in-text photographs from 1990 to 2010.

the researchers. While it may be the case that researcher interest impacted topic selection, it is certain that male researchers were sometimes denied access to women's private-sphere rituals. Women in ethnomusicology sometimes have an advantage in regard to gaining such access, which makes their ongoing participation in the field critically important.

Issues of access aside, early materials that featured male world music traditions often failed to address the absence of women. Nor did they discuss how gender perceptions and roles vary by culture.[9] To better understand how cultural perspective impacts understanding of gender roles, let us think through multiple meanings of the banning of women's voices in Orthodox Judaism.

KOLISHA
"the voice of woman"; Orthodox Jewish belief that women must not sing in the presence of men due to the potential to distract men in prayer

MARIACHI
Latin American ensemble originally from Mexico; traditionally features a variety of guitars as well as two or more of each of the following: violins, vihuela, guitarron, trumpets

GAMELAN
percussion-dominated ensemble prevalent in several regions in Indonesia

The practice of **kolisha** might be viewed as both restrictive and liberating for women. For women who embrace the practice, it is a way in which they realize their divine purpose.[10] For other women, the practice seems oppressive. Opinions are strong on both sides. The main problem with this type of situation is not one of determining a correct "answer," but rather that the practice is discussed in terms of culturally specific gender roles. Early materials ignored those discussions. They also failed to point out that there were other musical activities in which women participated in the cultures that were highlighted.

Disagreement remains regarding what should be the focus of study in women's world music activity. Some researchers condemn studies that investigate women's involvement in traditions that were originally constructed as "male." Thus the study of all-women **mariachi** groups and **gamelan**

Figures 3.6 and 3.7
Although the djembe (left) is often shown in male hands, historical accounts of its origins state that the instrument and its rhythms originated with women. Women often worked in groups of two or three, alternating the pounding of their pestles into large mortars to grind grain. The polyrhythmic sound probably informed djembe rhythms. Also notice the similar shape of the mortar and the djembe.

ensembles, for example, would be considered a "second best" solution. These scholars prefer to address "matriarchal" music-making, viewing it as the unique and culturally powerful contribution of women. They claim that the control-oriented, time-driven music of male ensembles needs to be presented with an alternative view.[11] Opponents of this perspective acknowledge that culturally defined gender roles exist, but hold fast that sex is not a factor in creating, performing, or consuming music, and thus any field in which women participate should be considered.[12]

WOMEN'S ROLES IN WEST AFRICAN RITUAL: OUTSIDER ASSUMPTIONS AND INSIDER REVELATIONS

To address the role of researcher perspective in creating narrative, this section of the chapter investigates an insider's perspective on women's roles in one traditional West African music-based ritual. Interview data from a master drummer of Ghana tells a story that is quite different from the often-told narrative.

Perhaps no world music topic has captivated America more than the music of West Africa. By the end of the twentieth century, folk singers such as Raffi delighted children with songs such as "Akan Drum" and "Anansi," while senior citizens exercised mind and body in drumming circles. What many people called "African drumming" was actually a specific West Coast polyrhythmic style that American ethnomusicologists first studied in the 1940s and 1950s.

Consumers who wanted to learn how to *play* "African drums" had a vast number of alternatives. Self-motivators could select from "teach-yourself-to-play" books, audio-visual materials, and online lessons. Those who wanted actual lessons could turn to local community classes or private teachers. Both academic and commercial materials consistently presented the expert drummers as male. To master drummers such as Kwesi Brown, there is much more to the **Akan** ritual than the drumming.

AKAN
ethnic group of West Africa

An Interview with Kwesi Brown

Kwesi Brown's personal history is one of dualisms. His grandmother, a fetish priestess in the Akom ancestral religion of his culture, allowed him access to rituals that were forbidden to men. His father, a Methodist minister, punished him for his trips to his grandmother's shrine. Kwesi's love of drumming compelled him not only to return to the shrine as a youth but also to revisit his culture as a researcher. Today, he is both a master drummer and a trained ethnomusicologist. One of the first things that Kwesi explains is that drumming roles for women vary depending on audience and setting:

> Women and drumming changed a lot in Ghana because of globalization and Western influence. A lot of cultural groups moved from the village to attract tourists. Drumming groups have adopted many things just to be different from other groups. So if you have a woman who plays the role of master drummer, which is not a common thing even among men to acquire that position, you attract more customers. The Ghana Tourist Board uses such groups to generate income for the nation. But you only see this in the cities . . . Tourists don't understand that you won't find the same thing when you put this dance in context.[13]

In the traditional context, women have a very different role, one that is often viewed as restricted because it has nothing to do with drumming. In Kwesi's **matrilineal** culture, however, women's ritualistic musical roles mirror the importance that women have in society. Women such as Kwesi's grandmother have tremendous power in the community. He explained:

MATRILINEAL
tracing ancestral descent through the maternal line

> The priestess, or akomfu, is like a body guard for the community. It is a matriarchal society. They were the owners of the land. A priestess sees everything. If a king or a queen is in trouble, they go to a priestess. The akomfu knows everything . . . These women serve as the watchdog of the community. They check wrongdoings in a community. They are there to protect the community, and they are there to punish . . . You respect them, and you fear them based on the deity they work with. You respect them and you love them.

While cultural outsiders often turn their focus to Akan drumming, the drummer actually serves a higher purpose: to enable the priestess to enter into spirit possession. Kwesi believes that it is the outsider's association of drumming with ultimate power that impacts the perception that women are being excluded. The greatest power, he says, is found in the song and dance performed by women. In addition, it is a Western mindset that artificially separates the musical elements of the ritual:

OKOMFO/AKOMFU
priest or priestess in the Akan tribal religion

> The role of the drummer—the master drummer—is to work with the traditional priest or priestess to inspire possession. Most of the **akomfu** are women. You hardly see male **okomfo**. Drummers, they use the men . . . The spirits like "music." The whole ritual is based on "music." I use music in quotation because music in the Western world can be drumming, dancing, or singing, and in our vocabulary you cannot take these apart. You'll say, "That dancer can sing the movement. This drummer can dance the rhythm."
>
> So the drum and the drummer play a major role in the ritual; the drummer brings the spirit to possess the akomfu. But while the spirit is there, there is a *focus* on what the *women* are saying, found in the song. When they get

Figure 3.8
Fetish priestesses celebrating Swedru Akwambo festival in Ghana.
Source: Photo courtesy of Kwesi Brown

> possessed there is information in the song; the song is where the information lies. You see that men will sit and women will stand in the ensemble. Why? When you are up the sound travels; you can project to the world. Women have that role because they are very powerful in what they say . . . Their song is always focused on the welfare of the people.

The gender-specific roles of this ritual hold deep meaning for Kwesi. I asked him to speculate why the significant role of women in song and dance is sometimes absent in the typical narrative. Along with suggesting that outsiders cannot fully comprehend the spiritual aspects of the ritual, Kwesi admits that researcher interest and access are also issues:

> It's up to the scholar. He or she—mostly he—goes into the field and he looks for male things. Also, the woman priestess probably isn't comfortable talking to men. So when women researchers go, they get more information. Women would be more open to talking with another woman.

Kwesi also points out that women do play instruments in his culture, but that the ceremonies are not accessible to men. Many of the **life-cycle rituals** occur infrequently, sometimes only once per year. Interestingly, the gender tables are turned when it comes to tourism, as men sometimes perform women's rituals for tourists:

LIFE-CYCLE RITUALS community events that celebrate important rites of passage such as birth, puberty, marriage, and death

> Women's ensembles in Ghana are a very old tradition. In traditional women's ensembles, you find shakers, you'll find bells or castanets, or they will stretch their cloth and then play, or do hand clapping. There's one ensemble you'll find where they use clay with snake skin stretched on it. These ensembles are used for rituals such as the Dipo, a ritual for girls going through their puberty rights. They do this dance called tokwe, which is an initiation dance for the rite-of-passage. Again, if you go to Ghana, most of the culture troupes are performing it, and you see guys doing the dance. I call it the chicken dance because so many things have changed in it. Guys perform tokwe now and people don't care. But if you go to the village, males don't do it. It's the same thing with women playing drums.

Kwesi Brown's story is just one example of how researcher perspective impacts narrative in ethnomusicology. As a cultural insider, Kwesi's access to authentic sources, particularly his grandmother, significantly impacted his perception of musical gender roles. His narrative subsequently differs from the often-told story of West African "drumming." At the same time, Kwesi tells his story from a male perspective, and his narrative may differ from that told by a woman. Some women feel strongly that traditions such as this purposefully and systematically withhold women from participation, a topic that is discussed in some detail in Chapter 10.

MAMA, SING ME THAT SONG: THE POWER OF MATRIARCHAL MUSIC

> *The rabbis came back to the orphanage at bedtime and all the children were going to sleep. The rabbis quietly walked up and down the aisles and they started singing the Shema, and they heard the children cry "Eema, Eema, Eema!"—"Mother," in Hebrew. Nothing could erase the underlying* ***knowledge*** *and* ***power*** *of their mothers singing that prayer to them. And when I heard that story, besides crying with my friends, we all vowed that we would start singing it to our children.*[14]
>
> Michelle Wallach, Mother of Noah and Samuel

Knowledge and power: What two words have been more widely connected with the male sphere? And yet, when one looks beyond the history books, men and women throughout the world commonly articulate the role of mother in conveying knowledge and power to her family, her people, her culture. Often, this knowledge and power is conveyed via music.

Here we deviate from the historical-analytical model as we experience alternative methods of researching, preserving, and presenting knowledge about women in music. Using interview data and narrative-style documentation, the stories of three mothers demonstrate the power of music in the hands of women.[15] These women are keepers of their children's personal history, but also acknowledge their motherly role in helping their children negotiate inevitable change.[16]

The stories included here provide a glimpse of the role of music in a growing segment of the world population, those who have been **culturally displaced**. At the same time, the narratives allow a deeper understanding of matriarchal music-making. It is often self-created, sometimes improvised, frequently oral, and often performed without the use of tools, electronics, or instruments. It is commonly acknowledged as life-sustaining, powerfully simple, and open to listening.[17] The folk songs, prayers, lullabies, and teaching songs addressed in this portion of the chapter remind us of the timeless musical role of mothers, composer-creators of some of the most powerful music ever performed.

CULTURAL DISPLACEMENT
the separating of people from their native culture

Story One: Creating Cultural Identity in a "Third Culture" Kid

He is divided in two worlds.[18]

Lucy Vergara

Thinking Back

When Lucy Vergara remembers her childhood in Mexico City, her memories are permeated with the sound of her mother's voice in song. At home, in the car, and at school, it was her mother's untrained, unaccompanied voice that carried tradition to Lucy and her three siblings in a variety of informal settings. Today, as Lucy raises her young son in the Midwestern United States, it is this body of song that she shares as she counteracts an often inauthentic presentation of Mexican culture and music in a variety of public venues, including public schools. The musical traditions that Lucy is handing down to her son come from her mother's informal repertoire, a vocal tradition that was in turn learned from Lucy's grandmother. The mother's role in transmitting musical tradition is longstanding in Mexico, and remains the role of mothers of Mexican descent today, says Lucy:

> Whenever I meet a Hispanic family, I see it is the mom who brings the traditional music. For example, we have "nine days before Christmas" parties, and that's very traditional. I think in most Latin American countries there's a religious part of the celebration where you will pray, and many of the prayers are sung. Then after *that* there's a big party, and there's always tons of food involved, and listening to music and dancing. It's the mom who's going to bring the recordings and the songs into play.

Following the tradition of most Mexican families of the 1960s and 1970s, Lucy lived with her parents until she was married at age twenty-five. When she and her husband of three years left Mexico to seek their graduate education in Texas, she felt torn from her family and had every intention of returning to Mexico:

> It took two days to get to Texas. I cried pretty much the whole ride. I wanted to come, but it was like physically ripping me up from my roots, just going to the unknown. I think I was in the Ph.D. program when I knew we weren't going back. My husband really didn't want to go back. He'd say, "Look at all the work we've done and we're going to go back and get the same job."

And so they stayed, each seeking academic positions in American universities. After taking positions in two Midwestern schools, they settled in to their careers and began to raise their infant son in a new land.

A Sense of Cultural Identity: A Mother's Hopes and Fears

THIRD-CULTURE KID child whose parents reside outside of their passport country for extended periods of time

As a **third-culture kid**, Lucy Vergara's son, Rafael, is a child of two countries: the one of his parents' birth, and the one in which he is being raised. His mother is keenly aware of how her son continually negotiates his identity:

> What I am seeing now—I don't know if he can even articulate this—is that he is divided between two countries. And that's going to be rough for him as he grows up. He has gone through stages here where he felt he wanted to hide it. At five, he didn't want people to know that he spoke Spanish. I think the biggest advantage for him is that he's going to be more open to diversity. He's going to grow up in a world that is becoming more and more global. He's really, really going to be aware of racial differences and the struggles of some people and the advantages of other people . . . We go from a very comfortable situation here (in the Midwest) and we go to Mexico in these villages (where) the food is not the same, the level of comfort is not the same. He has asked, for example, when he sees people asking for money on the corners—he will ask why. That's one of my worries. The more he grows and learns about Mexican government and the things that happen there, because he didn't grow up there, he may lose that sense of pride.

The Role of Music in Creating Identity

To help her son understand parts of his identity that are not available to him daily, Lucy continually makes efforts to connect her son with Mexican culture, and one of the most effective tools for doing so is music. Whether at home in the United States or at home with family in Mexico, folk songs, patriotic songs, and traditional "family songs" are important parts of daily life:

> Every time I go to Mexico I get him music and tales; audio books of children's tales and books, of course. We read a lot, do tongue twisters and songs. I got the national anthem and I wanted to play it every Monday for him just as I grew up every Monday listening to the national anthem. I felt that he needs to have both. They do that in his school all the time, so I thought he needs to hear both anthems. I am a strong believer that music gives culture, more than if I were to just explain to him what culture means. The melodic terms, the rhythm, the environment you create with a song or a dance—I think it's a big part of my son being comfortable at home (in Mexico). There's a sense of recognizing some cultural things because of the music.

Lucy's belief in a connection between musical elements and identity construction is echoed across cultures. Cultural "world views" are often expressed in the actual construction of traditional music. For example, in many Native American cultures, cyclical time is important, and musical representations of the circle metaphorically express important spiritual concepts. When the performer or listener links musical elements such as rhythm and melody to a philosophy of life, the music enables a deep connection with self.[19] Native Estonians cite music, particularly singing, as one of the most essential means of constructing, preserving, and expressing national identity,[20] and renowned Hungarian music educator Zoltán Kodály proclaimed the critical importance of the folk music style, notably basing his methodology on what appeared to be the simplest of music.[21] Latino communities commonly use music to construct and maintain community, articulate values, and define ethnicity.[22] For third-culture kids such as Rafael, however, there is a chance that they will receive an inauthentic version of their musical heritage. The role of the mother is thus critical. Says Vergara:

> I don't see how authentic culture will be preserved unless I work very actively to preserve it. One day they told Rafael at school that they were going to do an "authentic" Mexican song. The teacher asked, "Can we put a big hat on your son, because he's going to represent Mexico." I got nauseated, and thought, "No, you're making a big cliché out of my son." But in that moment I thought I needed to play along and be flexible so they can do their multicultural program. When I got to the program I saw my son coming out with this huge hat, and they're playing *Feliz Navidad* by Jose Feliciano (who is from Puerto Rico). And they had told him, "This is from your heritage. This is authentic."

And indeed, Lucy is not alone in expressing her concern about authenticity in the classroom. Though educators are increasingly seeing their students as the best sources of authentic music,[23] the risk of losing the authentic traditions is very real for a third-culture kid.

> It's a tough thing, I will say, as an immigrant, to know whether your child will continue to pass along that tradition, because the only place he really gets to do that is at home. It's a big competition between what he does at home and with his friends. I think it's important for him to know about Mexican culture and be proud of it and to keep it because that's what he is. And at the same time I know he is divided in two worlds.

Recognizing Her Son's Heritage: A Mother Listens

> I had to understand at some point that I also had to learn *his* heritage. I also need to sing songs for him that are American, because that's what he is. I had to learn that and open the door at home for that. There was a moment when we were getting some stuff for Fourth of July, and they were selling the small flags—he has a Mexican flag in his room—and we were getting ready to pay and he said, "Will you buy one for me?" And my automatic "mom" reaction when he asks for something in the checkout line is to say no, but he said—he had his flag in his hand—"Why not? I have one from Mexico." And that just turned my head around. "You're right." Why would he have one and not the other? And I told him, "You're completely right." So he now has two flags on a pole in his room together. To me it was very symbolic that he was telling me, "Hey, hello! I am both!"

Story Two: Learning the Language of Her Children: Bicultural Kids and the Musical Role of Mother

> *Kemunto was born about a year after we were married and she is named after her Kenyan great-grandmother on her father's side. During the early migration days, history has it that the Kisii tribe migrated from the North. During this long trek, men were charged as providers, so the responsibility of keeping the family intact fell to the women. As they moved between locations, they needed a leader who would give them strength, guidance, and hope in order to survive the dangerous terrain. Those who took that leadership role were known as Kemunto.*[24]
>
> Wendy Mogaka

Worlds Apart

As a child, Wendy Mogaka never dreamed that she would be the mother of Kenyan-American children. Raised in a rural farm community in Wisconsin, she was the daughter of a stay-at-home mother and a factory worker. They were European-Americans who never traveled outside of the Midwestern United States, let alone across the globe. Her school days were filled with activities that revolved around family, church, and music-making, and she was especially involved in the school concert band. As much as she loved music, she chose a career in mathematics, and today balances her work at a world banking firm with the work of raising four children.

Half a world away, Wendy's future husband was living in the village of Kisii, Kenya, in a home with a grass-thatched roof, walls and floor made of dirt, and no running water. John Mogaka's father worked for British colonial residents, doing housework, yard work, and carpentry, and he taught himself to write and speak English. John's mother stayed at home, like all rural Kenyan women of the mid-to-late twentieth century, and only left the house to perform necessary tasks, such as selling excess vegetables at market. The role of John's mother as singer of the everyday song etched a permanent memory in the mind of her first-born son, and remained with him as he traveled to the United States to seek a college education.

John and Wendy met at a small liberal arts college in Iowa, dated, and were soon married. Within a year of their marriage, their first daughter, Kemunto, was born, and three additional children were born to the Mogaka family within the next ten years. Their first-born son, Sagana, was named after his grandfather (Mogaka Sagana) and his great-grandfather, Sagana. The twins, Misiani and Moruri, were named after John's aunts. Wendy has proudly embraced the role of helping her children understand their dual heritage, and with the help of her husband, has used music to carry on traditions that John learned from his mother in Kenya:

> We started singing African songs to Kemunto right after she was born. John sang a song to her, and I picked up on it. For me the biggest thing is that I have not completely learned Swahili. I know greetings and things like that, but it was a way for me that I could sing and teach her some of the Kisii and Swahili that I already knew. I think it was actually around the time that our second child, Sagana, was born that John also then taught us a song that they used to teach children how to learn their numbers in Kenya.

A Family Musical Heritage

John remembers the musicianship of his aunts, for whom the twins were named, and the important role they had in the life of his family. Moruri was a singer and Misiani was a singer and dancer:

> My dad did not sing a lot, but once in awhile for special occasions. If the family was getting together to celebrate a special occasion like Christmas, my

> Dad would sing. Everyone would see Dad was really singing. Wow. Everyone would see his face smiling. When his sisters came to visit him, because his sisters were good singers and dancers, then you'd see him really join the singing. They would be singing, praising him. I could see that when his sisters came to visit him that there was a lot of joy on his face. One of the reasons I have the kids (twins) named after my father's side of the family is that they were good singers and good dancers, and loved their only brother dearly.[25]

Life in Kisii was steeped in music. John recalls that there was no radio in his childhood home, and the musical memories that he wanted to transmit to his American family were based on the music of everyday living:

> My mom sang. Many moms, I think that's how they start talking with their kids. That's how they get them to start talking, a lot of singing. Moms sang every day, even when the baby was not asleep. It is a part of entertainment. Singing is everywhere. Walking, people are singing. Picking or harvesting, people are singing for entertainment because there is not (recorded) music around. Many people do not have running water in the house, so they are going downstream to fetch water. For entertainment they are singing. Besides all of that, the kids are singing everywhere. Singing is part of life, part of communication, part of passing along a message.

Conveying the Message in a New Land

Wendy knows that passing along that message is important, and that it lies, to a great extent, in her hands. While John conveyed a body of lullabies and teaching songs to her, it was her role as mother to sing them every day, replicating the experience that her husband had with his own mother:

> I want my kids to know their African heritage. It's very important for them to know both cultures, especially since we live in the United States. I want to make sure that they don't lose their Kenyan background. Music is an important part of who you are. It forms who you are. I would sing Kemunto American songs, but usually when I sang the Swahili song it seemed like the one that put her down easiest. And the twins especially. The counting song is to this day their lullaby. Now that Kemunto and Sagana are older they are starting to do their own music and singing to the little ones.

Listening to the Next Generation: An Authentic Blending of Cultures

An initial hearing of the Mogaka family lullaby might lead one to think that this isn't traditional "African" music, or that Wendy, as an American mother, altered the song musically. The Mogaka version sounds somewhat like the French/British *Are You Sleeping*? and the lyrics are topically related. But Kisii in the days of John's youth already reflected a variety of influences that intertwined to create John's cultural childhood. He explains, "There are Catholics. There are Protestants. And if you go out there are people that practice Islam. Tribal religion, no. Tribal traditions, yes."

It makes sense that John's musical experiences are permeated with French and British musical culture, but like all evolving music cultures, there is local musical nuance, local meaning in the lyrics, and a definite use of the song for teaching. Not only is the song in Swahili, but John learned it in his local Kisii dialect. For Wendy as mother, a key reason to sing is transmission of language. Numerous studies have examined the mother's role in facilitating language acquisition via song,[26] and Wendy's choice to facilitate the learning of both Kisii and English is notable. Along with teaching her *children* Kisii, she is simultaneously improving her own skills.

The fact that Wendy, not John, became the daily singer of these songs reflects not only matriarchal tradition but also a physiological and psychological connection between mother and children. It is Wendy's hope that her children will learn about their complete heritage via *her* voice, even as she simultaneously learns about her own children more deeply. The

LISTENING EXPERIENCE 3.1

Kisii Lullaby (recorded 2010)
Sung by Kemunto Mogaka
Companion CD Track 3

LISTENING FOCUS

As you listen to Kemunto Mogaka sing the family lullaby, notice the ways in which the song reflects the French/British "Are You Sleeping?"; also notice how the song varies in terms of phrase endings, pitches, and rhythm. In addition, Kemunto personalizes the lullaby for one of her twin sisters, calling her by name.

TEXT

Mtoto Misiani, Mtoto Misiani, *Child Misiani, Child Misiani*
Noraire? *Are you sleeping?*
Noraire? *Are you sleeping?*
Noigwete eke'ngere? *Can you hear the bell ring?*
Noigwete eke'ngere? *Can you hear the bell ring?*
Ding Dong Do
Ding Dong Do

LISTENING EXPERIENCE 3.2

Kisii Counting Song (recorded 2010)
Sung by Sagana Mogaka
Companion CD, Track 4

LISTENING FOCUS

In this example, Sagana Mogaka sings the "counting" song in Swahili, a tradition that he is able to effectively practice by singing to his younger twin sisters.

TEXT

Moja, Mbili, Tatu, Nne, Tano, Sita, Saba, Nane, Tisa, Kuuumi

One, Two, Three, Four, Five, Six, Seven, Eight, Nine, Ten

transmission of a Kenyan song through Wendy's European-American voice is wonderfully symbolic of her children's racial and ethnic heritage. And while no one can predict what the Mogaka children will choose to retain from this experience, twelve-year-old Kemunto and nine-year-old Sagana are already singing the traditional songs to their younger siblings.

And so, a tradition is both alive and transformed; the songs that were sung by a mother in Kisii continue to be sung in Chicago. When the Mogaka children remember the songs of their childhood, the music that echoes through their minds will no doubt resonate in the timbre of their mother's voice.

Story Three: The Role of Mother in Conveying Spiritual Tradition

Michelle Wallach was raised Catholic by parents who dedicated themselves to the Catholic Church. Both parents had once been part of professed religious communities but felt the call to marry and have children, living their life of devotion in a new manner. Their "conversion" experience was not to be the only one in their family. Michelle Wallach's conversion to Judaism was not a typical conversion that accompanied a life-cycle event such as marriage, as one might suppose, given that her husband is Jewish. Rather, Michelle says it was "meant to be."

This is a story that examines the exploration of personal spirituality beyond the birth family unit, and the role of a Jewish mother in teaching her children about a faith tradition that differed in many ways from her own childhood experience. Michelle's journey has been marked by surprise, disappointment, acceptance, and joy, as she worked to understand the role of women as musicians and mothers in a faith experience that she has only lived in her adult life:

> I met my future husband when I was seventeen. There's a term called bisheret —it was meant to be. In high school I had already started exploring Judaism, and I was taking classes at Hillel, which is a Jewish facility on campus. My journey just sort of took off from there. Between my twenty-first and twenty-second birthday I converted to Judaism on my own, which is a little bit unusual. Most people wait until a life-cycle event—marriage, death—before they would consider this sort of a change—usually marriage. For me, there was no dramatic, life-altering event. I just knew I was ready.

Dreams of Being a Cantor

As a classically trained singer who had a deep spiritual calling, Michelle longed to be trained as a cantor. As a Reform Jew, it was possible, and her aunt-in-law served as a mentor, being one of the first women in the Conservative movement to be ordained a cantor:

> Aunt Renee was one of the first. She was the second or third woman in the Conservative movement to be ordained as a cantor, at the Jewish Theological Seminary in New York, which is the main academic body for training for Conservative rabbis and cantors. She was really part of history in the making, at least for the Conservative movement. That was a really big step for them to start acknowledging women in music.
>
> I was accepted into HUC, Hebrew Union College in New York, which is the Reform movement's primary educational program. I did an intensive study right after we were married. I took Hebrew—I had taken it in college—but I started to develop a fluency that was necessary for the entrance exams. A lot of the prep work was just learning the prayers. During a trip to Israel I visited a Sephardic **shul**. I went upstairs, and I could barely see because they had this lattice-work screen, and it was very ornate, and I couldn't follow anything because the Orthodox Hebrew is just so fast. So I couldn't understand a single word. I didn't know what was going on. I was surrounded by women of all different ages, all nicely dressed, and here I am looking very schlubby—I had just been digging in a hole in the middle of the desert the day before at an archeological site. And these women are looking at me like *what is wrong with you*? Then in the middle of the service, somebody takes their siddur, a Jewish prayer book, and thumps me on the middle of the forehead. And I look at her and she only gestures—she takes her finger from her eye and points down—*look down*. I didn't realize it, but they were saying the *Shema*, and I was supposed to cover my eyes and look down.

SHUL
a synagogue

Motherhood: A Change of Plans

Michelle's plans to become a cantor rapidly changed when she and Dan learned that they were expecting their first child. It wasn't long before the role of mothering became Michelle's new calling.

> When I had my boys in 2004 and 2007, it was such an important thing for me to pass on what I had learned and what I'm continuing to learn, and have them experience it first hand by going to services and hearing me practice in the home. One of the most important things for me to pass on to them is learning the *Shema*. It is, besides the other prayer, the *Amidah*, a daily prayer that you say upon waking and before going to sleep. "Hear, O Israel, the eternal is our God. The eternal is one. Blessed is God's glorious majesty forever and ever." And it is, in my mind, the most important prayer that you can say. In Orthodoxy, Conservative, and Reform Judaism, they all highly value that prayer, so I've taught it to my children. We say it every night before bed. They can both say it—even Sam in his garbled two-year-old voice can say it with me. With children, religion is a sensory experience.
>
> For Judaism, especially for me and for Danny when he was growing up, music was such an integral part of how we learned our Hebrew, how we learned the vernacular of prayer. That could also be said about the Jewish tradition of cooking. So much of Judaism is about food and wine. It's the actual "doing" process, and experiencing and smelling the challah that's baking in the oven on Shabbat. When you smell the chicken soup, you know it's Shabbat. But the same goes with music. Music has always been something that is celebrated. It's been a really important part of how we identify with our different religions: Catholicism and Judaism.

Teaching a Heritage

> What really made it an emotional moment—knowing that I was doing the right thing musically with my children—was when I heard this story that I'll relay to you.
>
> In Alsace-Lorraine in 1945, two rabbis, one from America and one from London, England, had gone to help liberate some of the camps and to ease the transition for the survivors of the camps in World War II Nazi Germany. But in Alsace-Lorraine they came across information that there were young children who had been separated from their parents before transporting them to camp. The parents had left their children in the hands of orphanages, Catholic orphanages to be specific. And there was one in this particular province where they went, and they decided to make it their mission to find these children, take them under their wing, and perhaps find another family for them later on. But when they approached the priests who ran the

orphanage, the priests were very protective because they didn't want anybody to identify these children as Jews for their own protection. They were doing their best. The priests said, "If you can't prove if specific children here are Jewish, you need to leave the property." One rabbi said, "Wait. We have one test that we want to do, and it won't cause any pain. Please let us come back at bedtime."

They came back at bedtime and all the children were going to sleep. The rabbis quietly walked up and down the aisles, and they started singing the *Shema*, and they heard shouts of "Eema, Eema, Eema!"—"Mother," in Hebrew. These children had been converted to Catholicism in a beautiful way, in a way to try and save them. That could not erase the underlying knowledge and power of their mothers singing that prayer to them.

And when I heard that story, besides crying with my friends, we all vowed that we would start singing it to our children. I had already started, but it really solidified the concept that it's my duty as a mother to teach my children how to pray, and what better way to do that than through song?

LISTENING EXPERIENCE 3.3

Singing of the *Shema* (recorded 2010)
Performed by Michelle, Noah, and Samuel Wallach
Companion CD, Track 5

LISTENING FOCUS

In the spirit of the matriarchal tradition, it is fitting to conclude this chapter by allowing the reader to simply listen and reflect as Michelle, Noah, and Samuel Wallach sing the *Shema*.

Figure 3.9
Michelle, Noah, and Samuel.
Source: Photo courtesy of the Wallach family

SUMMARY

Music is not a universal language in terms of how it is understood from culture to culture, but all cultures reflect and construct gender relationships via music. Through the study of musical traditions and practices, there is much to learn about culturally defined gender roles. Unfortunately, musical realities and cultural truths are presented inaccurately when women's perspectives are missing. The stories included in this chapter demonstrated a few ways in which world-music narratives can describe women's culturally defined roles and perspectives. If researchers are concerned about the validity of their selected "world music" portrayals, women need to be included in the picture.

QUESTIONS FOR CRITICAL THINKING AND DISCUSSION

1. Respect for tradition is a delicate balancing act for ethnomusicologists. How is respect for racial, ethnic, or religious diversity related to gender issues?
2. Have you ever participated in a musical experience in which you defied culturally defined gender roles? Explain the situation, including reactions you received, and your feelings about the overall experience.
3. What are the advantages and disadvantages of relying on **primary source** materials such as data derived from interviews?

IDEAS FOR FURTHER RESEARCH

1. The designation of music as matriarchal or patriarchal is laden with controversy. Investigate scholarship that both embraces this separation and negates it. What are some of the main arguments that scholars use to support their contentions? What are your conclusions? You may want to begin by examining the terms "matriarchal" and "patriarchal" outside of a musical setting.
2. Men's instrumental ensembles still prevail in world music textbooks. Conduct research on an all-women's ensemble of interest to you.
3. Do internet research and look at the cover art on world music materials marketed to the general public, including books and methods intended to teach amateurs to perform on instruments such as the djembe or didgeridoo. What do you notice about gender representation?

PRIMARY SOURCE
artifact that provides first-hand accounts of historical events or subjects; letters, diaries and original music manuscripts are examples

GUIDED RESEARCH PROJECT PART I

DEFINING FEMINISM

Part I of the text presented information about the importance of researcher perspective on the reporting of historical events and trends in music, but with little overt reference made to feminist theory and perspective. With the guidance of your professor, attempt to define feminism, and then assess your personal relationship to its many strands. If there is one key concept to take from this assignment, it is that there is not only one definition! As you proceed through the text, continue to refer to your list and identify the variety of perspectives that are included, including your own.

Some focus areas:

1. Quick association: what comes to mind when you hear or see the term "feminist"?
2. What are the historical roots of the connotation that you identified?
3. Identify the "waves" of feminism that are commonly referenced in the twentieth century:
    a. In which historical periods did they exist?
    b. How did they coincide with cultural phenomena of the time?
    c. What political and economic motivations were involved?
    d. How does race intersect with the various waves of feminism?
    e. How are they viewed from today's perspective?
4. Identify specific movements within feminism (for example, environmental, or riot grrrl). Do you find that you relate better to some movements than others? Which ones, and why?
5. Finally, are there overriding principles that allow you to make any generalizations about feminism?

PART II

Restricted Domains

GENDER SPHERES IN ART MUSIC

INTRODUCTION TO PART II

RESTRICTED DOMAINS

Gender Spheres in Art Music

Part II continues to follow the path of Western art music history, moving forward from the medieval roots that were addressed in Chapter 2 to include discussion of the Renaissance, Baroque, and Romantic periods. This segment of the book focuses on secular traditions in which women were involved as both performers and creators, and does so with a focus on strict societal rules that governed their work. Many culturally defined beliefs regarding women's musical roles between 1200 and 1900 still remain evident today.

In an age in which most women were not allowed to obtain an education, women who were employed in court music settings were not only musically educated but were also trained in a variety of intellectual traditions, ranging from poetry and visual art to writing and science. **Chapter 4** examines cross-cultural courtesan traditions in Japan and Europe, noting similarities in musical roles, and also noting the liberation and independence enjoyed by women who were engaged in these traditions. At the same time, it is noted that negative connotations were endured by women who accepted these roles, some of which continue to impact women who perform today.

Chapter 5 looks at women's musical employment as members of families who were engaged in music as a profession. During the period known as the Baroque, both royalty and wealthy families of the rising merchant class hired artisan-class musicians to provide entertainment. Not only did women perform and compose in these settings, but those who had the proper connections also had their works published. Despite the increased opportunity, however, women employed as musicians were restricted to specific musical tasks. The narrative included in this chapter focuses on just three women who became known outside of their restricted domains, only to disappear from written records for several centuries before they were eventually rediscovered.

Just when it appeared that women had broken into the public sphere and were gaining recognition as composers, the rising influence of middle-class culture moved women's musical activity back into the private sphere. The restricted domain of the upper-middle-class home is the focus of **Chapter 6**, and is told via the stories of Fanny Mendelssohn Hensel and Clara Wieck Schumann. In the period of music history labeled "Romantic," families who could most afford to educate their daughters did so with the intent of allowing them the honor of remaining in the home. Women remained musically active, particularly in salon settings, and continued to favor vocal and keyboard works, long considered acceptable for women. Despite their extensive activity, it was sometimes a struggle to get works published, and the restrictions were set in place not only by publishers but sometimes also by women's families, as was the case with Hensel. Clara Schumann's story is intriguing as well, in that she elected to remain in the public eye as a virtuoso performer but was suppressed in historical accounts that preferred to cast her as a dutiful wife and stay-at-home mother.

CHAPTER 4

The Renaissance and Beyond

Courtly Worlds of Women and Music

Once upon a time there was a world in which there were no computers, telephones, cars, or electric lights. Despite the physical separation of the people in this world, there arose among them common ways of living, negotiating, fighting, loving, and entertaining. They sang their own songs in their own languages, but the themes were strikingly similar . . .

There was a time, not long ago, when there was no middle class, and rulers reigned over segments of the earth, governing the land and its people. Most readers of this book would have been among those governed, wondering what it was like on the other side of the courtly walls. Today, we access that royal scene through a blur of fact-based fiction—images filtered through the ages. In Western culture, kings, queens, and armored knights are characters in a courtly story that has been told and retold. But there are lesser-told stories that go beyond war and conquest.

One of the global consistencies of court cultures is that of musical entertainment. Across cultures, the soft sounds of acoustic wind and stringed instruments mingled with voices, many of which were female. While the royal class performed at times, many of the performers were not of the nobility. From Japan, China, Korea, and India to Greece, Italy, France, and England, women of less-than-noble birth accessed the court via their musical skill. They were adulated, even adored, but they were also feared and demeaned. Educated and elevated, they were at the same time social outsiders. What follows is a glimpse of the musical traditions that were formed within their restricted domains.

COMMON COURTLY THEMES

Court performers were among the best-educated women in their respective cultures. In an era when most women did not learn to read, a court musician's education often included study of writing, poetry, and visual arts, as well as music. From this place of educational privilege, women musicians engaged in intellectual exchanges with their male patrons via debate, conversation, and artistic performance, often with greater skill than was possessed by the uneducated women of the home. Confidants as well as entertainers, female court musicians shared part of a musical world that belonged to men, and performed roles that were often inaccessible to other women.[1]

As isolated as various cultures were prior to the electronic age, many societies created strikingly similar intellectual exchanges between patron and performer that wed music and poetry. Male patrons often supplied poetic verse upon which women musically improvised. Thus, artistic song creation was a common court-based activity. This practice was fundamental to the development of European Medieval and Renaissance secular genres such as the troubadour song and madrigal, as well the Japanese kouta.

COURTESAN
female court attendant who is educated or trained as a performer in multiple artistic and intellectual areas

In many ways, the lifestyle of the educated female court musician, commonly known as a ***courtesan***, was glorious and desirable. It included access to education and independence, as well as connections to powerful men. It came with a price, however. In cultures where the role of a virtuous woman was to marry and have children, the unmarried educated woman was considered suspect. In cases where the wife was honored primarily for her role in preserving the bloodline, marriages sometimes aimed to assure political alliances rather than to provide love or intellectual compatibility. Courtesans often provided the companionship that people now expect in a marriage partner. Thus, unmarried performers risked being viewed or treated as morally corrupt. Musical skills elevated the courtesan, but threatened her image as a virtuous woman.

SIREN
half-human, half-animal female who tempts men via song

To make the courtesan's role even more socially tenuous, those who sang were additionally connected to the age-old concept of the **siren**, the alluring voice that is both desirable and dangerous. Although the siren took various cultural forms, she was usually half-human, half-animal, and lived on the border between nature and culture. Hans Christian Anderson's "Little Mermaid" is one siren story, in which the mermaid gives up her voice and temporarily loses her power to control the prince.[2] The courtesan's perceived role as a creature that could control man's reason placed her on society's border. She was powerful enough to command attention, but, for the patron, provided a potentially fatal attraction.[3]

In all, the story of the court performer is one of mystery, allure, and power. A brief examination of myth versus reality in the Japanese geisha tradition will allow useful comparisons to European court traditions that continue to impact Western perceptions of women and music.

THE JAPANESE GEISHA

> *There is an enormous gulf between the geisha's self-image and the way in which the rest of the world sees them.*[4]
>
> Lesley Downer, scholar who lived among geisha in 1999 Kyoto

To begin, it is important to understand a partial history of the term "courtesan." Although the current English connotation is one of simple prostitution, even the Oxford dictionary defines the courtesan as a person "attached to the court of a prince." Further, the *concept* of court attendant does not translate well into all traditions and languages. There is no English equivalent to the Japanese role of "gei-sha," which literally means "arts person." Similarly, the term "cortigiana onesta" references the well-educated and intellectual woman of the Italian court, while the Indian "ganika" was the "civilized woman" proficient in the arts. At the same time, many courtesan traditions did include performed displays of female beauty that were regulated by male patrons, and some traditions linked patron and performer in sexual relationships. In all, unraveling the mystery of these ancient traditions requires careful investigation.

One of the West's major clichés of Japan, the role of the **geisha**, is often misunderstood, even, at times, by inhabitants of Japan. Fully understanding the tradition is difficult, however, because of the secrecy that is part of the geisha's allure.[5] The fact that her performance involved formulaic flirtation only makes the geisha's courtesan role more difficult to define.

GEISHA
courtesan of the Japanese tradition associated with performance of traditional Japanese art forms such as song and dance

The roots of female court performance are deeply embedded in Japanese history, which is steeped in the belief that performance can embody mystical and spiritual power.[6] The Zen practice of controlled breathing in flute performance is just one example. Prior to the tenth century, the imperial court honored female performers whom they believed capable of communicating with gods and spirits. These women, not yet called geisha, enjoyed special privileges as a result of their skill. They were allowed to travel and did not have to pay taxes. The women eventually formed independent households that were financially supported by the emperor. With this support, they became increasingly autonomous. Many were mothers of high-ranking ministers.[7]

> *The romanticism of geisha life . . . ignores the poverty that drove many parents to indenture their daughters.*[8]
>
> Literary scholar Gaye Rowley

The thirteenth-century samurai viewed female court performers differently, however, and considered them sexual labor for commercial exploitation. With military might, the samurai took political control over the emperor, and one consequential change was a restriction of female entertainers to a designated, licensed district. As a result, the women lost political power and economic independence. Two classes of entertainers were licensed by the ruling powers, including one class that was licensed for prostitution. The artistic entertainers, however, received a separate license in acknowledgement of their differentiated role. Still, their placement in the district brought a lasting connotation. In addition, the artists eventually subdivided into various ranks, especially as financially desperate families sent their unskilled daughters to the district. The line between entertainer and prostitute was thus further blurred, even among the performers who came to be called geisha. Higher-class geisha, with superior artistic skills and training, were far less likely to engage in prostitution than were the uneducated, who had little choice.[9]

Even among the artist class, however, there was an aura of the erotic in performance. Geisha were trained to combine musical performance with subtle flirtation and teasing that utilized multi-layered costuming to veil the female body. Even the facial make-up, which left a small amount of unpainted skin exposed, created an impression of secrecy. The idea was to keep the patron wondering, and willing to return in the future.[10]

Links to a Cultural Heritage

EDO PERIOD
Japanese historical period from 1603 to 1868; associated with the development of many lasting Japanese artistic genres

KABUKI THEATRE
dance theatre of Japan that emerged in the Edo period; women were banned from this form of theatre

Many of the genres that artistically define Japan stem from the **Edo period** (1603–1868), and several are connected to the art of the geisha. Among the significant art forms that arose in that period are **Kabuki theatre** (a dance theatre with musical accompaniment), musical genres such as the kouta (short-song), and woodblock printing. The banning of women from Kabuki, beginning in 1629, was fundamental to the direction in which geisha artistically turned.

Unlike the separation of genres that often exists in Western cultures, the Japanese performance arts are tightly linked. Since theatre was a major performance venue for classical music and dance, women banned from the theatre were excluded from those art forms. They continued to perform in alternative venues, however. In teahouse performances, geisha transformed storylines from the theatre into their own setting, and also performed specific dances and excerpts directly from the Kabuki repertoire. The **shamisen**, a plucked, three-stringed instrument that originated in Okinawa, emerged as the primary accompaniment for these performances, and is strongly associated with the geisha.[11]

SHAMISEN
a plucked, three-stringed instrument of Japan; associated with the geisha

Along with accompanying their own voices in theatre-related genres, geisha used the shamisen to create musical accompaniments to fit their patrons' poetry. The genre that arose from this practice, the **kouta**, was a short song of one to three minutes' duration. Much of the poetic text was of an erotic nature, filled with imagery. Just as clothing and dance related to the geisha art is subtle, kouta lyrics feature a restrained sensuality that was masked by suggestive metaphors and puns. Lyrical lines often contained five to seven syllables, typical of much traditional Japanese poetry.[12]

KOUTA
Japanese "short song" of one to three minutes' duration, often with erotic, poetic text that is filled with metaphor; associated with the geisha tradition

Improvising to the verse was a musically challenging task, because the patrons were often musical amateurs. Geisha were expected to make even the most unskilled patron sound good by adapting the accompaniment to the poetry as necessary, resulting in rhythmic complexity. Performing effectively required extensive training.[13] For many women, the challenge and reward of performing in this manner was their primary motivation, rather than the entertainment of patrons.[14]

Despite the artistic freedom that geishas exercised, there were restrictions on the genres they could access, and kouta lyrics were regulated by male patrons. In addition, geisha remained tightly restricted to designated performance spaces that marginalized not only their moral character but sometimes also their physical safety. One of the most enduring and glamorized images of the geisha is that of the "floating world," the marshy entertainment district of Yoshiwara, that was often accessed via boat. Tales and artwork depicting the silent evening boat ride to the entertainment district captured many imaginations. When cultural outsiders envisioned the floating world, they did not likely envision performance art.[15]

The geisha tradition continues today. With education in reading, poetry, music, and visual arts, geisha intellectually engage with high-ranking and

Figure 4.1
"The House of Kinpeiro in New Yoshiwara," 1871. This is one of many woodcut prints that depicted the "floating world" of the entertainment district. Note two women playing shamisen (far left and right), and one woman in the center performing on the koto.

Source: Courtesy of the Library of Congress

Figures 4.2 and 4.3
The H. C. White Company of Vermont was a leading producer of stereoview photography at the turn of the twentieth century. One series of photographs featured women performers from around the world, labeled with such titles as "full of fun and saucy." That series included these photographs of Japanese geisha and Indian court dancers, along with other examples such as Hawaiian hula dancers and "veiled women of Cairo." The pictures are titled "Passing Away a Dull Hour—Geisha Girls Dancing," (1906), and "Professional Dancing Girls in the Streets of Old Delhi, India" (1907).

Source: Courtesy of the Library of Congress

powerful men, and often give indirect political advice. Lesley Downer effectively compares them to high-society hostesses or corporate wives who enter the world of business through informal settings where the deals of politics sometimes occur.[16]

Women who continue in the tradition are still drawn to the power of their art form. Far from the demure women of the storybooks, modern geisha are independent career women who elect to go into the profession for their own reasons, but certainly not prostitution. Those who continue the practice play an important role in the preservation of some of Japan's most revered artistic traditions. As fewer women enter the field, the future of those traditions is in question.[17]

IMAGES OF WOMEN MUSICIANS IN EUROPEAN COURTS

> *Once upon a time in another land, it came to pass that a knight loved a lady (but) she refused and rejected his love. Then one day she said to him, "My friend, I have put you off with words . . . now your love is recognized and proven, henceforth I will do as you desire." "My lady," said he, "Woe is me that you did not have this thought a while ago. Your shining face . . . has so deteriorated, my lady . . . too late, my lady . . ."*[18]
>
> From a thirteenth-century French song

Artistic works of the European courts reflect many notions regarding societal gender roles, and a significant number of those beliefs and practices still inform

Western culture. For example, despite the fact that the knight of the quoted excerpt grew old along with his higher-ranking lady, her aging face allowed him to reject her, evidence of gender-based differentiation in the desirability of aging that still exists. Other ideas that stemmed from this period specifically address music, including the assignment of designated instruments for women, as well as "proper" gender roles for vocalists, composers, and musical sponsors. Like courtesans in other cultures, European women encountered both musical freedom and social peril as they stepped out of those designated roles.

Between the fifth and twelfth centuries, medieval Europe was governed by a feudal system in which military might was used to retain interests in land and power. A hierarchy of lords, knights, and vassals worked beneath a ruler to maintain and control power. The human components of this system were sworn to obedience and loyalty to ensure victory and sustenance. With the exception of some royal women, it was a male hierarchy.

Primary goals of the royal marriage were to bridge political alliances and to ensure an heir to the throne. As such, it was not uncommon for an older king to marry a young girl of royal blood from another country to gain political advantage. Some of the women were betrothed as young as twelve or thirteen, and being in love was not a major consideration. Women who were able to bear a child, preferably male, fulfilled their expected role and were upheld on a pedestal of honor. Women who could not bear children, however, were at serious risk. If the king believed it necessary to move on to another wife to ensure his bloodline, the once-royal woman often found herself accused of impropriety, and was sometimes exiled or even executed.

Working within this domestic setting were female court musicians who provided companionship, entertainment, and intellectual stimulation for royalty. It is not difficult to imagine how the presence of the courtesan was inviting for the husband and challenging for the wife. Strong societal beliefs about the power and danger of music to spiritually and physically impact the individual only added to the difficulty of the situation. Although it was considered important to be exposed to the uplifting qualities of music, royal women were forbidden to sing due to notions about the sensuality of song. As such, the work fell to courtesans. The lasting impact of the courtesan's practice on Western music history will be addressed shortly. First, however, it is necessary to acknowledge the women of nobility who were serenaded by male court musicians. Interestingly, gender roles between musical performer/composer and royalty were reversed in the era of the troubadours.

TROUBADOURS AND TROBAIRITZ

In Chapter 2 we noted the sacred work of Hildegard von Bingen in her German convent during the twelfth century. Between 1170 and 1260, court-produced music in France addressed secular topics. In an area known as Occitania (in the south of present-day France) there arose a class of composers known as **troubadours**. Stereotypically depicted as lute-bearing wanderers, the troubadours were actually court-based poets, often of aristocratic standing. While others traveled and performed the troubadour's creations, the troubadours perfected the art of composition, delivering their poetic verse through musical recitation. The romantic-poetic love **song** was born, and the concept quickly spread to other European areas.[19]

TROUBADOUR
poet-composer of southern France in the twelfth and thirteenth centuries

SONG
musical work that is sung and has lyrics

FOCUS TOPIC 4.1

Resource Focus: The Orientation of Women to Music— A View from 1948

Sophie Drinker's 1948 *Music and Women* was a notable early work that traced women's musical roles from antiquity to the early twentieth century. An ethnomusicologist before the field was widely recognized, Drinker noted sociocultural environments that shaped women's musical activity in a variety of geographical regions. Drinker designated the troubadour era as a time of significant change in women's orientation to music, with the establishment of passive roles for women such as listener, sponsor, and source of inspiration. The perception of male as composer was further established by the printing industry, which did not preserve the improvisatory work of women court musicians.

The troubadour's audience included the lord and his peers, the wife and her attendants, and others who resided within the court. Especially known for the praise songs that he wrote to address the noble wife of his employer,[20] the troubadour expressed devotion and obedience in exchange for being made "a better man."[21] Although it may have led to romance in some cases, it was largely a symbolic gesture, an expression of love and admiration typical of the feudal obligatory system. The notion continued in the practice of chivalry, where the woman was upheld as the pure, weak, virtuous sex. Thus, **courtly love** was the subject of most troubadour songs, an expression of unattainable "worship from afar" that was to be met with rejection by the lady. The knight would in turn reply that he was "dying" from lack of returned affection.

COURTLY LOVE
"fin' amors" in Occitan; refined, unattainable love for one who is admired from a distance; associated with troubadour song

That the noble women of Occitania began to write songs expressing their own feelings about matters of love is not only interesting, it was unusual. The only known women troubadours were from that region, and their songs go on record as being among the first known secular works of women composers. "**Trobairitz**" were not of the knightly troubadour class but rather

TROBAIRITZ
female poet-composer of southern France in the twelfth and thirteenth centuries

FOCUS TOPIC 4.2

Genre Focus: Troubadour Songs

Troubadour songs are part of the **monophonic** song tradition, although evidence suggests that they were sometimes accompanied. They were sung in the vernacular language of the composer. Two forms of the genre emerged, including the **chanson** (a solo love song) and the tenson (improvised, and likely performed before an audience). The tenson often contained dialogue, and could be performed by more than one person.

Song construction reflected rhyme schemes and syllable counts, and texts were often set in **strophic form**. Consistent syllable counts in the poetry allowed subsequent verses to easily utilize previous melodic material. The exact manner in which troubadour songs were rhythmically performed remains speculative, since rhythmic indications in the notation are not obvious to modern musicians. Because the poetry was recited metrically even before it was set to music, it is likely that the original performers also delivered their songs with intentional rhythms.

MONOPHONIC
music having a single melody without accompaniment or harmonizing parts, as in chant

CHANSON
French secular song

STROPHIC FORM
form in which each poetic verse is set to the same music

were the noble women to whom the knights sang. As the main recipients of troubadour song, the women were well versed with the poetic-musical form. When they wrote their own songs, however, they expressed their thoughts uniquely. Unlike the men who penned symbolic ideas, the women often spoke of intimately personal issues, including their own happiness, anger, and desires.[22] The most famous trobairitz song, written by the "Countess of Dia," expressed the noble woman's love for the troubadour himself.

Biographical information on the "Countess of Dia" is somewhat unclear. Like the Occitanian troubadours, the countess kept a biographical vida, but her information does not completely correspond with historical fact. It is believed that she was born c. 1140 and that she may have lived in the diocese of Dia. There is some evidence to suggest that she may have been named Beatriz, and that she was romantically linked to the well-known troubadour Raimbaut d'Aurenga (c.1147–1173).[23] What is definitive is that she was a woman of noble birth, one to whom troubadour songs would have been sung. Of the relatively few surviving trobairitz poems, four were believed to have been written by the Countess of Dia. Her "A chantar m'er de so" is the only surviving trobairitz song with a known melody. [24]

In "A chantar" (see Figure 4.4) the countess expresses her love for a troubadour, a love that was not returned. From her royal standing, this unattainable love held a very different meaning than it did for the male singer. Whereas troubadour song addressed love that was impossible due to differentiated social ranking, the countess expected reciprocation. Her lyrics therefore expressed not only anguish, but also anger and disbelief.

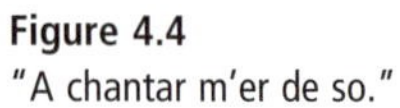

Figure 4.4
"A chantar m'er de so."

LISTENING EXPERIENCE 4.1

"A chantar m'er de so" (c.1175)
The Countess of Dia
Playlist

LISTENING FOCUS

Listen for a neumatic setting (in which there are no more than three notes per syllable) and a narrow range. Each line features eleven syllables. This recording features an accompaniment, and includes three complete verses.

FORM AT A GLANCE

Three verses, each containing seven lines, melodically set in the pattern A B A B C D B.

TIMED LISTENING GUIDE

0:00 instrumental introduction

Verse One

0:16	A material: "I must sing of what I'd rather not"
0:33	B material: "So bitter do I feel toward him whose friend I am"
0:46	A material: "For I love him more than anything"
1:00	B material: "With him, mercy and courtliness don't help me"
1:15	C material: "nor does my beauty, my rank, or my intelligence"
1:27	D material: peak range: "For I am every bit as *betrayed* and *wronged*"
1:37	B material: "as if I were completely ugly."

Verse Two

1:59	A
2:10	B
2:21	A
2:32	B
2:46	C
2:55	D
3:07	B

Verse Three

3:29	A
3:40	B
3:52	A
4:01	B
4:15	C
4:25	D
4:37	B

Repeat of Final Lines to Close

4:56	D
5:07	B

MUSIC OF THE EUROPEAN RENAISSANCE: AVOIDING THE COURTESAN CONNOTATION

Despite the involvement of women in the troubadour song tradition, women's public-sphere musical roles remained strictly limited, even at the outset of the Renaissance. The Renaissance (literally "rebirth") took place in Europe from about 1420 to 1600, and encompassed philosophical thinking that looked to classical antiquity for inspiration, particularly the culture of ancient Greece. Human values, reasoning, and scientific discovery informed the dominant philosophy of the period, known as **humanism**. Humanistic thought was reflected in multiple artistic areas, ranging from visual art and architecture to music.

HUMANISM
philosophy that emerged in the Renaissance in which ancient Greek and Roman culture inspired the study of human knowledge

The Renaissance was not a completely secular age, as is sometimes mistakenly believed. Church music was still prevalent, and most courts had their own chapel within the castle walls, as well as court composers who wrote and oversaw performances of religious works. Masses, motets, and new Protestant genres were written and performed primarily by men, as the church ban on women musicians still prevailed. At the same time, the court additionally sponsored secular entertainment, including songs and dances. By the end of the era, roles for women in secular music performance dramatically changed.

Italy is considered the birthplace of the Renaissance. The arts were financed by a growing merchant class that engaged in home music-making, as well as by prominent rulers such as the Gonzaga, Este, and Medici families, who commissioned artwork for the church, but also provided secular entertainment for their guests.

Musical activity for the noble woman of the home was highly regulated, and beliefs about women's roles in instrumental music governed their performance activities. Noble women were restricted to private performance using small keyboards, lutes, and other stringed instruments that did not require the use of facial distortion or "unladylike" body positions. Loud, blaring instruments and drums were restricted to the male domain. This practice so entered Western thought that the tendency to align women with instruments such as acoustic guitar and keyboards, rather than brass and percussion, still persists.

Because of notions regarding the sensuousness of song, noble women were discouraged from singing in public. The Renaissance belief that music could inflame the soul and make the listener lose control placed public vocal performance out of the realm of the noble woman. As in other cultures, courtesans were much more likely than noble women to fulfill singing duties during the early Renaissance.

The musical work of courtesans was likely significant, as is evidenced by numerous European paintings and literary works. Solid musical evidence is difficult to find, however, since the courtesan's music was often **improvised**. With the advent of the European printing press circa 1440, the work of male composers hired by the courts became increasingly preserved. It was the published work of courtly centers of artistic sponsorship that became the subject of lasting interest to musicologists.[25]

IMPROVISE
to compose, or simultaneously compose and perform, on the spur of the moment

For women court musicians, what can be better documented is the diligence with which they sometimes fought to escape the derogatory connotation that was connected with their court employment.

As a **virtuoso** singer of the latter half of the sixteenth century, Maddalena Casulana (c.1540–1590) was referenced in print as both "muse" and "siren," terms strongly linked to courtesan culture. The concept of women singing in public was new, and the technical ability and powerful sound of vocalists such as Casulana placed them in special danger of social disconnection. Casulana's work as a composer, however, suggests that she may have attempted to overcome that image. She is known today in great part because of her connection to the powerful Medici family, particularly her sponsor, Isabella de' Medici, and her subsequent access to publication.

VIRTUOSO
performer who possesses astounding technical skills

Figure 4.5
"Concert of Women," 1530–1540. The work of an anonymous artist depicts a trio of women performing on lute, flute, and voice.
Source: Public domain

Being a published composer was a rare thing for a woman during the Renaissance, and Maddalena Casulana was well aware (and proud) of her unique status. In her first group of published madrigals, she expressed that she wished to "show the world the vain error of men, that they alone possess intellectual gifts and think those gifts are not possible for women."[26] In an era in which madrigals were still often written in three-voice **homophonic** settings, Casulana's rhythmically complex settings featured four- and five-voice parts, with alteration between **polyphonic** and homophonic textures.[27]

HOMOPHONIC
musical texture in which multiple lines move together rhythmically

POLYPHONIC
musical texture in which two or more independent melodic lines sound simultaneously

The fact that Casulana published her work is cause for interesting speculation. Was she really one of the few women who composed written work during this era, or was she simply lucky enough to have the necessary connections by which to publish? [28] Did Isabella de'Medici, her sponsor, live vicariously through Casulana in having the composer's work published? The noble woman, betrothed as a mere youth of eleven, herself aspired to sing and compose, but was restricted by her royal status. It has also been suggested that Casulana might have viewed publication as an avenue by which to escape the courtesan image that haunted singers of her era, as courtesans rarely published. Further evidence of her concern for erasing that connotation lies in her careful text settings. Not only did she avoid the virtuosic vocal displays of which she was technically capable, she took great care in how she embellished sexual metaphors that were musically highlighted by other composers.[29]

Whatever her reasons, there is significant evidence that Casulana was highly regarded for her compositional work. Renowned composer Orlando di Lasso conducted one of her five-voice works in Munich in 1568, and she was also connected with a number of other well-known composers and poets. It is additionally notable that she was a teacher of composition. Casulana's first book of madrigals, published in 1568, is thought to contain the first printed works by a woman in European music history.[30] She wrote sixty-seven madrigals, almost all of which were published.

In the end, Isabella de'Medici did not fare as well as did Casulana. Accused of impropriety, she was summoned to her husband's room and was murdered at the throat, in dreadful reference to her musical aspirations. She was just thirty-four years old. Casulana continued to publish after the death of her patron, with musical and textual references to Isabella's obedience.[31]

"MORIR NON PUÒ IL MIO CUORE"

MADRIGAL
Italian secular vocal genre that utilizes poetic texts; stylistic traits and number of voice parts change by historical period

The **madrigal**, like many musical genres, changed over time. While the genre existed as early as the fourteenth century, it is the sixteenth-century madrigal that carries the most historical weight. Like the troubadour song, it is both a poetic and musical form, and centers on secular themes. By the sixteenth century, it utilized three or more voices, with additional voices added as the genre developed throughout the century. Most madrigal composers utilized **word painting** to depict text. (For more information on madrigal text meanings and changing cultural notions of the madrigal, see Focus Topic 4.3.)

WORD PAINTING
in texted works, using musical gestures or elements to reflect movement and emotion in the text

FOCUS TOPIC 4.3

Genre Focus: The Madrigal: Higher Art or Suggestive Pop Tune?

Cultural perceptions of madrigals have changed dramatically over time. Not unlike Japanese kouta texts, many madrigal texts contained metaphors for sexual longing and satisfaction. Madrigals were first sung by groups of men in settings that we might compare to informal gatherings of the guys. With the entrance of female virtuoso singers into madrigal performance in the 1560s, the performance orientation changed. Rather than participate, the men became audience members, and the women were praised for their looks as well as for their singing.

Over time, published and preserved madrigals received a higher art connotation, and were often sung by elite chamber groups because of the musical difficulty involved. It is likely that many current-day madrigal singers do not fully understand the original meaning of the texts, as evidenced by performances in public school settings, among other venues.

Casulana's madrigal in the listening example features four voices, and alternates between polyphonic and homophonic textures to accentuate textual meaning. Polyphonic sections are linked to textual dialogue. While the topic and setting might appear mundane or even somber by today's standards, many of the words would have originally been understood as sexually suggestive. Casulana was careful to avoid over-embellishing those words, marking a significant difference in her madrigal settings compared with other composers of the era.

PROFESSIONAL SINGING LEGITIMIZED

By 1580, views on public musicianship for women began to change in Italy. Partly due to the rise of the commedia dell'arte (professional theatre), women's musical performance was considered respectable if it was practiced within designated and regulated settings. The courts at Florence, Mantua, and Ferrara were particularly active in terms of women's musical performance, as evidenced by extensive court records. The founding of the **concerto delle donne** (group of singing ladies) in the Ferrara court signaled groundbreaking change.[32]

CONCERTO DELLE DONNE
"group of ladies"; professional female court singers

LISTENING EXPERIENCE 4.2

"Morir non può il mio cuore" (1566)
Maddalena Casulana
Playlist

LISTENING FOCUS

Listen for alternating polyphonic and homophonic text settings and word painting as the composer metaphorically sets the text setting "to die."

TEXT

Morir non può il mio cuore: ucciderlo vorrei,
Poi che vi piace,
Ma trar no si può fuore dal petto
Vostr'ove gran tempo giace;
Et uccidendol'io, come desio,
So che morreste voi,
Morrend' anch'io[33]
Text Translation
My heart cannot die: I would like to kill it,
since that would please you,
but it cannot be pulled out of your breast,
where it has been dwelling for a long time;
and if I killed it, as I wish,
I know that you would die, and I would die too.[34]

TIMED LISTENING GUIDE

0:00	polyphonic setting as voices enter separately and overlap on the text "morir" (die)
0:14	opening phrase ending in unison on cuore (heart)
0:15	homophonic setting of "I would like to kill it" expresses unified desire for pleasure
0:25	polyphonic setting of "but it cannot be pulled out" expresses effort and struggle, a reluctance to pull the heart from the breast
0:42	homophonic setting of "where it has been dwelling for some time"
0:46	longer note values express the lingering of the heart
1:01	polyphonic setting of "I know that you would die, and I would die too"; chromaticism, ascending pitch, and peak rhythmic activity signifies tension
1:26	repeated musical setting of final line of text
1:40	anti-climatic ending signified by unison and slowed rhythm

The original members of the concerto delle donne at the Ferrara court —singers Laura Peverara (d. 1601), Anna Guarini (1563–1598), and Livia d'Arco (1565–1611)—were not only artistically able; they came from the noble class. The idea for creating the group is attributed to Duke Alfonso d'Este, at whose invitation Peverara (whom he had heard sing in Mantua) and other members of the original ensemble became associated with the court. As official ladies-in-waiting to the duchess, their presence was both acceptable and well within an established court-based tradition. Nonetheless, it appears that the Duke made several concessions to further protect his singers from negative associations.

Whereas the courtesan class usually composed their own music, the women of the concerto delle donne performed works by male composers.[35] Their audience was carefully selected. Documents show that the women appeared regularly in sessions called **musica reservata** (or musica secreta), a chamber music setting only open to invited nobility that featured intensely expressive performances. To distance the women from the courtesan tradition, the Duke ensured that the women were provided dowries, and were properly married to nobles. Along with a salary, Laura Peverara was also provided living quarters in the Duke's palace. On the one hand, this was a substantial fringe benefit. On the other hand, it could be viewed as an extra-zealous attempt to control and protect the singer.

MUSICA RESERVATA
music reserved for an elite, invited audience; often featured virtuoso performers; term used in the sixteenth and seventeenth centuries

The virtuosic music of the concerto delle donne tradition, written by male composers and executed by women's voices, brought the Ferrara court honor and renown (see Figure 4.6). Within a decade of the inception of the ensemble, every significant Italian court began to assemble groups of their own.[36] As the Renaissance drew to a close, women of the mercantile class were actively preparing for careers in music, and the emergence of opera in the first decade of the seventeenth century led to even further opportunities.

SUMMARY

Women court musicians were among the best educated women of their time. Along with the freedom to perform on instruments and sing in spaces forbidden to other women, they often were afforded societal freedom to earn money, move freely, and live independently. At the same time, their performance art was not entirely in their own hands. Their genres and performance practices were often defined by male patrons who asserted approval over standards of performance, sometimes to the point of regulated licensing. Songs and dances often focused on the erotic, with song lyrics written by male patrons. As court cultures and courtesan roles dissolved, court-based arts traditions changed. In some cases, traditions ceased to exist; at other times, genres were reinvented. At worst, artistic elements were entirely lost, and were replaced by mere prostitution.

The courtesan connotation did not dissolve with the courts, however. Women who continued to sing in public in subsequent eras still risked being considered morally corrupt. At the same time, they often were revered by men who were attracted to their perceived non-traditional sexuality. Is it going too far to connect the glamour and attraction of the modern pop diva to the court singer? After all this time, are women still singing in a restricted domain?[37]

Figure 4.6
An excerpt from "O dolcezz'amarissime," a 1601 madrigal by Ferrara court composer Luzzasco Luzzaschi (1545–1607), who wrote works for the concerto delle donne. Although this particular work was written after the dissolution of the original group of singers at the court, its technical difficulty is typical of the literature that the women performed. Note the three soprano voice parts (with lyrics) and the extended virtuosic passages.

QUESTIONS FOR CRITICAL THINKING AND DISCUSSION

1. Discuss the questions posed in the final paragraph of this chapter. Considering performance practices, costuming, and popular song lyrics, do you believe that court-based notions regarding women and music still persist?
2. Discuss the current status of gender perceptions of male singers. Are male singers also confined to a restricted domain?
3. Are popular songs still constructed according to rhyme schemes and syllable counts? Take one of your current favorites and explore the musical-text connection. Do you think that this work will become art music in the future?

IDEAS FOR FURTHER RESEARCH

1. Investigate the history of another courtesan culture to further explore cross-cultural perceptions of women and music. As a starting point, you might research the history of Indian musicians, including devadasi temple musicians of the Hindu tradition, or the court-based ganika. Other possibilities include court traditions in Korea, China, and ancient Greece.
2. The madrigal is not the only art music genre that was originally considered popular music. With the help of your instructor, explore other genres that underwent a similar transformation. Speculate as to why this phenomenon occurs.

CHAPTER 5

Baroque Keyboard and Vocal Genres

Gender Roles in Musical Families

Bach, Mozart, Gabrieli, and Strauss: the pages of Western music history are liberally sprinkled with the names of musicians from extended musical families. Although this phenomenon once sparked debate about whether prolific musical activity within families was due to heredity or proximity, it rarely led to speculation about what had happened to the women in the family! Of course, the gender-limited view is no longer prevalent, and the either/or approach to nature versus nurture is also long past the debate stage. Most people now believe that a combination of biological and contextual factors contributed to musical achievement within families, and that women were withheld from public view due to cultural restraints.

This chapter addresses women of the Baroque who gained musical notoriety due to social class and family connections. Unlike the female members of the Bach and Mozart families, Francesca Caccini, Barbara Strozzi and Elisabeth-Claude Jacquet de la Guerre did not curtail their musical activities when they reached adulthood, and all were well known during their lifetimes. Even as late as the 1980s, however, these prominent musicians were missing from textbooks and discographies, their stories lost in centuries of reformulated narrative. By the turn of the twenty-first century their stories re-emerged, pieced together from court employment records, publications, written correspondence and earlier historical accounts.

This chapter highlights the work of three prominent composers as it also addresses how composers in Western art music have traditionally achieved lasting renown. At the same time, it addresses the issue of gender-designated genres to which these women were restricted, an association that remains deeply connected to the present.

UNDERSTANDING THE BAROQUE

A linear sense of history often leads to the mistaken perception that opportunities for women in music increased as time progressed. Interestingly, women's documented musical activity in the Baroque (approximately 1600–1750) surpasses that of the Classical era (approximately 1750–1800). Women of the Baroque were involved in a wide array of musical activities, including paid vocal performance, publishing, and instrument building. In family businesses, women often worked with their husbands in partnership. Other women were members of artisan-class families that were court-employed.[1] With the rise of the middle class during and after the Enlightenment, women's public (and paid) musical activities were curtailed. Women who could most afford music education increasingly led their musical lives within the domestic realm. As the public concert increasingly became the venue for art music performance, the documented musical activity of women waned.

The Baroque style was shaped both by humanistic principles of the Renaissance and continued changes in the way the world was viewed due to scientific discovery and exploration. Galileo Galilei proclaimed that the sun was the center of the universe, and Isaac Newton explained planetary motion by the principles of gravity. Europeans of great wealth sent explorers around the globe to discover and conquer new territory, many lands were colonized, and the European slave trade was established to provide agricultural labor in the Americas.

Many of the wealthy families who sponsored the explorers abroad spent lavishly on the arts at home, and surrounded themselves with vast numbers of artisan-class employees. The Medici, Este, and Gonzaga families in Italy are among court families who used the arts to glorify their names and to increase their political power. Following the lead of women such as Margherita Gonzaga d'Este, who promoted women's musical and theatrical activities in the late-Renaissance court, women of the Baroque continued to establish ensembles of women performers and actors. Like Margherita, these courtly women often lived vicariously through the arts, taking on roles that were forbidden in their everyday lives, and expressing their independence and power through artistic production.

Unlike the Classical aesthetic with its form-driven structure, symmetrical balance and objectivity, the Baroque aesthetic was one of emotion, irregularity and energy. In theoretical terms, the era saw a shift from **modal** to **tonal** systems, and an increased use of chordal harmony. **Consonance** and **dissonance** were purposefully controlled to express aesthetic nuance. Musicians were expected to execute embellishments and elaborate on melodies as they performed against the backdrop of **basso continuo** lines that harmonically guided performance in a manner not unlike blues improvisation.[2] **Virtuosic** displays

MODAL
music that is based on modes (sequences of whole and half steps) other than major or minor

TONAL
related to major and minor scalar systems, as opposed to modal systems; in actual practice, a tonal musical work will be organized around a given note or key

CONSONANCE
combination of tones that creates a sense of stability or calm

DISSONANCE
combination of tones that sounds unstable; sometimes considered harsh, or in need of resolution

BASSO CONTINUO
"continuous bass"; Baroque system in which a bass line is written out and an instrument fills in appropriate harmony

VIRTUOSO
performer who possesses astounding technical skills

of technical ability by performers were showcased in long, forward-spinning passages filled with melismas.

Baroque genres encompass a stylistic variety so great that it is difficult to consider the era as a unified whole. Works such as Claudio Monteverdi's (1567–1643) opera *Orfeo* mark the beginning of the era, while J. S. Bach's (1685–1750) cantatas and George Frederic Handel's (1685–1759) oratorios rest on the other end of the spectrum both chronologically and stylistically.

DOCTRINE OF THE AFFECTIONS
Baroque doctrine in which music was believed to elicit specific emotional responses such as sadness, anger, or joy

AFFECT
predominant emotion of an artistic work

DOCTRINE OF ETHOS
ancient Greek belief that upheld music's power to impact the soul of the listener

What brought the Baroque together, however, was an overriding affective goal. The Baroque **Doctrine of the Affections** espoused the purposeful eliciting of "**affect**" in those who listened, and it was as much the performer's role as that of the composer to bring forth the response. Moving the listener was more complicated than drawing out a simple emotional reaction. Inspired by the ancient Greek **Doctrine of Ethos**, proponents of the Baroque aesthetic believed that human beings benefited from alteration of body, mind, and spirit via music. It was believed that this was best accomplished by focusing a single work on a single affect. Perhaps an easy way to understand this by today's standards would be to consider the impact of a "good cry" after exposure to a "moving" song, theatrical production, or movie. In Baroque terms, the "moving" of the listener was considered literal, with physiological reaction of the body's fluids in response to the affect (in this example, the rising and shedding of tears).

PRIMA PRATTICA
"first practice"; referencing seventeenth-century text setting in which the music sometimes overshadows the text; sometimes associated with polyphony

SECONDA PRATTICA
"second practice"; referencing sixteenth-century text setting in which textual clarity takes precedence over music; associated with the monodic style

OPERA
a dramatic work that is entirely sung

CASTRATO
castrated male singer who sings in the soprano or alto range

MONODY
style that features a vocal soloist with an instrumental accompaniment

BAROQUE GENRES AND GENDER SPHERES

While many women were involved in music performance in the Baroque, their activities were focused in specific areas, particularly vocal music and instrumental chamber music. Baroque vocal music linked music and text to stir the passions of the listener. Whereas the contrapuntal text-setting style of the Renaissance **prima prattica** (first practice) often obscured the text (and was often written and performed by men in relation to the church), the **seconda prattica** of the Baroque focused on clear musical-textual execution. Text and emotion literally rose as one from the body of the singer, and because singing was an act that required physical execution, it rested well in the female sphere. Already, the Western split between mind and body had placed women into the bodily realm, and men into the realm of the mind.[3]

As new vocal genres emerged in the Baroque, women had increased opportunities to participate as performers. Women found roles in **opera** in many geographical locations, although the use of the **castrati** in Rome and in the Papal states exemplified the Church's continued prohibition of women's voices in church and on stage. The **monody**, a solo song with accompaniment, quickly displaced the multi-voiced madrigal as the Baroque progressed, and was deemed suitable for performance by women in designated venues.

Monodies were a vehicle for the expression of affect, and an entire system of singing was created to assist the singer in achieving aesthetic goals. Even the instruments used to accompany monadic singing, such as the lute and harpsichord, were considered suitable for women.

Instrumental music moved beyond accompaniment in the Baroque, but as the orchestra developed, women were restricted to small stringed instruments and keyboards of the chamber. Instruments such as these allowed demure physical presentation of the woman's body and alleviated concerns about obstruction of the face. Even the size of the woman's hand was deemed superior to men's for harpsichord performance.[4] As independent keyboard genres emerged, women were involved in both performance and composition.

PART OF THE FAMIGLIA: MUSICIANS AMONG THE MEDICI

Throughout the course of Western music history, geographical centers of musical innovation and activity shift. Opera, oratorio, sonatas, and concertos all formed in Italy. The predominance of the Italians during the Baroque led to international adaptation of Italian musical markings, and common use of Italian musical terms. Whereas the church was a primary driving force in the medieval period, the influence of courts rose to prominence in the Renaissance, and continued to impact the Baroque. The court and the church were far from separated in Italy, however, as many wealthy court families embraced both secular and religious thought. Among the leaders in upholding this dual identity was the Medici family of Florence.

The Medici dynasty had risen to tremendous power by the fifteenth century, attaining immense wealth and political influence in Florence's international banking industry. Stories of the Medici still captivate the imagination of the modern world, with tales of assassination and deceit adding intrigue to other narratives that detail the broad interests of the family. Caught between a world of the secular and the sacred, the Medici used their wealth and power in both realms. The family produced several popes and numerous cardinals, and subsequently commissioned artwork for the church, sponsoring artists such as Michelangelo and Leonardo da Vinci. The Medici were also champions of **humanist** thought in the Renaissance and the Baroque, with connections to some of the most well-known scientists in history. Galileo Galilei tutored Medici children, for example.

HUMANISM
philosophy that emerged in the Renaissance in which ancient Greek and Roman culture inspired the study of human knowledge

The Medici family members most relevant to the story of Francesca Caccini are women who were born in the sixteenth century, married to Medici men who lived during the second full century of the dynasty. Christine de Lorraine (1565–1637, married to Ferdinando de'Medici) was Caccini's sponsor for thirty years, and Maria Magdalena d'Austria (1589–1631, married to

Christine and Ferdinando's son Cosimo II) also commissioned work by Caccini. Both Christine and Maria were widowed, and because Maria's son was too young to assume power when Cosimo II died, the two women served as regents, or heads of state, for the Medici family for many years. It was to these powerful women that Francesca was assigned.

Francesca Caccini (1587–1641)

There are no official visual images of Francesca Caccini. She was not a wealthy aristocrat who had her portrait painted, or her figure cast in plaster. Caccini was from the artisan class, her parents both court musicians. Caccini's mother was the singer Lucia Gagnolandi, who died when Francesca was only four years old, and her father was Giulio Caccini (c. 1551–1618), who worked for the Medici as one of many court composers. The Caccini family was included in the larger Medici famiglia, a network of Medici blood relatives, their attendants, and their servants. Giulio Caccini was one of the best-known singers and teachers of singing of his time, and his 1601 *Le nuove musiche* (The New Music), a book on the art of singing the new monadic style, acknowledged his name in an era when composers often were kept anonymous to greater glorify their employers.[5]

Giulio Caccini taught his daughters not only his singing method but also instrumental performance skills. Along with her sisters Settimia and Pompeo, Francesca learned to play harp, harpsichord, lute, and guitar, and also her father's prescribed singing methods, which focused on speech-like intensification of words via breath control. Techniques such as the gorgheggiando, a rapid starting and stopping of sound production created by passing air through the vocal folds, required extensive training and precise body control.[6]

Francesca was recognized as a singer before she was known as a composer. One of the first women musicians known to tour, she traveled with her family to France as a teen and so impressed her audience that Henry IV asked to procure her services. The Medici family quickly responded by formally signing Francesca into their own service in 1607. Thus began a thirty-year connection between Francesca Caccini and her patroness, Christine de Lorraine.

Despite the privilege afforded by association, court musicians were treated as objects of the court. Christine quickly arranged for Francesca's marriage (to another court musician) so that Francesca could officially be put on the payroll. Within a year of the marriage, a baby girl was born, and Francesca eventually trained her as a singer as well, in keeping with the Caccini family trade.

Francesca did not live within the walls of the court as one might expect, but instead lived in the city and traveled to the various buildings held by the Medici family throughout Florence. In her home, she composed, did copying, and spent significant time teaching composition, instrumental performance, and voice, both to artisan-class students and to children of her patrons. Widowed twice in her life, Francesca returned to the service of the Medici after a short absence during her marriage to her second husband, a wealthy music lover. In all, she led a productive musical life in the Medici court, where she composed at least seventeen theatrical works and hundreds of chamber music works. Like much music of that period, only a small fraction of her written compositions survive today, including thirty-six songs and duets in the *Primo libro delle musiche* from 1618, and a published score of a balletto-opera called *La liberazione di Ruggiero dall'isola d'Alcina* (The Liberation of Ruggiero from the Island of Alcina) from 1625.[7]

Although Francesca was primarily associated with Christine de Lorraine, Caccini also worked collaboratively with men. The fact that she was at one time the court's highest paid musician suggests a court culture that was gender neutral for the Medici artisan-class. Caccini frequently collaborated with Michelangelo Buonarroti the Younger (nephew of the visual artist), a writer of many of the texts that she set to music. She also worked with men for events outside of the women's court, co-writing the play *La Fiera*, and writing the *Ballo delle zigane*, which was performed at the Pitti Palace (one of several Medici buildings) in 1615.[8] Her duties required that she frequently performed for men, including many appearances before Cosimo II to console him during his extended illness. Despite the ban on women's voices in the church, Caccini performed for the Cardinal de'Medici on many occasions, and sang before Pope Urban VIII as a gift of the Medici family to the newly elected pontiff, a non-Medici family member.

Maria, dolce Maria

Caccini was thirty years old when she wrote the *Primo libro delle musiche* collection. Dedicated to the Cardinal de'Medici, it contained nineteen works on sacred themes along with seventeen secular works. It was almost certainly a pedagogical collection, as it systematically presented a variety of techniques and styles. The collection is the most extensive of Caccini's generation and, like her father's songbook, bore her name. The deliberate fusion of words and music is evident throughout its pages.

Suzanne Cusick provides a fascinating way to view Caccini's work in "Maria, dolce Maria," a **sacred madrigal** that unites the power of Mary with the power of the singer in control of her own spiritual ecstasy. As the vocalist releases the meaning of the text, she combines a Christian and secular power that is not unlike the Medici dynasty itself. In the manner of the Baroque aesthetic, Caccini uses embellishment not just to decorate the melodic line, but to help express the text. Maria is described as "sweet," "gentle," and "consecrated," with a reverent musical setting, but when she "enraptures" the heart of the singer, and "inflames" her with love, the setting reflects emotion with

SACRED MADRIGAL
solo vocal work with a sacred text

Figure 5.1
A segment of Francesca Caccini's "Maria, dolce Maria," in which the text "io canto" is expressed with a long melisma. This shows Caccini's original notation, while Figure 5.2 (opposite) is a modern transcription.

Figure 5.2
A modern transcription of Francesca Caccini's "Maria, dolce Maria" (see Figure 5.1).

FOCUS TOPIC 5.1

Genre Focus: The Monody

By the late Renaissance, vocal music featured as many as five or six voices that performed polyphonically without instrumental accompaniment. The monadic style that emerged at the turn of the seventeenth century was a completely new style, in which a solo vocalist was accompanied by an instrument such as the harpsichord or lute. Not only did this thinner texture help listeners hear the text, it allowed the solo singer a great deal of freedom to improvise. Virtuoso singers improvised melodically and rhythmically complex passages to bring intense textual messages to life, in keeping with the Baroque aesthetic that favored the expression of emotion.

increased musical movement. On the phrase "io canto" (I sing), the reserve explodes into a melismatic passage in which text is lost. Both singer and listener are taken beyond words, signaling the height of spiritual experience. The harmony works in like manner, with just two chords performed in the stagnant opening, followed by rapid movement through a harmonic progression that leaps by fifths in a circular fashion, also suggesting spiritual rapture.[9] See Figure 5.1 for the original notation and Figure 5.2 for a modern transcription.

Composing for the Women's Court

The concept of the women's court may be unfamiliar to twenty-first century readers because of a historical tendency to tell stories of the male court. It was not uncommon for women of the court to live apart from men. In many cases, marriages were arranged primarily to ensure a proper heir rather than to celebrate true love and affection. In the case of the Medici, the women's court was physically located outside of the city, in part due to fear of violence (indeed, there were several Medici family murders) and probably also to control and isolate the women.

LISTENING EXPERIENCE 5.1

"Maria, dolce Maria" (1618)
Francesca Caccini
Score available in the *New Historical Anthology of Music by Women*
Playlist

LISTENING FOCUS

Listen to the monodic style, featuring a solo vocalist with accompaniment. Vocal ornamentation and word painting express spiritual ecstasy in this sacred madrigal.

TEXT

Maria, sweet Maria
Name so gentle
That pronouncing it enraptures the heart
Name sacred and holy
That inflames my heart with celestial love
Maria, never as long as I sing
Can my tongue a happier word pull from my breast than to say "Maria?"
That name consoles every grief, tranquil voice that quiets every agitation
(Name that) . . . makes every heart serene, every soul happy."[10]

TIMED LISTENING GUIDE

0:00	opening instrumental chord establishes calm reverence
0:03	reverent expression of "Maria, sweet Maria"
0:23	rhythmic movement on "enraptures the heart;" vocal ornamentation on "core" (heart)
0:36	melisma on "consecrated"
0:42	harmonic circle progression and rhythmic movement on "enflames me with celestial love"
1:04	extended melisma on "io canto," (I sing) expresses spiritual ecstasy
1:23	melisma on "felice parola" (happier word)
1:47	rhythmically calm expression of words "tranquil voice that quiets agitation"
2:06	melodic sequencing on repeated text "that every heart is serene"
2:23	melodic sequencing again on repeated text "that every heart is serene"
2:35	melisma on "every soul happy"

The women's court had a vibrant life of its own that included significant musical activity. Suzanne Cusick brings to life the women's court setting as she describes an extensive group of female cousins, nieces, duchesses, princesses, and an unimaginable array of people who served them. The women had access to gardeners, cooks, wet nurses, poets, musicians, and tutors, among many other assistants. Leisure activities included horseback riding, hunting, games, dancing, and theatrical productions. Dames from aristocratic families were companions to the princesses, and donne, girls from the middle class, assisted with dressing, bathing, hairstyling, and entertainment, including singing and dancing.[11] In charge of the entire court was Francesca Caccini's sponsor, Christine de Lorraine, along with her daughter-in-law Maria.

La Liberazione di Ruggiero dall'isola d'Alcina is Caccini's one surviving staged work, erroneously called an opera. The work was written for a performance during Carnival, 1625, commissioned for the betrothal of Maria's twelve-year-old daughter to a Polish relative in a political move intended to strengthen political alliances. Performed at the country estate Villa di Poggio Imperiale, the performance was clearly in the jurisdiction of the women's court geographically and topically.[12]

The subject of the performance was the liberation of a lovesick knight, Ruggiero, who was put under a spell by a sorceress, Alcina.[13] It was a sophisticated production that included operatic conventions such as **recitative**, **aria**, choruses, and **ritornelli**, and its elaborate staging included an opening aquatic scene and the setting of an actual fire. The cross-dressing sorceress Melissa appears in disguise as a man as she liberates Ruggiero from the spell of Alcina's seduction. Alcina, rather than succumbing to tears at the release of her captive, leaves stage on the back of a dragon and starts a fire that consumes the island. The power of women to captivate and control the man on stage reflected the power of the women who hosted the production. Not only were they running the women's court, but the entire Medici family. That a woman was selected to write the balletto and was allowed to publish it under her name was probably not coincidental.[14]

RECITATIVE
technique found in opera, oratorio, and cantata in which the text is sung in a speech-like manner, as opposed to the lyrical aria style

ARIA
lyric song for solo voice; also found in several large-scale genres, including opera and cantata

RITORNELLO
a short musical passage that returns throughout a work in the manner of a refrain

Barbara Strozzi: Adopted Daughter of the Academy

Unlike Francesca Caccini's court-based life, Barbara Strozzi (1619–1677) lived in relative seclusion among the secretive male world of the academy, a group of intellectuals who met privately in homes to discuss and debate philosophical issues, politics, and literature. Born in Venice, Italy, she was likely the biological daughter of Giulio Strozzi, a member of the Academy of the Incogniti (Academy of the Unknown) and Isabella Garzoni, one of Strozzi's household servants. Giulio Strozzi had a strong musical influence on his adopted daughter, and purposefully built her career as a singer and composer. Barbara essentially was adopted into the academy as well, a placement of a

Figure 5.3
A painting widely considered to be the image of Barbara Strozzi, by the painter Bernardo Strozzi (not believed to be Barbara's relative). In visual art, the exposure of the left breast is often associated with motherhood, while the exposure of the right breast usually has erotic connotations. Given the uncertainty that this was an image of Strozzi, there is little reason to speculate about what the painter was attempting to portray.
Source: Public domain

woman among men that linked her to the courtesan culture of Venice. Her story is one of both liberation and captivity as she attained high social status and fame within a restrictive setting.

The intellectual life into which Barbara Strozzi was born was a closed world of men. As freethinkers, literary people, and politicians, academy members shaped the political life of Venice and the world of opera. The men not only met in private but often published their work anonymously, using formats such as poetry, essays, and opera **libretti** to address topics that were often considered immoral.[15] Through the blending of their political activity and literary work, academy members not only supplied libretti to leading composers but also created an environment that led to the 1637 opening of the world's first public opera house, the San Cassiano theatre. For the first time, opera extended beyond the courts, and citizens who could afford a ticket could attend.

LIBRETTO
the written story of an opera

Despite multiple connections to the world of opera, Barbara Strozzi's musical life was restricted within the walls of the academy. Her compositions and performances were intended for an intimate male audience, and only via her publications did she access the outside world. Giulio Strozzi gave his daughter the best musical education he could afford, including private compositional study with leading opera composer Francesco Cavalli. Along with her compositional skill, Strozzi possessed a prodigious voice, and she began to perform for the men of the academy as a young teen. It is likely that Giulio Strozzi formed the Academy of the Unisoni (a sub-group of the Incogniti) specifically to promote Barbara's musical career.

By all accounts, Barbara Strozzi had rare vocal talent, which was compared to the "harmonies of the spheres."[16] Composer and academy member Nicolo Fontei wrote two volumes of song for Strozzi after hearing the teen sing for the Unisoni. Strozzi's own compositions, the majority of which were written in her range, featured demanding passages that required virtuosic technique.

Barbara Strozzi's exceptional vocal ability, education, and her intellectual exchanges with men of the academy strongly linked her to the courtesan culture of Venice. She enjoyed a musical and intellectual life unlike most women of her day, and she served both as a hostess and musical entertainer for academy meetings. It is difficult to know for certain how she was perceived within the academy. While the city on the outside believed that knowledge of music threatened a woman's modesty, the academy members themselves espoused feminist views and collaborated with women they respected, including nuns, via written correspondence.[17] Strozzi's father also made a point of defending Barbara when outsiders attacked her character. Whatever the truth, Barbara Strozzi's life among the academy must have been a fragile balance of participant and object. Women singers were considered of ornamental value in that era, and the beauty of their voices and bodies were viewed as one.[18] While she was included in an intellectual and musical circle of men, she must have stood on the outside of that circle at the same time.

Even with Strozzi's prolific compositional output, she would probably remain unknown today if it were not for her publications. Due to Giulio Strozzi's connections to the Venetian printing industry, Barbara was able to disseminate her work beyond local geographical boundaries. Eight volumes of song were printed in her name, making her one of the most published composers of her time, male or female. Though she was usually absent in twentieth-century musicological narratives, she was highly regarded during her lifetime, with over one hundred solo vocal works to her credit. She wrote more secular cantatas than any other composer of her era.[19]

Through publication, Barbara Strozzi became known to the world that existed beyond an academy of men among whom she lived and worked. She composed for her own voice, and performed before a designated, limited audience. Despite her placement in a city engaged in opera, she never used her compositional or singing voice on stage. Strozzi's association with the outside world was both enabled and limited by her father. While she had limited patronage of people such as Emperor Ferdinand III of Austria and Anna de'Medici, written correspondence indicates that Strozzi struggled to maintain important musical connections without her father. Within a decade of his death, the world heard little else from Barbara, and even the exact date of her death is speculative.

"Amor dormiglione"

CANTATA
based on the Italian "to sing"; sacred or secular vocal work with performance forces ranging from soloist, to chorus and orchestra

Unlike the multi-voiced sacred cantatas of Bach and other late Baroque composers, Strozzi's **cantatas** were secular solo works that highlighted poetic texts via melismatic melodies, melodic sequences, and rhythmic shifts.[20] Strozzi is considered a link between the early and middle Baroque in terms of formal constructs, being one of the first composers to place both recitative and aria within a single solo work. With her exposure to the literary minds of the academy among whom she lived, she was keenly aware of textual nuance, and was able to use music to emotionally persuade the listener.[21] At the same time, her music simultaneously displayed features that were considered feminine—spontaneous, graceful, ornamented, and topically centered on love.[22]

LISTENING EXPERIENCE 5.2

"Amor dormiglione" (1651)
Barbara Strozzi
Playlist

LISTENING FOCUS

Listen for the monadic style, with solo voice against a simple accompaniment. Also listen for extended melismatic passages by the vocalist.

FORM AT A GLANCE

Multi-section cantata with refrain at beginning and end: A B C A.

TEXT TRANSLATION

Love, dear love
Open your eyes! Rise, waken, cease sleeping!
For while you slumber all joys are dormant and only sorrow keeps vigil.
Beware, Love lest indolence claim you!
Arrows, fire, arise!
Open your eyes, you stupid and slothful, unwise, unseeing, fainthearted Cupid.
Ah! I must remain ardent with longing while you sleep, which only adds to my misery! Arise!

TIMED LISTENING GUIDE

0:00	A opening refrain urges love to sleep no more; Arise! waken!
0:32	B new material; "beware lest indolence claim you! Arrows, fire arise!"
1:02	C another new section; "you stupid . . . fainthearted Cupid! I must remain ardent with longing while you sleep."
1:36	A return to opening refrain; "Arise, waken, cease sleeping!"

Figure 5.4
Elisabeth-Claude Jacquet de la Guerre (1665–1729).
Source: Public domain

THE FRENCH COURT AND THE ARTISAN FAMILY: ELISABETH-CLAUDE JACQUET DE LA GUERRE (1665–1729)

While Italy was the flamboyant center of the early Baroque musical world that was supported by wealthy families, the French cultivated their own important contributions under the auspices of the monarchy. Much artistic development of the French Baroque took place in the court of Louis XIV, who used the arts to promote national cultural supremacy and to support his personal political agenda. The center of Louis' artistic and political world was the court at Versailles, where Louis moved his government in 1682. Located just outside of Paris, the Versailles palace contained 700 rooms, over 2,000 windows, and more than 60 staircases. The building was set amid an enormous estate that contained miles of geometrically ordered gardens and numerous fountains that were run by a sophisticated hydraulic system. During his seven-decade reign, Louis sponsored all forms of the arts, including architecture, ballet, painting, literature, and opera. The court hired as many as 200 musicians at a time, who served in three divisions: chapel musicians for religious services, chamber musicians for indoor entertainment, and musicians who performed at military and outdoor events.[23]

While women were not permitted to perform in the church realm in court settings such as Versailles, they were involved in chamber music for the court, and the prominent new chamber instrument of the era was the harpsichord (*clavecin* in French). Elisabeth Jacquet was born to an artisan-class musical family that boasted harpsichord builders, performers, and teachers. Her ability to perform and improvise on the harpsichord was so spectacular that she caught the attention of Louis XIV and his mistress, Madame de Montespan, when Elisabeth was only five years old. Legends of the child prodigy grew as she continued to perform in the court: "For four years a wonder has appeared here. She sings at sight the most difficult music . . . She composes pieces, and plays them in all the keys asked of her . . . and she is only ten years old."[24] Her connection with the "arts king" ensured years of patronage, including publication rights. With the backing of Louis XIV, she published her first book of *Pièces de Clavecin* (*Works for Harpsichord*) at age twenty.[25]

Maintaining her artisan-class status, Elisabeth married the organist and harpsichord teacher Marin de la Guerre in 1684, and they subsequently moved to Paris and had a son. Like Francesca Caccini, Guerre continued to work as a married woman, living in her own home and working for the court off-site. Both her son and her husband preceded Elisabeth in death. She remained an active performer and composer in her widowhood, performing in public as well as in her home.

With the patronage of Louis XIV constant throughout her career, Guerre received significant notoriety for her achievements. She was included in musical catalogues and dictionaries of the period, including entries by Charles Burney and John Hawkins in England, and Johann Walther in Germany. Walther's article on Guerre was longer than that of Francois Couperin (1688–1733), a French composer who received significantly more coverage than Guerre in subsequent years.[26]

Guerre's work was impressive in scope and quality. Her five-act opera *Céphale et Procris* was the first work by a woman performed at the Paris Opera. In addition, she wrote biblical cantatas, a ballet, and a Te Deum (hymn of praise) that acknowledged the recovery of Louis XV from smallpox. Her sonatas were creative, with bass lines that dialogued with the violin line in an innovative new style. Guerre was the only French composer to publish sets of harpsichord works in both the seventeenth and eighteenth centuries.

FRENCH STYLE AND THE KEYBOARD SUITE

The French were more musically conservative than the Italians, favoring musical control, refinement, and restraint. The French historical connection to the ballet de cour, or court ballet, became infused into French opera and impacted other countries that emulated the style. As the style extended beyond the borders of France, dance-related titles and styles were utilized in several genres (for more information, see Focus Topic 5.2).

FOCUS TOPIC 5.2

Genre Focus: The Dance Suite

The dance suite has its roots in the Renaissance, where paired dances were accompanied by consorts of like instruments. Repeated sections alerted dancers to changes in direction or motion. The Baroque suite extended the concept by joining multiple dance styles to form a complete work, often unifying them by key. While dance suites were not actually used for dancing during the Baroque, the rhythmic character and style of original dances were musically evident, and the repeated musical phrases were usually retained. The allemande, courante, sarabande, and gigue formed a common core of the suite, and other dances such as the minuet, bouree, gavotte, and loure were frequently added. The stylistic characteristics of the keyboard suite eventually extended to the orchestral suite as well.

Harpsichord Suite ♯1 in D Minor

Like the work of French composer François Couperin, Guerre's works showcase her virtuosic keyboard skills and evidence her improvisatory style. The highly ornamented melody is indicative of the Baroque aesthetic, and the use of the **agrément** is consistent with the French practice of artistic control and restraint.[27]

AGRÉMENT
French for "charm;" refers to an ornament in music, usually indicated by a written sign in the music

LISTENING EXPERIENCE 5.3

***Harpsichord Suite ♯1 in D Minor*, III Courante (1687)**
Elisabeth-Claude Jacquet de la Guerre
Playlist

LISTENING FOCUS

Listen for the ornamentation, typical of the French harpsichord style. See notation for the first section in Figure 5.5.

FORM AT A GLANCE

Two sections, each repeated.

TIMED LISTENING GUIDE

0:00	section one
0:34	section one repeated
1:09	section two
1:50	section two repeated

Figure 5.5
Excerpt from Guerre's Courante from the *Harpsichord Suite in D Minor.*

SUMMARY

The pages of history that erased the work of Caccini, Strozzi, and Guerre have been replaced by other narratives that acknowledge the musical activity of women of the Baroque. Once seen as anomalies, the three women highlighted in this chapter more accurately represent a significant number of other women who were engaged as opera singers, keyboardists, instrument builders, composers, and engravers. In the venues of the court and the familial circle, women were often conduits of aesthetic ideals that embraced culturally defined feminine notions of affect and emotion. The placement of singing and keyboard playing into the feminine sphere, along with a focus on bodily performance of these genres, continues to impact Western art music culture and popular music performance alike.

QUESTIONS FOR CRITICAL THINKING AND DISCUSSION

1. Conduct a "mystery listening" exercise in which you listen to recordings of French and Italian Baroque works. With the help of your instructor, try to determine the geographical source of each work based on information provided in the chapter. Then attempt to summarize the overall aesthetic feel of both Italian and French music of this period.
2. Investigate elements of the Classical aesthetic and compare it with the Baroque. Discuss how Classical aesthetic ideals might have defined musical roles for women.
3. Western culture has long associated the mind as the male sphere and the body as the female sphere. Is that belief still in evidence today? If you believe that it is, speculate how it impacts modern music.

IDEAS FOR FURTHER RESEARCH

1. Research the historical development of genres such as the madrigal and the cantata in terms of their changing meaning over time. As the genres evolve, are there musical characteristics evident that allow them to better rest in the female compositional sphere?
2. Compare and contrast a keyboard suite written by Elisabeth-Claude Jacquet de la Guerre with one written by François Couperin. Detail stylistic similarities and differences and investigate why Guerre was often significantly overshadowed by Couperin in secondary source materials. When did the shift in documentation occur?
3. Investigate and outline a brief history of women in the workforce from 1200 to the present. How do historical changes in women's work status impact music history?

CHAPTER 6

Romantic-Era Performer/Composers

Walking the Public/Private Line

After a promising increase in activity among women musicians in the Baroque era, the musical eras labeled "Classical" (approximately 1750–1800) and "Romantic" (1800–1870) were times of musical restrictions on women who could afford an arts education. As in the Baroque, eighteenth- and nineteenth-century musical families still generated a cohort of well-educated and well-known musicians, and many women from these families received formal music instruction that rivaled that of their male siblings. But while men could aspire to careers in music, women's music education was a preparation for expected roles in the home as entertainer, musical centerpiece, and, if wealth allowed, promoter of the arts.

SOCIAL CLASS AND MUSICAL EXPECTATIONS

When the general public is asked to list names of famous composers, it is not uncommon that many Romantic-era musicians are recalled by last name: Schubert, Schumann, Mendelssohn, Chopin, Tchaikovsky, Grieg, Brahms, Wagner, Liszt, and more. The post-Enlightenment rise of the middle class led to expanded opportunities for musicians to perform and compose music, and the large number of recognized composers from this era is indicative of change in the art music world. Musical families still existed, but a new group of musical unknowns composed "on the side," often making a living by other means. Some had limited formal music education.

EXTRA-MUSICAL
musical work that contains non-musical references such as a story or program

Whether formally trained or not, Romantic-era composers often produced music with melodic and **extra-musical** components that proved in many ways more accessible to the less musically educated masses than the form-based works of the Classical style. Despite widening inclusively in art music, however, the religious, moral, and cultural mores of the Romantic era made it difficult for women to enter the public musical arena. The Romantic ideal of the individual genius, which included the "great composer" notion, was decidedly male.

Restrictions on women in art music were particularly strong in Germany and Austria. In this region, where there arose composers such as Mozart, Beethoven, Schubert, Brahms, and Wagner, women were called "inferior beings who had no right to expect full integration in society." Arthur Schopenhauer famously wrote in 1851 that women existed "solely for the propagation of the species," and that they were "bereft" of any sensibility for music, poetry or fine art."[1] German historian Gordon Craig asserts that anti-feminist rhetoric was sometimes on a par with anti-Semitism, and subordination was evident in German law, religion, and custom.[2]

Despite the backdrop of suppression, Fanny Mendelssohn Hensel and Clara Wieck Schumann rose to surprising levels of notoriety in their lifetimes, only to diminish on the pages of recorded history thereafter. Focusing on the concept of primary and secondary source material, this chapter explores the constant reshaping of women's music history.

PRIMARY AND SECONDARY RESOURCES

Historians make use of a variety of resources when they do research. **Primary sources** are artifacts that provide first-hand accounts of historical events and subjects. In the music world, these include such items as letters, diaries, musical instruments, and original music manuscripts. **Secondary sources** are documents that have been interpreted by someone other than the direct source. In music, secondary resources would include a newspaper review of a concert or a textbook. Notice the varied views of Fanny Mendelssohn Hensel displayed in these two resources:

PRIMARY SOURCE
artifact that provides first-hand accounts of historical events or subjects; letters, diaries, and original music manuscripts are examples

SECONDARY SOURCE
document that has been interpreted by someone other than the direct source; in music, a newspaper review of a concert or a textbook are examples

> It isn't easy being a child prodigy. And if you discover that your younger brother is even more gifted than you are, does that make it better or worse? Most of us don't have such problems to deal with. Anyone who does might want to study the example of Fanny Mendelssohn.[3]
>
> Excerpt from *Women Composers*, 1988. Secondary source material

> He has no musical advisor other than me; he never puts a thought on paper without first having submitted it to me for examination.[4]
>
> Excerpt from correspondence written by Fanny Mendelssohn Hensel regarding her brother Felix. Primary source material

While primary resources are advantageous in many ways, such sources must not be considered infallible. The validity of primary materials is impacted by such things as editing, translation errors, and the individual researcher's knowledge of cultural context. With this in mind, we can turn to the use of both types of resources as we investigate the life and music of Fanny Mendelssohn Hensel.

FOCUS TOPIC 6.1

Style Focus: Romanticism

Romanticism was a nineteenth-century intellectual, literary, and artistic movement that was an ideal venue for musicians to explore. Visual artists, writers, philosophers, and musicians espoused and expressed the Romantic ideals of freedom, equality, and fraternity in their work. It was an era in which individual freedom was stressed, evident both in artistic works and in the breakdown of the patronage system. Emotional thinking overpowered the emphasis on rationalism prevalent in the Classical era, and the artist was often emotionally linked to the artistic work. A fascination with nature in both beautiful and destructive forms permeated musical works, particularly as the composer showcased the Romantic ideal of people struggling against the environment. Nationalism was evident in musical works as well, as folk and regional musical characteristics were infused into art music scores.

Musically, the form-driven balance and poise of the Classical era gave way to less strict formal structure. Extra-musical stories and programs often accompanied a musical work, sometimes demoting music from this era to a lower status in the eyes of musicians who valued the formal construction of the Classical style. On the other hand, the emotional connection between composer and music, and its subsequent transmission to the audience, has made Romantic-era music extremely popular among consumers of art music.

FANNY MENDELSSOHN HENSEL 1805–1847

When music history sources address Mendelssohn, it is almost always in reference to Felix Mendelssohn, 1809–1847. Despite the growing awareness of the work of Fanny Mendelssohn Hensel that occurred in the latter part of the twentieth century, she was omitted in many widely distributed collegiate music history materials at the turn of the twenty-first century, and remains underrepresented in current reference works. When Fanny Mendelssohn-Hensel *is* included in written materials, she is usually cited as the "sister of Felix Mendelssohn," portraying her as musically inferior to her brother.[5]

Fanny Mendelssohn was the eldest child born into the Abraham and Lea Mendelssohn family of Berlin. Her grandfather was the famous philosopher

Figure 6.1
Fanny Mendelssohn Hensel, by artist Wilhelm Hensel.
Source: Public domain

Moses Mendelssohn, widely known for articulating Enlightenment thinking pertaining to the integration of the Jewish people into new social structures such as middle-class education.[6] Like her brother Felix and two other siblings, Fanny was given superb private instruction in general educational studies, as well as musical studies in piano and composition. Both Fanny and Felix studied with the highly regarded composer and teacher Carl Zelter, who steeped the Mendelssohn siblings in rigorous theoretical work such as the contrapuntal writing of Johann Sebastian Bach. As such, both Fanny and Felix wrote progressive Romantic works that also reflected the technical skills of well-educated composers.

Fanny and Felix shared many musical opportunities and experiences, and both were child prodigies. Fanny performed Bach's entire *Well-Tempered Clavier* by memory at age thirteen, and Felix wrote several major works, including *Midsummer Night's Dream* before he turned eighteen. Both composed a significant number of works in their teenage years, and they regularly exchanged and critiqued each other's compositions. This artistic exchange continued in their adult years and is documented in written correspondence between the siblings. Despite the propensity of biographical dictionaries to portray Fanny as musically inferior to her brother in terms of keyboard performance, Felix considered Fanny his superior, ranking her above the leading pianists of their time, male or female.[7]

As a converted Jew and a woman of some wealth, Fanny Mendelssohn would have compromised her social position, and that of her family, by receiving money for professional musical work of any kind, including composition and performance. While her brother toured Europe, became published, and soared to fame, her work as a professional musician was curtailed by societal expectations regarding her expected domestic role. Unlike some women musicians in this situation, however, Fanny continued to write music, composing over 400 works in her short lifetime. In addition, she had significant influence on a wide range of musical activities that took place in her home.

Important Work in the Private Sphere

> *You can well imagine, however, how it is for me—to whom she was present at all time, in every piece of music, and in everything that I could experience, good or evil.*[8]
>
> Felix Mendelssohn, in a letter written after Fanny Mendelssohn Hensel's death

Before we look at Fanny Mendelssohn Hensel's limited foray into the publishing world, we should not ignore the work that she contributed in her private-sphere endeavors. This included a continual artistic influence on her brother Felix, as well as the creation of works published under his name. In additional, Hensel played an important role in the **salon** scene in Berlin, and helped to ignite the "Bach revival" that is often solely credited to her famous brother.

SALON
a regular gathering of distinguished guests; in music, often references a meeting of literary or artistic people in a home

Fanny's correspondence and musical collaboration with her brother Felix had a significant impact on his compositions both in terms of editorial work and in his development of genres that were not associated with the male sphere in nineteenth-century Germany. Written correspondence between Felix and Fanny indicates that she critiqued his works in great detail, and that they debated particulars, such as use of ornamentation. He returned the favor with equally strong artistic criticism of her work, which he considered of the highest quality.

Although Fanny Mendelssohn's influence on Felix's lyrical piano works is generally ignored today, music critics during the Mendelssohns' lifetimes openly criticized Felix for succumbing to the feminine influence of his sister in his *Songs without Words*, a set of piano works in eight volumes, accessible for amateurs. History now favorably credits Felix Mendelssohn with creating the novel programmatic piano genre that inspired other composers to write similar works, but German music critics of the day attributed this genre in part to Fanny's influence on Felix, usually disparagingly. Theorist Adolf Marx indicated that Felix was "dallying" in the "feminine sphere," and Hermann

Zopff wrote that female influence "was the insidious poison that was more and more to strangle the high aspiration for which nature had endowed him." Yet another article indicated that Mendelssohn feared his sister and that she had a "restraining influence on his Romantic musical style."[9] That Fanny was Felix's musical collaborator in this genre is fairly certain, as at one point he sent one of his *Songs without Words* home to Fanny so that she might write the second part.[10]

Fanny's private composition in the home also surreptitiously impacted the public when Felix published some of Fanny's songs under his name in his opuses 8 and 9 in 1827 and 1830. While many authors have debated Felix's intent in publishing his sister's work as his own, it seems that he at least acknowledged Fanny's songs as her work when the opportunity arose. When Queen Victoria performed one of Fanny's songs in this collection in 1842, and naturally assumed it was Felix's work, he admitted that it was really his sister's composition. "I was obliged to confess that Fanny had written the song, which I found very hard, but pride must have a fall."[11] Music critics of the day declared that some of Mendelssohn's best songs were actually written by his sister Fanny, another indication that Felix must have acknowledged his sister's work.

Along with impacting her brother's extensive work, Fanny Mendelssohn Hensel's work in the Berlin salon scene was significant. For many years, the Mendelssohn family hosted the *Sonntagsmusik*, a series of Sunday salon concerts at the Mendelssohn estate. Because this music took place in the home, Fanny was permitted to continue the family tradition even after her marriage to Wilhelm Hensel. These weekly performances were a significant part of Berlin musical life, and were attended by the aristocracy of the city as well as the affluent middle class. In this venue Fanny showcased her true musical abilities as she performed on piano, premiered her brother's works, conducted groups (including a professional orchestra) and presented her own original compositions. Berlin audiences were introduced to the music of J. S. Bach and Christoph Willibald Gluck in this salon setting, reflecting the Mendelssohn influence from Zelter. Felix Mendelssohn is usually given full credit for the Bach revival in Berlin, but Fanny's continuous salon performances almost certainly helped to propel Bach into the revered position in the Western canon that he holds today.[12]

Despite remaining in the private sphere, Fanny Mendelssohn's abilities were sufficient that she was known as a musician in her lifetime, not a small feat for a woman in nineteenth-century Germany. We have seen that music critics wrote of her works during her lifetime, and her work in the salon setting made her a well-known name in musical circles as well. Despite the fact that she was permitted to present only one public performance on piano, her abilities as a performer were respected and known to the point that one male pianist indicated that he was frightened to play for her: "And to think that this terrible person should be a lady."[13] Although Fanny Mendelssohn Hensel was known during her lifetime, the power of written history was to downplay her abilities for the next 150 years.

Ethnicity, Social Class, and the "Suppression" of Public Work

Unpacking Fanny Mendelssohn Hensel's story is a complex task and yields a variety of interpretations. What seems certain is that Fanny aspired to be a published composer, and that some members of her upper-middle-class family felt vulnerable about her entering the public sphere as a published composer. The role of significant people in her life in impacting the initial suppression and eventual publication of her work is an important part of her story, and the additional role of her son and nephew in releasing edited primary source documents also impacted the telling of her story in secondary source materials.

Since 1980, scholars have attempted to explain why the Mendelssohn men (father Abraham and brother Felix) discouraged their daughter and sister from public music involvement, basing much of their argument on primary source materials such as letters and diaries. Post-enlightenment Berlin was a setting where women from accomplished social circles were highly educated, but it was expected that a woman's true happiness would be found as wife and mother. Musicologists often cite Abraham Mendelssohn's written correspondence to his daughter on her twenty-third birthday as evidence that her aspirations were suppressed: "You must become more steady and collected, and prepare more earnestly and eagerly for your real calling, the only calling for a young woman—I mean the state of a housewife." Another frequently cited document is Felix Mendelssohn's June 1837 response to his mother's request that he help Fanny publish some of her works. He wrote, "To persuade her to publish anything I cannot, because this is contrary to my views and to my convictions . . . She is too much all that a woman ought to be for this."[14]

It is difficult to find documentation that portrays Abraham Mendelssohn as anything but a man who discouraged his daughter's musical career, and that patriarchal influence was undeniably strong. The popular portrayal of Felix Mendelssohn as suppressor of his sister's work is more frequently debated. While Felix consistently expressed concern about Fanny's publication of works, he also indicated that he would assist her if she did decide to publish. He certainly understood her immense talent and had a unique opinion of women's musical abilities because of his exposure to his sister. When famous violinist Joseph Joachim expressed incredulousness that Clara Schumann could write intense, complex music, Mendelssohn reportedly laughed at his naiveté.[15]

Some scholars argue that primary source materials from Felix Mendelssohn were actually edited by male members of the Mendelssohn-Hensel family, including Fanny's only son Sebastian, and Fanny and Felix's younger brother Paul. These scholars speculate that Sebastian Hensel and Paul Mendelssohn probably altered family correspondence prior to publication so that it would reflect a "proper" attitude about the role of women in their family. It seems reasonable to believe that men of this era would have supported the notion of male suppression of female musical involvement to maintain respect for the family name. While it is difficult to prove that Sebastian Hensel's 1879 release of edited primary source materials reflected concern about the aspirations of the somewhat unusual women in his family, the excerpted letters and diaries initiated faulty thinking that surrounded Fanny Hensel's story for many decades. In fact, some of that material is still cited in the twenty-first century.

Throughout the twentieth century, secondary source materials ranging from books to highly regarded reference materials portrayed a subservient Fanny Mendelssohn, who dutifully adored her "more talented" brother and promoted his career. This 1988 book excerpt is indicative of that perspective:

> Fanny's talent was immense and immediately apparent . . . but Felix, who was four years younger, soon began to outstrip Fanny in every musical field . . . She idolized her brother and tended to neglect her own work in order to promote his.[16]

Primary source materials tell a different story, in which Fanny ardently longed to make public the music that she felt compelled to write. These sources also reveal a loss of creative impulse when her work continually was withheld from public consumption, and a creative resurgence upon receiving public affirmation of her work. Following a trip to Rome in which she received high praise among the arts community she wrote, "I compose a great deal now, for nothing inspires me like praise."[17]

In spite of her husband's encouragement, Felix Mendelssohn's influence over his sister made her reluctant to publish. She wrote:

> Hensel, on the one hand, is for it, and you, on the other hand, are against it. I would of course comply totally with the wishes of my husband in any other matter, yet on this issue alone it's crucial to have your consent.[18]

Sebastian Hensel's materials did not negate the struggle that his mother endured while deciding whether or not to pursue publication, but his publication of family documents did exonerate the Mendelssohn men from liability. This excerpt written by Fanny to Felix supports the notion that she sought publication despite being afraid of displeasing and disgracing the family. "I trust you in no way will be bothered with it, since, as you can see I've proceeded completely on my own in order to spare you any possible unpleasant moment."[19] Along with standing up for herself within her domestic circle, Fanny Hensel had to pursue publication with some aggression. In a letter to her brother Felix, in which she referred to songs that were eventually published, she said that she had "shoved them down Schlesinger's throat," referring to the publisher who eventually became her advocate.[20]

Regardless of her repressive environment, Fanny Hensel recognized her ability. "My own delight in music and Hensel's sympathy keep me awake still. I cannot help considering it a sign of talent that I do not give it up."[21] The fact that she composed over 400 works is testament to a woman who believed that most of her works would not reach the public.

Support from Wilhelm Hensel and Lea Mendelssohn

Two lesser-examined roles in the story told by primary source materials are those of Fanny's mother Lea and Fanny's spouse, artist Wilhelm Hensel. Despite evidence that Lea Mendelssohn clearly supported Fanny's publication aspirations (and wrote to publishers on behalf of Felix as well) she has been historically dismissed from promoting Fanny's work. Nonetheless, having her mother's support must have been a source of reassurance in deciding to publish against her father's and brother's wishes.

Though sometimes marriage meant an immediate curtailing of musical activity for women, Wilhelm Hensel apparently wanted his wife to expand her public musical activities. This excerpt from a Felix Mendelssohn letter to his mother Lea is one of several references to the wishes of "Hensel" to promote Fanny's publication:

> If she resolves to publish, either from her own impulse or to please Hensel, I am, as I said before, quite ready to assist her so far as I can, but to encourage her in what I do not consider right, is what I cannot do.[22]

In addition to moral support, Fanny's life with Hensel the artist allowed her to be deeply steeped in and connected to the arts world and to experience travel and social situations beyond her restrictive Berlin environment. The Hensels collaborated on joint artistic works and enjoyed dual connections with the artistic public as well.

Visits to Rome, Milan, Venice, and Florence allowed an artistic inspiration and freedom that provided renewed confidence for Fanny. Italian contacts found her work not only compelling, but extraordinary. After her trip to Rome, composer Charles Gounod wrote, "Madame Hensel was a musician beyond comparison, a remarkable pianist, and a woman of superior mind."[23] Encouraged by her husband and inspired by a new circle of people who highly acclaimed her work, Fanny at last began actively seeking publication of her work under her own name.

Figure 6.2
Shown here is the first page of Fanny Mendelssohn Hensel's *Piano Trio in D Minor*, Op. 11, first movement. The aggressive energy of the opening prevails throughout most of this movement, causing speculation that Hensel purposefully avoided adding the contrasting lyrical theme usually found in sonata form. In writing a boldly aggressive instrumental work, Hensel's trio defied more than one gender-based connotation. For more information on gender notions and sonata form, see, for example, the work of Susan McClary (1991) and Suzanne Cusick (1994), cited in the bibliography.

SONATA FORM
frequently found in the first movement of a sonata or symphony; usually consists of an exposition with contrasting segments, followed by a development of the opening material, and a recapitulation which returns to the original key or tonality

LISTENING EXPERIENCE 6.1

Piano Trio in D Minor, Op. 11, Movement I (published 1850)
Fanny Mendelssohn Hensel
Companion CD Track 6

LISTENING FOCUS

Listening Experience 6.1 is the first movement of a three-movement piano trio, scored with the usual instrumentation of piano, violin, and cello. Listen for the exchange between the voices as they take turns leading with the melody.

FORM AT A GLANCE

Sonata form

Exposition	Development	Recapitulation	Coda

TIMED LISTENING GUIDE

Exposition

0:00	A theme in key of D minor heard in violin and cello, supported by virtuosic scalar material on piano
0:52	transitional theme in piano begins in B♭ major
1:35	B theme in F major in cello, accompanied by measured tremolo in piano; theme passed to violin
2:32	transition to development

Development

2:40	development begins in F minor in piano
3:49	A theme fragments, frequent modulation
5:14	B theme in cello, then piano
5:48	fragments of A theme and transitional theme (6:05)
6:16	sequencing leading to recapitulation

Recapitulation

6:30	A theme in D minor heard in the piano, strings now have opening scalar passages
6:58	return of transitional theme from exposition
7:16	A theme fragments
7:39	B theme in strings as in exposition, but in D major; B theme in piano (8:06)

Coda

9:41	piano introduces coda with opening scalar passage, along with cello on A theme

LISTENING EXPERIENCE 6.2

"September: At the River" from *Das Jahr* (1841)
Fanny Mendelssohn Hensel
Playlist

LISTENING FOCUS

This is one movement from a fifteen-movement solo piano cycle that depicts the months of the year via musical association rather than lyrics. Hensel subtitled the September movement "At the River." The changing of the seasons is depicted in shifts between major and minor tonality, while the movement of water is suggested in the rhythmic motion of the work.

FORM AT A GLANCE

A B A

TIMED LISTENING GUIDE

0:00	Introduction
0:11	A section, with theme in key of B minor; modulation leading to B section (0:58)
1:23	B section begins in G♯ major, transitions to E♭ minor (1:32), modulates back to A section
1:56	A section, returning to key of B minor
2:37	Closing section

FOCUS TOPIC 6.2

Genre Focus: Chamber Music

Chamber music refers to music written for a small ensemble, usually not in excess of ten performers, with each performer assigned an individual part. Chamber music was popular in the Classical and Romantic eras, and the rising middle class took a new role in supporting its production and performance. Like the Classical symphony, chamber music often was built upon strict formal structures. The piano trio, string quartet, brass quintet, and woodwind quintet are among many common chamber ensemble combinations for which volumes of music have been written. Since chamber music was often performed in private performance venues accessible to women, nineteenth-century women tended to write for chamber ensembles rather than large-scale forces such as symphony orchestras.

CHAMBER MUSIC
music for performance by a small group, usually with one performer to a part, as in a string quartet; originally for small audiences

An Early End to Publishing

Fanny Mendelssohn Hensel's story takes on a tragic ending because of her early death. After spending the majority of her compositional years as an unpublished composer, her decision to actively seek publication could have made her historically famous. Her death from a stroke at age forty-one occurred just one year after her decision to publish, and as such, the vast majority of her work remains in the family archives in Berlin. The early publications largely comprised **lieder** and choral works, generally more accepted as part of the limited and emerging female canon. This unfortunately hides the fact that she was also adept at writing instrumental works. Her brother Felix, who died six months after his sister, had several of Fanny's works published after her death, including the *Piano Trio Opus 11*, an energetic and captivating work that has been subjected to gender decoding because of its predominance of so-called "male" aggressive characteristics.

LIED
German for song; in formal music study, usually refers to German art song

History is slow to correct omissions and errors, and at the turn of the twenty-first century, Fanny Mendelssohn Hensel still stood in the shadow of her brother. The musical world still has much to learn from the unpublished material that remains in private collections, and it is certain that her written story is far from complete. Felix Mendelssohn appropriately expressed Fanny Hensel's compositional ability when he said of her work: "Truly there is music which seems to have distilled the very quintessence of music, as if it were the soul of music itself . . . I know of nothing better."[24]

PROGRAM MUSIC
instrumental work that tells a story or suggests a non-musical idea; may actually be associated with a written program, but sometimes only includes a suggestive title

CHARACTER PIECE
quasi-programmatic piece for piano that emerged in the nineteenth century that suggested a mood or feeling via title or overall aesthetic; tended to be fairly simple in structure

ABSOLUTE MUSIC
music that does not seek to suggest a story or scene, but is concerned with formal construction; distinguished from program music

Contrasting Absolute and Programmatic Works of Fanny Mendelssohn Hensel

In Listening Experiences 6.1 and 6.2 compare the musical qualities of absolute and programmatic music. Hensel's **programmatic** *Das Jahr* is reminiscent of Felix Mendelssohn's **character pieces** for piano, and stands in contrast to the **absolute** style of Hensel's trio.

CLARA WIECK SCHUMANN (1819–1896)

> *Though much has been written about Clara Schumann, she is . . . known to us only through the eyes and minds of her own era.*[25]
>
> Nancy Reich

Clara Schumann's life has been the subject of novels and films, and it is not surprising, as the vignettes of her life include all of the elements of Hollywood: Clara the child prodigy, separated from her mother and controlled by her father; Clara the young woman who eloped with Robert Schumann; Clara,

Figure 6.3
Virtuoso pianist and composer Clara Wieck Schumann.
Source: Public domain

the married woman who lived with her husband's mental illness, suicide attempt, and early death; Clara, the widowed mother who traveled the world and raised seven children on her own; and Clara, the woman who fell in love with composer Johannes Brahms.[26] No doubt Clara Schumann was an unusual person in terms of her life story as well as her musical gifts, but what is fact and what is fiction?

The novelized version of Clara Schumann's life often portrays a child prodigy who traveled extensively until she got married, then gave up her career to embrace duties as mother and housewife. This narrative typically portrays Clara's return to the concert stage as necessitated by her motherly devotion and the need to feed her children after her husband's death.[27] In truth, Clara Schumann never relinquished her performing career during her married years and collaborated extensively with some of the most prominent musicians of the Romantic era. During her fourteen-year marriage, she frequently corresponded with composer/conductor Felix Mendelssohn, performed extensively with the renowned violinist Joseph Joachim, was a chief interpreter of the works of Frederic Chopin and Robert Schumann, and commenced a lifelong collaboration with Johannes Brahms.[28]

It is interesting to note that although Schumann was one of the greatest performing artists of the nineteenth century, she sometimes received more musicological recognition as a composer, almost to the point that her performance career was overshadowed. We will address Clara Schumann's compositional work shortly, but will first attempt to revitalize her life as a performer for readers who might consider composition her primary focus.

The sources that lend an air of legitimacy to Clara Schumann narratives are primary source materials that were commonly kept in the nineteenth century. Letter writing was as common then as electronic communication is now, and keeping a diary was an ordinary occurrence. Clara wrote a diary both as a child and as a married woman, and Robert and Clara Schumann kept a joint marriage diary. These preserved documents, along with travel and financial records, reveal rich detail about the life of this prominent artist. We have already examined the role of editing in the Fanny Mendelssohn Hensel narratives, and Clara Schumann's materials were also edited by family members and historians before they were released to the public. The amount of available Schumann material alone necessitated selectivity, and passages and excerpts that might have seemed improper or irrelevant to earlier researchers have been reexamined by others, none more so than Schumann scholar Nancy Reich. Reich extensively examined original documents in the Robert Schumann archives, and re-translated materials to ensure accuracy. In addition, Reich's work is guided by a feminist perspective that is shaped by her twenty-first century view of how women were regarded in nineteenth-century Germany. As we study the work of Schumann, we will simultaneously study the work of Reich.

Clara Schumann: The Performer

Robert Schumann lives boldly on the pages of documented music history, but in the 1840s it was often Clara Schumann who received the most attention. Robert was highly regarded during his lifetime, but like many innovative composers, he was not as celebrated during his life as he was after his death. It was Clara Schumann the virtuoso who was better known, and often it was she who secured more income than her husband. However, Clara performed for more than money. She craved an audience and artistic recognition, and in spite of the repressive culture in which she lived, she persisted in maintaining her artistry. Widely known as the major interpreter of the work of Robert Schumann, Frederick Chopin, and Johannes Brahms,[29] Clara Schumann ignored gendered roles in her lifetime, but was still subjected to them on paper after her death.

Clara Wieck was born in 1819 to Friedrich and Marianne Tromlitz Wieck. Her father was a well-respected piano instructor in Leipzig who also sold and rented pianos. Although not an outstanding performer himself, Wieck's teaching methods were widely admired. Marianne Wieck, Clara's historically ignored mother, was ostensibly the connection to musical ability that Clara's father capitalized on with his pedagogy. Marianne was a gifted pianist and taught most of the advanced piano students in the Wieck studio. But by the time Clara was five years old, her parents were divorced, and Clara became the property of her father, consistent with German law.

In an era when many parents invested in piano instruction as a means of finding a proper husband for their daughters, Friedrich Wieck's intent was to create a piano virtuoso, and there were no gender barriers in his mind. Along with structuring a rigid life of education, physical exercise, and diary writing, Wieck enforced a grueling piano regimen that resulted in shaping a child prodigy. Clara began performing publicly at age eleven, and embarked on an eight-month international tour at age twelve. A performance at Weimar during that tour drew this response: "I caught myself admiring a precocious talent: perfect execution, irreproachable measure, force, clarity, difficulties of all sorts successfully surmounted . . . she feels what she plays and knows how to express it; under her fingers the piano takes on color and life."[30] By age sixteen Clara was widely recognized as a performing phenomenon.

Friedrich Wieck is sometimes portrayed as a father-hero for supporting his daughter's immense talent, and though it is undoubtedly true that his pedagogical techniques and concert management propelled her to stardom, his motivation for doing so seems less noble. Wieck's showcasing of his young daughter brought him fame as a teacher and, with it, significant amounts of money. Clara's brothers were not musically gifted, and Wieck had little time for them, even indicating in correspondence with his second wife that the boys were to be sent away from home until they could be useful and successful.[31] Other primary sources indicate a brusque attitude about Clara's wellbeing on the road, with a greater focus on her moneymaking ability. At the same time, Wieck's legacy to his daughter was undeniable. He had promotional and financial savvy that Clara drew upon later in life as she managed her performance career, and he also infused her with the belief that gender had nothing to do with artistic ability. In an age where girl prodigies were commonly pulled from the public performance circuit when they became adults (a notable example being Nannerl Mozart), Clara Wieck was encouraged to continue. When Robert Schumann asked for Clara's hand in marriage, it is not surprising that Wieck vehemently declined.

Connection with Robert Schumann

The decision by Robert Schumann (1810–1856) to become a piano virtuoso came at the relatively late age of eighteen. He took his dream to Friedrich Wieck upon hearing a performance by nine-year-old Clara. Schumann moved in with the Wieck family, and despite Clara's young age, began a lifelong musical collaboration and a friendship that turned to love. Robert's performance dreams were dashed for more than one reason, including an injury to his hand. Even prior to that, he had struggled with his lack of progress, and was both captivated and discouraged by Clara's ability. "With Clara it just comes pouring out," he confided in one entry as he considered his future.[32] Already known as a virtuosic performer by the time Robert joined the household, Clara Wieck began to perform and premiere Robert's compositions, and they exchanged compositional ideas years before their marriage. Robert increasingly turned to composition, an area in which he was to become one of the giants of nineteenth-century Romanticism.

Friedrich Wieck was so opposed to Robert Schumann's marriage proposal that the young couple eventually took Wieck to court, as Clara was a minor. Wieck attempted to retain all of the concert proceedings that Clara had earned, and even demanded that Clara pay him for the lessons that she had received throughout her childhood.[33] The young couple eloped in 1840, just one day before Clara's twenty-first birthday.

The marriage of Clara Wieck and Robert Schumann is often discussed with the notion that Clara became a subservient Romantic-era housewife who never played the piano until Robert's death. Fictionalized and scholarly materials utilized excerpts from letters and the marriage diary that led to this notion. Less frequently quoted excerpts reveal that Robert actually wavered back and forth in his support of Clara's career, torn between wanting her home and wanting her to achieve success.[34]

The addition of eight children to the Schumann household in ten years is also assumed to have ceased Clara's performance career. Although it was true that Clara managed the busy household, she did so with the help of household servants, typical for European families of that era and social class. Clara Schumann's connection to motherhood was far from the domestic idyll of mother gathered around the hearth with children. She was a concert artist who struggled with the increasing size of her household in terms of its impact on her career.[35]

Despite her concerns, Clara performed 139 public concerts during her fourteen married years, and simultaneously juggled ten pregnancies, eight live births, the death of a young child, and the suicide attempt and institutionalization of her husband. She concertized throughout her pregnancies, almost unthinkable in an era when pregnancy was hushed and concealed, and returned to the concert stage immediately upon giving birth. Clara's celebrated concert tour to Russia, sometimes erroneously portrayed as taking place after Robert's death, actually required that she leave young children at home without parents, as she was accompanied on the trip by the already ailing Robert. As her husband's health diminished, Clara became the family spokesperson and managed business affairs. She defended her husband staunchly against his critics, and even though she was a world-class soloist, she accompanied her husband's rehearsals on piano to assist him as he struggled in his final conducting position. She sat by his bedside, managed the household, toured, and practiced.

Nancy Reich asserts that Clara Schumann almost always took the career route when faced with a decision between home and performance, even to the point that she was absent for the children during severe illnesses. Second daughter Eugenie expressed this perception of her mother: "We knew that in our mother woman and artist were indissolubly one . . . We would sometimes wonder whether our mother would miss us or music most if one of the two were taken from her, and we could never decide."[36]

This was not the type of women's narrative that was portrayed prior to the late twentieth century, but became more familiar with an increased recognition of the emotional tug of working mothers. Clara Schumann's guilt and confliction seems to foreshadow that of women of a future generation. From a modern vantage point, one can speculate that it might have been because of her gender that Schumann felt she could not cancel a performance or let down her professional persona. Her expressions of concern for her children's health and well-being were evident in volumes of letters and diary entries, but were obscured by a determined, disciplined artistic presentation to the public. Images of guilty mother *and* stoic performer were omitted by a generation that deemed neither of those versions the "proper" Clara Schumann.

Robert Schumann's early death left Clara with seven living children to support, and as the thirty-five-year-old widow had a socially acceptable reason to work, she began to travel even more extensively. By the end of her sixty-year performance career, Schumann had traveled to France, Austria, Hungary, Denmark, Russia, Holland, Belgium, Denmark, Switzerland, England, and Bohemia, and she made return visits to many of those sites. By 1888, she had performed thirty-eight extensive foreign tours and additionally performed enumerable times in Germany, seventy-four times at the Gewandhaus in Leipzig alone.[37]

Clara Schumann: The Composer

Considering that Clara Schumann was one of the greatest performing pianists of her era, it is interesting to note that she became known to late twentieth-century musicians as a composer. This is probably due in great part to the tendency of historians to dwell on composers and their works; it is exacerbated by a lack of recording technology that could have captured Schumann's ability. Although Clara Schumann wrote many instrumental works, it is not surprising that it was art song that first appeared in historical materials such as Donald Grout's *History of Western Music*, fitting the "proper" compositional

ART SONG
a song written by a trained composer to convey a specific artistic idea, as in projecting the mood and meaning of a poetic text

sphere of women. Her "Liebst du um Schöenheit," a simple, strophic **art song** included in the Grout anthology, was frequently performed in recitals by the end of the twentieth century and often was included in recorded compilations of "women's" compositions.[38]

Although Clara Schumann wrote many art songs, it was literature for solo piano and instrumental chamber music that she first published. Clara Schumann's compositional career at first paralleled her performance career, with her first publication at age eleven. In this review of her piano concerto, one can see that Clara's compositional work was nearly as celebrated as her playing, but was subjected to gender analysis: "One has to marvel approvingly at the masculinity of the spirit that pervades (the work) and the technical difficulties leave absolutely no doubt about the widely admired virtuosity of the composer."[39]

As a frequent performer of chamber music that incorporated piano, Clara Schumann also brought a deep understanding of chamber genres to the compositional table. Her *Piano Trio in G Minor* (Op. 17) is an excellent example of Schumann's expertise with large forms, showcasing her ability to write an extended work in four-movement format.[40]

Numerous scholarly studies link a number of Robert Schumann's works to Clara's earlier works in regard to melodies that he borrowed from his wife, but perhaps overemphasize what was more likely musical collaboration. Reich reports that Clara also borrowed freely from Robert, as their musical relationship was symbiotic: they studied scores together, read poetry that they set to music, and explored similar genres. Robert obviously thought highly of his wife's abilities, as he asked Clara to arrange some of his most famous works when he was too busy to complete them. Clara additionally worked on piano transcriptions of many of his songs.[41]

Despite her ability and success, Clara Schumann's connection to composition remains an area of speculation and debate. She was fierce in her persistence to remain a performing artist, but seemed reticent to fully embrace the title of composer. Her discussions of composition were marked by conflicting signs of self-doubt balanced with knowledge that she possessed unusual compositional ability.

Clara Schumann's work as a composer ceased after Robert Schumann's death, and one can only hypothesize why she stopped composing. Speculation ranges from lack of perceived ability to unwillingness to battle gender bias. Others say it was simply a lack of time.

Variations on a Theme by Robert Schumann

Throughout her life, Clara Schumann remained a faithful champion of her husband's compositions and did extensive editorial work after his death. Even in her own work, she paid tribute to Robert. Like many of her compositions,

LISTENING EXPERIENCE 6.3

***Variations on a Theme by Robert Schumann*, Op. 20 (1853)**
Clara Wieck Schumann
Score available in the *New Historical Anthology of Music by Women*
Companion CD Track 7

LISTENING FOCUS

Listen for the Classical form and restraint of this Romantic-era work.

FORM AT A GLANCE

Theme and variation form

Twenty-four measure theme in ternary (A B A) form, followed by seven variations and a coda.

TIMED LISTENING GUIDE

0:00	A section of 24 measure theme in F♯ minor
0:22	B section of theme
0:41	A section
	See Figure 6.4
1:08	Variation One: rhythmic variation with triplet figure in left hand
1:54	Variation Two: more rhythmically varied, slight extension to 27 bars
2:57	Variation Three: new key of F♯ major; back to simple rhythm of the theme
4:09	Variation Four: return to F♯ minor with theme now in the left hand
	See Figure 6.5
4:59	Variation Five: faster tempo, with intense rhythmic accompaniment
6:10	Variation Six: canonic treatment of the theme between left hand and right hand
7:20	Variation Seven: final variation, with virtuosic flourishes
8:45	Coda: return to F♯ major

THEME AND VARIATION FORM
segmented musical form in which an original theme is first utilized, and subsequent segments of the work vary the original theme via manipulation of musical elements such as rhythm and harmony

Figure 6.4
Schumann theme.

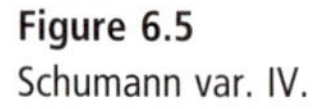

Figure 6.5
Schumann var. IV.

her *Variations on a Theme by Robert Schumann* was written as a gift to her husband. Published in 1854, it was one of the later works that she wrote before she ceased composing.

This work does not display the virtuosity that Clara revealed in other compositions to showcase her mastery of the piano, but rather demonstrates the restraint and clarity of form that she embraced as a "classic" Romanticist. Clara used a theme from Robert's Op. 99, No. 4 as the material upon which she created seven variations. The twenty-four measure theme is in ternary form (A B A) and undergoes changes in harmony, dynamics, key, and style throughout the variations. For a woman whose musical life was so centered on the piano, it seems a fitting closing to this chapter on her life.

SUMMARY

Germany was at the center of the Romantic musical world. At the same time, it was one of the most restrictive environments for women in Western culture in the nineteenth century. That Fanny Mendelssohn Hensel and Clara Wieck Schumann rose to musical prominence in this cultural setting is testament to women who were at once musically gifted and tremendously tenacious. Known to the musical world in their lifetimes, they were initially erased from the pages of documented history in the country where musicology was born. For over a century, they received limited attention in historical materials, and when they were mentioned, it was usually in reference to the musical men in their lives. Today, the "sister of Felix Mendelssohn" and the "wife of Robert Schumann" appear to be returning to the position of prominence that they deserve.

QUESTIONS FOR CRITICAL THINKING AND DISCUSSION

1. Why do music history narratives often focus on composers rather than performers? How does this impact the perception of the modern-day reader?
2. How might electronic communication impact the telling of history from your era?
3. In your own words, describe how theme and variation structure differs from the structure utilized in Hensel's *Das Jahr*.

IDEAS FOR FURTHER RESEARCH

1. Compare and contrast recorded excerpts of Felix Mendelssohn's *Songs without Words* and Fanny Mendelssohn Hensel's *Das Jahr*. Focus on musical elements such as form, harmony, and melody rather than on your general reaction to the works.
2. Investigate research that attributes portions of Robert Schumann's compositional work to his wife Clara. Critically analyze the evidence presented.
3. Investigate a composer of your choice and compare primary and secondary source material.
4. Early studies of women who composed music often attributed the women's success to men who in some way assisted them in breaking down barriers. Revisionist historians often disagree. Investigate both sides of the argument.

GUIDED RESEARCH PROJECT PART II

WRITING THE CLASSICAL CHAPTER

Part II of the text presented information on three major historical periods in Western art music, commonly known as the Renaissance, Baroque, and Romantic eras. In these chapters, you were introduced to the connection between gender notions and aesthetic trends in these eras, as well as the importance of primary and secondary source materials and author perspective in historical documentation. One major historical period left out of this text is the Classical era. Given the following prompts, assemble the data needed to write your own version of the Classical chapter. This project can be done by individuals or in groups. Compare your final products, noting how access to data and personal perspective resulted in various versions of the Classical story.

Consider the following as starting points:

1. What are the traditional dates of the Classical period?
2. In which geographical area did much documented compositional activity take place, and how does that impact perceptions of women in music?
3. Which scholars are considered experts on women who composed during this era?
4. Can you find references to women's musical work in primary source materials?
5. How do secondary source materials compare to primary sources in their descriptions of women's musical activities?
6. Identify genres that emerged during this period. How do these genres fit into pre-existing notions about musical roles for women?
7. Similarly, describe the overall Classical aesthetic and make connections to gender perceptions.
8. Identify key individuals and works that you might discuss. If possible, find recordings and bring them to class.

PART III

Visual Images in an Aural World

INTRODUCTION TO PART III

VISUAL IMAGES IN AN AURAL WORLD

At first glance, the phrase "visual images" might seem to be redundant. In the world of music, however, aural imagery is frequently discussed. This portion of the text explores the connection between the two, looking at both visual and aural imagery in women's musical performance. While it would be just as valid to address this topic using an art music lens, this segment turns to popular-music history, an area that has involved significant numbers of women. The advantages and disadvantages of visual imagery in music marketing are discussed, and one of the key concepts investigated is that of the **gaze**. The gaze has been in existence in many arts areas, ranging from Renaissance visual art to twentieth-century film. In music, the spotlighting of women as visual objects has sometimes negated their musical ability.

GAZE
the sexual objectification of a body by an empowered viewer

Chapter 7 paints a picture of American popular music, beginning the narrative just before the dawn of electricity. Before the advent of records, radios, and other playback devices, popular music was an acoustic world that relied exclusively on live performers. Women's roles in the American parlor song tradition, circuses, theatre, and other forms of live entertainment are examined both in terms of what women were able to attain, and in terms of how they were visually portrayed. Stage presentations of female performers and visual portrayals of women on written materials such as advertising and sheet music are discussed.

Gospel and blues are focus topics in **Chapter 8**, in which the potential power of the visual image is explored. While it is undoubtedly true that women were sometimes exploited by marketers who used visual images to sell musical products, women have often used their fame to spread messages of cultural and spiritual importance. The chapter digs deeply into the artistic merits of both gospel and blues, a focus sometimes forgotten amid the compelling stage presence of the performers.

Chapter 9 moves forward historically to the post-1950 period, investigating both opportunities and challenges for women involved in rock and popular music connected with visual marketing strategies. The roots of the manufactured popular-music model are examined with a focused study of the girl group phenomenon of the late 1950s and early 1960s. The story continues by exploring the historical roots of music video, and concludes with a discussion of the internet and interactive advertising media.

CHAPTER 7

American Popular Music 1895–1945

Musical memory occupies a strong and poignant place in the mind. Most readers have probably been transported to another place and time by an old familiar tune. How does popular music capture our memories and feelings in this manner? The first response to that question is a musical one. Popular music is distinctive by time period, and rapid stylistic changes make it easy to pinpoint a date of origin. Much as a teenage girl takes the basic element of her hair and fashions it to reflect the latest style, the composer takes basic melodic, rhythmic, and harmonic structures and twists them into the trendiest popular sound. Even if you were born long after the 1950s or 1960s, for example, you probably can accurately date music of those decades, and perhaps hairstyles and clothing as well.

It is more than the music itself that captures our imaginations, though. Popular music serves as a medium through which we recall places, spaces, and activities that we once frequented. Dance venues, cars, movie theatres, and live concerts are just a few of the settings where music paints the backdrop of our daily lives. While it overtly links time and place, popular music more subtly embeds cultural values into our collective psyche. Consider dance settings of the 1950s versus the 1960s, for example. Societal mores were evident in the way in which the dancers moved, touched, and dressed. In fact, it is often in music-related venues such as this that cultural change is formulated. Popular music not only entertains; it also challenges social structures.

Because popular music is so culturally powerful, it is critical to examine women's involvement as contributors, consumers, and producers. In a sense, music is a window into the world of time-specific gender beliefs. As we focus on a fifty-year period from 1895 to 1945, it will be with an eye toward women's musical work, challenges, and triumphs in American popular music. It is also important to note ways in which women were expected to project specific visual imagery as they participated in the world of popular music, as many practices from this early period are still reflected today.

TROUBLING LABELS

Before we begin the journey, let's revisit the labeling of music as "art" or "popular," particularly as it intersects with gender. Although differences in structure and complexity exist in music, the relationship between art and popular genres is best understood as a continuum that is impacted by era, performer, audience, setting, and musical creator. For example, sixteenth-century madrigals were popular music in their day, but now reside in the collegiate art music curriculum. Similarly, the orchestral music of "waltz king" Johan Strauss II (1825–1899) has floated between the art and popular labels since the nineteenth century. In the professional concert hall and textbook, it is art music—in the dance hall and park pavilion, it has a popular music nuance.

Gender also impacts the placement of musical activity in art and popular music spheres. Orchestral and band performance has been historically segregated by gender, with professional groups limited to the male domain. Women's groups have often been considered "entertainers" even when their ensemble instrumentation and repertoire have been similar to that favored by men. Similarly, songs produced by women in the Victorian parlor were sometimes published as popular music, even though the compositions were structurally similar to art-music works composed by men. Musicologists' reticence to address dance as art music is also notable, reflecting an overall tendency to analyze and historically revere musical structure rather than the bodily performance of music. This has resulted in scholarly dismissal of a significant amount of women's musical activity throughout time and throughout the world.[1]

Finally, it is important to note that racial bias further blurs the labeling of art and popular music. With the societal elevation of art music to an "elite" status, styles that originated in minority communities were often considered solely entertainment despite the music's structural complexity. For example, because of its origins in the black community, as well as its early performance settings and dance connections, jazz was once ignored by scholars.

POPULAR MUSIC BEFORE ELECTRICITY

The world of music at the turn of the twentieth century was a world of live performance that involved men and women from every social class. Electricity distribution was still limited, and although new inventions were about to change the sound of music, most music was heard live. Audiences traveled on foot or via horse to access musical entertainment, and venues ranged from the city park to local theatres. Minstrel shows, vaudeville acts, and circuses all featured performers who moved from town to town via train, setting up tents to shelter the audience and to create a performance venue.

Performances by traveling artists were not everyday events, however. Americans most often performed music for themselves, and song was a backbone of popular music repertoire. Ukuleles, mandolins, and keyboard instruments such as the piano and parlor organ were commonly found in homes, and were often played by women and girls to accompany singing. Young women of sufficient financial means were given music lessons in an attempt to achieve social status.

Keyboard performers who could read music often accessed sheet music inside the pages of women's journals and magazines. *Godey's Ladies Book*, published between 1830 and 1898, presented fashion and etiquette advice much like popular magazines today. Its inclusion of sheet music, however, indicates the importance of musical performance in women's everyday lives prior to 1900. *Godey's* also impacted cultural notions of what it meant to be musically "ladylike," by presenting images of women performing on specific instruments, such as the violin. *The Etude* (published from 1883 to 1957) was a music-specific magazine that contained both sheet music and pedagogical advice.

Figure 7.1
The parlor organ was a staple in many American homes at the turn of the twentieth century. Women and girls were especially encouraged to play keyboard instruments. This photo dates from 1896.

Source: Courtesy of the Library of Congress

BREAKING INTO THE STRING WORLD

Gender connotations of musical instruments change over time, and by the turn of the twentieth century, the violin had become an acceptable instrument for the proper "lady." From today's perspective, it might seem that instruments such as the violin and flute were always in the female sphere, but time and culture define what is acceptable. Even in the nineteenth century, Europeans defined the violin as unladylike. As European puritan ideas faded, however, women increasingly fought for equal rights, and the mores that governed gendered musical roles began to bend in America.[2] In the span of one hundred years, the violin went from being "unsuitable" for women, to an instrument that was highly encouraged. By the 1890s, many accomplished women violinists performed in America, and even more women participated as amateurs. Virtuosos such as Camilla Urso (1842–1902) spoke publicly about the need for professional ensembles to admit capable women performers into their groups, but the established professional orchestras remained closed to women.[3] As such, the expanding ranks of women violinists sought alternative opportunities.

With sex-based prejudice restricting access to professional groups, many women turned to amateur ensembles. All-women groups from Europe had toured America as early as the 1870s, and probably inspired the expansion of gender-segregated groups in America that followed. "Ladies' orchestras" were often acknowledged for excellent musicality, but even the finest ensembles were considered curiosities. Audiences wanted to *see* women play as much as they wanted to hear them play. An 1874 *New York Times* review of the Viennese Ladies' Orchestra foreshadowed the type of response that American women's ensembles often received throughout the twentieth century in venues ranging from jazz to rock:

> The orchestra presents a *coup d'oeil* attractive enough to compel the sternest critic to lay down his pen, supposing he may have anything unkind to say. But, happily, the Viennese ladies, with their uniformity of pretty costumes and (may it be added) their uniformity of pretty faces, are no mere pretenders.[4]

Restricted from the concert hall, the performance venues of the women's ensembles clearly placed them in the non-professional sphere. Women performed at parties, at fairs, and in park pavilions, and the interjection of vaudeville acts and "light repertoire" made public performances tolerable by societal standards. Performing an entire concert from the core canon was socially reserved for the professionals.[5] At the Columbian Exposition at the World's Fair in 1893, a suffrage publication announced the expected performance of an orchestra of sixty-five women who were to perform alongside the Sousa band, a common pairing of women's orchestral groups with entertainment-oriented wind ensembles.

In the cities, music clubs provided additional opportunities for women to perform for each other and for small audiences. The clubs also facilitated skill development and championed women's compositions. Rose Fay Thomas, wife of Chicago Symphony Orchestra conductor Theodore Thomas, led a national convention of women's clubs in 1893, and simultaneously led a movement to move the clubs beyond their self-serving focus to expand on educational outreach for children and communities.[6] (At the time of writing, the National Federation of Music Clubs awards $750,000 in fellowships for young musicians annually, and still honors Rose Fay Thomas with fellowships in her name.) The music club idea expanded to include a wealth of other string ensembles called "orchestras" during this period as well, a trend that was extremely popular for the first two decades of the twentieth century. Mixed ensembles of guitars, mandolins, and violins began to operate as clubs at universities, and also emerged as part of the curriculum in preparatory schools.

WIND ENSEMBLES

Brass bands and concert bands were popular sources of musical entertainment, particularly between 1895 and 1925. With historical roots in the military, the band medium maintained racial and gender segregation that was reflected in amateur and professional groups. By the turn of the twentieth century, the initial utilitarian tasks of bands on the battlefield had increasingly melded with entertainment functions. As with orchestras, the ensembles designated as professional were white and male. Military-based concert bands were widely popular across America and Europe, with one of the most famous traveling groups being the John Philip Sousa band. Sousa (1854–1932) drew large crowds of people who set down blankets in parks and tapped their toes to the music. The band's soloists were as well known as popular artists are today. The crowd anticipated virtuosic solos performed by trombonist Arthur Pryor and cornet player Herbert L. Clarke. Even the famous piccolo solo on Sousa's 1896 "Stars and Stripes Forever" was played by a man.[7]

Sousa's band was the model for other traveling concert groups, and they all had one primary role for women, as featured vocal soloist. Like the male instrumentalists, the female singers were widely known. The Sousa band's Estelle Liebling (1880–1970), who was trained as an opera singer, created such a sensation with the American public that the *New York Times* announced her 1905 engagement with a large headline: "Estelle Liebling, Sousa Band's Prima Donna, Engaged."[8] Along with vocal talent, the women who stood in front of the band provided a striking visual image in white or light-colored evening gowns that stood in strong contrast to the dark military-style uniforms of the men behind them.

Figure 7.2
All-women marching band in the National American Woman Suffrage Association parade held in Washington, DC, March 3, 1913.
Source: Photo courtesy of the Library of Congress

Inspired by the professional bands, amateur groups formed across the country, both in industrial sites, such as factories, and in small towns. Small-town bands in particular were valuable sources of entertainment and community pride. These amateur ensembles, along with college groups that formed during the same era, followed the gender-segregated model of the professional groups well into the twentieth century.

Figure 7.3
In 1937, the University of Iowa band did not include women. Some collegiate groups, particularly marching bands, did not integrate until the 1970s.
Source: Harris and Ewing Collection, Courtesy of the Library of Congress

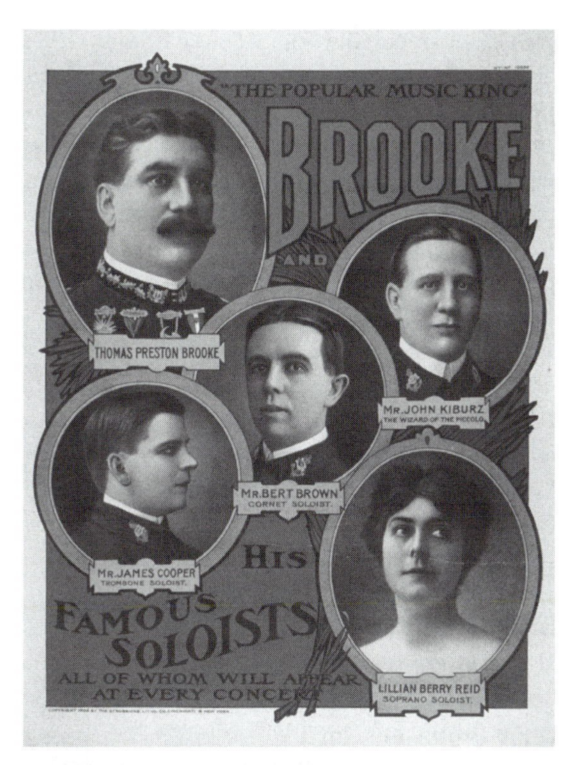

Figures 7.4 and 7.5
Women vocal soloists of the professional concert band era stood in contrast to male band members both musically and visually. In this poster from 1903 (Figure 7.4), vocalist Lillian Berry Reid is shown with male instrumentalists with the Brooke band. The notion of a woman vocal soloist fronting a group of male instrumentalists was later replicated in jazz ensembles and rock groups. In Figure 7.5 (below), a group of women are seen dancing in front of the Boyd Atkins Band during a cabaret floorshow at Dave's Cafe in Chicago c.1941.
Source: Courtesy of the Library of Congress

Beyond the well-documented world of Sousa, however, there were women involved in bands, and some of them were professional groups. Until D. Antoinette Handy (1931–2002) published research on black women in bands and orchestras in 1979, many Americans had no idea that black women were active instrumentalists, even prior to the First World War. Handy used photographs, newspaper accounts, and interviews to tell the story of women who led and organized brass bands, concert bands, dance bands, and orchestras. Their performance venues included circuses, carnivals, minstrel shows, riverboat rides, and vaudeville shows. Although many of the women photographed in the groups were unnamed, there were a significant number of named groups and soloists as well, especially in the gender-integrated groups. In all, the extent of women's involvement was noteworthy. Examples of those fortunate enough to be recognized by name include the following: the Mahara Minstrels, who gave concerts on the streets of Indianapolis; the Hart family orchestra, which featured sisters Hazel and Clothilde on drums;[9] Irma Young, sister of jazz saxophonist Lester Young, who performed in the Young Family Carnival Band; and Viola Allen, who was a cornet soloist with the "Colored Female Brass Band" of East Saginaw, Michigan. The work of black women in the band world of this era foreshadowed the involvement of black women in the jazz age, women who also were largely unrecognized outside of the black community until the late twentieth century.[10]

While black women were providing functional music under the circus tent, the role of white women in the circus venue was sometimes quite different. Live music played an important role in creating suspense and ambience as high wire acts and elephant riders entertained the crowd. Circus band music was technically difficult and required great stamina, as the musicians played almost continuously throughout the show. The bands that provided the behind-the-scenes music were almost always staffed by men. While musically excellent women's ensembles also performed, they had a dual function as they also served as a visual attraction. Women instrumentalists were sometimes

Figure 7.6
This Barnum and Bailey circus poster from 1898 clearly indicates that the women's orchestra was one of many sideshows. Dubbed as part of the "largest zoological exhibit on earth," the small print also reads "tremendous, strange, and curious."

Source: Image courtesy of the Library of Congress

displayed front and center, even blatantly advertised as sideshows. It was a sadly accurate portrayal of a widespread societal attitude about women in instrumental music.

WOMEN OF TIN PAN ALLEY

Back in the home setting, the greatest amount of music-making remained centered on accompanied song. Beginning in the 1890s, subscription magazines that marketed music met some stiff competition in a new industry that dominated the white popular music market until 1950. **Tin Pan Alley** was a sheet music industry that disseminated a variety of popular styles and genres on paper, and later coupled its sheet music sales with recordings. Named in part for the centralized geographical region of its publishers in New York City, Tin Pan Alley also came to signify a popular music style. **Song demonstrators** were hired to promote the sale of Tin Pan Alley sheet music, sometimes performing the newest tunes live on the city streets. The popular music world of this era can be seen on millions of pieces of sheet music published by the Tin Pan Alley industry. Boxes of sheet music can still be found at estate sales and auctions, and even the most popular hits of years past are available online

TIN PAN ALLEY
popular music style associated with the sheet music industry between 1880 and 1950; also a physical location of the publishing firms in New York

SONG DEMONSTRATOR
person who performed sheet music for customers who were considering a purchase

Figure 7.7
Baseball was a frequent focus of early Tin Pan Alley songs, reflecting America's fascination with the game. In this 1911 work by Nellie Nichols, the composer also posed on the sheet music cover.

Source: From the collection of the author

today for relatively low cost due to the original volume of sales and the number of sheets printed. Many of the songs that were popular at the turn of the twentieth century are still known today, including the number one popular tune in America in 1908, "Take Me Out to the Ballgame." That particular song is an excellent example of Tin Pan Alley musical style from this era. While the verses were often forgotten, the choruses were widely known and remembered. Harmonization was relatively simple, limited to a few chords for the ease of amateur performance.

Sheet music allowed families to replicate popular music for themselves at social gatherings, where it was often the woman's role to perform for guests. Tin Pan Alley utilized marketing schemes that catered to women as musical consumers in the home, addressing topics ranging from tender love songs to First World War hits about missing a soldier. On the production end of the industry, however, roles for women were much more limited. When women did compose, their names were often concealed by pseudonyms. (For a discussion of women's extensive publications in jazz and ragtime, see Chapter 13.)

CARRIE JACOBS BOND AND THE PARLOR SONG

Women were very involved in the performance of popular song but, overall, men dominated Tin Pan Alley composition and printing. Despite the odds, Carrie Jacobs Bond persevered and built a publishing company that became known worldwide. Her story allows a glimpse at the discrimination faced by women in the industry during this period.

PARLOR SONG
simple popular song performed by amateurs to the accompaniment of piano, parlor organ, or small stringed instrument

Prior to Tin Pan Alley, the **parlor song** tradition had long roots in America, dating back to the late 1700s. The topic of parlor songs was not unlike popular music of today—all things to do with love. Intended to be sung "in the parlor," the intended performers and audiences of the parlor song were usually amateurs. Still, the line between art song and parlor song was sometimes tenuous. "Classical" European works were often reprinted as parlor songs in America, and composers such as Carrie Jacobs Bond often wrote difficult piano arrangements and expanded vocal ranges that were beyond the abilities of amateurs.

A gifted pianist and child prodigy, Carrie Jacobs Bond (1861–1946) was born in Janesville, Wisconsin. Despite notable musical ability, Bond did not immediately engage in music professionally, and instead married and had a son. Her first marriage ended in divorce, and her second marriage, though good, ended tragically with her husband's accidental death in 1894. It was sometimes by necessity that women entered into the professional music world, and such was the case with Bond. A financially destitute widow at thirty-two, she wrote some songs and sent them to a Chicago publisher. Using the excuse that her work was "too classical" for the popular sheet music industry,[11] her intended publisher suggested that she limit herself to children's songs, mirroring the common belief that woman's compositional work belonged in the educational or children's literature areas.

Undaunted, Bond continued to write and promote her work, singing recitals in homes and at informal gatherings. She quickly gained a large enough following to support the start of her own business. After moving to Chicago in 1896, Bond established C. J. Bond and Son, the first music publishing firm in the United States run by a woman. The "Bond House" initially operated out of a corner area of the rented rooms where the composer and her son lived. Although Bond had to hire out the printing, she did everything else herself, including the artwork for the sheet music covers. The quality and appeal of her work was embraced by an enormous clientele and resulted in extensive royalties. Bond's biggest hits were "I Love You Truly," published in 1901, and "A Perfect Day," published in 1910. "A Perfect Day" sold eight million sheet music copies alone. Having decisively resolved her financial trouble by the end of 1910, Bond moved business operations out of her home and into a Chicago-area building. She subsequently moved her company to other locations, eventually settling in Hollywood, California. Bond is a classic example of a musically gifted woman who survived professionally by operating in the entertainment industry, persevering and prospering in a male-dominated marketplace by carving her own niche.[12]

LISTENING EXPERIENCE 7.1

"I Love You Truly" (1901)
Carrie Jacobs Bond
Playlist

LISTENING FOCUS

Listen for a vocal range that spans just over an octave, with simple piano accompaniment.

FORM AT A GLANCE

Strophic form (A A)

TIMED LISTENING GUIDE

0:00	Piano introduction
0:10	A Verse One
0:51	A Verse Two

STROPHIC FORM
each poetic verse is set to the same music

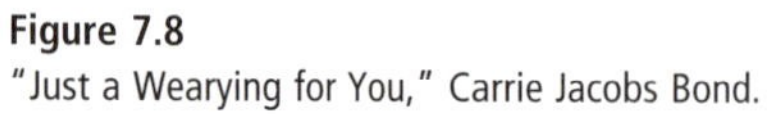

Figure 7.8
"Just a Wearying for You," Carrie Jacobs Bond.

Figures 7.8 and 7.9
This segment from Carrie Jacobs Bond's 1901 "Just a Wearying for You" (Figure 7.8) demonstrates her classical training, and exhibits art song characteristics. Along with the difficult key and expanded vocal range, the piano accompaniment imitates the sound of birds, referenced in the lyrics. The cover for Bond's 1910 "A Perfect Day" (Figure 7.9) is typical of her early sheet music covers, which she designed and painted herself.

Source: From the collection of the author

WOMEN ON STAGE: OPPORTUNITY AND EXPLOITATION

Before Broadway and Hollywood, sheet music sales were connected to a wide variety of staged productions. While paid roles for women in the music-related entertainment role were somewhat limited for composers, music-related stage shows and theatre held many opportunities. Vaudeville, minstrel shows, and the burlesque had their start as traveling "tent" entertainment popular in the 1890s, much like the circus. These genres interspersed musical acts with animal tricks, comedy, and magic shows. Minstrel shows, with roots in the South, were originally performed as early as the 1820s by slaves for plantation owners, but by the 1890s they were frequently performed by white performers who used **blackface** and made fun of the genre. Minstrel shows led to the development of ballads and comic songs known as "**coon songs**,"[13] a racist genre that stereotyped black Americans and sold in great numbers in the sheet music industry. Over 600 such songs were published in the 1890s alone.[14]

BLACKFACE
theatrical make-up used in vaudeville and minstrel shows that portrayed racist stereotypes of black Americans

COON SONG
late nineteenth-century popular song that presented a stereotyped view of black Americans; often performed by white singers in blackface

REVIEW
in staged musical productions, a variety show with music, but no plot

The **review** format was alive and well through 1915, and pre-Harlem New York was an active area with shows in revue format that featured singing and dancing. Black performers sang and danced in segregated houses, with both black and white audiences in attendance. Aida Overton Walker (1880–1914) was an international star who performed authentic black-derived genres such as the ragtime and cakewalk, along with her husband's popular "Williams and Walker" act. Like many women in the variety show world, Walker possessed multiple talents in singing, acting, dancing, and theatre.[15]

Vaudeville acts such as the Hyers Sisters similarly showcased the talents and versatility of female musicians. Along with providing entertainment, these groups often addressed serious topics such as discrimination.[16] Family groups such as the Musical Spillers were outlets for women who might have

Figure 7.10
Tin Pan Alley promoted and sold music related to a variety of stage shows. In this sheet music from 1904, star Aida Overton Walker is visually connected to the role of temptress in the song "Why Adam Sinned." The music industry has long used women's images to sell products.

Source: Historic American Sheet Music Collection, Duke University Rare Book, Manuscript, and Special Collections Library

had difficulty gaining access to gender-integrated instrumental groups without the family affiliation. Isabele Taliaferro Spiller (1888–1974), who married into the Spiller family as well as the performing group, played alto and baritone saxophone, trumpet, and piano, and was just one of the many women who performed on multiple instruments.[17]

With all of the musical activity in theatres of this era, theatre orchestras were in high demand and provided employment for many musicians. Marie Lucas' Orchestra performed in Harlem's Lafayette Theatre, one of the first theatres in the country to desegregate.[18] One of the best-known women's theatre ensembles of this era was the Fadettes, a nationally known group based in Boston. Had the Fadettes not been women, they probably would have been employed in professional orchestras. Many of the group members had studied with members of the Boston Symphony, but since the orchestral venue remained closed to women, the Fadettes turned to paid performance opportunities in theatre. After one successful theatre tryout in Boston, they were hired to replace an all-male ensemble from the Boston Symphony, some of whose members had been the women's former teachers. Boston was just the beginning for the Fadettes, and they continued to perform vaudeville shows in theatres across the country,[19] logging over 6,000 performances under the direction of conductor Caroline Nichols. As was often the case with women instrumentalists, the Fadettes adapted their repertoire to suit a wide variety of audiences and settings. Along with their more serious performance segments, they also became known for their entertaining stage antics.[20]

White theatrical shows such as the Ziegfeld Follies, which ran from 1907 until 1931, usually placed women in prominent roles as singers and dancers rather than as instrumentalists. Like vaudeville, the Follies featured a series of scenes and popular dances rather than a plot or storyline. One of the best-remembered Follies features was a line of chorus girls who wore revealing costumes and performed choreographed dance maneuvers. While men in the show were fully dressed in pinstriped pants and top hats, the women's costumes were clearly made to display sexuality, in bare-shouldered dresses draped in feathers. It was very rare to see male performers in advertising and sheet music related to the Ziegfeld show. The era of the pin-up poster was born long before the rock era.

Women continued to have many opportunities to perform on stage in the 1920s. Musical revues and variety shows developed into full dramas known as **musicals**, and **Broadway** was the center of activity. The new genre placed the focus of the entertainment on a storyline that was interspersed with song and dance. With over fifty new shows appearing in some seasons, there were ample opportunities for women to perform alongside men. Like the variety show venue, however, much behind-the-scenes activity remained in the male domain. While a number of women were involved in choreography, a high percentage of composers and directors were men.

MUSICAL
a theatrical production that includes singing and dancing; utilizes a plot

BROADWAY
New York theatre district associated with musical productions; also used in reference to the productions themselves

Figure 7.11
In this sheet music from 1918, the Ziegfeld female performers are visually displayed as a garden of beautiful women in connection with one of the songs included in the publication, "Garden of My Dreams."

Source: Historic American Sheet Music Collection, Duke University Rare Book, Manuscript, and Special Collections Library

TIN PAN ALLEY BETWEEN THE WORLD WARS

Popular songs of Tin Pan Alley were still prominent in American culture between the two world wars. Names such as Irving Berlin (1888–1989) and George Gershwin (1898–1937) are deeply associated with Tin Pan Alley, but during the height of the industry, nearly 200 women joined ASCAP (the American Society of Composers, Authors, and Publishers), and many were influential popular song writers. Women such as Dorothy Fields (1905–1974)

Dana Suesse (1909–1987), and Kay Swift (1897–1993) got limited press in the long run, but their songs were so well known that current readers may still know them today: "You Ought be in Pictures," "The Way You Look Tonight," and "I'm in the Mood for Love," are just a few. Perhaps best known of this group was Kay Swift who had a long career in the popular music industry.

Kay Swift was a classical musician and composer who studied with Charles Loeffler at the Institute of Musical Art. She met George Gershwin in 1925, and he encouraged her to write popular music, which she first did reluctantly. Gershwin consulted Swift frequently about his work throughout their relationship, and their long extra-marital affair led to Swift's eventual divorce. Aside from her collaboration with Gershwin, Swift had great success writing her own songs and, in 1929, composed what was to become an all-time jazz classic, "Can't We Be Friends?" One year later, Swift's musical *Fine and Dandy* became a huge Broadway hit as well. George Gershwin died in 1937, but Swift continued to collaborate with his brother Ira. Swift's musical credits are numerous, and she enjoyed a career in the popular music industry that spanned much of the twentieth century.

The standard **ballad**, or lyrical love song, remained a top seller for Tin Pan Alley. Much like the movie industry today, consumers in the early twentieth century enjoyed hearing music that was associated with their favorite show, and thus a symbiotic relationship formed between the sheet music industry, Broadway and Hollywood.[21] As elements of jazz and pop began to blend with rhythm and blues, new recording labels entered the market and promoted their female vocal stars. First to the tune of big bands, and later with smaller ensembles, performers such as Billie Holiday (1915–1959), Sarah Vaughan (1924–1990), and Ella Fitzgerald (1917–1996) were heard on records and on the radio.

BALLAD
in the blues and popular music tradition of the twentieth century, a smooth, lyrical song often about love; in the folk tradition, a song that tells a story of everyday life

Talented performers such as Ethel Waters (1896–1977) and Hazel Scott (who was a pianist as well as a singer) crossed over into Hollywood. As these women stood in front of the band or in front of the camera, they were frequently objectified. For example, when Hazel Scott was interviewed by a *New York Post* columnist shortly after she filmed *The Heat's On*, the title of the interview read: "Keeping Abreast of Hazel: Hazel Scott Boasts Buxom Bust and Deft Touch on the Piano."[22] Not unlike the movies of today, the female star was often the subject of the male gaze, with male characters and camera shots that focused lingeringly on the woman's body. Often, a woman's musical ability was overshadowed by her physical appearance.

Along with solo acts, the **girl group** movement that began with the Boswell Sisters in the 1930s continued with the Andrews Sisters in the 1940s. With good looks, tight vocal harmony and wartime songs such as "Boogie Woogie Bugle Boy," the Andrews siblings sold over seventy-five million records and traveled abroad numerous times to entertain military personnel in live shows. They also starred in at least seventeen movies during the 1940s alone. The

GIRL GROUP
a small ensemble of female vocalists who sing popular music

Figure 7.12
A 1940 photograph of Ella Fitzgerald.

Source: Carl Van Vechten Collection, Courtesy of the Library of Congress

LISTENING EXPERIENCE 7.2

"Can't We Be Friends?"(1929)
Written by Kay Swift, performed by Ella Fitzgerald and Louis Armstrong
Playlist

LISTENING FOCUS

Listen as Ella Fitzgerald and Louis Armstrong take turns soloing and improvising over the repeated 32-bar form of this jazz classic.

FORM AT A GLANCE

Three choruses of 32-bar song form.

TIMED LISTENING GUIDE

0:00	Piano Introduction
Chorus One: Sung by Ella Fitzgerald	
0:08	A section, eight bars
0:25	A section, eight bars
0:43	B section, eight bars, modulates
1:00	A section, eight bars
Chorus Two: Sung by Louis Armstrong	
1:17	A section
1:34	A section
1:50	B section
2:08	A section
Chorus Three: Armstrong and Fitzgerald	
2:25	A section; Armstrong trumpet improvisation on chordal progression
2:43	A section; trumpet improvisation continues
3:00	B section; Fitzgerald and Armstrong take turns singing
3:18	A section; Fitzgerald and Armstrong sing together

girl group movement peaked in the second half of the century, with groups such as the Chantels and the Supremes topping the charts. Like the Andrews Sisters, the post-war girl groups delivered both a vocal sound and a visual image as part of their entertainment package. (For an extensive discussion of the girl groups, see Chapter 9.)

THE DANCE HALL

Popular music is often strongly tied to dance, with new dance styles related to emerging music genres. Dancing was a popular American pastime throughout the early twentieth century, and new dances crossed over from the dance hall into staged shows and movies. Known as the "ballroom decade," the 1910s provided musical employment and entertainment in dance halls that were built on rooftops and in restaurants. Vernacular dances known as "animal" dances, with styles based on black syncopated styles from the minstrel tradition, entered the mainstream music market. Among the many new dances were the turkey trot, bunny hug, grizzly bear, and snake. In white venues, the new dances were as controversial as they were exciting, disturbing a generation that had been accustomed to Victorian-style dances.[23] The shaking hips and acrobatic lifts of the animal dances were a distinct change of pace from the waltz and polka.

Several black dance forms were revised by white dancers who modified the styles to allay the concerns of white Americans who were worried about social acceptability. Vern (1887–1918) and Irene Castle (1893–1969) were an iconic couple during this period, teaching from their stylish "Castle House" studio, located on a rooftop venue in New York City. Americans who could not get to New York could still learn from the Castles by purchasing a copy of their popular dance manual entitled *Modern Dancing*. Vernon was killed in the war in 1918, but Irene continued to dance in vaudeville, and also appeared in silent films. Many women of the 1920s emulated Irene Castle's attention-getting sleeveless styles and sheer dress material, along with her thin figure.[24] Even though their career as a couple was cut short, the Castles helped to change the course of modern dance in American culture, marking one of many times when widely popular dance styles were adapted from ethnic and minority styles. The jitterbug, born in the Savoy Ballroom in Harlem in the 1920s, was one of the most popular dances of the swing band era.

COUNTRY MUSIC ROOTS

Seemingly a world away from the New York-based popular music world, markedly different popular music styles were forming in various regions of the country. Along with the rhythm and blues of Chicago and Detroit, white hillbilly music of the rural South was soon to become a marketable product known as country music. Musical aspects of R&B and country blended together to formulate early rock and roll by the 1950s. As the 1940s drew to a close, so did the reign of Tin Pan Alley.

The roots of modern country music were strongly shaped by the women of the Carter family, a country music group that formed in 1927. The Carters

Figures 7.13, 7.14, and 7.15
(Clockwise from above)
With its focus on the bodily art of performance, dance was a form of popular music entertainment that embraced women performers. Shown here are: Vern and Irene Castle in a c.1913 pose (Figure 7.13); dancers in a Washington DC jazz club c.1938 (Figure 7.14); and jitterbug dancers on a dance floor in 1938 (Figure 7.15).

Sources: Figure 7.14 from the William Gottlieb Collection. All photos courtesy of the Library of Congress

lived in the backwoods of Virginia, where they used folk instruments such as autoharp and guitar to accompany folk songs, ballads, gospel, and blues. Alvin (A. P.) Carter married Sara (Dougherty) Carter (1898–1979) in 1915, and Sara's cousin Maybelle (Addington) Carter (1909–1978) married Ezra Carter shortly thereafter. Together, A. P., Sara, and Maybelle formed the basis of the original Carter family singers. Sara sang and played guitar and autoharp, and Maybelle accompanied with guitar and harmonized with vocals. The Victor Record Company found great success selling the Carters' music, and radio broadcasts from WSM in Nashville further built what was to become a country music empire.

Although they did not receive publishing credits, Maybelle and Sara Carter composed lyrics and did arrangements for the Carter group. The women often wrote about women's "lot" in life, and aside from blues lyrics, the Carters' depiction of women was fairly uncommon in popular music of the time. The Carter women probably had plenty of personal experience to inspire them. Both women raised kids, did chores, wrote and arranged music, traveled, and recorded. The original Carter group recorded approximately 300 tracks before Sara and Alvin divorced.[25]

Maybelle Carter's guitar playing revolutionized the role of the instrument in country music, as she used her thumb to play melodic lines on the bass strings while she strummed chords with her fingers on top. This technique, still known as the "Carter Scratch," made the guitar a lead instrument rather than a rhythmic accompaniment device. In the 1990s, Maybelle was named one of the top guitarists of all time by *Musician* magazine, her technique having impacted not only country music but folk styles as well. Maybelle solidified the Carter legacy by performing with daughters Anita, Helen, and June in the 1940s. June eventually married performer Johnny Cash and, like her mother, wrote songs, co-writing one of Cash's signature hits, "Ring of Fire."[26]

The Carter family, along with other women country music stars, long retained a more conservative stage presentation than did women in other genres. As country music branched out into the "country and western" subgenre associated with the widely popular "Western" film genre, female stars dressed in cowboy hats and Western-style checkered shirts. The off-the-shoulder dress of the circus, musical reviews, and Hollywood film star would not come for country music performers until much later.

SUMMARY

Women found both success and notoriety in popular music venues prior to 1945, but underlying themes of discrimination and marginalization limited their participation to areas that were socially defined as acceptable for their sex. While women such as Carrie Jacobs Bond and Kay Swift made a living in the popular music world, other women, particularly instrumentalists, often settled for performance experiences as an avocation rather than a profession. Gender segregation was common in instrumental ensembles, and all-women groups were scrutinized for their visual appeal as much as their musical ability. Vocalists and dancers received significant notoriety in popular music, but with fame came the price of being sexually objectified. Whether amateur or professional, behind the scenes or in front of spotlights, women in popular music negotiated their space by being as flexible and creative as they were musically able.

QUESTIONS FOR CRITICAL THINKING AND DISCUSSION

1. Discuss gender roles in popular music that you access today. Do you notice any parallels between modern and historical trends?
2. Black women were far more likely than white women to perform in gender-integrated instrumental ensembles. Discuss why this might have been the case.
3. Ask some older family members about popular singers and dancers that they admired when they were young.

IDEAS FOR FURTHER RESEARCH

1. The Tin Pan Alley industry was largely run by men. Investigate the people behind today's music industry and compare the situation to the pre-1945 era. Who is writing today's popular hits?
2. Further investigate gender roles in the world of theatre. Outside of stage-related performances, what were the roles of women "behind the scenes" in theatre prior to 1945?

CHAPTER 8

Empowered Voices in the Public Eye

Women of Gospel and Blues

Wade in the water
Wade in the water, children
Wade in the water
God's gonna trouble the water . . .
You know chilly water is dark and cold
(I said) God's gonna trouble the water
You know it chills my body and not my soul
(I said my) God's gonna trouble the water . . .
Wade in the water
Wade in the water, children
Wade in the water
(I said) God's gonna trouble the water

Traditional spiritual

Spoken words can be musical. Patterns of repetition, length of phrase, rhyme, and alliteration all help words come alive, especially when text delivery is performed in a musical way. Perhaps the most famous American speech of the twentieth century is Dr. Martin Luther King Jr.'s "I Have a Dream," delivered at the Lincoln Memorial in Washington DC on August 28, 1963. Think about how Dr. King enhanced textual meaning with musical technique. To draw attention to literary devices such as metaphor and repeated textual passages, Reverend King's speech featured intensification of selected words within phrases. He purposefully changed the speed at which he spoke, sometimes pausing, and the pitch of his voice traveled into high and low registers. In addition, he listened to the response of the audience gathered around him, and altered his delivery based on their communication back to him.[1] The words and the music of his voice worked together to make the speech an unforgettable experience not only for those who heard it that day but for generations who have heard the recorded version. Imagine the sound in your mind: "I have a dream . . . that . . . *I have a dream* . . . that . . . *I HAVE A DREAM* . . ."

Women also have used musical text delivery to speak important social messages, and while they were less likely to serve as preachers, they effectively spread their messages via a musical pulpit. For many working-class black women of the early twentieth century, music was a powerful means by which to resist oppression. Not only did singers depict everyday realities, they aimed to create change. Patricia Hill Collins points out that in an era when many working-class black women could not read, early blues recordings preserved their activist work in much the same manner as written materials were used in white culture.[2] Blues and gospel artists spoke to the needs and concerns of their audiences, inspired them to seek justice, and helped them build community. As they expressed knowledge, they also expressed deeply personal feelings, a wedding of politics and the aesthetic.[3] While the wide variety of musical work of other black women is included elsewhere in this text, it is important to consider the deeper meaning of blues and gospel, and women's roles in conveying sociocultural meaning via these genres.

American media sources have historically overdramatized the lives of blues and gospel artists in movies, plays, and documentaries, often masking the artistic, historical, and cultural significance of their musical art. Just as black women have been subjected to other stereotypes, so have they been cast into a stereotypical role in the blues and gospel.[4] We have thus been exposed to movie images of the "tragic" Billie Holiday and scenes from *Sister Act* with little detail about the actual music and the richer context in which the music was formed. It is impossible to understand the role of women as *more* than a stage presence without addressing how women of blues and gospel negotiated a music industry that catered to the male gaze. The glamorous dresses and sexy attitude of the blues singer, and the jewelry and wigs of the gospel star, are part of a performance milieu that needs to be understood in greater depth. As such, an important goal in this chapter is to investigate the performer's battle to remain in charge of content and presentation as she balanced the demands of the industry that allowed her message to be widely disseminated.

TRACING AFRICAN TRADITIONS INTO AMERICA

In America today, the term "African-American" has many shades of meaning. For some, it references only people of African descent whose families were taken into slavery during the trans-Atlantic slave trade. For others, it includes the people who willingly immigrated to the United States in the twentieth and twenty-first centuries. As immigration history evolves, there will be continued debate and probably some definitional changes. While not wanting to negate the telling of narratives that address the wider population, the stories presented in this chapter are clearly connected to people whose ancestors were slaves, taken out of Africa between the sixteenth and nineteenth centuries. An estimated nine to twelve *million* people were captured, bought, and sold. Allowed to bring no material goods, they carried traditions and rituals with them internally, and deposited rich cultural treasures in new lands. Musical rituals and performance practices were a fundamental part of maintaining and transforming identity and community. In the end, the migration of these practices transformed the course of music history throughout the world.

Ethnomusicologists continue to study and debate the African origins of blues and spirituals. Rhythmic traditions have perhaps received the most historical attention, along with **call and response** and melodic ornamentation. More recent studies cite other connections as well, including evidence that one-stringed instruments and mouth bows in several West African areas were likely reborn as one-string diddley bows and harmonicas in the rural South. The musically accompanied sung text tradition of the West African **griot** is also considered a predecessor of blues performance, where sung text is accompanied on stringed instruments.

The **blues scale** has historically been presented as an American adaptation of a seven-tone European scale with "flatted" third, fifth, and seventh tones. Some compelling studies suggest, however, that **pentatonic** and **modal** melodic systems in areas such as Mauritania, Morocco, Algeria, Ghana, Mali, and Nigeria closely resemble elements of the blues sound. Undeniably, there is a common sense of pitch flexibility, rather than adherence to a rigid scalar system, which is common in African cultures, as well as frequent use of **melismatic** vocal passages.[5] In all, the salient features of gospel and blues are deeply rooted in Africa.

Tribal worship traditions from Africa also impacted the development of blues and gospel. The blending of African and Christian worship styles was common in nations where African slaves were taken, and **syncretic** religions are still in evidence in many of those nations today. Readers may be familiar with syncretic traditions in nations such as Mexico, Haiti, Cuba, and Jamaica. Likewise, in America, tribal worship and spirit possession blended with Christian traditions in the South. This was evidenced in the use of rhythm to invoke spirit possession, speaking or singing in tongues, speaking or singing testimonials, and dancing as the spirit moved the worshiper. Just as women played key roles in conveying spiritual messages in many African rituals, they continued to play key roles in the black Christian church. They were far more likely to give a spirit-inspired public testimonial than were men, and women were leaders in church singing as well.[6] (The reader may wish to reference

CALL AND RESPONSE
a musical form where one (or more) musician performs a musical phrase or statement (the call), and another soloist or group answers with another phrase or statement (the response)

GRIOT
West African musician-historian

BLUES SCALE
in Western terms, a major scale with flatted third, fifth, and seventh tones

PENTATONIC
a five-tone melodic system

MODAL
music that is based on modes (sequences of whole and half steps) other than major or minor

MELISMA
a succession of multiple pitches sung on a single syllable

SYNCRETISM
the blending and merging of two or more distinct cultures into a distinctive new culture

the spirit possession ceremony detailed in Chapter 3, noting the role of women in that tradition.)

SPIRITUALS IN THE RURAL SOUTH

FIELD CRY/FIELD HOLLER
improvised monophonic song with flexible pitch and rhythm, sung by workers in the fields

SPIRITUAL
religious music of black Americans that originated in the time of slavery

The transformation of music ritual into blues and gospel is linked to the nineteenth-century spiritual. In times of slavery, women and men participated equally in work and in music-making, both of which often took place in the fields. The music of work, including **field cries** and **hollers**, existed side by side with **spirituals**, an umbrella term for black religious music in the time of slavery.[7] Blues-related scalar systems, moaning, and flexible melodies of the fields are believed to be the direct predecessors of blues and gospel style. The use of call and response is also notable, as this tradition became a key feature of many black genres, ranging from jazz to gospel.

BEYOND THE MUSIC

The sociological use of music by women in the nineteenth century also foreshadowed twentieth-century women's performance practice. Women such as Sojourner Truth (b. 1797) and Harriet Tubman (b. 1820) both used vocal music in practical and inspirational ways. Along with creating her own works, Truth used known hymns and secular songs to convey messages about equality and freedom. To the tune of "Auld Lang Syne," she sang:

> I am pleading for the mothers
> Who gaze in wild despair
> Upon the hated auction block
> And see their children there.

Tubman also used music to instruct slaves who were moving on the Underground Railroad via signal songs that indicated when and where it was safe to move. "Go Down, Moses," for example, was used to signal that the way was clear:[8]

> Go down Moses, way down into Egypt's land,
> tell old Pharaoh, let my people go.

Textual references often carried double meaning, a tradition that was carried on in gospel and the blues. The "chariot" of "Swing Low, Sweet Chariot" thus referenced carrying the enslaved people home to heaven, but also referenced a ride to a new land where there could be freedom on earth.

Figure 8.1
Harriet Tubman, c.1880.
Source: Courtesy of the Library of Congress

Figure 8.2
Sojourner Truth c.1864.
Source: Courtesy of the Library of Congress

Harriet Tubman's use of the song "Wade in the Water" not only instructed people to step into the water to avoid being tracked by dogs but also encouraged perseverance. Scholar Bernice Johnson Reagon notes a long history of women's song that expresses the necessity of walking *through* trouble, not around it, on the path to ultimate freedom.[9]

IMPACT OF THE GREAT MIGRATION

The end of slavery in America did not create true freedom for African-Americans. Many families remained separated due to financial problems, and some families were never able to reunite with family members who had been sold during times of slavery. Life for most freed slaves meant subsistence farming in sharecropping situations where there was little hope for financial freedom.[10] Poverty, discrimination (including numerous lynchings), boll weevil infestations, and drought all prompted blacks to move out of the rural South, and in the early decades of the twentieth century, many moved to Northern cities in what came to be known as the **Great Migration**. When the Mississippi River flooded in 1927, the Delta farming area was further decimated, exacerbating the plight of the populace in the South, prompting another wave of migration.

GREAT MIGRATION
mass movement of Southern black Americans to Northern cities in the early decades of the twentieth century

By conservative estimates, at least 1.5 million blacks moved from the rural South to urban centers in the North by 1930.[11] What they found in the North were crowded conditions, segregated housing, a need for employment, and continued discrimination. Community was maintained and built in safe spaces, among them churches and nightclubs created by and for the black community. The church and the night club were musically and socially connected in interesting ways, for in these public spaces, women musicians spoke candidly to the community about continued difficulties, as well as hope for the future.

GOSPEL CHURCH: THE MUSICAL CRADLE

GOSPEL
black religious music that emerged in urban centers during the early decades of the twentieth century

SANCTIFIED CHURCH
an umbrella term for a number of black Baptist and Pentecostal churches

The spiritual remained alive in the black church in the form of gospel music. **Gospel** generically references religious music that emerged in urban areas in the early twentieth century, and covers a number of subgenres such as quartet singing, arranged choral singing and solo work. The term was first applied in the 1920s, but the genre really began in the 1910s as the church grew in urban areas.[12] Two branches of the black church existed during this developmental period. A more conservative, reflective style of worship was favored in mainline traditions such as Methodism, while a more exuberant style was used in the **sanctified church**. The sanctified movement encompassed a number of Pentecostal and black Baptist churches and was unified by a worship style that allowed worshipers to move with the spirit. Elements of traditional African musical ritual such as dancing, moaning, using body percussion, and invoking spirit possession with rhythm were transformed into the "sanctified" gospel sound,[13] a sound that still impacts popular music today.

Church was a place of community for women, a haven to escape and combat prejudice. For many, it was a means of spiritual and emotional survival.[14] Women comprised the strong majority of church members and church musicians in the early twentieth century. Some scholars cite a two-to-one ratio of women over men in churches of that era, and others claimed the ratio was as high as fifty to one.[15] The church community supported women musicians in numerous ways, including musical training, leadership, moral support, and sometimes monetary support for education of church members. The urban church that took up residence in small buildings and storefronts in the early part of the twentieth century was the birthplace of a huge music industry by the end of that century. Both inside and outside of the church, women were at the forefront of gospel and became some of the biggest stars in the commercial world. It would be impossible to recount the number of women in twentieth-century popular music who had their start in the black church. Toni Braxton, Tina Turner, Aretha Franklin, and Big Mama Thornton are just a few.

Figure 8.3
Photo from the 1959–1961 Storefront Church Series.

Source: Photograph © Milton Rogovin (1952–2002). Used by permission

Analyzing the Gospel Sound

Marion Williams (1927–1994) is considered by many to be the most accomplished gospel singer of the twentieth century. In 1993 she received an Honors Citation from the Kennedy Center, marking a lifetime of musical achievement. As she received her award, Little Richard shouted, "Marion, you're the one who gave me my whoo!"[16] Using "Surely God is Able," performed by Marion Williams, we can familiarize ourselves with the gospel sound and also note its connection to popular music of the later twentieth century.

VAMP
a repeating musical accompaniment common in jazz, gospel, soul, and musical theatre; usually outlines a single harmony or harmonic progression over which a soloist improvises

LISTENING EXPERIENCE 8.1

"Surely God is Able" (c. 1948)
Performed by Marion Williams
Playlist

LISTENING FOCUS

Marion Williams' gospel style directly impacted early rock. Listen for the high, ornamented wail, the pitch bending, the growling sounds, and the emotion. Also notice call and response between Williams and the chorus.

FORM AT A GLANCE

Verse/chorus with **vamp** segments.

TIMED LISTENING GUIDE

0:00	opening wail
0:06	first call and response verse, moving to vamped instrumental groove as Williams adds lyrics
0:55	chorus
1:13	second call and response verse, moving to vamp
1:48	Chorus

Expanding the Female Pulpit: Moving Gospel to the World's Stage

For women, gospel was a ministry parallel to male preaching.[17] Women understood that music was a way to hold the attention of people in spiritual need, and they took their music to the street, to revivals, and to other venues. Church music and the blues shared a symbiotic musical relationship during this period. Women such as Arizona Dranes (c.1891–early 1960s), a blind pianist of the sanctified church, played with a driving **barrelhouse-style** rhythm,[18] a blues-inspired style that combined elements of ragtime and **boogie-woogie** bass patterns. While church instrumentalists incorporated jazz and blues rhythms to accompany church choirs and soloists, blues singers in the nightclubs adopted vocal techniques from the sanctified church.[19]

Church women recognized an opportunity to expand their evangelical role by using emerging technology. Recording technology developed rapidly in the 1920s, and in that decade an astonishing ten million blues and gospel records were sold per year.[20] Many of the record companies were controlled by white entrepreneurs in what came to be known as the **race record** market, which targeted sales to the African-American community. African-American companies such as Black Swan Records also arose during that era. Arizona Dranes was just one of many gospel musicians who used the recording studio to reach a wider audience. But as these women came increasingly into the public eye, they simultaneously had to defend their identity and their mission.

BARRELHOUSE-STYLE
piano blues style that combined rag-inspired melodies with boogie-woogie bass lines

BOOGIE-WOOGIE
piano style that emerged in the 1930s; featured syncopated melody against driving, repeated bass figure

RACE RECORD
music industry term for recordings of black artists that were primarily marketed to black consumers

The Battle of the Image

The black community continued to eagerly purchase records into the 1930s, but another world of expansion was just around the corner with the rapid growth of radio usage. Women who led the development of gospel within the church also led the way in the commercialization of the genre to a nationwide community, and Sister Rosetta Tharpe epitomized women who moved into the commercial world. Tharpe made gospel known to the American populace but, as she did so, drew conflicting responses from members of the black church community, some of whom began to doubt the sincerity of her message.

Sr. Rosetta Tharpe (1915–1973) began her gospel career in the manner of most women in the gospel tradition—firmly entrenched in the work of the church. Sister Rosetta had a gift for music, recognized in her community as God-given. She started playing the guitar at age six and traveled across the country with her mother, the evangelist Katie Bell Nubin. The portability of the guitar provided an excellent way to spread the gospel and was often used instead of the piano at revivals and in store-front churches. Wherever Sister Rosetta evangelized, she beat out a rhythm that transfixed her audience. She "made the guitar talk" by playing single notes rather than chords, and presented a sort of spoken dialogue between guitar and vocal passages.[21]

By 1938, Tharpe had moved to the nightclub and theatre scene, initially so she could reach even more people with her message. By 1939, she caught the attention of *Life* magazine, and her "swinging spirituals" came to the attention of a huge national audience.[22] The subject of the *Life* feature was a performance at the Cotton Club (named in reference to a stylish plantation) in New York in 1939, and it marked Tharpe's foray into the more secular

Figure 8.4
Sr. Rosetta Tharpe.
Source: © Michael Ochs Archives/ Getty Images

mainstream. The Cotton Club catered to a white upper-class audience and featured some of the most talented black performers of the 1920s and 1930s, including Duke Ellington, Bessie Smith, and Louis Armstrong. Media coverage at the club helped to launch many careers, as radio coverage extended to black and white listeners.[23] While the gospel message was still present in Tharpe's work at this time, her stage presence changed. Tharpe abandoned her conservative dress for stylish gowns, and she was accused of being a "holy roller" due to her rhythmic stage movements. Tharpe was also accused of using clever wording in an attempt to capture both sacred and secular markets. Neutral phrases such as "I need you in my life" are still used in the contemporary Christian market today.

Rosetta Tharpe influenced a significant number of country, gospel, and rock artists along the path of her long career. As early as the 1940s, she was connected with the Nashville music scene and got significant air time on Nashville radio. In 1952, she recorded a duet with white country artist Red Foley, a commercial collaboration between a black woman and white man that was unheard of at that time. Country fans liked her virtuosic guitar playing and fun lyrics, and when it came to speed in picking the guitar, she was unmatchable. Her gospel style and guitar playing inspired performers such as Johnny Cash and Elvis Presley, who both grew up listening to southern gospel and blues.[24]

Throughout the 1950s and 1960s, Sister Rosetta continued to market herself to a wide audience. In 1952, she celebrated her third marriage in a baseball stadium, selling tickets to the event and performing in her wedding dress. From the famous "wedding concert," she took her music to other public spaces throughout the 1960s, including ballparks, theatres, and other stadiums.

Sister Rosetta's musical life in the dual world of the sacred and the secular was controversial among members of the sanctified church, the birthplace of her musicality and style. She had bridged the gap between church and a wider audience, but some church members thought that the cost was too great. In her later years, Tharpe's manager had a difficult time booking her in some of her original venues, and when she died in 1973, she was given relatively little attention in the black press.[25] Tharpe's influence on the world of popular music, however, was immense. For commercial gospel singers, she had paved the way to reaching the masses.

The Gospel Audience Grows

With stars directly from the church in the lead, the door into the secular world was wide open in the 1950s, and that decade saw the peak of commercial gospel popularity. Almost all of the gospel greats of that era were women, some of the most successful being Clara Ward (1924–1973) and the Ward Singers, Marion Williams, and Mahalia Jackson. Producers bought into the genre because it was a big money maker. The gospel singer stage presence was not provocative, but it was flashy, with glittery dresses, dangly earrings, and high-piled wigs. Many gospel singers of this era wore choir robes to reflect the church tradition, but the robes were bedecked with rhinestones or jewels.

Some critics believed that the glittery costuming was not the only problem with commercialized gospel. Comments about Mahalia Jackson's "belly dancing" and Clara Ward's alto "moan" indicate that for some, there was a fine line between sexuality and spirituality.[26] The strain between members of the church community and the singers continued, as they debated the value of reaching a wider audience versus succumbing to secular influences. Further complicating matters were white producers who were taking commercial advantage of the genre's success, while they dictated presentation style and sometimes even the spiritual message.

Mahalia Jackson (1912–1972) was a gospel singer who successfully walked the sacred-secular line, and was generally regarded as a devout carrier of the gospel message. She was a gifted singer who delivered the word with a blues-inspired sound, and she knew how to connect with a variety of audiences. Jackson remained current with emerging commercial changes throughout her career, adapting from a traditional gospel sound to the sound of "studio string" accompaniment. She also embraced new media as it developed throughout

Figure 8.5
Gospel singer Mahalia Jackson.
Source: Carl Van Vechten Collection, courtesy of the Library of Congress

the century. A star for Decca records in the 1930s, she later tapped into the radio market with CBS radio, and in 1956 made an appearance on the *Ed Sullivan Show*, a popular television variety show that showcased talent before a national audience. Jackson remained a beloved figure throughout the 1960s, beginning the decade by singing for John F. Kennedy's inauguration in 1961 and remaining visible throughout the Civil Rights Movement. Like her church sisters before her, she used her commanding voice to convey a powerful message, and paved the way for new artists in R&B and soul to do the same.[27]

THE BLUES ON STAGE: ANOTHER PUBLIC FORUM FOR WOMEN

Just as women were performing gospel in the black churches and city streets, the night club scene of the 1920s featured another group of women who were to forever impact popular music: the blues singers. Like their counterparts in the church, women blues performers forged a powerful connection between music, lyrics, and stage presence.

The blues singer of the early twentieth century drew attention to black women in a new way. Long the subject of stereotypical images ranging from Mammy to Jezebel, the blues performer projected an image of confidence and control rather than contented servant or promiscuous temptress.[28] At the same time, blues lyrics spoke volumes about history, culture, and the state of race, class, and gender oppression. Like the women of the West African lament tradition, the blues singer stood before the community and used music to deliver a message. She became the voice of her people and mirrored the role of her lamenting ancestors by freely expressing emotion in a public venue.[29]

Scholarly study of the blues has historically presented a "gendered" division of two blues styles. The main focus traditionally has been on the male-gendered **rural blues**, usually presented as the "authentic" blues style. The **classic blues** was an urban style where women predominated, and has been presented as less authentic because the performers often sang to someone else's accompaniment and sometimes did not write their own works. Aside from the fact that classic blues singers wrote more works than they were credited for,[30] the typical discourse also negates the significant tradition of interpretation and its impact on meaning. In addition, it fails to recognize the role of black women in expressing working-class resistance.[31]

RURAL BLUES
blues that originated in the rural South; accompanied with acoustic guitar or simple stringed instrument such as a diddley bow

CLASSIC BLUES
blues that emerged in urban centers in the 1920s; often accompanied by piano and drums

Despite her glamorous stage appearance, the blues performer spoke to middle-class audiences about the challenges of everyday life. The reconstruction-era South was only a few decades past, and the topics of lost love, broken families, and separation mingled with current realities of poor housing, having to work all day, and keeping the family functional. Sexuality was a frequent topic as well, with songs addressing everything from cheating men to the exploration of newfound sexual freedom in the first generation beyond slavery.

How could drawing overt attention to sexuality provide freedom from the gaze? In a tangible way, blues performers expressed to their audiences that they were in charge of their own sexuality. In addition, the elegant look of tiaras, jewelry, feathers, and fans all signaled a luxury that was now attainable for black women. Audiences responded to beauty that was at once sensuous but also beyond surface level. The propensity to call singers "Empress," "Queen," and "Mother" signified a sense of pride that the audience had in blues performers, and the tradition carried on throughout the twentieth century.[32] Blues performance allowed black women to be publically deified in an entirely new manner.

The freedom and control of the classic blues singer is not only found in her outward stage presence, however. In her interpretive musical manipulation of the literary elements of the blues, the stage afforded the blues singer a venue from which she could make social commentary. At once, a "rat" eating through the walls of a house could reference a rodent found in poor housing conditions or a man causing trouble for a woman. Both meanings were appreciated by the audience. Even more specific meaning could be gained by musical manipulation of the lyrics.[33] Like the presentation style of Martin Luther King Jr.'s *I Have a Dream* speech that we noted earlier, one had to be present in the audience to get the full impact of the message. For example, Bessie Smith's "In the House Blues" depicts men and women in the domestic sphere in a situation where the lyrics seem to say that the woman is trapped and weak as she wrings her hands and waits for "her man" to come home. With a deep growl on the word "weak," however, Smith transmitted an entirely different meaning to the audience—the woman is suddenly strong and aggressive.[34] This illustration of the interpretive role of the singer recasts the authenticity of classic blues as being quite powerful. Clearly the performer is not just a mouthpiece for someone else's lyrics.

Leaders of the Classic Blues Style

Because of the historical tendency to place less value on the cultural significance of the classic blues tradition, many performers have been ignored as well. Therefore, it is important to showcase the work of a few major innovators here. Not only did these artists significantly impact their immediate audiences, but they also influenced future generations.

Gertrude "Ma" Rainey (1886–1939) was a critical link between rural and classic blues styles. She was one of the first people to chronicle an encounter

Figure 8.6
Gertrude "Ma" Rainey.
Source: Public domain

Figure 8.7
Bessie Smith.

Source: Carl Van Vechten Collection. Photo courtesy of the Library of Congress

with the blues, confessing that a "strange and poignant" song sung by a girl in a tent show in 1902 compelled her to incorporate the sound into her own acts.[35] Rainey began to replicate the sound in carnivals, minstrel shows, and vaudeville acts that she presented before working-class audiences. She became a model for other blues singers of the twentieth century.

The wider dissemination of the blues in the early twentieth century is tied to the development of the phonograph record. Despite recording innovations that emerged as early as the late 1800s, the recording industry was still largely closed to African-Americans prior to the 1920s—until Mamie Smith (1883–1946) was discovered. Her 1920 recording of "Crazy Blues" on Okeh Records is considered the first recording by a black blues artist. Sales of Smith's recordings astonished Okeh's German-American managerial staff; when the black community purchased 75,000 copies in one month, record company entrepreneurs quickly tapped into the new market.

The blues artist who probably used the recording industry to her greatest advantage was Bessie Smith (1894–1937). In 1923, Smith's "Gulf Coast Blues" and "Down-Hearted Blues" together sold almost 800,000 copies, and that was just the first year she recorded.[36] Dismissed as an inauthentic star in earlier discourses because she often sang songs written by others, she more recently has captured the attention of other scholars who recognized her sociocultural and musical legacy.[37] Smith sang of the feelings of black female workers,

LISTENING EXPERIENCE 8.2

"In the House Blues" (1932)
Bessie Smith
Playlist

LISTENING FOCUS

Notice how Smith's musical interpretation of the lyrics clarifies her stance as a strong woman. Also notice call and response between Smith and the instrumentalists throughout the performance, as well as the form.

FORM AT A GLANCE

Twelve-bar blues, with repeated harmonic progression.

TIMED LISTENING GUIDE

0:00 Introduction, piano, trumpet, and trombone

Verse One

0:17	A	initial melody and lyrics	I	I	I	I
0:26	A	initial melody and lyrics repeated	IV	IV	I	I
0:35	B	new melody, new lyrics	V	IV	I	I

Verse Two

0:44	A
0:53	A
1:01	B

Verse Three (note the change in delivery, especially on the word "murder")

1:11	A
1:19	A
1:28	B

Verse Four

1:37	A
1:46	A
1:54	B

Verse Five

2:04	A
2:12	A
2:21	B

Verse Six

2:30	A
2:38	A
2:48	B

expressed thoughts about power relations with men,[38] and made it clear that she was not just a sex object. Smith was also a teacher of the blues via the aural tradition. Records were a major way in which the blues style was learned. Bessie Smith's voice was one of several urban voices that taught the blues to people in rural as well as urban areas. Indeed, many people are still learning from Bessie Smith's recordings today.

Although Memphis Minnie (1897–1973) is a woman who does not fit the classic blues mold, her influence on the music industry is far-reaching. It is also important to investigate how this woman negotiated the male-dominated rural blues tradition. Born Lizzie Douglas in the Mississippi Delta region in 1897, Memphis Minnie was steeped in the rural style. She accompanied her hard-edged vocals on guitar and wrote many of her own songs. Throughout her long career, she was able to adapt and transform her technique from a virtuosic picking style to a smoother post-Depression era approach.

Like the classic blues singers of her day, Minnie favored a feminine stage presence that featured provocative clothing and stances. At the same time, she was described as tough in dealing with male performers in rural blues venues. She was known for beating up men who went after her and sometimes displayed a pistol. Her hard-playing blues style matched her personality.

Figure 8.8
Memphis Minnie, 1941.
Source: © Frank Driggs Collection/Getty Images

Notably, Minnie was one of the first guitarists, male or female, to use an electric guitar, and her electric guitar recordings from 1941 are among the first of the electric blues style.[39] Many accounts of Memphis Minnie reference "Memphis Minnie on the Icebox," written by Langston Hughes and first published in the *Chicago Defender* in January 1943. Hughes described a woman who captivated her audience not only with music, but also with an ability to express community and history:

> Memphis Minnie sits on top of the icebox at the 230 Club in Chicago and beats out blues on an electric guitar . . . Midnight. The electric guitar is very loud, science having magnified all its softness away. Memphis Minnie sings through a microphone and her voice—hard and strong anyhow for a little woman's—is made harder and stronger by scientific sound. The rhythm is as old as Minnie's most remote ancestor . . . Through the smoke and racket of the noisy Chicago bar float Louisiana bayous, muddy old swamps, Mississippi dust and sun, cotton fields, lonesome roads, train whistles in the night, mosquitoes at dawn, and the Rural Free Delivery, that never brings the right letter. All these things cry through the strings on Memphis Minnie's electric guitar.[40]

Minnie's virtuosic skill was legendary, and she impacted future artists in a wide range of genres, including rock and roll and country blues. She repeatedly won "cutting contests" that displayed the skills of top performers. Minnie went head to head with big-name performers such as Big Bill Broonzy (1898–1958) and Muddy Waters (1915–1983) and routinely won. Blues performer James Watt recalled a contest between Minnie and Waters:

> They used to have these contests, the one who win the contest, they would get the fifth of whiskey. And Memphis Minnie would tell Muddy, "I'm getting this fifth of whiskey." She'd get it every time, though. She would get it *every* time . . . I saw her beat ten different artists one night.[41]

ONGOING BLUES IMPACT: ARTISTS AND STYLES

Although blues women often are omitted from recorded history after Bessie Smith, in reality, blues women did not disappear. Many stars lived "under the radar" of the wider music industry, and some suffered discrimination. Willie Mae "Big Mama" Thornton (1926–1984) was the daughter of a gospel church singer and a preacher, but spent most of her life performing and writing blues tunes. When she recorded "Hound Dog" in 1952, it spent seven weeks on the R&B charts. Her version, which commences with a growl and features typical blues woman manipulation of the lyrics, clearly depicts men as dogs.

When Elvis Presley heard the song, he **covered** it as a rock and roll tune. Seven million copies later, the song was known by almost every American as an "Elvis" tune. Many consumers did not know what the lyrics really meant, and even fewer knew that it had been first recorded by an African-American woman.[42] Thornton's own composition "Ball and Chain" was covered by Janis Joplin in the 1960s and became a signature tune for Joplin as well.

COVER
recording made by an artist that replicates the recording of a previous artist

Ruth Brown (1928–2006) remained an active artist throughout the twentieth century and became a champion for performers' rights. Credited with formulating the rock and roll sound, Brown recorded under R&B labels but was restricted from the rock and roll charts by the industry. Meanwhile, white artists such as Patti Page received fame and fortune covering her songs. Brown had a string of hits on the Atlantic label in the 1950s, to the point that Atlantic was dubbed "the house that Ruth built." Although her records sold in the millions, she was told that she owed the company recording costs and received little royalty money. Brown was not the only singer who battled contract issues. Her dispute with Atlantic was settled in 1988, and the monetary settlement led to the establishment of the Rhythm and Blues Foundation, which gave grants to pioneering performers and championed performers' rights. Brown's obituary in the *New York Times* highlighted her activism in speaking out against exploitative contracts for musicians.[43]

Figure 8.9
Ruth Brown.

Source: Leonard Feather Collection. Photo by permission of the University of Idaho

Other blues artists continued to carry the message of the blues into the latter half of the century. Margie Evans' "Mistreated Woman" is a great example of the continuation of blues topics from the 1920s. In addition, her work as a spokeswoman, educator, and motivational speaker is notable. Evans was joined by other artists such as Nina Simone (1933–2003), who was a strong Civil Rights activist, and Koko Taylor (1928–2009), who displayed a more traditional blues style (and was dubbed yet another "Queen" of the blues). More recent artists such as producer-guitarist Deborah Coleman (b. 1956) continue to sound a variety of blues themes in the female voice.

SUMMARY

Gospel and blues styles have impacted a wide array of popular genres in the twentieth and twenty-first centuries. Country blues, country gospel, doo wop, rhythm and blues, and rock and roll are just some of the genres that blended elements of gospel and blues. The tradition lived on in the Civil Rights era in **soul** music. The term "soul" itself became associated with black power, pride, and freedom.[44] As with blues artists, funk and hip-hop performers defied cultural restrictions on lyrics and commented on urban issues of their day.

SOUL
gospel-influenced popular style that peaked in the 1960s

Aside from the continuation of musical traditions in the public venue, the black church remains an important center of community and activism for black women. Choir directors, pianists, drummers, and solo singers still have leadership roles in the worship service, and women in the church continue to be pillars of the community.

As gospel and blues blended and shared musically, the genres were simultaneously forged in part by a music industry eager to make money. What were the pros and cons of mass marketing? For some, there was a loss of the sacred, for others, a loss of authenticity. Sometimes there was monetary loss for the performer, and sometimes there was exploitation. At the same time, there was an avenue for empowerment. As such, women of gospel and blues are increasingly being recognized as key players in the formation of modern black identity. Whether in times of slavery, reconstruction, economic turmoil, civil rights, or equal rights, women have come together as community in musical settings to find healing, restoration of spirit, bonding, and a means of survival. While these women have had to battle the commercial music industry to avoid objectification, they also learned to utilize the industry to do greater good.

QUESTIONS FOR CRITICAL THINKING AND DISCUSSION

1. Aretha Franklin's "Respect" is considered a seminal song in the feminist movement. Investigate how Franklin reworked Otis Redding's original version to create an empowering song for women.
2. Musically compare and contrast recordings of "Hound Dog" as recorded by Big Mama Thornton and Elvis Presley. Analyze both versions using the blues form model found in this chapter, and use elements of music language to highlight differences in melodic and rhythmic style. After you are done, describe how the two versions impact you personally.
3. Research the topic of covers in the music industry, particularly in terms of early rock and roll artists who covered the work of black artists.

IDEAS FOR FURTHER RESEARCH

1. Investigate women pop singers in the mass music market today in terms of their musical background and training. Are there still connections to the black church? Identify women whose musical sound is impacted by the sanctified church tradition.
2. Research roles for women in West African spiritual traditions and make connections between those traditions and the black church in America. How was gospel music particularly impacted?

CHAPTER 9

Visual Media and the Marketing of Women Performers

You are on stage, a microphone almost touching your parted lips. The lights are low, your voice is powerful, and the audience is yours.

If you have lived the fantasy of the glamorous singer captivating an audience, chances are that you are a woman. In fact, the music industry works diligently in the hope that female listeners *will* imagine themselves on stage. If marketing is successful, not only does music sell, so does a wide array of other merchandise. Interestingly, the seeds of the singer fantasy were sown as early as the seventeenth century, when Euro-American ideas pertaining to women and singing took shape in the European Renaissance and Baroque. Even then, culturally defined music roles were related to gender characteristics. In public, men were supposed to suppress their emotions, and women were supposed to let them flow. Men were supposed to be able to control mechanical devices (read: instruments) and women were supposed to allow their bodies to connect directly with the audience. Men were supposed to analyze and create the arts, women were supposed to enact bodily performances of those creations.

As noted elsewhere in the text, the idealized fusion of beauty in body and song has been longstanding in the female sphere. So persistent is the body image connection to women vocalists that a lack of physical beauty sometimes causes automatic dismissal of potential talent. In 2009, for example, a middle-aged woman named Susan Boyle took the stage on a British television show called *Britain's Got Talent* and stunned the audience with her performance of "I Dreamed a Dream" from the musical *Les Misérables*. A video of the performance rapidly circulated around the world on the internet, and viewers noted visible jaw dropping among Boyle's audience. Why did the listeners expect so little from Boyle before they heard her sing? Simply put, they did not expect the image they saw on stage to project a good sound. This chapter will address the connection between the aural art of music and the visual world of music marketing, using popular music from the late twentieth century as a focal point.

A BODILY ART

Music is often presented academically as a cerebral art. Textbooks such as this often lean on verbal descriptions and analytical presentations of musical scores that focus on the creative process, rather than on musical performance. The telling of music history then becomes a tale of musical creators, or composers, rather than a story of performers. In reality, it was often the performers who were better known in their day.

With the exception of computer-generated music, music is a bodily art that features a human being interacting with an audience. Before the era of recorded sound, the physical interaction between performer and audience was a given. There could be no music without the performer. While creation of music has been constructed as male (associated with the cerebral in Western culture), bodily performance of singing and dancing has been connected to the female sphere. In vocal music and dance, nothing stands between the performer and audience; thus singers and dancers invite audiences into a personal space. The audience is captured not only by the music but also by the sight of the performer.[1]

Electronic media such as television and video changed the way in which women's images were projected in the music world, but the concept of the **male gaze** is longstanding. The gaze, in which a woman's body is objectified by the empowered male watching her, has long lived in the arts. In visual art, the gaze appears as a nude Renaissance woman, deified and encircled by admiring (clothed) men; in movies, it is found in the lingering shot on the curves of a woman's body; in music, it is found under a spotlight that is focused on a woman singing. In music video, the gaze objectifies the woman in front of a male audience that exists both on and off the screen.[2]

MALE GAZE
the sexual objectification of the female body by an empowered viewer

Women particularly have been subjected to visual perfection, to the point that critique of musical performance is sometimes skewed in favor of bodily performance. The priority is reversed so much that popular artists often commercially succeed with only marginal vocal ability. Art music is not averse to promoting sexual imagery either. The "gaze" is evident in written music reviews when reviewers report on the musical ability of male performers but comment at length about the attire of women who were involved in the same performance, often even as featured soloists. Like any other form of advertising, music marketing plays on youthful good looks and holds women to hypercritical standards, while men are allowed to age and expand their girth. Just as in the world of news and sports broadcasting, young women rotate in and out of the music business, while aging men remain in the business for decades.

THE VOICE AND SEXUALITY

Aside from the body from which a voice emanates, the voice itself is tied to notions of age, sexuality, and emotion. Sight unseen, most people can determine the age of a speaker's voice within ten years, but a speaker can also deliberately change the timbre of the voice to project sexuality. Think about how one might manipulate the voice to produce a vulnerable childlike tone versus a seductive sound. Singers manipulate vocal sound to convey emotion and sexuality as well, surpassing the ability of speakers to do so because of expanded range and volume capabilities.[3]

Boys' voices noticeably convert to men's voices at puberty, but the changing of a woman's voice is more subtle. It is not known for certain when a woman begins to project her adult voice. Scholars such as Suzanne Cusick speculate that this may contribute to the perception that women are "lesser adults." Without the male authoritative timbre, the woman projects her childlike voice, and with it projects a childlike vulnerability—unable to make decisions for herself, unable to speak forcefully, or with authenticity. Conversely, the male *singing* voice has long been viewed as effeminate in Western culture, to the point that many school choirs have difficulty recruiting men.[4] In short, the vocal/sexual connection is deeply and specifically embedded in culture.

Early rock and roll provides a good avenue for examining the combination of aural and visual elements in music marketing. Along with its dramatic stage presentations, rock's lyrical emphasis on love and sexuality created an opportunity for the music industry to capitalize on culturally defined perceptions of music–body–sexuality, resulting in immense profits. This has sometimes led to the exploitation of women performers, and has contributed to a rising expectation that women deliver a visual, as well as aural, image.

THE BIRTH OF ROCK AND ROLL: GIRLS IN A "MAN'S WORLD"

Post-war technology paved the way for 1950s rock and roll. Innovations in electronic instruments and mass production made electric guitars and amplifiers easily attainable and affordable. The Fender bass was mass marketed in 1951 and rapidly replaced the acoustic string bass, a hallmark of the 1940s jazz-oriented sound. Similarly, recording technology improved in quality while it simultaneously became cheaper. By 1950, a recording studio could be equipped for under a thousand dollars.[5] It was inexpensive to produce records, and it did not take a huge run of recordings to realize big profits. On the consumer end of the spectrum, there was a market for recordings among an increasingly youthful population. Post-war affluence left American youth with money to spend, cars to drive, and trouble to raise. Rock was the voice that allowed them to express their freedom.

Despite the pioneering work of Ruth Brown, Big Mama Thornton, and other rhythm and blues artists who paved the way for rock and roll, 1950s rock appeared to be a man's world. There was a strong perceived connection between technology, electricity, and the male sphere, and most rock performers who were visible to the public were men who manipulated electronic instruments and equipment. Behind the scenes was a male-dominated industry of producers, songwriters, publishers, and recording engineers hungry to make money. Rock took the country by storm, and the smooth jazz-based popular music of the late 1940s (such as that of Billie Holiday, Ella Fitzgerald, Bing Crosby, and Frank Sinatra) died quickly among the teenage population. Rock was more than music; it was a form of rebellion that spoke of sexuality from a male perspective. Teenagers purchased millions of records by performers such as Bill Hailey and the Comets, Elvis Presley, Buddy Holly, and Richie Valens. Like all popular music, however, the stylistic pendulum was due to shift, and the rock and roll of the early 1950s reached old age within a decade.

In the gap between the early rock and roll groups and The Beatles was a phenomenon that rocked the country in a new way, and one that reached out to a new segment of the popular music market. The airwaves of the late 1950s and early 1960s were full of the sounds of groups with names such as The Supremes, The Chantels, The Ronettes, The Shangri-Las, The Shirelles, The Crystals, The Blossoms, The Angels, and The Marvelettes—the **girl groups** had entered the marketplace. Girl groups dominated the pop charts for the better part of a decade, and were only surpassed when The Beatles entered the American market, soaring to fame in part due to their appeal to the girl groups' audience.

GIRL GROUP
a small ensemble of female vocalists who sing popular music

The entry of girl groups into the popular music scene signified the first widely recognized work of women in rock and an important time of crossover between black and white markets. It also marked a turn toward music-related consumerism that intensified in ensuing decades, with sales expanding beyond music to include clothing, make-up, and products plugged by performers. Many women who were teenagers during the girl group era continue to laud the genre for its ability to address *their* needs and interests—it offered a woman's view of topics that were important to her, including sexuality and fashion. Prior to the girl group era, rock lyrics put men in the driver's seat. Girl groups provided a new perspective, cleverly couched in a dialogue between women on stage that also included the audience in the conversation. As the lead singer debated her love life with the chorus, audience members decided which part they wanted to sing for themselves as they constructed their own meaning.

Girl groups were historically present in the era of Civil Rights and Equal Rights, and the genre addressed both issues in many ways. Music, like professional sports, was a bridge between races where the consumer could forget about race and simply appreciate the performance. In an era when the country was coming to grips with a long history of discrimination, music, like athletics, gave minorities a chance to be viewed and revered for their accomplishments. Groups such as The Supremes were widely popular in all markets.[6]

For all of these reasons, girl groups can be seen in a positive light, especially considering that many composers of the biggest girl group hits were women. The flip side of the record is that individual girl group members did not always fare well in their professional lives. Music marketers viewed young musicians as raw products destined to make money. Marketers altered visual images of the girl group "product" at will and created interchangeable parts that could be replaced, if the need arose, to keep production moving.[7]

LOSS OF INDIVIDUALITY

Popular marketing today is often about the individual performer, to the point that many pop stars and movie stars are simply known by their first names. Consumers follow every move of the celebrity, from exotic trysts on the beach captured in photos snapped by paparazzi to details of the stars' trips to the grocery store. In many ways, the marketing of male performers in the early rock era was similar in terms of promoting the individual. Consumers in the music market could name all of The Beatles as individuals (and could buy posters of their favorite one), but girl groups primarily were marketed as groups. Entrepreneurs such as **Motown**'s Berry Gordy did plug some lead singers such as Diana Ross in the years after The Beatles arrived, but most of the early girl groups maintained a consistent group name that masked frequent personnel changes. Biographers sometimes refer to Motown's "stable" of performers, and in a sense it was a stable. If one unit faltered, had a baby, or needed to be fired, the next one could be called in, and, in the best case scenario, the audience would hardly notice. Identical choreography and dress ensured a consistent visual image. All a new member needed to do was blend in on the vocals, learn the moves, and put on the matching dress. The Supremes, a trio that existed from 1961 to 1977, involved at least ten different singers, many of whom were relatively unknown as individuals: Diana Ross, Mary Wilson, Florence Ballard, Betty McGlown, Barbara Martin, Cindy

MOTOWN
record company originally based in Detroit, Michigan; named for the city's nickname, the "motor city"

Birdsong, Jean Terrell, Lynda Laurence, Scherrie Payne, and Susaye Greene. Despite the combination of individuals, the group was always "The Supremes."

Music, Consumers, and Girl Fashion in the Music Industry

Long before girls looked at fashionable images on the internet, music videos, and hand-held electronic devices, they accessed a world of glamour, fashion, and make-up on record album covers. Girl groups were packaged as lookalikes not only to conveniently keep the group in business but also to help the girl at home to imagine that *she* was standing on the stage. Girl groups were not always the subject of the male gaze, but were just as often marketed to young women instead, as the upper-middle-class "girl next door." Prom-style dresses and sparkly gowns were adorned with bows, ribbons, buttons, and lace, while accessories such as headbands, red nail polish, and white gloves completed the look. The conformity in look was extreme. Along with identical clothing, hairstyles, jewelry, and accessories, small details such as the curve of the eyeliner, the tilt of the head, and the type of smile (wide or demure) were unified in publicity photos. The idea was to create an image in which all parts of the unit were the same, and the tight vocal harmony added to the illusion. Just as a group of girlfriends might call one another to decide what to wear to school the next day, the girl groups invited their fans to join in their look and sound. It was a clever marketing tool.[8]

Figure 9.1
The Supremes, 1964. From left to right, Florence Ballard, Mary Wilson, and Diana Ross.
Source: © David Farrell/ Getty Images

> *Phil was first taken by their appearance—they wore heavy eye makeup, tight dresses and slacks, and all had matching hairdos piled high on their heads. He quickly decided that he wanted to record them, and later on when he actually heard them sing, was surprised at just how good they sounded.*[9]
>
> Phil Spector's reaction to meeting The Ronettes

BRILL BUILDING
office building on Broadway in New York that was a central focus of girl group music production in the late 1950s and early 1960s

The **Brill Building** in New York was the center of the girl group production universe. An office building on Broadway, the building held everything a singer needed to be successful in the music industry, except, perhaps, a chance of making it on her own if she stepped out the door. With a team of composers, arrangers, studio musicians, and contract specialists on hand, entrepreneurs such as Phil Spector, Berry Gordy, and Luther Dixon negotiated their way to great wealth, while girl group members saw minimal financial reward. A millionaire by age twenty-one, Spector "developed" over a dozen big-name acts, including The Ronettes and The Crystals, as well as male groups such as The Righteous Brothers. Spector wrote much of the music, located singers, and directed all aspects of production. Young girls without experience in contract negotiations were often taken advantage of, and some found their careers over by age twenty-one. With no marketable name recognition, they had little chance to pursue solo careers. Luther Dixon, who managed The Shirelles, not only controlled the songs and arrangements, but even held the singers' money in a trust account. By the time expenses were covered for recording and marketing, very little was left for the performers.[10]

Musical input varied, but most women had limited artistic control. Singer Eva Harris claimed that songwriter Gerry Goffin consulted her to be sure that his lyrics expressed what black teenage girls would say, but Dee Dee Kennibrew of The Crystals said, "We were never allowed any say in what we did at all . . . We would have liked some input. But no way! There was nothing we could do. Phil Spector was our record company, our producer, our everything."[11]

Perhaps most notorious for his controlling ways was Berry Gordy, who led the Motown production empire. Although he protested negative depictions of his management style, there is evidence to suggest that he ran the label much like a company town, owning everything he needed to control personnel and maximize his own profits. Singers recorded in Gordy's studios, but had to pay for recording costs. They signed away publishing rights to Jobete Publishing (Gordy's firm), and their contracts were negotiated with Gordy's talent-management company.[12]

The look and style of individual performers were also completely controlled by managers. When Gordy realized that there was huge potential to make money in a multi-racial market, he worked to create visual images that would substantially broaden his consumer base. Gordy "redesigned" his black performers to be acceptable to middle-class whites, requiring that they attend talent-training classes. They received makeovers and learned how to walk, talk, and act in public. Black performers had their hair straightened and styled in a fashion that would appeal to white and black audiences, ranging from long, sleek styles to piled-high bouffants. Martha Reeves of The Vandellas recalled members of The Supremes, The Marvelettes, and other Motown groups gathered together at the training school, and she remembered the speech that they received from the staff expert when they arrived: "You're not the prettiest girls in the world and you're not the best singers, but what I'm going to teach you will give you all the charm, finesse and glamour you need to take you through the rest of your life."[13] While black artists were taught to "take the edge off," white groups such as The Shangri-Las could afford to be presented as tough girls without hurting their marketability. Their attire often included leather pants and boots, and props such as a man on a motorcycle were sometimes added to solidify the bad girl image. Clearly it was more than music that was for sale.[14]

> *Girl groups were devoted to the things teenage girls cared about—parental control, boys, reputations, and marriage. These were my concerns and I heard them articulated every night, under my pillow, on a transistor AM radio.*[15]
>
> Donna Gaines, journalist and sociologist

WOMEN COMPOSERS, PRODUCERS, AND CONSUMERS

While performers lost their personal style and expression to the industry, women who consumed and composed girl group music found it a source of empowerment. Black performers had more collective success on the charts during the girl group period than at any other time in American popular music history, and it happened in large part because composers who understood girl-talk were writing many of the songs. While producers are given credit as the minds behind the industry, several of the most important songwriter-producers of the girl group genre were women.[16]

Carole King, Ellie Greenwich, and Cynthia Weil were all part of teams that penned some of the most long-lasting songs in popular music history. With then-husband Gerry Goffin writing lyrics, Carole King wrote the music for such familiar songs as "One Fine Day," "Will You Love Me Tomorrow," and "A Natural Woman." Ellie Greenwich, along with Jeff Barry, wrote "Be My Baby," "Chapel of Love," and "Do Wah Diddy Diddy," among many others, and Cynthia Weil, along with Barry Mann, wrote such favorites as "You've Lost that Lovin' Feeling" and "On Broadway." On the Weil-Mann team, Weil was the lyricist, and she tackled themes that addressed social consciousness, using the voice of girls to diffuse challenging messages. The Brill Building songwriters spoke to gut-level feelings that related to their audiences' lives. Like the visual aspect of marketing, girl group lyrics tapped into middle-class values and expressed everyday hopes and dreams rather than unattainable lifestyles. Almost all young listeners could relate to being vulnerable or losing their first love.[17]

Lyrical Content Condemned

King, Greenwich, and Weil collectively ended up with more than 200 songs on Billboard's Singles Chart. For the first time, rock was not just about male expression, but verbalized women's perspectives.[18] The romantic sound of studio strings, blended with vocal harmony, belied the fact that the lyrics were often about rebellious feelings that teenage girls had about their sexuality, and toward their parents. The girls onstage lamented parental control, and songs such as The Shirelles' "Will You Still Love Me Tomorrow?" played on the girl's feelings about her vulnerability compared with that of her boyfriend. If she gave herself to him, what would be the consequence? "Her" reputation is a common theme in the genre.

It would be incorrect to state that all was rosy with girl group lyrics from a feminist perspective. Many of the lyrics were written in the passive voice, creating a genre that critics believe reinforced a subservient role for women. While the Rolling Stones and Jimi Hendrix pronounced love from a position of power and control, girl groups often mouthed youthful insecurity and a preoccupation with "wanting to be wanted." Lyrics such as "won't you say you love me" stand in stark contrast to lyrics sung by male rockers of the 1960s, and there are numerous other examples of the passive tone. In The Chantels' "Maybe," the girls contemplate a "what if" mentality that pins their happiness solely on finding her guy: "Maybe if I pray every night you'll come back to me, and maybe if I cry every day you'll come back to stay." The Shirelles sang, "Say you need my love, say you need my lips, say you want my heart," while The Chiffons sang, "One fine day, you're gonna want me," and The Supremes declared, "My world is empty without you."

Other hits placed women in even more vulnerable positions. The Crystals' 1962 "He Hit Me (and It Felt Like a Kiss)" describes a girl whose boyfriend hits her after she cheats on him. The song projects that all is well, however, because the boyfriend's reaction lets the girl know that she is loved. Beyond submissive, the woman in this story is so desperate to be loved that she will withstand physical abuse.[19] While most songs did not go this far, many songs espoused the power of the girl's unfailing love no matter the boy's character. Even when the boy was bad or dangerous, the girl who stood by his side could redeem him with her love. As the girl groups sang the lyrics of domination, they smiled. The sweet-sounding, overly dramatized music, along with the movement of long false eyelashes and white-gloved hands, further projected a sense of dependence and vulnerability.

Despite the fact that many of the girl groups lacked powerful singing technique and were often mouthpieces for passive lyrics, the genre nonetheless expressed concerns that were real for many teenage girls in the 1950s and 1960s. From a marketing perspective, female fans constituted a vast new

LISTENING EXPERIENCE 9.1

"Be My Baby" (1963)
Performed by The Ronettes
Playlist

LISTENING FOCUS

Listen to the lyrics, the interplay of soloist and chorus, as well as the studio "**wall of sound**," produced by Phil Spector.

WALL OF SOUND recorded tracks in which massed instrumental and vocal parts were heightened with echo

FORM AT A GLANCE

Verse/Chorus.

TIMED LISTENING GUIDE

Introduction

0:00 instrumental

Verse One

0:08 vocal soloist takes first eight bars

0:21 chorus adds harmony

Chorus

0:34 soloist and chorus in call and response "dialogue"

Verse Two

0:51 soloist with chorus harmonizing

Chorus

1:18 soloist with chorus in call and response

Instrumental bridge

Chorus

1:49 chorus as before

Drum transition

2:08 chorus material, mechanical fade

revenue stream, and the coupling of fashion, stage image, and performers had only just begun, accelerated to warp speed by a new marketing tool that defined the female star even more stringently by her looks.

SCREEN IMAGES AND THE FEMALE POP STAR

While the work of women in popular music throughout the 1960s and 1970s is examined in Chapters 14 and 15 through the lens of studio technology and production, this segment will briefly address the music video industry, beginning with MTV. This will lead to the guided research project for Part III, your investigation of women as producers of music-related visual imagery.

A new wave of women pop stars came to widespread public attention in the 1980s, and many of the most commercially successful women owed their notoriety to MTV (Music Television). At the same time, the music video industry has been widely condemned for sexism and the portrayal of violence toward women. How did the video industry begin, and how did women fit into that world? MTV debuted in 1981, in an era that predated the internet and existed just as cable television was expanding its outreach across the country. Cable provided unprecedented competition for the "big three" syndicates (NBC, ABC, CBS), all of which had dominated the airwaves since the earliest days of television. The choices open to television consumers in the cable era were vast, and one of the most popular new channels in the early 1980s was MTV.

Readers who have always accessed the internet may have a difficult time imagining what it was like to encounter MTV for the first time. Prior to MTV, glimpses of the stars were available on album covers, teen magazines, posters, and live concerts. MTV provided touch-of-a button access to the latest music and artists, all packaged in an appealing film format that was at once outlandish and compelling. Cleverly, producers managed to convince consumers that they were watching a television show, when in fact they were viewing a continuous commercial. Not only were products plugged during traditional commercial breaks, but the music video itself was an advertisement that promoted music, fashion, and products that were strategically placed in view. While the video format varied in some ways, there were predictable elements, and one of them was exposure of the female body. Like other advertising, music videos used sex to sell a product, and the venture was aimed at men and women alike. Women could aspire to be the performer on the screen, emulating her fashion and style, and men could consume the image of the female body.

Some fairly standard visual portrayals have existed on music video for decades: a single, clothed male surrounded by multiple, lesser-clothed women; fully dressed men watching women strip and shower; women being whipped or hit and appearing to enjoy it; men pushing women against walls, throwing objects at them, or spraying them with alcohol. Music videos frequently present images of women who welcome sexual advances from strangers, and many images dehumanize women by letting the camera rest on specific body parts rather than focusing on the whole individual.[20] Few people disagree about the problem of violence toward women that has been displayed in some segments of the music video market, yet **misogynist** violence has succeeded commercially.

MISOGYNY
a hatred of women or girls

Genres such as hardcore rap and heavy metal that featured misogynist lyrics have linked their violent content with video images since the 1980s, and the marketing of women's bodies on MTV easily crossed over into the advertising and video game world. Lyrics from metal group Mötley Crüe's "Too Young to Fall in Love" single included the following: "We're both sinners and saints/not a woman, but a whore/I can just taste the hate/well, now I'm killing you/watch your face turning blue . . ." Along with its use in music videos, the song re-emerged in the widely criticized 2002 videogame "Grand Theft Auto: Vice City," where the game gives players "life force" for driving a car to a secluded spot, having sex with a woman, and then "beating her down" when she gets out of the car.[21] This is especially disconcerting because marketing of the gaming industry is aimed at children as well as adults.

By the early 1990s, a segment of rap known as hardcore used images of male sexual domination that crossed over into depictions of pain and violence toward women. The group 2 Live Crew made videos with candid shots of men standing over naked women's bodies, and frequent use of names such as "hoe," "slut," and "bitch." Despite widespread condemnation of such videos, video marketing that exploited women made big money, and some bands used the video medium almost exclusively for advertising. Groups sometimes marketed "clean" versions too, but the originals usually outsold them by a huge margin.[22]

Images Produced by Women

Women have not always been objectified by male music video producers, however. Even in the early years of the industry, some women began to produce their own images and, over time, more women became involved as executives in the industry. Women-produced videos embraced women as sexual but often altered both the restrictive and misogynist aspects of the genre. At the same time, it is important to understand that some feminists refuse to watch music videos entirely, blaming the phenomenon for widespread negative representations of women in popular culture. One way to examine this dualism is to address the work of entertainer Madonna, who drew praise and blame from vastly differentiated constituencies.

Born in 1958 as Madonna Louise Ciccone, Madonna became a one-name wonder in the early 1980s. At a surface level, Madonna's video imagery did not appear much different from the usual music video. Her "Like a Virgin" video (1984) was compared to soft porn by her critics,[23] and focused the camera lens directly on her body. In 1990, even MTV executives believed that Madonna had gone too far, and refused to air her "Justify My Love" video because of its sadomasochism. What was different, however, was that the woman of focus in the video was Madonna herself. Her advocates lauded her refusal to conform to cultural expectations regarding how women could portray themselves sexually, and believed that she intentionally defied the industry's consumption of women's bodies using irony and humor. Madonna not only controlled the gaze, they claimed; she used her voice to express the

Figure 9.2
Madonna on tour, 1985.
Source: © Richard E. Aaron/ Getty Images

ridiculousness of the male view of women's sexual roles. Her high-pitched girly voice in "Like a Virgin" and "Material Girl" are part of the storytelling and the mockery.[24]

Even if it was difficult to discern whether Madonna hurt or helped women's cause in music video, other women used the medium to more directly express resistance. Pat Benatar's "Sex as a Weapon" used visual images of scantily clad women next to a variety of products (ranging from beer to detergent) to make a strong statement about the exploitation of women's bodies in advertising. Queen Latifah and Salt 'n Pepa (discussed in more detail in Chapter 15) directly addressed rap's misogynist element, and country stars such as Martina McBride focused on such topics as domestic violence.[25]

The Voice versus the Look

Thus far we have focused extensively on visual imagery in video music marketing, but what has been the impact of the industry in terms of marketing vocal talent? Just as Madonna's voice was the subject of much discussion in relation to the juxtaposition of vocal talent and bodily image on stage, commentary about vocal quality continued into the twenty-first century. As noted earlier, the wedding of female voice and body has existed in Western culture since at least the Renaissance, and one consistency was the expectation that women vocalists should project both a desirable look *and* a desirable sound. Examples of women who fulfilled this dual expectation are as musically diverse as nineteenth-century Swedish opera star Jenny Lind and twentieth-century jazz vocalist Billie Holiday. In the video age, however, vocal talent was not a given. While many artists at the turn of the twenty-first century had well-trained voices, a significant number suffered from pitch inconsistency,

LISTENING EXPERIENCE 9.2

The "Material Girl" versus Laurie Anderson Playlist

The elements of music (introduced in Chapter 1) help listeners formulate value judgments about music. **Timbre** is perhaps the most surface-level element that hits the ear as listeners decide whether or not they "like" a voice. In Western culture, high, thin, crackly voices tend to be perceived as inferior, whereas strong, rich timbres tend to elicit positive responses. Using "Material Girl" as an example, try to assess why critics declared that Madonna had a "bad" voice. Further, examine this issue from a gender perspective. Is the positive valuation of rich, deep timbre a gender issue as well as a musical one? After you finish this analysis, access the work of Laurie Anderson, available in numerous online video excerpts. Discuss the messages that Anderson conveys with her multiple voices.

TIMBRE
the characteristic quality of sound that distinguishes one voice or musical instrument from another; "tone color"

limited range, and poor sound, even to the point of embarrassment in public performance when technological support failed them.

As the music industry saw profits decrease due to internet sales and file downloading, it relied increasingly on marketing performers as part of an entire merchandise package. Girl stars with developing voices, such as Miley Cyrus, were marketed to preadolescents via a variety of screen formats, including a television show. The music was marketed along with multi-million dollar accessory lines that included toys, backpacks, and clothing that children "needed" to remain popular. When female stars begin to "age" in the industry, which sometimes occurs when women are as young as sixteen or seventeen years old, marketing strategies become more overtly sexualized.

The vocalist's ability to prosper within the cult of celebrity became increasingly connected to long-term success, and the pressure of notoriety caused some women to collapse. Britney Spears had a nervous breakdown that resulted in a very public head-shaving incident (and a subsequent need for psychiatric help), before she returned to the public. By 2008, however, Spears was re-beautified, and ready to rise to fame again. Joining other stars ranging from Jennifer Lopez to Reba McEntire, Spears launched a clothing line[26] and, by 2010, she had sold 83 million recordings worldwide.

Impact Beyond Music

As noted earlier, the commercial roots of MTV easily branched into various forms of visual advertising, ranging from television commercials to the gaming industry. Provocative visual imagery has created pressure for young girls and women, not only to attain material goods but also to attempt to achieve a look that includes airbrushed perfection of face, hair, and body. Some research studies have linked the video age to a rise in the number of eating disorders, and there is documented evidence that young girls who watch music videos experience lowering of self-esteem.[27] Web-based marketing increased the speed at which new images could reach the consumer. Young girls not only aspired to sing like the latest pop star; they wanted to look like her, too. Female fans projected themselves on stage much as they did in the age of the girl groups, but did so attempting to attain electronically manipulated standards of physical perfection.

As the power of the video marketing industry increased, most commercial music genres adopted visual imagery. The Nashville Network, VH1, and BET (Black Entertainment Television) are among the networks that came on board after the emergence of MTV. Country artists who were formerly marketed as the "cowboy's girlfriend" were transformed into idols with low-cut dresses, high heels, and facial makeovers. By the late 1990s, the country music television website (cmt.com) looked surprisingly like that of other commercial genres. A common homepage display included men in cowboy hats and black t-shirts juxtaposed with scantily-clad women in white or light-colored attire. In the crossover marketplace, altering the image of the female country music star was the only way to survive in an increasingly manufactured music industry.

> *Have we really reached the point where only the slim or the beautiful need apply?*[28]
>
> San Francisco Chronicle reporter, regarding the firing of opera star Deborah Voigt

By the turn of the twenty-first century, even art music began to increase the sexualized marketing of women performers. Once the last bastion of "music for the sake of music," marketing promotions for women violin soloists, chamber music ensemble members, and opera stars began to feature publicity shots that portrayed women with fan-blown hair, revealing clothing, and seductive poses. Most often, men were still pictured in the traditional tuxedo, complete with bow-tie-encased neck. The visual demands on women performers received widespread attention in the operatic world in 2004 when Deborah Voigt, then considered one of the world's greatest opera stars, was fired from a Royal Opera production in London because of her weight. The singer recalled, "I got a call saying that . . . I was not appropriate because of the costume that Ariadne (her character, and her signature role) was meant to wear in this production, and that they were canceling my contract."[29] Citing the need to use tight-fitting costumes rather than the traditional toga-style opera gown, the director decided to replace Voigt with another singer. Rather than fight the establishment, Voigt decided to lose weight. Lighter by 135 pounds, she returned to the opera stage healthier, but also having succumbed to a world that demanded even opera stars to look, not just sound, the part.

SUMMARY

Technology in the latter half of the twentieth century allowed rapid dissemination of popular music and related video advertising. The consumer could download a video, chat with a star, or view the artist in a variety of clothing styles at the touch of a button. Just as easily, the female fan could buy the artist's latest hit (along with a karaoke version) to live out the pop star fantasy. The strategy of the girl group marketers lived on, but was delivered at a frenetic pace.

Women vocalists in the popular music industry have some difficult choices to make as they decide whether or not to join the celebrity world. By the turn of the twenty-first century, former girl stars such as Christina Aguilera and Jessica Simpson had made the switch to the women's realm of music marketing, while Disney's youthful Miley Cyrus was just coming to grips with the changes she was facing as she "aged" in the industry, even prior to her eighteenth birthday.

At that uncertain time when a girl's voice becomes the voice of a woman, a performer must decide: does she leave behind her career with the voice of her childhood, or does she embrace the critical glare of an industry that critiques her body as much as her voice?

QUESTIONS FOR CRITICAL THINKING AND DISCUSSION

1. Do your own analysis of a music video and consider camera angles, use of music, and visual imagery as it relates to the overall impact on the viewer. Do you notice differences between depictions of men and women in the videos?
2. Discuss your thoughts regarding whether or not images found on music video affect how viewers pursue visual and sexual ideals for themselves.
3. Analyze the vocal ability of a well-known woman or girl on the popular music market today. Considering all marketable aspects of this performer, try to predict her future.

IDEAS FOR FURTHER RESEARCH

1. Investigate the current state of music production in America or other countries, and attempt to determine the ratio of men to women in the field today. If you are successful in locating this information, attempt to discover if there are major differences in finished product based on the producer's sex.
2. Go online and access popular music from other cultures. How do marketing techniques compare between the American market and markets such as Bollywood?
3. Investigate the history of male "manufactured" groups such as the Backstreet Boys and the Jonas Brothers. How is sexual imagery used to promote these groups?

GUIDED RESEARCH PROJECT PART III

WOMEN BEHIND THE LENS

Part III primarily focused on women as the object of the gaze in a variety of popular music genres throughout the twentieth century. As the century progressed, however, women increasingly took control of their own imagery, and sometimes turned the visual tables as they metaphorically and literally stood on the other end of the lens. In this project, it is your assignment to discover the work of women who took control of music video production and to record the results of their work in terms of how men and women were visually depicted.

Some areas to consider:

1. Chronicle the current status of the music video market. Where are the videos being produced, and by whom?
2. Identify a group of women who are currently involved in music video production, and attempt to estimate their numbers compared with men in the industry.
3. In which genres are women more likely to be involved in music video production? Why do you think this is the case?
4. Select several music videos that represent various popular music genres and bring them to class. Compare and contrast the work of male and female producers in terms of their depictions of men and women. Discuss your findings as a class.
5. Compare music video production in a variety of countries and cultures. Do you notice similarities and differences regarding the representation of men and women in these videos? Who are the producers?

PART IV

A Century of Change

THE IMPACT OF EDUCATION ON WOMEN'S ART MUSIC ACTIVITY

INTRODUCTION TO PART IV

A CENTURY OF CHANGE

The Impact of Education on Women's Art Music Activity

In one century, women gained greater public recognition for their musical work than in all other centuries combined. For this reason, three chapters are devoted to art music of the twentieth century, a time of stunning cultural change. Long-held beliefs about women in culture were largely abandoned and, throughout the century, women enjoyed increased opportunity and unprecedented educational advantage. Such sweeping change does not come easily, however. Thus, as the abundant work of women is discussed, it is also imperative to acknowledge ongoing challenges.

Chapter 10 focuses on the story of gender integration in the world of professional instrumental performance. Despite women's access to private study and collegiate course work, it was difficult for women to find professional performance opportunities at the beginning of the twentieth century. A focused case study of the professional orchestral system provides an excellent lens through which to view the sometimes painful process of integration. From the complete exclusion of women from the ranks of professional ensembles to the achievements of women who led those ensembles as conductors, a century of true change is outlined.

LARGE-SCALE WORK in music, refers to genres that require large numbers of performers (such as symphonies and opera); also refers to genres that are of significant length

CHAMBER MUSIC music for performance by a small group, usually with one performer to a part, as in a string quartet; originally for small audiences

As was noted in Part II, women were very involved in designated compositional areas prior to the advent of the twentieth century, particularly song and keyboard composition. The twentieth century, however, brought widespread change for women who composed. **Chapter 11** highlights representative **large-scale works** of women, an area that was restricted prior to women's access to music education. From the powerful sounds of Amy Beach's *Gaelic Symphony* to Chen Yi's inspired *Chinese Myths Cantata*, this is an exciting chapter in women's music history.

Chapter 12 focuses again on **chamber music**, a category that continues to see prolific activity by women. This is not the chamber music of the past, however. In particular, this chapter focuses on experimental and contemporary works, since connotations regarding the experimental world were not readily connected to perceptions of women, even in the modern age. Representing just a small fraction of the significant compositional output in this area, six composers and representative works are examined in detail with the hope that readers will continue to explore the abundance of chamber music written by women.

CHAPTER 10

Gender Integration in Twentieth-Century Instrumental Ensembles

News Flash: *New York Times*, July 24, 1938

—Antonia Brico First Woman to Conduct Philharmonic!

News Flash: *The Guardian*, London, January 10, 2003

—The Vienna Philharmonic has Appointed its First Female Musician . . .

—Performance Seen by Millions Around the World

News Flash: *Time Magazine*, July 25, 2005

—Marin Alsop Breaks New Ground in a World of Male Maestros, but not without a Fight

Perhaps it is not surprising that Antonia Brico's debut as conductor of the New York Philharmonic made the news in the 1930s, but why the strikingly similar headlines nearly seventy years later? Phrases such as "woman conductor," and "female musician," suggest that "real" musicians, by default, are men.

Integration is a long, painful process that initially involves pioneers who possess the talent and the personality necessary to endure discrimination and harassment. As we explore the topic of women in twentieth-century instrumental music, we will highlight the work of some of those pioneers. At the same time, this phenomenon warrants investigation of how instrumental music became associated with the male sphere in the first place, and why gender-bias still persists. We will begin the chapter by looking at connotations of power in instrumental music throughout the world, and will then narrow the focus by looking at gender integration of professional orchestras, a venue long considered the purview of men. After identifying the manner in which women have negotiated space within the orchestral system, we should be able to better understand gender dynamics within a variety of male-defined musical networks.

It is important to note that some women avoid the discrimination discussion for fear that it reinforces negative stereotypes, and many believe that integration has been achieved. While the turn of the twenty-first century marked significant improvement in terms of integration, however, women continued to report problems with access and opportunity in instrumental music. In 1996 alone, five American orchestras were in the midst of current or recently settled gender-discrimination lawsuits.[1] Women remain banned from many instrumental ensembles throughout the world, and in other ensembles they still receive undue attention due to their sex, particularly when they take leadership roles. As long as "woman" remains an adjective rather than a noun in instrumental music, it seems that we have a topic that is worthy of investigation.

MUSICAL UNIVERSALS: GENDER SPHERES IN MUSIC

One of the longest-standing clichés in the arts is that music is "the universal language." Thanks to the work of ethnomusicologists, we now better understand that context defines music differently from culture to culture. Listening to music from outside one's own culture sometimes leads to stereotyping and judgment rather than acceptance and understanding. At the same time, there are "universals" in music. Music is a metaphor for deep cultural beliefs throughout the world, and music often facilitates the conveyance of values. There are universal purposes for music, including education, courting, worship, and entertainment, but also culturally specific shades of meaning that exist within those purposes.

Cultures throughout the world assign relationships between gender and instruments. Music, along with literature and visual art, has long played a role in communication about cultural values regarding sexuality—it establishes understanding about gender roles and power, and is connected to arousal and desire. Whereas art, literature, and texted music overtly address sexuality, instrumental music's connection to sexuality is not as obvious. It is difficult to prove that a particular rhythmic pattern or melodic ornamentation is intrinsically sexual. As such, people sometimes fail to see how culture mediates gendered meaning in instrumental music.[2]

If we think about it, however, sexual symbolism is present in instruments throughout the world. Parts of instruments are named for human body parts: the head, the neck, the belly, the throat. In many cultures, instruments are connected to gender-specific spirits, and in other parts of the world instrumentalists bestow a human name on their instruments, usually a name of the opposite sex. For example, one of the most famous named instruments in America is B. B. King's guitar "Lucille." No matter what the instrument, there is power in the creation of instrumental sound as the performer manipulates the object, essentially "bringing the sound to life." Similarly, gendered connotations of power and control are evident in the naming of chiming clocks such as Big Ben and Great Paul in England.[3]

Instrumental timbre is also associated with culturally defined gender characteristics. Thus the booming sound of a drum or the blaring of a trumpet is often connected with male characteristics of authority and power, while the ephemeral sound of the harp is gendered female, expressing delicacy and gentleness.

Physical size, strength, and endurance are also connected with ideas about gendered roles in music, and sometimes intersect with non-physical power constructs. Even today, some people cite physical strength and size as reasons why women cannot effectively play the tuba or the Japanese taiko drum. As women prove skeptics wrong, however, it becomes apparent that control of tradition may be the underlying concern. Documentation from legal cases of the late twentieth century provides hard evidence that some male conductors still cited lung capacity as a reason to remove women from the professional orchestral ranks.

Physical allure in performance has been a consistent concern of those who have wished to ban women from certain aspects of instrumental performance. Music making is a physical act that requires specific body positioning, facial alignment, and movement. Many European court cultures forbade instruments that compromised a woman's physical presentation, while instruments that were played in a modest, seated position were allowed. Thus, keyboard instruments such as the harpsichord and the piano were considered acceptable for women, while instruments such as the cello and the bassoon were not. Instruments on which the performer can move gracefully and avoid facial distortion such as the harp and guitar are often gendered female. Interestingly, many of the instruments historically considered proper for women were instruments on which the woman could accompany her own singing voice, further embedding vocal music into the female sphere.[4]

The distortion and obstruction of the face has often been specifically cited as a reason for restricting women from brass instrument performance. Women jazz personnel from the swing band era revealed that male managers required them to stain their lips red to maintain a feminine look while dealing with practical matters—you cannot play a brass instrument while wearing lipstick![5]

Rituals, Gender Roles, and Power

The universal role of instrumental music in spiritual and religious ritual is worthy of special note, not only because of the large number of rituals that exist throughout the world but also because these rituals often set precedent for other non-ritualistic musical traditions. Religious rituals were often initially performed in public spaces banned to women, and this restriction still exists in many cultures throughout the world. While some cultures deny instrumental access out of respect for women, many times access is denied out of fear. Ethnomusicologist Ellen Koskoff suggests that performance restrictions are in place to deny access to spiritual power. She notes a triangular connection between performer, instrument, and spirit in which the performer attains spiritual power via manipulation of the instrument. For example, spirit possession rituals in Ghana and Zimbabwe, facilitated via drumming and mbira performance respectively, allow the instrumentalist to control both the instrument and the connection to a higher power. Closed systems help performers maintain control of musical/spiritual relationships, and some systems are even governed by hereditary or caste-oriented structures.[6]

Not all instruments are gendered male, but it is important to point out that many of the "female" instruments are presented as "male" in reported research. The vina (or veena), for example, is the main melodic instrument in Indian Karnataka music, and is associated with the Hindu goddess of wisdom. Despite the fact that the vina symbolizes feminine spirituality (even the shape of the instrument represents a woman's body), the instrument is often pictured in the hands of male performers in textbooks. The Chinese zither suffers the same fate. In addition, life-cycle rituals such as puberty rites are celebrated by men *and* women in segregated ensembles throughout the world, but women's rites are rarely mentioned, while male rites have been extensively documented. Musicologist Susan Cook suggests that this is probably due in part to the tendency of researchers to negate the validity of female consultants.[7]

Along with cultural ideas regarding instruments that are proper for men and women, there are gendered notions related to performance practice. In this regard, traditional communication styles between orchestral conductors and ensemble members serve as a good example. The role of the conductor is "leader," and methods of communication between conductor and ensemble members have historically been direct and not subject to argumentation. Conductors still joke that the ensemble is not a "democracy," and some conductors have indeed been compared with the cruelest of dictators—the more professional the ensemble, the more the gag rule applies. The conductor sometimes manipulates the members of the ensemble professionally as well as musically, in terms of rank and position. Even social stature within the group is impacted by the wielding of the conductor's analytical role. This system of performance practice has made women's entrance into instrumental conducting difficult due to cultural notions of gender-specific personality traits.

Throughout the world and across cultures, the persistence of gendered musical roles can be attributed to some method of maintaining tradition.

Figure 10.1
The Fetish priestess of Ghana is involved in many community music rituals, but receives far less documentation than the all-male drumming ensembles that accompany her.
Source: Photo courtesy of Kwesi Brown

Required knowledge is supplied, and necessary training is provided. Those who have access via inheritance, education, tradition, or exposure are equipped to function within the system. Lack of access denies both entrance and successful participation.[8]

CASE STUDY OF ORCHESTRAL GROUPS IN THE UNITED STATES AND EUROPE

Women's involvement in professional instrumental music has not guaranteed equal opportunity or pay. Like other professions, women have had to fight for their place, demanding opportunities that people in positions of power have been reluctant to give. Perhaps more than other professions, however, the overtones of sex-based bias in orchestral music have rung longer and more loudly.[9] As such, the integration of women into the orchestral system serves as an excellent case study.

Anyone who has seen a school band or orchestra knows that a significant number of performers are girls. In fact, women already comprised the majority of the nation's music student population in 1925.[10] Even today, however, when a television camera pans across professional orchestral personnel in concert, viewers see far more men than women. Statistics back casual observation. By the year 2000, the most prestigious orchestras in the United States had a surprisingly low percentage of women in their ranks: 31 percent in Baltimore, 25 percent in Boston, 25 percent in Chicago, 23 percent in Cleveland and Detroit, and 18 percent in Philadelphia. In terms of principal players (section leaders), the numbers of women were astoundingly low: only two women principals in Baltimore, Boston, and Philadelphia; three women principals in Cleveland and Detroit; and none in the Chicago Symphony.[11] And the situation in the United States is better than in some other countries.

The gender disparity in orchestras caught the attention of an unlikely audience in 2000, when two economics professors wrote an article on the impact of so-called "blind" auditions on the hiring of female orchestral musicians. Professional orchestras were the perfect site for their research. First, it was one of the rare job interview scenarios where a candidate for the position could be assessed for their ability unseen. In addition, the size of the organization is fairly standard (95–105 members per group), thus multiple "work sites" could be assessed as part of one larger data pool. Once hired, "workers" in ensembles tend to stay, often for life. As such, the orchestral situation allowed a multi-decade look at the proportion of women hired without creating concern regarding changes in the occupation or composition of the workforce. Using extensive data analysis, the economists concluded that the practice of using a screened audition, which began in the 1970s and 1980s, led to a significant rise in the number of women in America's five most prestigious orchestras. Beneath the surface of the hiring process, however, there were other issues that the economists did not address in their research. We can take their labor market analysis a bit further by looking at discrimination and retention among female "employees" as orchestras became integrated.

As female membership slowly rose in ensembles that permitted women to audition, work conditions were sometimes strained. Many women lacked access to dressing rooms and restrooms while on the road, despite the fact that opera and ballet companies had addressed this issue years prior; they had no choice, since their genres required the participation of women.[12] Sexual harassment and unfounded criticism in rehearsal sometimes led to complicated court battles where both parties in the suit had to back their claims amid the difficulty of quantifying musical ability. To better understand what led to this male-dominated environment in the first place, it is important to address the historical development of orchestras.

HISTORICAL FORMATION OF ORCHESTRAS

The "hallmark" of success in American and European classical music is membership in the professional orchestra. The historical roots of the organization help to explain how and why orchestras became associated with the male domain. The modern European orchestra, consisting of an ensemble of strings, winds, and percussion, had its roots in the Baroque era (1600–1750), and, like many aspects of Western music, its performance venues were the church and court. Aside from groups in all-girl schools or orphanages, orchestras were closed to women. Church-related ensemble work initially served the purpose of accompanying singing. St. Mark's Cathedral in Venice was an early developmental site for instrumental music, and its double choir lofts showcased not only double choirs, but antiphonal brass as well.

Orchestral ensembles grew in size and expanded in purpose throughout the Baroque, so that by 1700 they frequently functioned as separate entities. Court orchestras were prevalent, and many of the world's most famous composers were men who were employed to direct all aspects of court-based musical activity. Court musicians composed and had orchestras under their direction, and a large number of new instrumental genres were developed by men in these settings.

By the Classical era (c. 1750–1800), separate orchestral genres were firmly established. As the orchestra developed and grew in size, performance practice was increasingly regimented, and genres such as the symphony rose to prominence. Men continued to dominate both performance and composition, as access to ensembles and access to education severely limited women's participation. By the nineteenth century, Romantic-era music was performed by an orchestral ensemble that replicated modern proportions, utilizing as many as 90–110 members.

While smaller orchestras did not utilize or need a conductor, the increasing size of the orchestra, as well as changing performance practices, led to the adoption of the conductor-led ensemble. French opera composer Jean-Baptiste Lully (1632–1687) is considered one of the first conductors. Known for insisting on uniform bowing and precision as well as coordinated ornamentation, Lully also "conducted" the group with a long staff, pounding it on the floor rather than holding it in the air. If music students remember nothing else about Lully, they tend to remember that he died from conducting: he contracted gangrene after hitting himself in the foot with his staff.

The composer-conductor connection continued strongly to the modern era, cementing a bond that firmly defined orchestral performance practice as male. Many composers conducted their own ensembles: Louis Spohr, Carl Maria von Weber, Felix Mendelssohn, Robert Schumann, Ludwig van Beethoven, and Leonard Bernstein are among them. Only in modern practice is there a separation of musical roles and an expansion of the role of conductor to serve as interpreter of the score. With this history, it is easy to see how the prestige of orchestral music had to do not only with performance settings but also with a socially constructed reverence for a body of works.

THE TWENTIETH-CENTURY ORCHESTRAL WORLD

The opening of orchestral ranks to women was slow and difficult. Women who played violin and harp had the first opportunities to enter into the professional orchestral sphere, though women harpists sometimes were hired only because a male harpist could not be found. It was not uncommon for orchestras to feature guest appearances of women violin soloists who performed in elaborate attire in front of the ensemble. Integration into the ranks of the orchestra itself, however, was very rare even until the 1960s.

Whereas women who performed in jazz and popular music genres of the early twentieth century often had to supply a photograph with their job applications, the art music world resisted a glamorous stage presentation for women ensemble members until the final decades of the century, and even then reserved the visual scrutiny for soloists and chamber groups.

Figure 10.2
Violin virtuosos such as Camilla Urso (1842–1902) and Wilma Norman-Neruda (1838-1911, pictured here) were sometimes featured guests of professional orchestras. Their attire stood in stark contrast to that of the ensemble accompanying them. The tendency to showcase women violinist soloists continued into the twenty-first century with soloists such as Hilary Hahn.
Source: Public domain

The professional orchestral scene was supposed to be about the music itself, and thus it would seem that capable women would have enjoyed equal opportunities. Although musicality was the main criterion on the surface, gender did have a major impact on hiring and retention.

The Business Metaphor

In essence, the orchestral world is a "business." Roles of employee, supervisor, hiring committee, and board of directors all exist, and the bottom line in keeping the organization functional is to remain financially solvent. Ticket sales are only one part of the financial equation. Like today, art music relied on patronage in the early twentieth century, and wealthy board members were common. While the performers onstage were almost all male, a significant percentage of board members were women, and these patrons of the arts not only donated their own money but also headed fundraising efforts. It is well documented that male *and* female board members were hesitant to hire women. Even faced with shortages of male personnel during the Second World War, women on the Boston Symphony board openly expressed reluctance to save money by hiring women.[13] The plight of the aspiring conductor was even more abysmal. Despite Antonia Brico's earlier success in Europe, Arthur Judson, manager of both the New York Philharmonic and the Philadelphia Orchestras, refused to allow Brico to conduct, claiming that women subscribers did not want to see a woman on the podium. Concert manager Minnie Guggenheimer was just as indignant as Judson, and only a petition with 4,000 signatures on Brico's behalf convinced Guggenheimer to change her mind.[14]

Aside from board members, ensemble members also have had a historical role in hiring new orchestral personnel, a practice that still remains in effect in some ensembles. The "boy's club" tendency of section leaders to recommend and hire their own students for open positions strongly impacted access to knowledge about available work. For decades, job openings in professional orchestras were not even advertised. Lack of invitation to social networking sites, ranging from the bar to the golf course, kept even the most distinguished women out of the hiring loop. "Word of mouth" remains common practice in the music profession today, ranging from jazz gigging to conducting jobs. It is one of the most difficult practices to combat due to its covert nature.

Historically, the most influential decision maker in the hiring process has probably been the conductor. Given the prestige conductors are afforded, they have not been hesitant to voice negative generalizations about women musicians. In 1916, New York Symphony conductor Josef Stransky indicated that women would have to be "better than men" to apply for positions,[15] while renowned conductors such as Zubin Mehta, conductor of the New York

Philharmonic until 1990, was heard to say, "I just don't think women should be in an orchestra."[16]

To negate the concern that women were being discriminated against in the hiring process, many organizations began to use screened auditions in the 1970s and 1980s. As noted previously, this enhanced the chance that a woman would advance out of the preliminary round, and likely explains the increased proportion of females among new hires between 1980 and 2000.[17]

Women who were hired by professional orchestras during this era explained that the screen was not always effective, however. Sometimes the screen was opaque, and many orchestras only used screens for the preliminary round. Some organizations use a carpeted surface to counteract the gender betrayal caused by shoes tapping on the floor.[18] When trombonist Ava Ordman auditioned, for example, another auditioner who thought Ordman won the spot asked a committee member why "number six" (Ordman's number) didn't get the job. The committee member replied, "Oh, you mean the girl."[19]

Discrimination in the Workplace

The means to which organizations must go to assure a fair audition indicate a continued reluctance to admit women into the professional ranks. It is not surprising, then, that the work environment for those hired has sometimes been difficult. After the 1970s, many conductors recognized the foolishness of making blatant public condemnations of women. Still, the profession's continued reverence for the conductor sometimes resulted in overt actions aimed toward women. Jeanne Williams Holder, at the time of writing a professional freelance performer and educator, indicated that she once had a young conductor who began to harass and fire women in the orchestra, starting with the oldest. When the conductor began to repeatedly address musical issues with Williams during rehearsal, other ensemble members began to avoid her, and Holder suspects that they feared for their own positions. She ultimately decided to freelance, calling the situation a "battleground."[20]

Demotions and dismissals from professional orchestras are normally rare, as most performers are granted tenure after a short probationary period. A significant number of women, however, have had to deal with conductors who attempted to demote them despite their tenured status. Trombonist Lorin Maazel was tenured as a co-principal player in her ensemble, but the conductor demoted her anyway, assigning second trombone parts. When the orchestra posted auditions for a new opening in the section, Maazel was told that a man would be playing first parts most of the time—even prior to the auditions. Maazel counted herself among the women who initially would have thought that women who were experiencing problems "had a chip on their shoulder." Now she feels differently. Trumpet player Susan Slaughter, member of the St. Louis Symphony since 1969 and the first woman principal trumpet player in a major American orchestra, believes that assignment to the role of principal player makes things even more difficult for women due to leadership connotations.[21]

Sex bias can be very difficult to prove in any field, but the process of critiquing musical performance makes discrimination in the orchestra world especially tricky. The eleven-year legal battle of trombonist Abbie Conant versus the Munich Philharmonic exemplifies how hard women sometimes fought to retain their stature once admitted into an ensemble.

One of the most highly regarded trombonists in the world, Conant won a principal position with the Munich Orchestra via a screened audition in 1980, besting a field of thirty-two male trombonists. It was soon apparent that her conductor, Romanian Sergiu Celibidache, was not happy with her hire, and he soon reassigned Conant to second chair. Throughout the course of the legal procedure that followed, Conant underwent physical tests of her lung capacity as well as inhalation and exhalation demonstrations, all of which proved in her favor. Although the court ruled for Conant, she still was held to second chair by the conductor, and subsequently received less pay. Conant was told she did not have the physical strength to lead the section, and the conductor openly called her derogatory names.

Even Conant's appeal to the Munich Women's Equal Opportunity Office was in vain. They said that they would need "supernatural powers" to change Celibidache. In subsequent court appeals, Conant was required to audition for an external expert witness, who declared her skill outstanding. In 1993, thirteen years after she won her audition, Conant won her legal battle, and the court ordered that she receive principal parts and equal pay. She left the organization of her own accord to take a full professorship at the State Conservatory in Trossingen, Germany. She had been the only woman solo brass performer with a top German orchestra, and when she left, none remained. Interestingly, the Munich Orchestra quit doing screened auditions after Conant's audition in 1980.[22]

> Three women are already too many . . . By the time we have 20 percent, the orchestra will be ruined. We have made a big mistake.[23]
>
> Vienna Philharmonic Orchestra Member, 2003

Geographical location impacts the status of women in professional groups differently. In England, women were first admitted to orchestras in the 1910s, and the percentage of women in the ranks is higher than in America. In Germany, however, discrimination persisted longer, as noted in the Conant case. The Berlin Philharmonic first admitted women in 1982, and the Vienna Philharmonic was still making world headlines in the twenty-first century, admitting its first non-harpist woman, violist Ursula Plaichinger, in 2003. Prior to that time, it had only employed harpist Anna Lelkes on an auxiliary basis.

The admission of women to the Vienna Philharmonic came only after the Viennese government threatened to withhold funding to the organization.[24] Organizations such as the International Alliance for Women in Music joined in protest of the Vienna group in the early twenty-first century, and reported that the ensemble still included only three women in 2010.

Four Conductors, Four Coping Mechanisms

While it was difficult for women to become members in professional orchestras in the twentieth century, women's access to the role of conductor was even more restrictive. We have already discussed the power of the conductor in terms of leadership roles and decision making. Along with perceptions that women could not wield such power, they were faced with the additional problem of accessing ensembles to gain conducting experience. With almost any other musical performance area, musicians can practice on their own, perfecting skills for as many hours as they care to work. Not so with conducting. This predicament was brought to light in the 1970s when Judy Collins filmed a documentary about pioneering conductor Antonia Brico.

Antonia Brico (1902–1989) immigrated to the United States in 1908, and was both a pianist and a conductor. She graduated from the University of California-Berkeley in 1923 and studied conducting in Berlin where she became the first American graduate of the State Academy of Music of Berlin. She was the first woman to conduct the Berlin Philharmonic in 1930, as a youthful twenty-eight year old. She continued to conduct throughout Europe and America in the 1930s, with engagements in Germany and Poland and a performance at the New York Metropolitan Opera House with the Musicians Symphony Orchestra. Brico's career seemed well on its way, but she began to experience significant problems finding work in the United States due to concern about her sex. Brico found that prominent male soloists sometimes refused to work with her, and symphony boards and managers feared the repercussions of hiring a woman to conduct. Despite the high regard that musicians such as Arthur Rubenstein and Jean Sibelius had for Brico, many managerial staff members in America were afraid of public reaction and refused to engage her services.[25]

Unable to access "an instrument to practice," Brico founded her own ensemble, the Women's Symphony Orchestra, and subsequently added men to the ensemble, renaming it the Brico Symphony.[26] Like many women's orchestras of that era, it failed financially. Although Brico fought the system and sought opportunities to conduct, the American marketplace remained difficult, and she spent the majority of her long conducting career working with amateur groups in the Denver area.

Another conductor of Brico's era was Ethel Leginska (1886–1970), a flamboyant public figure who had a personality that fit the defined role of

NEW YORK WOMEN'S SYMPHONY ORCHESTRA

ANTONIA BRICO
Conductor

CARNEGIE HALL
57th STREET AND SEVENTH AVENUE

TUESDAY EVENING
FEBRUARY 23rd
at 8:45

Assisting Artist
LAURA ARCHERA
Violinist

Photo by Valente

PROGRAM

IDOMENEO OVERTURE .... *Mozart*

VIOLIN CONCERTO in A Major .... *Mozart*
Allegro
Adagio
Tempo di Menuetto
Allegro

—INTERMISSION—

INTRODUCTION AND ALLEGRO .... *Goffredo Petrassi*
For Solo Violin and eleven instruments

LA GIARA .... *Alfredo Casella*
Symphonic Suite
Prelude
Sicilian Dance
General Dance
Finale

NEGRO HEAVEN .... *Otto Cesana*
Symphonette

Tickets: Box Seats $3.00, $2.00; Orchestra $2.50, $2.00; Dress Circle $1.50; Balcony $1.00, $.75.

Management Richard Copley, 113 West 57th Street, New York, N. Y.

The Steinway is the official piano of the New York Women's Symphony Orchestra

Figure 10.3
A concert program featuring Antonia Brico as conductor of the New York Women's Symphony Orchestra at a Carnegie Hall performance. The group existed from 1934 to 1937.

Source: From the collection of the author

conductor. Born in 1886 in England, Leginska was a renowned pianist who had studied in England, Frankfurt, and Vienna before coming to the attention of the American public in 1912. The *New York Times* archives are full of headlines that indicate how much Leginska captured the American imagination as both a pianist and a conductor. In 1924, she diverted her attention away from piano performance and began conducting professionally, leading the London Symphony, Berlin Philharmonic, and Munich Orchestras all in the same year. Her non-musical activities, including a very public child custody case, became part of her stage presence—Leginska knew how to market herself. Like Brico, Leginska founded a group of her own in 1931. Unlike Brico's group, however, Leginska's Boston Philharmonic consisted of all men except for the harpist and pianist. She also worked with women's ensembles that she established in the New York area. Leginska openly addressed the public perception that a conductor should be male. She bowed to male tradition in practical yet attention-getting ways, abandoning traditional bare-shouldered gowns for a black velvet jacket with a masculine collar and cuffs. She was vocal in her belief that women had to emulate men in dress and hairstyle to

Figure 10.4
Conductor and pianist Ethel Leginska abandoned gowns in favor of masculine jackets, believing that women had to emulate men in order to succeed in professional instrumental performance venues.

Source: Courtesy Library of Congress

Figure 10.5
Along with her work in the field of teaching, Nadia Boulanger was a pioneer in the field of professional orchestral conducting. She is pictured here with Sinsinawa Dominican musician Sr. Edward Blackwell, O. P.

Source: Courtesy of Sinsinawa Dominican Archives

succeed in the public performance sphere.[27] Leginska's self-promotion ability, leadership skills, musical ability, and notoriety as a soloist all combined to help her successfully negotiate the field of conducting. Interestingly, she voluntarily left the conducting field and returned to piano-related work.

On the opposite end of the personality spectrum was a third woman who debuted with several professional orchestras of the early twentieth century, French conductor and pedagogue Nadia Boulanger (1887–1979). Better known for her work as a composition teacher, Boulanger was a highly respected force in the musical world and was accustomed to being a minority in the room —her teaching studios were usually filled with male students. (For more on Boulanger's work as an educator, see Chapter 11.) Along with being the first woman to conduct the Royal Philharmonic and the BBC Symphony Orchestra in England, Boulanger was the first to conduct the New York Philharmonic, the Boston Symphony Orchestra, and the Philadelphia Orchestra. When Igor Stravinsky fell ill for the premiere of his *Dumbarton Oaks Concerto* in Washington DC, he called on Boulanger to take over as conductor. Known as the "tender tyrant," Boulanger was a no-nonsense personality who wore demure clothing and displayed a serious countenance.[28] She was all about the music, and everyone understood that she knew her art. Boulanger is the champion of women who prefer not to bother with the discussion of gender issues in music. Pressed by reporters about what it was like to be the first of her sex to conduct the Boston Symphony Orchestra, Boulanger retorted, "I've been a woman for a little over fifty years, and I've gotten over my initial astonishment. As for conducting an orchestra, that's a job. I don't think sex plays much part."[29]

A generation after Brico, Leginska, and Boulanger had their professional conducting debuts in America and Europe, women were still having difficulty entering the field. Margaret Hillis (1921–1998), slipped in to the orchestral world by establishing herself as conductor of a symphony chorus. Although Hillis' "first love" was orchestral conducting, she pursued choral conducting because there were "virtually no orchestral conducting opportunities" for women in the 1950s. After studying choral conducting with Robert Shaw, Hillis quickly rose to prominence in the choral world, and in 1957, at the invitation of Chicago Symphony conductor Fritz Reiner, she established the Chicago Symphony Chorus. Along with earning accolades for her work with the chorus, Hillis increasingly worked with the orchestra as well, and by the 1970s, opportunities opened for Hillis across the country. Her forty-year career with the Chicago Symphony was filled with challenges as well as rewards, but Hillis dealt with prejudice by using a sense of humor. She quipped, "There's only one woman I know who could never be a symphony conductor, and that's the Venus de Milo."[30]

Thus four pioneers of the orchestral conducing world took various approaches to negotiating their place on the podium. Brico continued on her journey by creating her own gender-segregated ensemble and working with amateur groups. Leginska emulated personality traits, clothing, and hairstyles that were defined as male, and openly asserted that "acting male" was the only means of survival. Boulanger engaged in music making and dismissed references to gender, while Hillis entered the field through a path that was considered acceptable to women. Despite the work of these pioneers, orchestral conducting remained a difficult point of entry for women in professional music throughout most of the century.

Separate but not Equal: Women's Ensembles in the Twentieth Century

Like Antonia Brico, many women who were unsuccessful at attaining long-term positions as performers or conductors turned to gender-segregated ensembles as a means to perform their art. As we noted in Chapter 7, women's groups often played lighter music, and were restricted to informal venues such as parks, hotels, and restaurants. If the groups generated any income at all, it was minimal. Between the 1920s and 1940s, approximately thirty women's orchestras existed in the United States, but most had disbanded by the conclusion of the Second World War. The Cleveland Women's Symphony Orchestra, established in 1935, was one of the few that remained active, and that group celebrated its seventy-fifth season in 2009–2010.[31]

The practice of segregation is decried by many women. Women's ensembles have been inconsistent in terms of musical quality, and most women's groups lack the social status and monetary backing of long-established professional groups. Many performers believe that segregation simply delays full integration of women into professional music.

At the same time, some women have found a purpose in segregated ensemble work. Groups such as the Cleveland Women's Orchestra not only perform but also encourage and showcase the work of women in composition and conducting. Segregation can provide a supportive environment where musicians focus on music making rather than negotiating their space. Less experienced musicians also appreciate encountering accomplished women role models.

Segregated ensembles have also existed in instrumental venues other than orchestra. All-women jazz ensembles, concert bands, drum corps, percussion groups, and rock bands have been common in the United States, and many segregated groups still exist. In the world music venue, women's ensembles are commonly utilized in traditional ensembles such as mariachi groups, gamelan groups, and West African drumming. Like their counterparts in the orchestral world, women in these ensembles enjoy the camaraderie and the opportunity to make music, but many would gladly integrate if given the opportunity.

AT THE TURN OF THE TWENTY-FIRST CENTURY

After examining twentieth-century gender integration in orchestral performance in such depth, it is important to return to the broader scope and reflect on the status of women in instrumental music in the twenty-first century. We have already noted the continued minority status of women in professional orchestras, particularly in principal positions. Breaking into professional conducting remained challenging for women during this period, but there were signs of hope.

In 1998, JoAnn Falletta (b. 1954) was appointed music director of the Buffalo Philharmonic Orchestra, at that time the highest orchestral appointment for a woman in American orchestral music. Falletta had done impressive work as conductor of the San Francisco-based Women's Philharmonic from

Figure 10.6
With her appointment as director of the Buffalo Philharmonic Orchestra in 1998, JoAnn Falletta attained the then-highest ranking orchestral appointment for a woman in American orchestral history.

Source: Photo by Cheryl Gorski, Courtesy of JoAnn Falletta

1986 to 1997, championing the work of women via commissions and premiere performances. The group dissolved in 2004, but had done critical work in promoting the music of women. (A recording of the group performing Chen Yi's *Chinese Myths Cantata* under Falletta is discussed in Chapter 11.) Falletta continues to be highly regarded as a promoter of contemporary music and music by women, and has won numerous prestigious awards for conducting and programming.

Reservations about the ability of women to hold music director roles were again brought to light in July of 2005, however, when Marin Alsop's appointment to director at the Baltimore Symphony (BSO) was strongly contested by orchestra members. When the BSO board announced their intent to hire Alsop, a committee of seven performers asserted that 90 percent of the ensemble wanted to continue the search.[32] In Alsop's case, the board overruled the musicians, but the newly appointed conductor was faced with standing before an ensemble whose opposition to her appointment had involuntarily become known to her.[33]

By the early twenty-first century, women were slowly gaining recognition in the professional orchestral conducting field. Cuban-born Odaline de la Martinez, founder of the contemporary ensemble Lontano and the European Women's Orchestra, enjoys an international career, as does Cuban-born Tania León. The Kapralova Society, a non-profit arts organization based in Toronto, Canada, honors the name of outstanding Czech conductor Vita Kapralova (1890–1973), via promotion of women's achievements in conducting and other fields.

As an indication of continuing bias toward women conductors, however, JoAnn Falletta was called upon to lead a seminar for "women" conductors in 2009, sponsored by the League of American Orchestras, at which she addressed communication skills, self-promotion, perceptions of authority, and other

Figure 10.7
Marin Alsop conducting the Baltimore Symphony Orchestra.
Source: Photo by Grant Leighton, Courtesy of the Baltimore Symphony Orchestra

"specific challenges of on-podium leadership for women conductors."[34] For conductors in particular, there is much progress yet to be made in terms of full gender integration.

THE AMATEUR RANKS

Is the attitude about women in instrumental music as difficult in the amateur world as in the professional realm? Like orchestras, twentieth-century concert bands, collegiate marching bands, and drum corps were often reserved for boys and men, and although many groups opened to women in the 1960s and 1970s, there were issues of hazing and sexual harassment throughout the ensuing decades. At least two sexual harassment claims associated with collegiate marching bands made national headlines in the first decade of the twenty-first century.

In 2010, there were still instrumental ensembles in the United States that excluded women entirely. At this writing, the Cavaliers and Scouts drum corps still do not accept women, citing their historical roots in the Boy Scouts as the reason. The concert band profession also remains male dominated. As of 2010, twenty-one out of twenty-three past National Band Association presidents were men, and the organization's hall of fame listed forty honorees in 2010, thirty-nine of whom were men.[35]

SUMMARY

Women's methods of working within instrumental music systems differ. Some women take pride in saying that they are "one of the boys," and relish their place as unique. They are as likely as men to believe that they are a phenomenon for their sex, and as they frequent social networking sites, they take on socially defined personality characteristics that allow them to fit an expected role.

Other women tire of the bias they perceive in integrated situations, and decide to either exit the profession or continue in gender-segregated ensembles. Those who are in integrated ensembles often state that they must work harder and perform better than men in their groups. Many assert that they keep a low profile to avoid conflict.[36]

In the world music marketplace, gendered roles in instrumental performance are also being challenged. The Australian didgeridoo, the Shona mbira, and the Japanese taiko drum are just a few of the popular "world music" instruments that are being embraced by women. Cultural outsiders who access these instruments often do so without much thought to cultural restrictions, while women in the original settings sometimes remain banished from performing on the same instruments.

The professional instrumental music realm is difficult to access regardless of gender. Aside from the need to possess exceptional skill, aspiring musicians must have access to private study, performance opportunities, and social connections to break into the professional ranks. In many cases, social class and race are as much to blame for restricted access as is gender. Still, traditional practices in instrumental music have made progress for women especially slow, and pioneering women continue to make the headlines. Perhaps in your lifetime the frontier will finally cease to exist.

QUESTIONS FOR CRITICAL THINKING AND DISCUSSION

1. Compare the challenges for women described in this chapter with women in current rock/pop ensembles. Are gender-segregated groups still in existence? Why?
2. Discuss your thoughts regarding women's access to world music instruments that are banned for women in the culture of origin. Should women outside of the original culture perform on those instruments?
3. Compare public perceptions of women's leadership roles in music with perceptions toward other societal leadership roles, such as political positions.

IDEAS FOR FURTHER RESEARCH

1. Using an instrumental ensemble of your choice, document how members of that ensemble obtained the musical and social knowledge they needed to be accepted as a group member. Was the process formal, informal, or both?
2. Select two women from this chapter and do an in-depth study of their educational backgrounds and personal philosophies regarding their involvement in music.

CHAPTER 11

Twentieth-Century Large-Scale Works

Contrasting Compositional Voices

LARGE-SCALE WORK
in music, refers to genres that require large numbers of performers (such as symphonies and opera); also refers to genres that are of significant length

The twentieth century marked a dramatic expansion in compositional activity for women. The increased opening of conservatory classes to women in the 1870s allowed unprecedented access to music theory and orchestration coursework—critical knowledge required of composers who aspired to write **large-scale works**. To make a living as a composer, however, it takes more than musical ability and education. In many ways, non-musical aspects of the composition profession in the twentieth century were even more difficult for women to attain, and thus delayed the full integration of women into the compositional world for much of the century. While many composers earned a living as college and university professors in the first half of the century, those positions remained largely closed to women. Other composers relied on fellowships, prizes, and commissions to make a living, but mentoring regarding such funding was also connected to the university system, and was thus sometimes lacking for women. Libby Larsen indicated that even as late as the 1970s, "The little kinds of support that men received from mentors were withheld from women, because there was genuine doubt that women could think compositionally."[1] Perhaps one of the greatest roadblocks regarding large-scale works, however, was gaining access to performing ensembles. Composers need to hear their work performed to make improvements, and while it is relatively easy to pull together a chamber ensemble, accessing a capable orchestra or opera company requires connections. Even the best-educated women sometimes fought to hear their compositions performed. Composer Ellen Zwilich still tells aspiring composers that hearing their work performed is the single most important thing they must do to succeed as composers.[2]

Although change has been slow, it has been steady. The suffragette movement was just one of the major sociocultural phenomena of the twentieth century that led to unparalleled educational and employment opportunities for women, and a resultant increase in the number of women working as professional composers. Although university music departments still reported women as the minority among composition students at the turn of the twenty-first century, the historical face of the compositional world had undoubtedly begun to change.

The focus of this chapter is to explore a sample of large-scale works that women composed between 1896 and 2003, spanning a critical century of development and professional achievement. Breaking the bounds of the chamber, these composers represent a rapidly growing number of women who successfully wrote symphonies, concertos, opera, ballet, and other extended length, multi-movement works during this period. It is only a small sample of the work of women in music composition, but provides a historical sense of change throughout this important century in women's music history.

A UNIQUE COMPOSITIONAL VOICE?

Even the women highlighted in this text strongly disagree as to whether or not a unique compositional style exists among women who compose. Libby Larsen guardedly suggests that perhaps women are more inclusive in their approach to composition, taking into account their potential audiences, and working collaboratively with performers. Others, such as Shulamit Ran and Joan Tower, emphatically state that sex has nothing to do with compositional style.

Male or female, composers are influenced by many factors beyond basic music education. These may include their own ethnic musical experiences, spiritual beliefs, family background, performance experiences, and other issues of personal interest. Undoubtedly, composition teachers also often have a profound impact on the stylistic development of their students. As such, it is important to begin this chapter with a tribute to a woman who is considered the top twentieth-century teacher of composition, Nadia Boulanger.

NADIA BOULANGER: NURTURING THE COMPOSITIONAL VOICE

> *Her real power as a teacher came from her extraordinarily acute critical sense. I had never previously had a teacher . . . who knew so instantly what one's music was about.*[3]
>
> Composer Virgil Thomson regarding Nadia Boulanger

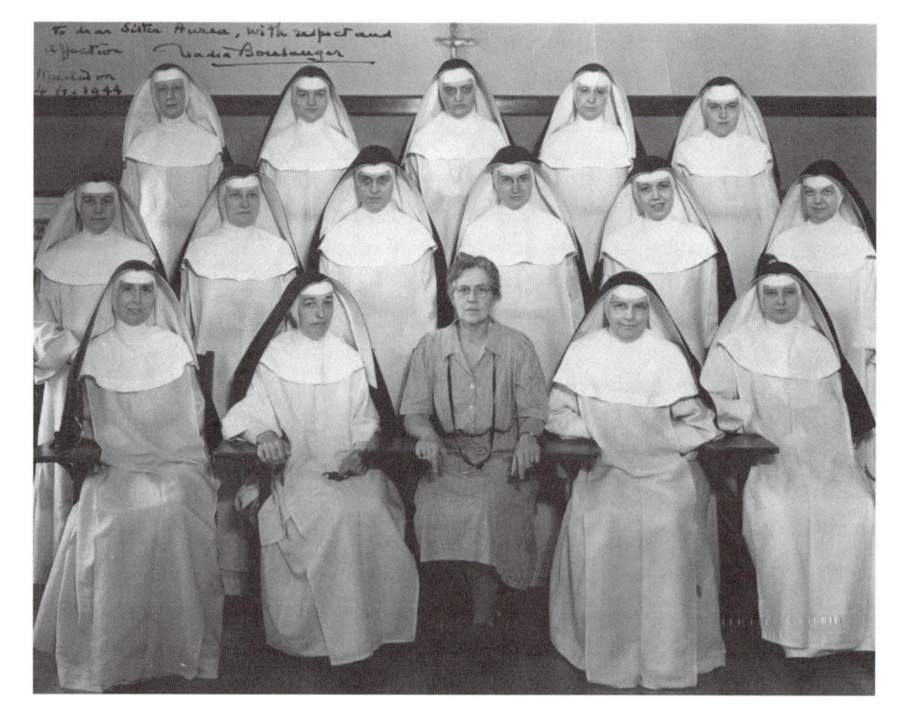

Figure 11.1
Nadia Boulanger in an unusual setting: surrounded by female students in a Second World War era summer session.

Source: Photo courtesy of the Sinsinawa Dominican Archives

Nadia Boulanger (1887–1979) is considered the greatest composition teacher of the twentieth century, and perhaps the greatest music pedagogue of all time. In a period when women were just beginning to widely access formal music education, Boulanger's achievement is even more stunning. The continued reverence of the musical world for Nadia Boulanger is testament to her immense musical and pedagogical ability.

Composing is a technical skill that requires knowledge of music theory concepts, forms, and structures. When orchestration is added to the formula, even more comprehension is needed, including mastery of instrumental ranges, technical capabilities, and transpositions. Nadia Boulanger's teaching was shaped and enhanced by her own extensive background in both composition and performance. Her mother, Raisa Mychetskaya, was a Russian singer, and her father, Henri-Alexandre-Ernest Boulanger, won the Grand Prix de Rome in 1835. Nadia studied with Gabriel Fauré (1845–1924) and Charles-Marie Widor (1844–1937), among others, and was a champion of the music of both Fauré and Igor Stravinsky (1882–1971). She won numerous prizes while a student at the Conservatoire, and took second place in the Prix de Rome in 1908. The next year she was asked to teach harmony at the Conservatoire. Younger sister Lili Boulanger (1893–1918), one of Nadia's first students, took first place in the Prix de Rome in 1913, the first woman to win the prize. Lili Boulanger was ill throughout her youth and died young. After Lili's death,

Nadia increasingly turned to teaching, conducting, and promoting her sister's compositional work.

In the 1920s, Boulanger began teaching at the American School at Fontainebleau, a conservatory near Paris that became popular for American students who turned away from German musical influences in the post-war period. She also taught at the prestigious École Normale and simultaneously maintained a teaching studio in her home. Boulanger believed in a disciplined approach to music study, and taught her students that every note must be meaningful.

Boulanger stood out among her peers not only because of superior knowledge but also because she helped each individual to recognize and utilize a unique compositional voice. While many composition teachers produce students who imitated the mentor's compositional sound, this was not the case in Boulanger's studio. Boulanger had the ability to find the essence of the student's distinctive sound and combine it with the theoretical discipline needed to make the music structurally excellent. Generations of students endured Boulanger's rigorous harmony, counterpoint, ear training, and keyboarding exercises. The list of her former students is far too immense to include here, but over 130 are listed in the *New Grove Dictionary of Music and Musicians* alone, with a range of work that extends from opera to jazz.

AMY BEACH (1867–1944)

> *I want you to know how much Mr. Parker and I enjoyed your symphony on Saturday evening . . . I always feel a thrill of pride myself whenever I hear a fine work by any one of us, and as such you will have to be counted in, whether you will or not—one of the boys.*[4]
>
> George Chadwick, member of the Second New England School of Composers, in an excerpt from correspondence with Amy Beach

George Chadwick's praise of Amy Beach's *Gaelic Symphony* is indicative of the musical world faced by an American woman born during the Civil War era. Beach was a decisive figure in the **symphonic** medium in a period when women often wrote only salon pieces and piano works, and today she is considered seminal in the expansion of women's compositions beyond the chamber. Beach's invitation to consider herself "one of the boys" indicates not only her ability level, but also a belief that she was an oddity among women. Far from being her only work, the *Gaelic Symphony* marked the beginning of a long and varied career in which this pioneer expanded her compositional range. She was able to accomplish this despite the fact that she was almost completely self-taught.

SYMPHONY
extended work for orchestra, usually with multiple movements

Figure 11.2
Amy Beach.
Source: Photo courtesy of the Library of Congress

A member of the Boston-based Second New England School of Composers,[5] Amy Beach and her compositional colleagues turned the musical eyes of America inward for the first time. American art music had been almost entirely focused on European musical education and ideals, and anyone who wished to pursue formal study previously had traveled abroad. Not only did members of this group compose original works, several were composition teachers in American schools of music, negating the need for aspiring composers to study abroad. Several were fundamental in establishing and working at the MacDowell Colony, an organization that has supported the work of thousands of artists since its inception in 1907.[6]

Born just after the American Civil War, Amy Marcy Cheney was raised in Boston, a developmental hub for American art music. Her mother, Clara Imogene Marcy Cheney, was a singer and pianist who claimed that the two-year-old Amy could improvise harmony to her mother's melodies. Her father was a mathematician and businessman whose success led to a comfortable lifestyle for the family. Amy was highly intelligent as well as musically gifted. She taught herself to read by age three, and by age four played the piano by ear. Formal piano study led to numerous public performances throughout her teen years. So outstanding were her performances that the Boston public believed Beach was destined to become a virtuoso. In 1885, however, the eighteen-year-old performer married Dr. Henry Harris Aubrey Beach, a forty-three-year-old surgeon. The marriage was to change her musical path profoundly (and unexpectedly) in the direction of composition.

Dr. Beach quickly put an end to his wife's performance career, making it clear that he was to be the sole financial provider of the family. The young wife dutifully limited her performances to infrequent charity events, and fulfilled the social expectations of the upper-middle class Boston wife. In an era when other composers such as Britain's Ethel Smyth (1858–1944) were involved in the suffragette movement, Beach sported conservative clothing and accepted a domestic-based lifestyle. She remained Mrs. H. H. A. Beach on publications, maintaining the expected formal status of a married woman of her era and subsequently honoring her husband's name on paper. This is perhaps one reason why he allowed her to publish.[7]

Dr. Beach encouraged his wife to write compositions, including large-scale works. Compositional work took place in the home, a far less public activity than was piano performance. Amy Beach's symphony, mass, and concerto were written during her marriage, and with her husband's encouragement. Publisher Arthur P. Schmidt, a strong proponent of American men *and* women composers of the period, became associated with Beach and maintained a long-term publishing relationship. Almost all of her 300 works were published and most were performed. Hearing her music and getting it published were critical elements to Beach's development and fame.

Beach's compositional expertise was attained with surprisingly little formal study. Denied a composition teacher when she made inquiries, she began intensive study on her own.[8] Her extreme intelligence is confirmed by her ability to teach herself the technical art of orchestration. Along with manuscripts of works by numerous composers, including contrapuntal work of J. S. Bach, Beach obtained a copy of Hector Berlioz' 1844 *Traite de l'Instrumentation* (*Treatise on Orchestration*), translated it from French to English, and memorized its contents without outside assistance. She furthered her education by attending orchestra concerts and studying the conductor's scores before and after performances.

Although Beach is often cast as a Romantic-era throwback, she continued to grow and embrace compositional change throughout her career. When her husband died in 1910, she resurrected her performance career and simultaneously embraced new compositional styles and techniques.[9] Beginning in 1921, she spent the first of twenty annual residencies at the MacDowell Colony.[10] Although she never used extreme dissonance or **serialism**, she was inspired by composers such as Maurice Ravel (1875–1937) and Alexander Scriabin (1872–1915), and was known for incorporating birdsong into her works long before Olivier Messiaen (1908–1992) became known for doing the same.[11]

SERIALISM
an atonal compositional method that systematically orders musical elements according to a fixed series

Figure 11.3
The title page from Amy Beach's "Gaelic" Symphony.
Source: Public domain

LISTENING EXPERIENCE 11.1

"The Gaelic," Movement I from *Symphony Number One in E Minor* (1896)
Amy Beach
Companion CD Track 8

LISTENING FOCUS

Listen for themes and accompaniment inspired by Beach's song "Dark is the Night," as well as a Gaelic bagpipe tune; churning chromatic accompaniment depicts the sea.

FORM AT A GLANCE

Sonata Form: Exposition (with three themes); Development; Recapitulation.

TIMED LISTENING GUIDE

Exposition

0:00	churning chromatic accompaniment depicts turbulent sea
0:18	Theme A: stated in trumpets and horns; based on Beach's "Dark is the Night"
1:20	Theme B: contrasting lyrical material; taken from middle section of Beach's song
2:06	clarinet solo begins transition to third theme
2:44	Theme C: oboe solo in Dorian mode references bagpipe; drone and dance rhythm also evident; based on dance tune "Connor O'Reilly of Clounish"

Development

3:11	opening "churning" material begins the development; A and B fragments throughout
6:03	clarinet solo signals transition to recapitulation

Recapitulation

6:20	opening "churning" material
6:24	A theme
7:05	B theme
8:24	C theme in solo flute, then solo oboe; later in strings

Closing

9:55	trumpet signals transition to closure with fragments of A theme
10:21	final closing segment

Gaelic Symphony

When Czech composer Antonin Dvorák (1841–1904) suggested that Americans tap their own ethnic music by utilizing spirituals as a primary source, Amy Beach publicly responded in writing and suggested that European immigrant music equally shaped America's musical formation. In the *Gaelic Symphony*, Beach blended Irish melodies with traditional European orchestral timbres and forms, as well as her own original art song. By the end of her career, she turned to other ethnic sources as well, including Alaskan Eskimo melodies in her *String Quartet* of 1929, as well as Balkan-inspired themes.[12]

GERMAINE TAILLEFERRE (1892–1983)

> *Ladies and Gentlemen, you are looking at a person on whom the Americans would have laid bets for conservatory prizes. She never began a class which she did not conclude with first prize.*[13]
>
> French composer Georges Auric, at an awards presentation honoring Germaine Tailleferre

Germaine Tailleferre's compositional voice initially took shape as a member of Les Six, a group of French composers whose aesthetic was unified only by what they wished to avoid: both heavy German Romanticism and French Impressionism. Dubbed Les Six by a French journalist, group members embraced classical and popular forms, often integrating tongue-in-cheek humor into everything from symphonic genres to commercial film scores. The group members had vastly individual styles that incorporated a range of styles, from jazz to **neoclassicism**. Along with Tailleferre, group members included Georges Auric (1899–1983), Louis Durey (1888–1979), Arthur Honegger (1892–1955), Darius Milhaud (1892–1974), and Francis Poulenc (1899–1963).

NEOCLASSICISM
style that emerged in the early decades of the twentieth century, and bowed to Classical stylistic characteristics such as form-driven structure, transparent texture, tonality, and lack of extra-musical program

When Germaine Tailleferre initially expressed interest in formal music study, her father was strongly opposed. Germaine was just twelve years old, and her father did not think the conservatory was a proper place for a woman. Her mother, however, encouraged Germaine to persevere, and the young woman entered the Conservatoire in 1904, earning her own way by teaching lessons. Her financial situation was improved by the numerous scholarship awards that she won in ear training, harmony, counterpoint, and accompanying. Tailleferre received more first prizes at the Conservatoire than any other member of Les Six, almost all of whom received more attention on paper in ensuing decades.[14]

Much of Tailleferre's work was written between 1945 and 1983, well after the peak popularity of Les Six. She wrote a significant number of large-scale works, including two piano concerti, a violin concerto, three vocal concerti, a concerto grosso, four ballet scores, four full-length operas, and numerous shorter operas. Although Tailleferre received many prestigious commissions, a sign that she was well respected during her lifetime, it has only recently come to light that she composed such a wide variety of styles and genres. Like Clara Schumann, Tailleferre downplayed her compositional ability, and this, along with the prejudice against women composers of her era, made her a far lesser-known composer than was deserved. The fact that Tailleferre's most successful compositions were large-scale works also contributed to the lack of attention she received. In an era when chamber music was still considered a more suitable avenue for women, it was difficult for women to get repeated exposure for their large-scale works. Even when pioneering recording projects began to feature women's compositions, there were financial struggles to pull together the forces needed to record works outside of the chamber music realm. As a result, Tailleferre's best work remained hidden.[15] Today, Tailleferre's large-scale works are considered among the best work of members of Les Six, negating earlier textbook accounts that only mentioned her name in passing. Although two failed marriages made Germaine Tailleferre's personal life financially challenging, she made a living as a composer and wrote over 300 works before she died at age ninety-one.

Sonata for Violin and Piano in C♯ Minor

The 1920s were a productive period for Tailleferre, and one in which she began to receive a number of prestigious commissions, including a ballet and a harp concerto. It was also a time when she developed many international connections. Her harp concerto, for example, was commissioned by the Boston Symphony Orchestra and was premiered by the BSO under the direction of Serge Koussevitzky in 1927. Tailleferre's *Sonata for Violin and Piano in C♯ Minor* was completed in 1922 and was composed for violinist Jacques Thibaud, a leading French violinist of the era whom she had met in England in 1920. Thibaud, along with pianist Alfred Cortot, premiered the **sonata** in Paris in 1922. It is a four-movement work that is neoclassical in its formal structure, but also hints at French Impressionism with its modally inspired melodic lines. The **bitonal** segments were probably inspired by both Maurice Ravel and Igor Stravinsky.[16]

SONATA
genre for one or two solo instruments; features multiple movements

BITONAL
simultaneous use of two different keys

FLORENCE PRICE (1887–1953)

> *My Dear Dr. Koussevitzky,*
> *To begin with I have two handicaps—those of sex and race. I am a woman; and I have some Negro blood in my veins . . . I should like to be judged on merit alone.*
>
> July 5, 1943 letter from Florence Price
> to conductor Serge Koussevitzky[17]

LISTENING EXPERIENCE 11.2

***Sonata for Violin and Piano in C♯ Minor*, Movement I (1921)**
Germaine Tailleferre
Score available in the *New Historical Anthology of Music by Women*
Playlist

LISTENING FOCUS

Listen for modal melodic lines that reflect French impressionistic influence, as well as bitonal segments.

FORM AT A GLANCE

Sonata Form

Exposition (two themes); Development; Recapitulation.

TIMED LISTENING GUIDE

Exposition

0:00	A theme in C♯ minor in violin
0:20	B material in F major
0:33	A fragments in piano
0:46	A fragments move between violin and piano
1:10	B theme in C major in violin, against alternating C and C♯ tonality in piano

Exposition Repeated

1:29	A theme in C♯ minor
1:50	B theme in F
2:03	transitional A material
2:40	B theme in C major in violin, against alternating C and C♯ tonality in piano

Development

2:58	bitonality more evident
3:33	piano material taken from exposition accompaniment figure, elongated
3:51	A theme fragments in violin against bitonal accompaniment
4:09	bitonal and modally inflected transitional material

Recapitulation

4:46	A theme in C♯ minor
5:47	B theme in C♯ major
6:00	Coda

Florence Beatrice Price was the first African-American woman to gain national recognition as a composer. Fusing European art music models with black ethnic influences, she made a living as a composer in an era in which she was not only marginalized due to her gender, but also due to race.[18] She is now recognized as an important compositional voice who authentically utilized the material that Anton Dvorák suggested could represent nationalistic American art music.

JIM CROW LAWS
named for a minstrel character, these laws sanctioned the denial of equal rights for black Americans, including racial segregation in public facilities

Price was born in Little Rock, Arkansas, in 1887, prior to the establishment of **Jim Crow laws** that allowed legal segregation. Her father was a well-respected dentist, her mother a businesswoman and former elementary school teacher who provided Florence's first musical training. As a family of mixed racial heritage, fair complexions, and high educational attainment, the Price family lived in relative affluence. When Florence graduated from high school at age fourteen, she moved to Boston to study organ and piano performance at the New England Conservatory. Already a published composer at age eleven, Price expressed interest in studying composition at the conservatory, and George Chadwick accepted Price into his private compositional studio. It was an honor

Figure 11.4
ASCAP photo of Florence Price.
Source: University of Arkansas Libraries, Florence Price Collection, Series One, Box One, Folder 12. Used by permission

VERNACULAR
"of the people;" as opposed to work of the educated elite

reserved for only the most gifted students. Like Chadwick, Price shared a passion for incorporating indigenous and **vernacular** sources into concert music.[19]

Price returned to the South to teach, and eventually became head of the music department at Clark College in Atlanta. She married attorney Thomas J. Price in 1912, and although Little Rock had been a good home for the black middle class in the days of Florence's youth, the family decided to move to the North because of increased race-based violence. In Chicago, Price found a fertile artistic environment. She studied at several institutions in the city, including the American Conservatory, the Chicago Musical College, the Chicago Teachers College, and the University of Chicago. The stock market crash in 1929 led to financial difficulties for the Price family, however, and the marital strain led to a divorce in 1931. Florence was granted custody of the couple's two children, and she made a living by teaching lessons and writing popular tunes under a pen name. Still, she often lived with friends to survive.

One of the home stays was especially providential for Price. During the period when she lived at the home of her pupil Margaret Bonds (who also became a well-known composer), Price was introduced to many of the most

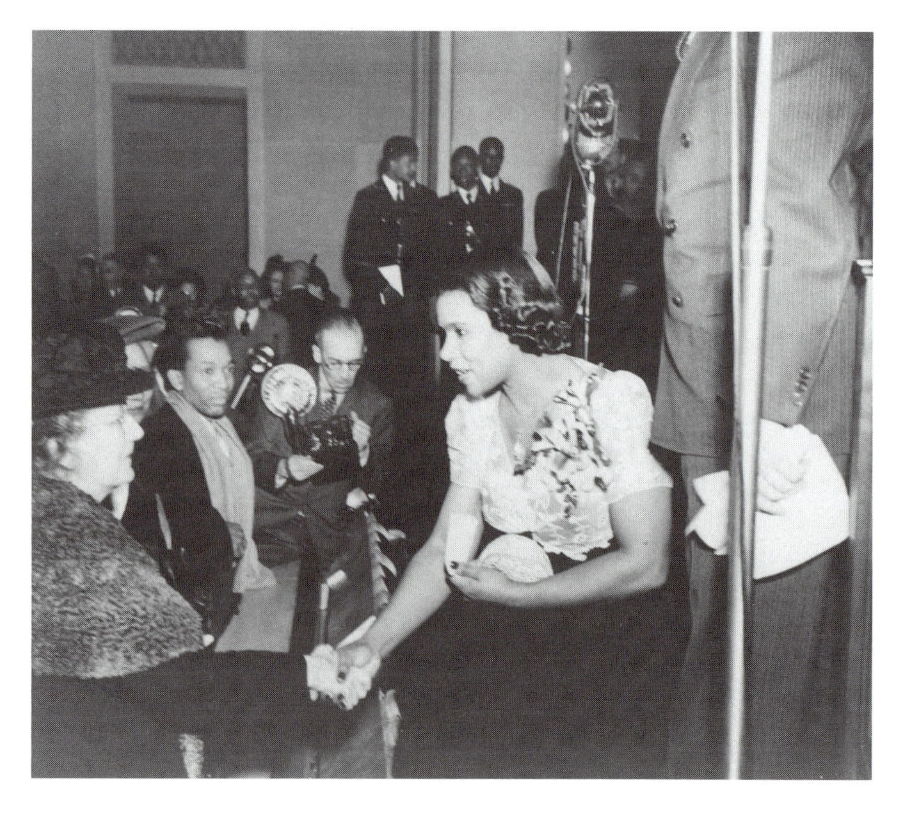

Figure 11.5
Marian Anderson's performance repertoire included fifty Florence Price art songs. Anderson's performance of Price's "Song to a Dark Virgin," based on a text written by Langston Hughes, propelled Price to further fame, when black artists such as Leontyne Price and Roland Hayes also began to sing Price's songs. Here, Anderson is seen greeting admirers after a performance.
Source: Photo courtesy of the Library of Congress

prominent people in the Chicago arts scene.[20] Over time, she became connected with leading musical and literary figures such as singer Marian Anderson (1897–1993) and writer Langston Hughes (1902–1967). Anderson eventually included approximately fifty Price songs in her performance repertoire, one of the most famous of which was "Song to a Dark Virgin." Like the artists of New York's Harlem, black artists on the south side of Chicago produced an outpouring of work that blended vernacular styles with the experiences of urban life.[21]

Despite the artistic and historical significance of Price's work, it was difficult for her to make a living. Price knew that her work was subject to discrimination due to her sex and her race, and her tenacity in self-promotion is evident in the number of times she wrote promotional letters. She wrote to Serge Koussevitzky of the Boston Symphony Orchestra nine times, for example, before he finally examined one of her scores.[22]

In seeking both financial reward and name recognition, Price entered numerous compositional contests. In 1932, her efforts were rewarded when she won the top prize for a symphonic composition in the Wanamaker competition for her *Symphony Number One in E Minor*. Along with the $500 cash prize, the award propelled her to national fame.[23] The work included characteristic African-American musical features, including **call and response**, the

CALL AND RESPONSE
a musical form where one (or more) musician performs a musical phrase or statement (the call), and another soloist or group answers with another phrase or statement (the response)

LISTENING EXPERIENCE 11.3

Piano Sonata in E Minor, **Movement II (1932)**
Florence Price
Playlist

LISTENING FOCUS

Listen for a lyrical theme and syncopated rhythms that are reminiscent of Price's solo vocal works. You may wish to obtain a recording of one of Price's spirituals to make a comparison.

FORM AT A GLANCE

Rondo Form: A B A C A

TIMED LISTENING GUIDE

0:00	A section; statement of syncopated lyrical theme in key of A minor
1:02	B section; new material in key of E major
1:48	A section; return to opening material in key of A minor
2:18	C section; expanded developmental section with modulation
3:49	A section; return to opening material in A minor

PENTATONIC
a five-tone melodic system

SYNCOPATE
to accent a note that falls between main beats

BLUES SCALE
in Western terms, a major scale with flatted third, fifth, and seventh tones

RONDO
musical form in which the opening section (A) recurs between contrasting segments; some sample rondo forms include A B A C A B A and A B A C A

pentatonic scale, **syncopation**, and **blues**-inflected melodies.[24] Price's *Symphony Number 3 in C Minor*, written as a Works Progress Administration project, also infused vernacular elements, but did so more subtly than in her earlier works. In the second movement of her *Piano Sonata in E Minor*, included here, Price utilized the lyrical, syncopated style of her spirituals in combination with a **rondo** form that reflects European-inspired compositional technique. The fusion of ethnic influences with European Romantic-style construction reflected upon life as it truly was at that time for blacks: a blending of rural traditions with the urban life they were living in America's northern cities.[25]

ELLEN TAAFFE ZWILICH (B. 1939)

Yet another symphonic first for a woman in the twentieth century occurred when Ellen Taaffe Zwilich won the Pulitzer Prize in Composition for her *Symphony Number One* in 1983. Zwilich represents a new era for women in composition, one in which educational opportunity truly opened doors. Her skillfully crafted compositional designs, coupled with her ability to aurally appeal to audiences, made Zwilich among the most sought-after composers of the late twentieth century and beyond.

Zwilich credits her musical formation in part to her high school public music program, where she played violin, trumpet, and piano. Her high school

Figure 11.6
Ellen Taaffe Zwilich.
Source: Photo: Florida State University

teacher often created written exercises on the spur of the moment to demonstrate musical concepts during lessons. As such, Zwilich learned to view composition as a very natural activity. Along with attaining early compositional experience in high school, she was also afforded early opportunities to conduct. It was important knowledge for an aspiring composer.[26]

Zwilich earned both bachelor's and master's degrees from Florida State University (in 1960 and 1962). She performed as a member of the American Symphony Orchestra under Leopold Stokowski from 1965 to 1972, in an era when relatively few women were hired in professional orchestras. Zwilich's high-level performance skills, ensemble experience, and personal performance knowledge on piano, strings, and brass brought important compositional understanding to the table. Zwilich deems modern orchestral members capable of virtuosic technique, and therefore writes technically challenging passages for all sections of the orchestra, including low brass and percussion. Her music is as appealing to performers as it is to audiences.[27]

In 1975, Zwilich became the first woman to earn a doctorate in composition from Juilliard, where she studied with Elliott Carter (b. 1908) and Roger Sessions (1896–1985). In an era when surviving as a composer was difficult regardless of sex, she earned a living as a composer and only joined the faculty of Florida State University in 2000. Zwilich's list of awards and honors is extremely long, and includes multiple honorary doctorates and composer-in-residence appointments, multiple awards for best new works, and multiple Grammy nominations. She continues to receive a steady stream of commissions and the list of her works is long and varied.[28] She has composed a series of concertos for standard instruments such as violin, oboe, bassoon, horn, and, at the time of writing, has composed five symphonies, a ballet, works for voice and chorus, works for band, and chamber music works.

Zwilich's Compositional Voice

Zwilich's work spans numerous genres and styles, but she is consistently known for writing challenging music with a modern sound and attention to formal design. Her large-scale works, such as the one featured here, tend to be cast in traditional formats. She is known for writing aggressive, rhythmically intense music.

Developmental forms are commonly used to structure Zwilich's works, and are the mark of a well-educated composer. Developmental variation, in which a small amount of basic musical material is transformed throughout a work, provides unity and structure to her work.[29] By blending precise neoclassical forms with appealing neo-Romantic orchestration, Zwilich has found favor with music analysts and audiences alike.

LISTENING EXPERIENCE 11.4

Symphony Number One, Movement I (1983)
Ellen Taaffe Zwilich
Score available in the *New Historical Anthology of Music by Women*
Playlist

LISTENING FOCUS

Listen for developmental variation of the opening ascending minor third throughout the movement. The interval is transformed both melodically and harmonically.

FORM AT A GLANCE

Slow introduction; intense center section; slow ending.

TIMED LISTENING GUIDE

Part One: Introduction

0:07	ascending minor third (A–C), introduced by violas and harp; tonality and instrumentation gradually expands, with cello and English horn (0:16) moving in perfect fifths against the minor third
0:35	upper strings perform compound minor third (wide leap upward)
0:47	violins, flute, and oboe play falling and rising motive comprised of two sets of minor thirds; D–B falling, C–E♭ rising
0:56	compound minor third "leaping" motive in high strings
1:02	rising horn line
1:16	piccolo/flute eighth notes play new theme derived from minor thirds; other layers continue
1:53	minor third motive in trumpet, with piccolo, flute, and strings playing minor thirds at other pitch levels; acceleration
2:11	aggressive brass statement of opening material (minor thirds against perfect fifths)
2:23	harmonic stacking of thirds along with melodic motion

Center Section

2:39	horns present "soaring statement" based on narrow minor third and wide leap to compound major third
2:43	trombones, then trumpets respond to horn with harmonically stacked thirds (eighth notes)
3:08	brass play compound soaring statement; multiple voices join as timbres are added and subtracted
3:17	piano and strings play transformed eighth note theme
3:38	snare drum signifies transition
3:57	soaring statement in violin, trombone, and trumpet
4:06	piano and bass play derived eighth note theme
4:22	trombones present soaring statement

Ending

4:50	tubular bell sounds; tempo slows
5:00	eighth note motive fragments in piccolo, flute, and piano
5:15	tubular bell "tolls"
5:51	minor third in oboe
6:06	cello plays rhythmically elongated descending motive taken from bars 13–15
6:29	minor third in viola and cello
6:46	first violin moves up to E♭, foreshadowing subsequent movements

Zwilich's *Symphony Number One*

Originally titled *Three Movements for Orchestra*, Zwilich's first symphony features developmental variation of material found in the initial fifteen measures of the work. A simple opening statement of an ascending minor third transforms both harmonically and melodically throughout the three movements of the symphony. The **motive** undergoes shifts in rhythm and timbre, and is used to mark formal segments. Because the construction of the movement is theoretically complex, this analysis will provide only a general introduction to the idea of developmental variation. Readers who are interested in detailed analyses are encouraged to seek material suggested in the chapter notes.[30]

MOTIVE
a short rhythmic or melodic idea that recurs in a work

CHEN YI (B. 1953)

> *I want to speak in a natural way in my own language, and that is a combination of everything I have learned from the past—what I learned in the conservatory, and what I learned in the field collecting folk songs . . . If you just put them together as Eastern and Western, then it sounds artificial . . . But if you can merge them in your blood, then they sound natural together.*[31]
>
> Chen Yi

Chen Yi's compositional voice reflects a fusion of music of the East and the West.[32] The daughter of two medical doctors, she began studying both violin and piano as a three year old. During China's cultural revolution of the 1960s, she practiced in secret, muting both her piano and her viola. When she was fifteen years old, Chen Yi's family home was seized by the government, and all five family members were separated. She spent two years doing forced labor in the fields, where she carried rocks and planted rice. Despite the agony of her work, the young musician saw the assignment as a way to learn about the authentic folk music of her country. She learned traditional Chinese folk music of the farmers and laborers she encountered, and carried the music with her in her compositional work. "I learned Chinese music language very deeply, into my mind and into the spirit," she said.[33]

When she was just seventeen, Chen Yi was called by the government to assist with the Beijing opera, and she witnessed first-hand the blending of Eastern and Western instruments as Jiang Qing, Communist Party leader Mao Tse-Tung's third wife, decreed that Western instruments should be added to China's traditional opera ensemble. Chen Yi was made concertmaster of the opera company, and for an eight-year period she also wrote music and learned the fingerings for almost every traditional Chinese instrument. The blending

Figure 11.7
Chen Yi.
Source: Photo by Kuandi Photos. Courtesy of Chen Yi

of sounds that she experienced became an important element of her mature compositional style.[34]

In 1986, Chen Yi became the first woman in China to receive a Master of Arts in composition. After moving to the United States, she received a doctorate from Columbia, and has held numerous prestigious appointments. As composer-in-residence with the Women's Philharmonic, Chanticleer, and Aptos Creative Arts Program, she wrote the work included in this text, *Chinese Myths Cantata*. Chen Yi also has received fellowships from the Guggenheim Foundation and the National Endowment for the Arts, first prize in the Chinese National Composition Competition, the Lili Boulanger Award, and many other honors. She has held collegiate teaching positions as well, formerly at the Peabody Conservatory, and then at the conservatory of the University of Missouri at Kansas City, where she remains, at the time of writing.[35]

CANTATA
based on the Italian "to sing"; sacred or secular vocal work with performance forces ranging from soloist to chorus and orchestra

THROUGH-COMPOSED
works in which new music is used for each section, as opposed to forms in which segments regularly recur

Chinese Myths Cantata

JoAnn Falletta was the first American conductor to program Chen Yi's work. The recording featured on the playlist is by the Women's Philharmonic, under the direction of Falletta, along with the male vocal ensemble Chanticleer. Traditional Chinese instruments, including the erhu (fiddle), yangqin (dulcimer), pipa (lute), and zheng (zither) fuse with dance, chorus, screened projections, and Western orchestral instruments. Rather than using traditional

LISTENING EXPERIENCE 11.5

"Nü Wa Creates Humans," Movement II from *Chinese Myths Cantata* (1996)
Chen Yi
Companion CD Track 9

LISTENING FOCUS

Listen for a blending of chorus, Chinese instruments, and Western instruments as musical motives are used to symbolize elements of a Chinese creation myth.

FORM AT A GLANCE

Through-composed

TIMED LISTENING GUIDE

Presentation of Nü Wa and Nü Wa Roaming the Earth

0:00 interrelated motives of seconds and sevenths are presented by traditional Chinese instruments; multiple instruments and motives represent Nü Wa's complex nature

0:45 Western instruments enter to signify Nü Wa's ability to bodily transform

1:24 glissandi in strings alternate with traditional Chinese instruments to depict the swaying of Nü Wa's snakelike body as she roams the earth; orchestral winds enter

Nü Wa Reflects by a Pond

2:38 abrupt stop and brief pause indicate Nü Wa seated next to a pond

2:44 Chinese instruments represent Nü Wa, Western instruments represent reflection in the water

3:24 extended solo indicates Nü Wa's delight at her reflection

3:58 woodblock solo (fast, slow, fast) indicates Nü Wa contemplating her next action[36]

Nü Wa Creates Human Beings

4:16 Nü Wa creates first human being; 4:27 human voice responds

4:35 Nü Wa creates; 4:50 human voice responds

5:00 Nü Wa creates; 5:16 human voices respond

5:33 Nü Wa; 5:40 human voices

5:52 Nü Wa; 6:00 human voices

6:25 solo group of Chinese instruments featured, Western instruments add to intensity

6:37 increasing number of voices indicate faster creation of humans; percussion added

7:27 brass enter, texture thickens

7:43 voices swoop upward, depicting the twirling vine

8:05 brass and string glissandi whip upward to depict twirling vine

8:11 voices swoop up and down, moving with the vine; spattering mud drops become human

9:05 forceful glissandi and intense percussion depict population explosion

9:30 voices, including audience, laugh, yell, and speak in nonsense syllables, indicative of massive creation[37]

FOCUS TOPIC 11.1

Genre Focus: Multimedia Works

Multimedia works involve non-musical forces, which may include dancing, film, staging, and other special effects, as part of the performance. Listening to a soundtrack from a multimedia work can be equated to attending a movie while wearing a blindfold. One must remember that a significant aspect of the performance is missing. Still, some multimedia works, including Chen Yi's *Chinese Myths Cantata*, feature such intriguing music that stand-alone soundtracks are embraced by the public.

Chinese folk music and rewriting it for Western orchestra in a stereotypical manner, Chen Yi skillfully maintains authenticity via sophisticated writing that requires Western instruments to either maintain original melodic elements or to provide dissonant or percussive backdrops. To further assure authenticity, Chinese instruments always present themes initially and are echoed in selective ways by Western instruments.[38] Largely **atonal**, *Chinese Myths Cantata* utilizes tonal elements in the presentation of themes. The **programmatic** nature of the work also appeals to a variety of audiences.

ATONAL
lacking a tonal center, or "key"

PROGRAM MUSIC
instrumental work that tells a story or suggests a non-musical idea; may actually be associated with a written program, but sometimes only includes a suggestive title

Chinese creation myth says that after the giant Pan Gu created the heavens and earth, Nü Wa created humans. The second movement of the *Cantata*, included here, tells the story of Nü Wa. To symbolize the complexity of Nü Wa's nature (her snake-like body can transform appearance up to seventy times a day), Chen Yi utilized a multi-layered, changing motive created simultaneously by multiple Chinese instruments. Nü Wa's response to her reflection in water is characterized by Western instruments echoing the traditional instruments, while voices in the chorus represent the humans that the goddess fashioned out of mud. In live performance, the vocalists combine with increasing numbers of dancers on stage, representing the increasing number of humans on earth. Nü Wa eventually produces the humans en masse by dipping a vine into the pond and swirling it around, and as the numbers exponentially increase, the chorus on stage invites the audience to join in the sound. At the climax, the entire concert hall is involved in the powerful creation story.[39]

THEA MUSGRAVE (B. 1928)

Born in Scotland in 1928, Thea Musgrave began her studies with the intent of becoming a medical doctor. After she settled on a career in music, she attained a postgraduate scholarship for work with Nadia Boulanger from 1950 to 1954, and also studied with Aaron Copland. Musgrave's compositions are known for the discipline and importance of every bar that was instilled in all pupils of Boulanger, and in 1952, Musgrave won the Lili Boulanger Memorial Prize in composition, the first Scottish composer to do so. Musgrave has been extremely successful on both sides of the Atlantic, with commissions from BBC Scotland as early as 1954 and a teaching career at Queens College in New York beginning in 1987. She is also a respected conductor, having frequently conducted her own works. Musgrave has received major awards from the Koussevitzky Foundation, has been awarded two Guggenheim Fellowships, and has been awarded several honorary degrees. In 2008, she celebrated her eightieth birthday with the premiere of two new works.[40]

Throughout her long career, Musgrave has explored a wide variety of compositional techniques, including serialism, **electroacoustic** techniques, and a style she calls dramatic-abstract, in which instruments take on personages and perform dramatically without a program. In these works, the players have a freedom of expression in which they cue one another and are sometimes asked to stand during performance. Similarly, she has experimented with acoustics and spatial separation of performers, sometimes requiring them to move around on stage.[41]

ELECTROACOUSTIC
general term that describes multi-faceted music genres, all of which use electronic technology to allow access to sound

Musgrave's operas are among her most highly regarded achievements and showcase her keen sense of drama and staging. Prestigious commissions indicate the high regard with which her operatic work is held. *Harriet, the Woman Called Moses* (1985) was jointly commissioned by the Royal Opera and Virginia Opera, while *Simon Bolivar* (1995) was jointly commissioned by the Los Angeles Music Center Opera and Scottish Opera. Her widely popular *Mary Queen of Scots* (1977) and *A Christmas Carol* (1979) are among her most performed works. Musgrave's atonal language is made palatable to wider audience by her return to pitch centers, use of unifying devices such as **leitmotivs**, and her excellent sense of drama. In *Mary Queen of Scots*, for example, a "Mary" chord recurs throughout the opera while melodic themes for the main characters help with the drama and unification. The strength of the title character is powerfully shown amid the composer's excellent sense of dramatic presentation. Similarly, Musgrave's *Harriet, the Woman Called Moses* uses a flashback technique that portrays Harriet Tubman plotting to return to the South to free slaves.[42]

LEITMOTIV
German for "lead motive;" a musical idea that represents a person, event or idea in a dramatic work

Although highly regarded for her atonal work, Musgrave is equally adept at writing tonal music, as is evidenced in her 2003 six-movement work *Turbulent Landscapes,* commissioned by the Boston Symphony Orchestra. Musgrave's sense of the dramatic is keenly evident as she brings to life a set of paintings by English Romantic painter Joseph Mallord William Turner (1775–1851) with deep, dark timbres, sweeping chromatic passages, and crashing percussion. The listener is drawn to a story first told on canvas, now brought to life again via music.

LISTENING EXPERIENCE 11.6

"The Shipwreck," Movement II from *Turbulent Landscapes* (2003)
Thea Musgrave
Playlist

LISTENING FOCUS

"The Shipwreck" is the second movement of Musgrave's six-movement *Turbulent Landscapes*, based on the seascapes of Joseph Mallord William Turner (1775–1851), an English painter of the Romantic period. Three Turner paintings inspire this movement: *Staffa Fingal's Cave* (1832), *The Shipwreck* (1805), and *Dawn after the Wreck* (1841).

FORM AT A GLANCE

Through-composed, programmatic.

TIMED LISTENING GUIDE

Staffa Fingal's Cave/The Shipwreck

0:00	gathering storm; undulating strings reference Felix Mendelssohn's *Hebrides "Fingal's Cave" Overture*
0:35	rapid string passages and sweeping wind parts simulate wind and waves; storm building in intensity
1:28	cymbal crashes; winds in rapid chromatic passages as storm intensifies; dissonant blasts from the brass
2:20	massive cymbal crash, followed by descending pitch and slowing tempo indicate sinking of ship

Dawn after the Wreck

3:07	solo oboe represents lone survivor mourning for the dead

SUMMARY

The twentieth century is known for its musical diversity, with styles ranging from serialism to postmodern exploration, including the incorporation of popular music styles into art music works. It was a century in which many composers initially alienated their audiences and relied on university employment to make a living. It was also a century that saw a return to works and styles that were intended to engage audiences. Women were actively engaged in all aspects of this musical diversity, and while concern for audience and performers is evident in all of the works selected for this chapter, it would be equally easy to find works that negate this trend. The debate regarding the existence of a distinctive compositional voice for women will likely continue for some time, but what is abundantly evident is that women's compositional work in large-scale genres is here to stay.

In a famous article on sociological change and the diminishing role of piano performance as a primary musical expectation for women at the turn of the twentieth century, Judith Tick declared, "Passed away is the piano girl."[43] At the beginning of the twenty-first century, we can join in the song and declare, "Passed away is the relegation of women to the compositional realm of small-scale chamber works and vocal genres."

QUESTIONS FOR CRITICAL THINKING AND DISCUSSION

1. In an all-class discussion, discuss access to higher education for men and women in your family in the twentieth century. At what point did women in your family become involved, and what impact did it have?
2. Access one or two music history textbooks and investigate the portrayal of the women discussed in this chapter. Are they fully integrated into the story, or is their work treated separately? Discuss your findings.
3. Should the composer be concerned with reaching audiences and performers with music that is "pleasing?" Present arguments for and against this practice, and especially consider how societal expectations for women might have impacted the type of music they composed.
4. Access the Turner paintings that inspired Musgrave's *Turbulent Landscapes* (easily available online). Make comparisons between the visual and timbral palettes utilized by Turner and Musgrave.

IDEAS FOR FURTHER RESEARCH

1. Investigate the life and musical work of Ethel Smyth and compare it to that of Amy Beach.
2. Select three women who studied composition with Nadia Boulanger. Compare and contrast their compositional styles.
3. Investigate the libretti (written stories) of Musgrave's *Harriet, the Woman Called Moses*, and *Mary Queen of Scots*, and compare Musgrave's portrayal of female characters with characterizations of women in nineteenth-century German and Italian opera.
4. Investigate an Eastern "classical" tradition in terms of its inclusion of women. How does it compare to the Western tradition?

CHAPTER 12

Old Genres, New Sounds

Contemporary Music and Experimental Voices

This chapter highlights the work of women who were engaged in experimental and contemporary acoustic music in the twentieth century, with a particular focus on works for chamber ensembles of various sizes. The compositions included in the discussion are diverse, ranging from the experimental work of Elisabeth Lutyens, Ruth Crawford Seeger, and Meredith Monk, to the contemporary sounds of Joan Tower, Shulamit Ran, and Barbara Kolb.

Experimental music has historically been met with trepidation and resistance by many listeners. At the same time, however, those who created experimental music have been celebrated by those who record music history. Thus, composers who delve into the new and experimental realm often stand alone during their lifetimes, only to be revered when their groundbreaking work is considered in historical context. Women have been involved in experimental music since its inception, and arguably have not been subjected to any greater scrutiny than male experimentalists during their lifetimes. At the same time, the experimental work of women was often ignored by the community of scholars and writers who most embraced the **avant-garde**, and who captured the newest trends on paper for posterity.

AVANT-GARDE
a French military term, meaning to be in advance of others; in music, refers to those who lead the way to the artistic future, even at the expense of risk

FOCUS TOPIC 12.1

Genre Focus: Gender and the Avant-garde

Before you read on, use what you already know from other sections of the text to make some connections between gender connotations and the term "avant-garde." Even though women have long been associated with chamber music, how does the "avant-garde" designation impact issues of gender in music?

"NEW" AND EXPERIMENTAL

Some music terms are notoriously difficult to define, but the terms "new" and "experimental" yield an especially wide range of definitions, since they describe art music that frequently changes. Still, both "experimental" and "new" music are commonly understood to have twentieth-century roots. The **experimental music** label first came into use in the early decades of the twentieth century, when composers in Europe and America began to explore elements of music using new notation, techniques, and resources. When electricity became available, for example, experimental composers explored its musical possibilities. Other "experiments" included creation of new instruments as well as development of extended techniques that drew new timbres from old sources. (For example, rather than performing the piano in the traditional manner, an extended technique would be to reach inside the instrument and strum the strings.) Similarly, a vocalist might growl, or sing in extreme ranges. Experimental structures were diverse too. On one end of the spectrum was the strictest of formal designs, with musical elements such as melody and rhythm mathematically manipulated using set theory. On the other end was an absence of strict form, where works of **chance** were left to random procedures such as coin tossing. Tonality was often abandoned in favor of **atonal** and **polytonal** styles.

The "new music" label (also called contemporary music) has been widely associated with the period after 1945, and, like experimental music, is an umbrella term for many subgenres. Spectral and electroacoustic composition (defined and discussed in Chapter 14), **postmodernism**, and **minimalism** are just a few of the "new music" categories that emerged. A number of women who began their careers using **serial** techniques and atonal styles turned to music that was more accessible to audiences as part of a late-twentieth century aesthetic shift, and in so doing recaptured an audience that had grown weary of aurally challenging dissonance. Elisabeth Lutyens, however, remained dedicated to atonal music throughout her career.

EXPERIMENTAL MUSIC
a twentieth-century term associated with music that explores new and unusual sounds and compositional techniques

CHANCE
music in which random procedures (such as coin tossing) determine the outcome of a work

ATONAL
lacking a tonal center, or "key"

POLYTONAL
utilizes more than one key at once

POSTMODERNISM
an aesthetic that reflects fragmentation, rejects boundaries between high and low art, and is not opposed to embracing the past; *modernism* rejects the old in favor of the new

MINIMALISM
artistic movement that used small elements of repeated material that evolved slowly over time; emerged in the 1960s

SERIALISM
an atonal compositional method that systematically orders musical elements according to a fixed series

ELISABETH LUTYENS (1906–1983)

Examining the work of Elisabeth Lutyens is a good way to begin an exploration of women's work in experimental music. Although Lutyens is highly regarded today, she was a lone voice throughout much of her lifetime. Born in London in 1906 to renowned architect Edwin Lutyens and Lady Emily Lytton, Elisabeth Lutyens was not from a musical family, but neither did the family discourage Elisabeth's musical study. She studied piano and violin as a child, but initially composed in secret. Lutyens admired the work of French composers Claude Debussy (1862–1918) and Maurice Ravel (1875–1937) and went to Paris in

LISTENING EXPERIENCE 12.1

"Magnificat" (1965)
Elisabeth Lutyens
Playlist

LISTENING FOCUS

Like sonata or rondo form, dodecaphonic technique is a structural device. Listen for the opening soprano line, as it clearly sets forth the tone row used in this work. Also notice how Lutyens interrupts the row in order to highlight specific words in the text. While we will not attempt to follow the serial structure throughout the work, keep in mind that it is continually operating beneath the surface. As the listening guide progresses, frequent word painting is indicated.

FORM AT A GLANCE

Twelve-tone composition, opening with the following prime form, where T and E indicate pitches ten and eleven. See Figure 12.1.

TEXT (taken from the Gospel of Luke)

My soul doth magnify the Lord, and my spirit hath rejoiced in God my Savior, for He hath regarded the lowliness of His handmaiden

For behold, from henceforth all generations shall call me blessed, for He that is mighty hath magnified me; and holy is His name, and His mercy is on them that fear Him throughout all generations

He hath showed strength with His arm; He hath scattered the proud, in the imagination of their hearts; He hath put down the mighty from their seat, and hath exalted the humble and meek

He hath filled the hungry with good things, and the rich He hath sent empty away.

He, remembering His mercy, hath helped His servant Israel, as He promised to our forefathers, Abraham and His seed forever.

Glory be to the Father, to the Son and the Holy Ghost, as it was in the beginning, is now, and ever shall be, world without end, Amen.

TIMED LISTENING GUIDE

0:00	opening row heard in the soprano line
0:05	alto, tenor, and bass lines enter with the retrograde inversion of the original row, beginning at three different locations in the row
0:07	row interrupted to highlight the text "magnify;" row resumes
0:32	"savior" highlighted with chordal treatment; row resumes
1:24	"doth magnify" highlighted by women singing in octaves
1:38	"holy is his name" highlighted with pianissimo chordal treatment of the text
2:07	"He hath showed strength" highlighted by male voices
2:24	"scattered the proud" highlighted with rhythmic motion
3:15	"empty away" highlighted with rising solo bass line
4:25	"as it was in the beginning" highlighted with solo tenor line
4:53	final syllable of the "amen" moves to an F-major chord with an added B

Figure 12.1
The opening soprano line from Lutyen's "Magnificat."

1922 to study at the École Normale, before she returned to England in 1926 to study composition and viola at London's Royal College of Music with Harold Darke (1888–1976).

Lutyens' compositional voice was not inclined toward the work of English composers such as Ralph Vaughan Williams (1872–1958) and others of the Royal College. Instead, she discovered serial composition, inspired in part by the work of Anton Webern (1883–1945).[1] Her serial works of the 1930s were among the first composed in Britain, making her arguably the most radical British composer of her era.

PALINDROME
a row of letters or numbers that can be read the same way in either direction; in music, refers to a row of notes or rhythms

DODECAPHONIC
a type of composition based on the manipulation of a row or series of twelve chromatic pitches that are contained within an octave; often called twelve-tone technique

Although Lutyens explored neoclassicism and other styles, her serial vocal music is probably the most impressive of her work, where she utilized tight formal organization using **palindromes** and other **dodecaphonic** techniques. Even among serial composers, however, Lutyens was an experimentalist, as she personalized the style by employing a fourteen-note series, among other original structures.[2]

To offer support to young composers like herself who found little acknowledgement in Britain, Lutyens collaborated with Royal College of Music students Anne Macnaghten and Iris Lemare in 1931 to found the Macnaghten-Lemare concert series in London. The series was largely run by women, and the resident quartet was comprised entirely of women. The modern music featured in the concert series included works of Benjamin Britten (1913–1976) and Alan Rawsthorne (1905–1971), as well as the work of Lutyens herself and a number of other composers who became well known after first appearing in this series.[3]

Like many composers who favored serialism, Lutyens expanded her compositional range in part for financial reasons. As the sole financial provider for her three children, she frequently wrote music that was accessible to the general public, including music for film and radio, as well as cabaret-style songs. In the 1960s, Lutyens' compositional embrace expanded to include works for the musical stage and a more abstract style that featured sparse materials and a sense of timelessness created by rhythmic freedom and selective silence.[4] During the same era, she was able to blend her personalized serialism with the popular media industry when Hammer Films deemed her material suitable for films such as *Dr. Terror's House of Horrors* and *The Skull*.

Despite the fact that she favored an intense, dissonant style and technically challenging writing, Lutyens' ability to write lyrically is evident in her concert works as well as her commercial ventures. Although her serial works were aurally challenging, they also featured clear text projection and lyricism. In addition to more than 200 film and radio scores, Lutyens' compositional output included six operas, nineteen orchestral works, twenty-five works for voices and instruments, thirteen choral works, almost fifty chamber music works, over thirty solo songs, and works for piano and organ.

Lutyens' innovative compositional voice put her outside of Britain's art music mainstream for many years, and her main supporters were innovative musicians who were much younger than herself.[5] It was only when music of German serial composers Anton Webern (1883–1945) and Alban Berg (1885–1935) became better known in Britain that Lutyens gradually gained recognition for her pioneering work. In 1969 she received official recognition in Britain when she was made a Commander of the Order of the British Empire.[6] Today, Lutyens is remembered in Britain and elsewhere as a creative artist, an inspiring teacher, and a tremendous contributor to Britain's musical life, a musician "for whom compromise was impossible."[7]

"Magnificat"

British composers have a long tradition of setting English translations of the Latin "Magnificat" text, taken from the Gospel of Luke. Associated with the Office of Vespers, the "Magnificat" in England became part of the Evensong tradition of the Anglican church. Although Lutyens was engaging in a tradition with roots some fourteen centuries old, she painted the ancient text with decidedly twentieth-century tonal colors.[8] (For additional insight on serialism, see Focus Topic 12.2.)

RUTH CRAWFORD SEEGER (1901–1953)

Some readers may be familiar with the Seeger name in terms of the Seeger family connection to folk music. Indeed, Ruth Crawford Seeger was a familiar name in music throughout much of the twentieth century due to her extensive work as a music educator, folk music specialist, and preservationist. Until recently, it was lesser known that Seeger's experimental voice of the 1920s and 1930s was then considered among "the most independent, able and promissory of the new American composers."[9] She was a contemporary of experimentalists Henry Cowell (1897–1965), and Edgard Varese (1883–1965), and was the first woman to win a Guggenheim Fellowship in composition. A resurgence of interest in Seeger's experimental work was evidenced at the turn of the twenty-first century with the publication of numerous articles and books. In 2001, a festival celebrating her work was sponsored by the Institute for Studies in American Music and the Conservatory of Music at Brooklyn

FOCUS TOPIC 12.2

Technique Focus: Serialism and Twelve-Tone Composition

Serialism is a twentieth-century compositional technique in which rhythms or pitches are grouped into sets, and then those sets are repeated or altered to create music. Common forms of set alteration include transposition (changing the pitch level of the original set), retrograde motion (executing the original set in reverse), inverse motion (executing a mirror image of a set), and retrograde inversion (executing the mirror image in reverse order).

Twelve-tone composition is a specific form of serialism in which the twelve discreet chromatic pitches found within an octave are ordered in a "tone row" and used to form the basic structure of a work. To help facilitate the analysis of such works, each of the chromatic pitches are assigned integers. T and E indicate pitches ten and eleven. A set matrix identifies all possible transpositions, inversions, and retrogrades of a given set. In the matrix for Lutyens' "Magnificat," the soprano melody can be seen along the top of the matrix. Courtesy of Albert Pinsonneault.

Prime →
Inversion ↓

← Retrograde
Inversion ↓

Soprano →	2	4	E	1	0	6	T	9	7	8	5	3	
	0	2	9	E	T	4	8	7	5	6	3	1	
	5	7	2	4	3	9	1	0	T	E	8	6	
	3	5	0	2	1	7	E	T	8	9	6	4	
	4	6	1	3	2	8	0	E	9	T	7	5	
	T	0	7	9	8	2	6	5	3	4	1	E	
	6	8	3	5	4	T	2	1	E	0	9	7	← Bass
	7	9	4	6	5	E	3	2	0	1	T	8	
	9	E	6	8	7	1	5	4	2	3	0	T	
	8	T	5	7	6	0	4	3	1	2	E	9	
	E	1	8	T	9	3	7	6	4	5	2	0	
	1	3	T	0	E	5	9	8	6	7	4	2	
	Alto ↑							Tenor ↑					

↑ Retrograde
Inversion
Prime →

↑ Retrograde
Inversion
← Retrograde

Figure 12.2
Ruth Crawford Seeger.
Source: Used by permission of Kim Seeger

College, New York. It was a fitting tribute to a very deserving composer, a true leader in experimental music.

Born in Ohio, and raised in Florida, Seeger's musical training and intended career path were connected to piano performance. She abandoned the "usual" path for women, however, when she began her studies at the American Conservatory of Music in Chicago, eventually earning a Master of Music degree in composition. Her study with Djane Lavoie Herz (b. 1889), an expert on the music of Alexander Scriabin (1872–1915), piqued an interest in mysticism in music. She explored eastern religious thought and transcendentalism, steeping herself in the writings of Henry David Thoreau and Ralph Waldo Emerson, as well as the poetry of Carl Sandburg, whose work she set to music. From 1924 to 1929, Seeger focused on very dissonant and unusual harmony, connecting to a spiritual transcendentalism inspired by Scriabin and her readings.

After meeting Henry Cowell, who suggested that she study with his first teacher, Charles Seeger, Ruth Crawford became increasingly interested in serialism, and learned to utilize serial control over elements of pitch, dynamics, and rhythm. She experimented extensively with the piano as well, using unique pedaling techniques, ostinato patterns, and chord clusters. Thematic transformation, strong contrasting rhythms, and extreme keyboard ranges were also used. Ruth was a key proponent of Charles Seeger's **dissonant counterpoint**, a method that combined two or more dissonant melodic lines simultaneously. Using that technique, Crawford was able to create clean, rhythmically independent melodic lines that created a sense of a tonal center despite their atonal nature. She eventually helped Seeger write a book that explained his theoretical concepts, and the two musicians were married shortly thereafter. Within five years, she became the mother of three children.[10]

DISSONANT COUNTERPOINT
a compositional method in which two or more dissonant melodic lines are simultaneously combined

The 1930s brought a dramatic change to the Seegers' career path. Along with her husband Charles and Charles' son Pete, Ruth became involved in a folk music preservation project funded by the Works Project Administration (WPA). Collaborating with father-and-son ethnomusicologists John and Alan Lomax, Charles and Ruth were integral in developing the folk music archives

LISTENING EXPERIENCE 12.2

"Rat Riddles" from
***Three Songs for Contralto, Oboe, Piano, Percussion, and Orchestral Ostinati* (1930–1932)**
Ruth Crawford Seeger
Score available in the *New Historical Anthology of Music by Women*
Playlist

LISTENING FOCUS

Alto, oboe, percussion, and piano depict a dialogue between a poet and a wise rat; listen to the piano and oboe "chase" each other with rat-like scurrying.

FORM AT A GLANCE

Serial organization (recall Lutyens) mixed with free material; timbre and texture exploration as well, with musical phrasing that links to the poetic text.

TIMED LISTENING GUIDE

0:00	opening percussion
0:04	piano entrance, following by oboe at 0:05; note the "scurrying" rhythm (0:16)
0:28	voice of the poet enters; notice pitch centering on words "gray" and "green"
0:53	rat contemplates answer to the poet's question
1:06	poet's voice heard again; pitch again centers on A♭ on "green"
1:29	rat's response
1:39	poet describes the rat's response; pitch centering again on "green"
1:56	alto takes the part of the rat, with a deep, recitative-like text expression
2:44	rat scurries away; "and the tail of the green-eyed rat whipped and was gone . . ."
2:59	percussion and piano close

at the Library of Congress. Ruth edited and transcribed melodies from field recordings, and was instrumental in editing the folk song anthology begun by the Lomax family. The papers and music manuscripts of the Seeger family remain an important part of the American Folklore Center at the Library of Congress. Ruth also contributed to American music education by collecting three books of American folk songs for home and school use that were published between 1948 and 1953. The Seeger family legacy continued strongly after Ruth's death, with connections to the urban folk music revival in the 1950s and 1960s.

FOCUS TOPIC 12.3

Technique Focus: The Complexity Beneath the Surface of "Rat Riddles"

For listeners unaccustomed to experimental composition, works such as "Rat Riddles" may appear to be more structurally simple than is actually the case. Ruth Crawford Seeger's "Rat Riddles" takes just under three minutes to perform, but has been the subject of an abundance of graduate-level research papers and book segments for good reason: the structural design is phenomenally innovative and complex. While we cannot get a complete sense of the structure here, consider a few of the structures that underlie the melodic portion of the work. (We will not even consider the rhythmic and harmonic organization.) Readers who are interested may wish to access the analysis by Joseph Straus.[a]

Here is a condensed and simplified version of Straus' analysis of the melodic structure of this short work:

1. The first six notes in the vocal line form the basis for all that happens with the ensuing melody. Those notes immediately begin to overlap with an inverted expansion of the original notes.
2. The entire melody can be read from left to right, going down the page, thus the material is also vertically aligned.
3. The original six notes are restated twenty-one times, and at the end of each statement, the melody almost always leaps by tritone (dissonant interval of an augmented fourth) to the next variation.
4. The twenty-two melodic statements form larger units that conform to the structure of the poetry. Grammatical poetic units deliberately end in the middle of musical variations, contributing to the heterophonic effect.
5. Musical repetition within this structure corresponds with text repetition.
6. The "rat's" part in the oboe, perhaps appearing as simple rhythmic scurrying, features pitch organization that is similar to that of the voice part, and utilizes some of its motives.

[a] *The Music of Ruth Crawford Seeger*. Cambridge: Cambridge University Press, 1995.

Ruth Crawford Seeger had just begun to return to experimental composition when she became ill and died of cancer in 1953. Rather than seeing Seeger's dual musical career as two ends of a musical spectrum, Judith Tick posits that Seeger was a leader in connecting modernism to vernacular music, bridging a gap between two areas once thought to be incompatible. As such, she yet again led the way in American experimental music.

"Rat Riddles"

Few art songs approach the structural complexity of "Rat Riddles," the first of *Three Songs to Poems of Carl Sandburg* that Seeger wrote for contralto, oboe, piano, percussion, and orchestral ostinati. Premiered in 1930, the work depicts a conversation between a wise rat and a poet and is a good example of Seeger's use of dissonant counterpoint. Along with a vocal style that is declamatory rather than lyrical, the piano and oboe "chase" each other with a variety of accompaniment figures that allude to rat-like movement. Pitch repetition on key words helps to unify the work. Charles Seeger delightfully called the **tritones** and sevenths in the work "vicious little stabs of dissonance."[11] Crawford-Seeger added to the work in 1930, and again in 1932, by creating additional parts. The composer suggested seating the added performers in separate sections to further highlight the **heterophonic** texture of the piece.

TRITONE
a dissonant interval of an augmented fourth

HETEROPHONIC
texture in which a melody is performed by two or more parts simultaneously, but with variation; for example, one part may be more ornamented than the other

JOAN TOWER (B. 1938)

Although Grammy-award winning composer Joan Tower began her career employing serial techniques, she increasingly turned to lyrical works that were accessible to audiences. Today, with over seventy works to her credit, she is a widely-recognized composer of the latter half of the twentieth century. A champion of new music, Tower founded the internationally acclaimed Da Capo Chamber Players in 1969, and performed with the group as a pianist through 1984. (The group celebrated its twentieth anniversary in 1989 by commissioning Shulamit Ran's *Mirage*, discussed later in this chapter.) Tower was the first woman to receive the Grawemeyer Award in Composition (1990), and was inducted into the American Academy of Arts and Letters in 1998, as well as the Harvard University Academy of Arts and Sciences in 2004. Along with her work as a performer and composer, she has taught at Bard College since 1972 and has served as composer-in-residence for both the St. Louis Symphony and the Orchestra of St. Luke's.

Born in New York, Tower was educated in the United States after spending her childhood in South America, and received both master's and doctoral degrees from Columbia University. She credits her South American experience for making rhythm an important element of her compositional work, and is

Figure 12.3
Joan Tower.
Source: Photo by Bernie Mindich. Used by permission

LISTENING EXPERIENCE 12.3

***Fanfare for the Uncommon Woman*, Number I (1986)**
Joan Tower
Companion CD, Track 10

LISTENING FOCUS

Listen to the interplay of brass (three trumpets, four horns, three trombones, and tuba) with percussion as Marin Alsop conducts this three-minute fanfare.

TIMED LISTENING GUIDE

0:00	opening percussion announcement, as in the Copland fanfare
0:09	trumpet enters on motive that will recur
0:28	three gong hits
0:34	low brass featured in extended segment, with gradual crescendo
1:09	tempo slows
1:17	solo trumpet motive expands to a duet; other voices added
1:46	brass and percussion dialogue
2:10	final statement of opening trumpet motive
2:18	percussion finale leads to final brass chord

also highly regarded for her excellence in orchestration. Throughout her performance career as a pianist with the Da Capo Chamber Players, she was involved in premiering several of her own chamber works, and she continues to write chamber music, along with a substantial number of works for orchestra and other large ensembles.[12]

Natural images are frequently the subjective focus of Tower's work, and she often uses programmatic titles that allude to imagery, including examples such as the string quartet *Night Fields* and the orchestral works *Sequoia* and *Silver Ladders*. Although she does not use detailed programs in her compositional work, the referential titles provide a focal point for audiences. A long-time performer herself, she is known for her commitment to connecting with her intended performers and often knows the musicians for whom she writes.[13] She is also known for her musical tributes, including *Petroushskates* (a tribute to Igor Stravinsky and a reference to his ballet *Petrushka)*, her *Concerto for Piano* (a tribute to Beethoven), and the *Fanfare for the Uncommon Woman* (inspired by Aaron Copland's *Fanfare for the Common Man)*.

The popularity of Tower's first *Fanfare for the Uncommon Woman* led to the composition of four additional fanfares, and, as of 2010, they have been performed by over 500 ensembles.[14] Considered by some to be a feminist response to Copland's fanfare, Tower herself indicated that the first fanfare was intended to "honor women who are adventurous and take risks."[15] She dedicated the work to conductor Marin Alsop, whose recording is included on the playlist.

BARBARA KOLB (B. 1939)

Although her father discouraged her study of music, Barbara Kolb pursued a degree in music education before she turned toward clarinet performance and a master's degree in composition, which she received from the Hartt School of Music. Kolb performed on E♭ clarinet as a member of the Hartford Symphony early in her career, and in the 1960s, studied with Lukas Foss (1922–2009) and Gunther Schuller (b. 1925). She was the first woman to win the American Prix de Rome, and in 1968 was awarded a fellowship for work at the MacDowell Colony. She has since received many additional honors, including awards from the Fromm, Guggenheim, and Koussevitzky Foundations, as well as awards and commissions from the National Endowment for the Arts and composer-in-residence positions. In 1983–1984, she also served as composer-in-residence at the Institut de Recherche et Coordination Acoustique/Musique (IRCAM) in Paris, a prestigious center for electroacoustic and avant-garde composition. Her continued success enables her to live on commissions and grants.

Like Joan Tower, Barbara Kolb is known as a promoter of new music and, along with writing a wide variety of her own experimental works, was the artistic director of contemporary music at the Third Street Settlement Music School in New York, where she presented a new music concert series. Kolb's compositions often focus on texture and visual imagery. She has used multiple compositional techniques to create unique timbral and textural palettes, including the addition of sung or spoken texts to instrumental works, the blending of computer-generated music with live ensembles, and the mixing of unusual instrument combinations. Works such as *Solitaire* not only used musical quotations from nineteenth-century pianist Fredrick Chopin, but also did so via the use of two prerecorded tapes of piano and vibes that are combined and re-played along with a live pianist during performance. Studies in texture are found in works such as *Soundings*, in which orchestral sections play the same elements at different speeds.[16] In *Millefoglie*, a nineteen-minute work for chamber orchestra and computer-generated tape, vertical and horizontal layers of harmonic and rhythmic structures are superimposed.[17] Kolb has often incorporated jazz elements into her works as well, apparent in her ballet score *New York Moonglow* in which her typical dense textures are coupled with segments of improvisation.[18]

Kolb's intense music, with its focus on texture and appeal to expressivity, is often inspired by visual images and poetry, causing comparison to French Impressionism, even though the language of her earlier works was primarily atonal. At the same time, like Joan Tower and other American composers, Kolb began to shift toward tonal music later in her career and increasingly wrote for larger ensembles. In *Extremes*, a work from the late 1980s featured here, she painted a musical picture of opposing timbres and styles in an unusual duet for flute and cello.

LISTENING EXPERIENCE 12.4

Extremes (1988–1989)
Barbara Kolb
Playlist

LISTENING FOCUS

This flute and cello duet explores musical "extremes." Listen for opposite timbres presented by the instruments, as well as opposing rhythmic and stylistic features.

FORM AT A GLANCE

Two connected movements, each expressing stylistic extremes.

TIMED LISTENING GUIDE

Movement One

0:00	rhythmically active flute solo moves against static cello line, expressing rhythmic "extremes"
1:24	cello begins rhythmic movement, joined by flute in rhythmic battle
2:40	softer volume, descending pitch level, slowing tempo
3:16	cello and flute move to unison to close the movement

Movement Two

3:23	cello featured in rhythmic solo (opposite of first movement); flute accompanies with sixteenth note triplets
4:09	cello sustains pitch, then pauses; the duet slows and pitches are sustained
5:36	slow, soft unison, with gradual crescendo and rising pitch
7:03	pause, then duet partners move in rhythmically equal patterns
8:06	flute solo
8:13	return to rhythmic intensity and pitch level of the beginning of movement two

SHULAMIT RAN (B. 1947)

Shulamit Ran is an Israeli American whose dual citizenship is often reflected in works that span the wide variety of genres and styles that she creates. Winner of the 1991 Pulitzer Prize in composition, her early training began in Israel where she studied with Alexander Boskovich (1907–1964) and Paul Ben-Haim (1897–1984). A child prodigy, she came to the United States at the age of fourteen to study at the Mannes College of Music in New York. Along with piano teachers Nadia Reisenberg (1904–1983) and Dorothy Taubman, she studied composition with Norman Dello Joio (1913–2008) and Ralph Shapey (1921–2002). Shapey, a long-time professor at the University of Chicago and director of contemporary music for many years, invited her to join the faculty in 1973 when she was just twenty-six years old.

Ran explains that it is difficult to define a truly nationalistic Israeli style, since Israel is a musical "melting pot." Still, Ran infuses musical elements into her works that many composers recognize as indicative of Israeli music, including the use of Near-Eastern and Mediterranean tonal systems. As a child,

Figure 12.4
Shulamit Ran.
Source: Photo courtesy of Shulamit Ran

Ran often listened to the Jewish cantorial music that her father played on the radio, and she thus also uses such music as a compositional source. In her opera *Between Two Worlds—The Dybbuk*, for example, she uses the shofar in dialogue with brass.

At the same time, Ran's long years of residency in the United States have also impacted her compositional voice, and since she began composing so young, she has undergone many compositional transformations. She states that she is "not the kind of composer who writes the same piece over and over."[19] Ran indicates that she cannot imagine the second half of the twentieth century without Elliot Carter's influence, and that Ralph Shapey helped her to discover how voicing matters, even when the same notes are used. No matter the style, drama and expression are important in all of her works: "I often find myself thinking of musical instruments having souls, (and) . . .

LISTENING EXPERIENCE 12.5

Mirage **(1991)**
Shulamit Ran
Companion CD Track 11

LISTENING FOCUS

Listen for the interplay of five performers: B♭ clarinet, violin, cello, and piano, with one additional performer who covers piccolo/flute/amplified alto flute. The melody is reminiscent of Middle-Eastern modal music, but with chromatic saturation. Also note the extremely virtuosic passages required of the performers.

FORM AT A GLANCE

Asymmetrical arch form, loosely structured, with texturally dense central section.

TIMED LISTENING GUIDE

0:00	thin texture begins the arch with A material performed by solo amplified alto flute; soloist moves freely against static accompaniment in clarinet, violin, and cello
0:59	clarinet moves in counterpoint with flute; violin and cello sustain accompaniment
2:08	piano enters, then other voices join as texture thickens and rhythm intensifies; listen for special effects created by flutter tonguing on winds, string glissandi, and piano pedaling; peak of the arch reached in this extended section
5:52	march-like piano accompanies various combinations of unison pairs and heterophonic passages
7:41	unison passage involving all voices marks move toward thinner texture
8:12	slower tempo, thinner texture
9:32	return of A material featuring solo flute; thinning to nothing

the exploration of that soul is of never-ending interest." Ran treats groups of instruments as actors on a stage, moving them around by pitting one group of voices against another, then placing them side by side. Virtuosic technique is common in her work as well. Ran says that she likes to "push things to the limit." One performer explained it well by declaring that performing Ran's music was like performing a "high wire act."[20]

Mirage

Whatever the style, Ran composes for people and feels a deep connection between her music and her intended performers, whom she often knows. *Mirage* was written by commission of the Da Capo Chamber Players (co-founded by Joan Tower) for their twentieth anniversary. The work evidences Ran's timbral exploration, including the orchestral quality that she draws from the piano via special pedaling techniques, and the amplification of the alto flute. The flute is featured as soloist in the work, while the piano is the "glue" that holds the piece together. Ran explains that she utilized a loosely structured, asymmetrical **arch form.**[21] Expressive markings abound in the score, with ample areas in which the performers breathe life into the music by taking liberty with time and are allowed to interact with one another. Although not overtly programmatic, the image of a mirage appearing and evaporating is aptly captured by the whisper of the muted alto flute that begins and ends the work.

ARCH FORM
a sectional musical structure in which music progresses toward a midpoint and then retraces its steps, usually symmetrically

MEREDITH MONK (B. 1942)

Meredith Monk's experimental style centers primarily on the human voice, used as both compositional focus and inspiration. Monk's biographers find it difficult to describe her and often paint a broad picture of a singer, actress, dancer, choreographer, and storyteller. In her own words, she is a composer first. But composition for Monk is not composition in the traditional sense. With an improvisational yet structured creative process, she often records her ideas on tape, and keeps notes in notebooks prior to committing actual music notation to paper until she has lived with ideas for an extended period of time. For Monk, the voice is an instrument that flexes like a dancer. She usually avoids text, believing that language gets in the way of music's capacity to directly touch the heart. Her vocal music is both primitive and futuristic, using world vocal techniques such as glottal breaks and **ululation**, special effects such as growling and circular breathing, and excessive ranges.

ULULATION
a wavering, trilling vocal sound

Meredith Monk's childhood was steeped in music. She remembers listening to the sound of her mother's voice as she professionally sang commercials and jingles at radio stations. By age three, Meredith could read

Figure 12.5
Meredith Monk.
Source: Photo by Massimo Agus. Used by permission

music. It was at Sarah Lawrence College, however, that Monk's creativity came to life in a multidisciplinary fashion. Monk studied composition, voice, **Dalcroze eurhythmics**, and theatre at Sarah Lawrence, where the blending of the arts that she experienced was facilitated by faculty who encouraged their students to individualize their educational journey. Monk encountered and was inspired by the work of John Cage (1912–1992), Igor Stravinsky (1882–1971), Béla Bartók (1881–1945), and experimental composer Henry Cowell, as well as Janis Joplin's (1943–1970) gut-level primal quality and natural phrasing.[22]

DALCROZE EURHYTHMICS
an approach to music education based on movement and dance

Monk's work includes music for solo voice, opera, chamber groups, and video, including feature-length films. With a three-octave vocal range, she explores the sensuousness of sound, and has been compared with **Symbolist** composers and poets whose focus on the beauty of sound was a main objective. The range and diversity of her work includes such examples as *Dolmen Music* for six voices, cello, and percussion, *Book of Days*, her first feature-length film, and *The Games*, a theatre piece that viewed reconstruction after a nuclear holocaust.[23]

SYMBOLISM
a late nineteenth-century aesthetic popular in France and elsewhere, which embraced the musical sensuousness of sound and text; typical themes were mysticism and otherworldliness

Along with her hallmark textless vocals, Monk is known for addressing social consciousness, and has tackled topics ranging from community-based living to nuclear destruction. Her social ethic is evident not only in topics that she addresses in her works but also in performance practice as well as in The House Foundation, a company that she founded in 1971 to perform her theatrical works. All voices in the foundation are considered unique and important, as they contribute to production and management services. In works such as *Atlas*, featured here, Monk embraces a world view, casting global characters and addressing global issues using a textless technique that transcends language barriers.

Atlas

Writing a meaningful opera that is primarily textless is an experimental act in itself, but one in which Monk succeeded extremely well. *Atlas* was premiered in 1991 by the Houston Grand Opera, with Monk performing the lead role. The work fits into the chamber category in the sense that it includes just eighteen singers and a small pit orchestra, all of which engage in telling an allegorical spiritual tale that alludes to real-life explorer and spiritualist Alexandra David-Neel. The work uses nonverbal syllables, siren sounds, melismas, and ensemble sounds that are both harsh and beautiful. Sometimes called a minimalist, Monk rejects that label as well, but does often rely on extended **ostinati** as a foundational structure.

OSTINATO
a short musical pattern that persistently repeats

Performed in three parts, *Atlas* explores the chronological and spiritual life of character Alexandra Daniels. The journey begins when thirteen-year-old Alexandra dreams of traveling the globe, and her parents respond with agonizing wails and deep vocal utterances. The young girl nonetheless chooses two travel companions and takes on other guides for her spiritual quest.

LISTENING EXPERIENCE 12.6

"Travel Dream Song" from *Atlas* (1991)
Meredith Monk
Playlist

LISTENING FOCUS

Clarinet, horns, keyboards, and strings perform ostinato patterns while a solo vocalist alternates between textless vocal sounds and spoken words.

TIMED LISTENING GUIDE

0:00	keyboard ostinato established; listen for slight alterations in pattern
0:27	textless vocal part enters
1:44	spoken words: "mountains," "cities," "steamships," interspersed with textless segments as the character dreams of the world she would like to see; continued ostinato
2:57	string ostinato layer added to keyboard ostinato
3:01	horn adds another ostinato layer
3:30	clarinet ostinato added to the texture
4:16	textless voice performs over layered ostinato

In part two, "Night Travel," the three companions travel the earth to seek enlightenment and, in the course of the journey, stop at an agricultural community, a desert, and a militarized scene where they face the possibility of destruction. In section three, "Invisible Light," those who escape destruction ascend beyond earth to enlightenment as a chorus sings in otherworldly tones. As the opera closes, Alexandra returns to earth as an older woman and reflects on her journey. In *Atlas*, Monk explores a woman's entire life, from girlhood to older age, as she travels both outwardly and inside herself.[24]

SUMMARY

As we draw to the end of Part Four, it is important to summarize and reflect on the achievements of women in twentieth-century art music. At the beginning of the century, women were primarily involved in chamber music and were frequently barred from professional ensembles. Today, they conduct and perform professionally in significant numbers. In terms of composition, arguably still the most documented and revered portion of the art music world, the twentieth century brought unprecedented opportunity due to educational access and social change. As a result, in no other portion of the text have so many worthy composers been left unmentioned.

It is also important to project forward at this point, and consider how time and documentation might alter the perspective provided in this segment of the text. Who among the many women professionally involved in art music today will be known to future generations? In written documentation, how will they fare compared with men who are writing comparable work? And certainly, in a world of electronically-supplied musical choices, what will be the future of art music creation and preservation as a whole?

QUESTIONS FOR CRITICAL THINKING AND DISCUSSION

1. Return to Chapter 1 and revisit the work of Sofia Gubaidulina. Considering all that you have learned since you read that chapter, place her work into wider historical perspective.
2. Speculate as to why large-scale works are considered more prestigious than chamber works. How has this impacted women?
3. How many people in your classroom are art music consumers? Is there a future for art music?

IDEAS FOR FURTHER RESEARCH

1. With the help of your instructor, identify some composers of art rock. Where does it fit into the experimental music picture discussed in this chapter, and what roles have women played in the genre?
2. Minimalism, symbolism, and postmodernism all existed in art forms besides music. Select one aesthetic and make comparisons between visual art and music that share the same aesthetic label. Can you make connections between the visual and aural images? How are women portrayed in the visual art?

GUIDED RESEARCH PROJECT PART IV

OUT OF THE TEXTBOOK AND INTO THE CONCERT HALL

After reading Part IV, it should be obvious that the compositional work of women has grown exponentially. Still, if music is not recorded or performed, it quickly dies. This research project can be easily conducted from your computer. The goal is to determine the current status of programming in terms of gender balance. You can assess concert programs, repertoire lists, and public radio playlists online to compile your data.

Some suggested steps:

1. Find websites for major professional ensembles throughout the world. The class may wish to divide the labor, with some teams focusing on choral ensembles, others on orchestral groups or opera companies, and so on. Using a predetermined time period (for example, within the past year, or looking forward to the upcoming season), determine which works were programmed by the groups that you researched. List the composers' names and sex.
2. Given that many groups present a historically balanced program, you will automatically note fewer works by women. If you focus on twentieth-century programming, however, what do you find in terms of gender representation? Attempt to estimate an overall percentage of works written by women.
3. If possible, try to determine who makes the programming decisions for your selected organizations. Then, using the names of living conductors mentioned in Chapter 10 as a starting point, determine whether or not female and male conductors differ in their programming choices.
4. Take your research to the local level and determine the programming of your own school. How does it compare to the professional realm?
5. Finally, access public radio playlists available online. What kind of gender representation do you see there?

After completing your research, discuss the current situation as a class, and discuss possible implications.

PART V

No Longer "One of the Boys"

INTRODUCTION TO PART V

NO LONGER "ONE OF THE BOYS"

Increasingly, the world of music is viewed through an inclusive lens that erases the firm dividing line that once stood between art and popular music. As such, it seems fitting to conclude the text by presenting an integrated view of three areas that have been especially reluctant to include women: jazz, technology, and popular music production. Women who initially ventured into these areas were often considered anomalies, and were sometimes even proud to call themselves "one of the boys." Happily, by the twenty-first century, this designation is no longer necessary, and neither is it a badge of honor.

The study of jazz, the subject of **Chapter 13**, is an excellent way to commence this portion of the text. Not only has jazz existed in a culturally defined limbo between art and popular music, it has been notoriously reluctant to include women in instrumental roles other than keyboard. Even the significant roles of women have been largely ignored in terms of historical documentation. This chapter tells often-forgotten stories of women who participated as jazz performers and composers, while it also acknowledges the struggles that sometimes remain for women who wish to participate in non-vocal aspects of the genre.

Music technology impacted art and popular music in a symbiotic way. Phonographs, signal generators, radios, tape recorders, and computers were embraced by art and popular music enthusiasts alike, and, in both areas, women who participated were initially under-recognized and sometimes systemically denied access to equipment and training. **Chapter 14** begins by chronicling the immediate movement of electronic composition from the university laboratory to the popular music and film industry, and then addresses art and popular music creators who tapped the power of technology.

Chapter 15 brings the text to a close by focusing on the role of producers and promoters in rock and popular music. As women began to take charge of their own studio production and advertising, they increasingly used their power to shape their own lyrics, messages, and sounds. While some women abandoned the music industry system entirely, others broke into the system on their own accord and worked it to present new portrayals of women in popular music.

CHAPTER 13

Instrumental to Jazz
The Forgotten Role of Women

I thought I had two strikes against me—being a woman and being black. Then I realized I had three strikes: I was playing a man's instrument.[1]

Bass player Lucille Dixon

Histories of women in jazz almost always include discussion of women's lack of access to the jazz scene, including issues of discrimination that limited their participation, and we will address the topic throughout this chapter. However, it is also important to acknowledge the tendency in jazz historiography to focus on single "superstars" designated to represent specialty areas. For example, Scott Joplin is the one-name wonder of ragtime, even though he was only one of hundreds of published rag composers. Similarly, Mary Lou Williams is frequently the only woman instrumentalist listed in historical anthologies and documentaries, when there were in fact hundreds of other women pianists and horn players. Individuals such as Joplin and Williams deserve the accolades they have received. At the same time, the historical highlighting of one or two individuals per subgenre leads the general public to believe that the elected "hall of fame" members represent all of jazz. Consequently, this chapter not only highlights the work of women commonly recognized in the field, but also introduces a few of the less adulated participants who contributed to the genre. It is hoped that this will lead the reader on a journey of discovery that embraces a more inclusive history of jazz.

JAZZ ROOTS

RAGTIME
musical style from the turn of the twentieth century that featured a syncopated melody against a steady bass

Although many jazz narratives begin with the story of Scott Joplin and **ragtime**, the roots of jazz are much deeper. Jazz-inspired melodic systems, rhythmic devices, and improvisation are among the many West African influences that

ANTEBELLUM PERIOD
period before the Civil War

JUBA
slave dance adapted from African tradition; included rhythmic patting and supple body movements

SYNCOPATE
to accent a note that falls between main beats

COON SONG
late nineteenth-century popular song that presented a stereotyped view of black Americans; often performed by white singers in blackface

TIN PAN ALLEY
popular music style associated with the sheet music industry between 1880 and 1950; also a physical location of the publishing firms in New York

were transformed on American soil by slaves in the rural South. Women were significantly involved in the musical traditions that impacted jazz. The earliest rags were performed on banjo, not piano, and very few of the original performers were music readers. The foot stomping and hand-patting of **antebellum-period** singing games and dances such as the **juba** were directly transformed into the rag tradition and subsequently impacted jazz. In piano works, for example, the "stomping" juba rhythm can be seen in the left-hand part, while the right hand took over the **syncopated** fiddle and banjo melodies.[2] See, for example, Figure 13.2.

With the commercial success of black-derived genres such as the **coon song**, **Tin Pan Alley** publishers viewed the rag as another genre to market to white Americans. Professional arrangers wrote out rhythmically simplified rags, erasing musical complexity that would have been impossible to capture with notation. Song and piano "ragtime" arrangements were thus made accessible to average Americans, and a standard piano form emerged. A typical Tin Pan Alley rag almost always featured a pattern of repeated segments, most

Figure 13.1
African-American woman playing a singing game with children in Florida, 1935.

Source: Lomax Collection, Library of Congress

Figure 13.2
In May Aufderheide's "Dusty," one can see the foot-stomping juba pattern in the piano left hand, while the right-hand melodic material is reminiscent of fiddle and banjo tunes.

Figure 13.3
African-American man giving piano lesson to young African-American woman.

Source: From a collection compiled by W. E. B. DuBois for the Paris Exposition in 1900. Courtesy of Library of Congress

commonly in the form A A B B A C C D D. The formulaic recipe was used to produce thousands of rags. A genre that was rooted in dance quickly became associated with solo piano.[3] The increased manufacture of upright pianos further helped ragtime soar into popularity. Uprights could be tucked against a parlor wall, and quickly replaced grand pianos that overwhelmed the average home with size and sound.[4]

Ragtime's popularity was also fueled by piano rolls and records that spread the new sound across the country. Women were consumers of this music but were also involved as professional performers. Pianists such as Pauline Alpert (1900–1988) displayed remarkable technical facility in the ragtime pieces she recorded on piano rolls. Alpert alone recorded approximately 500 rolls.[5]

It should not be surprising that many rag enthusiasts were women, given the genre's connection to the piano. Women were still the primary pianists at the turn of the twentieth century, and millions were proficient enough to perform commercial rags. Many women also composed. The 1906 "Pickles and Peppers Rag" by Adaline Shepherd (1883–1950) sold prolifically, and, like many rags written for piano, was additionally arranged for band and orchestra. William Jennings Bryan used the tune in his 1908 presidential campaign, propelling it to even greater popularity; Flanner Publications of Milwaukee sold 200,000 piano copies in 1908 alone.[6]

Another prolific rag composer was May Aufderheide (1888–1972), a middle-class American woman whose father was in the banking industry. When May's father opened a publishing company in 1908, he promoted his daughter's work. Her tunes "Dusty," "Richmond Rag," "Buzzer Rag," and

Figure 13.4
This well-worn copy of Adaline Shepherd's "Pickles and Peppers" rag is one of thousands of copies of the popular tune that sold in the first decade of the twentieth century.

Source: Courtesy Library of Congress

"The Thriller" became widely known. Like many other women rag composers, however, Aufderheide's compositional output diminished significantly after she married.[7]

It is more difficult to trace the authorship of other rags composed by women due to veiled references to their names. Many women, such as Louise V. Gustin, a Detroit area music teacher, were assumed to be men because publishers often used initials to identify them on sheet music covers and advertising. A resurgence of interest in ragtime in the 1970s led to the discovery of over 400 women rag composers, many of whom were once assumed to be men.[8]

By 1917, America's fascination with ragtime diminished as a new genre, jazz, captured the imagination of the nation. The impact of ragtime had been significant. Americans fell in love with its syncopated melodies and swinging rhythms. Within a short time, many would prefer the swing style to the straight toe-tapping marches of the past.

LISTENING EXPERIENCE 13.1

"The Thriller" Rag (1909)
May Aufderheide
Score available in the *New Historical Anthology of Music by Women*
Playlist

LISTENING FOCUS

Listen for the syncopated "ragged" melody moving against the steady bass line.

FORM AT A GLANCE

A A B B A C C

TIMED LISTENING GUIDE

0:00	A section
0:19	A repeated
0:38	B section
0:57	B repeated
1:16	A section
1:35	C section with call and response between right and left-hand parts; no repeat of the C section in this recording

Figure 13.5
This advertisement for works by composer Louise Gustin masked her gender by referencing her only as "L. V. Gustin." It has only recently become known that there were over 400 women rag composers, since many were similarly identified.
Source: From the collection of the author

PIANISTS IN "THE JAZZ AGE"

Jazz is a fusion of ragtime, blues, and brass-band instrumentation, with syncopated rhythms that were made for dancing. The first instrumental groups called jazz ensembles were small combos that usually consisted of five or six performers playing some combination of clarinet, cornet, trombone, piano, banjo, string bass, and drums. Jazz ensembles in the earliest years of the new century featured **collective improvisation** and complex polyrhythms. The drum set added a new polyrhythmic density of its own, allowing one person to

COLLECTIVE IMPROVISATION
the simultaneous layering of individual solo lines to create complex polyrhythms

generate polyrhythmic lines that were formerly created by multiple drummers. It provided a fresh new sound as well as rhythmic vitality, and forever changed the world of popular music.

GREAT MIGRATION massive movement of Southern African-Americans to Northern cities in the first decades of the twentieth century

New Orleans was a primary developmental site of the emerging genre, but in the first decades of the twentieth century many bands moved north during the **Great Migration**. As such, jazz spread rapidly throughout the country. All along the Mississippi River on the journey north, jazz centers emerged, and groups such as King Oliver's Creole Jazz Band eventually moved all the way to Chicago, a city that became a hub of jazz development. Not unlike other New Orleans groups, King Oliver's band featured a woman at the keyboard. Her name was Lil Hardin.[9]

SONG DEMONSTRATOR person who performed sheet music for customers who were considering a purchase

Despite common belief, many jazz pianists were women.[10] The sheer number of women who played piano during the jazz era resulted in a significant body of able artists. Women such as Lil Hardin Armstrong (1902–1971) (at one time considered an anomaly and connected to the jazz world only via her famous husband) were actually key players in the early jazz scene. Hardin was established in her career long before she met Louis Armstrong. She studied piano as a child, playing classics and marches, before a cousin introduced her to jazz. She studied music at both the Chicago College of Music and the New York College of Music and took a job as a **song demonstrator** early in her career. The woman who hired Lil to plug music recognized the pianist's talent and encouraged Lil to go to New Orleans to audition for work.[11]

In New Orleans, Hardin quickly connected with several leading ensembles and was hired as a pianist by Joe "King" Oliver (1885–1938) in 1921. One year later, Louis Armstrong joined the ensemble as well, and the two musicians married in 1924, a union that lasted until 1938. Lil is credited with convincing

Figure 13.6
Lil Hardin Armstrong with King Oliver's Creole Jazz Band, 1920.
Source: © Michael Ochs Archives/Getty Images

LISTENING EXPERIENCE 13.2

"Boogie Me" (released 1961)
Lil Hardin Armstrong, Piano
Booker Washington, Drums
Playlist

LISTENING FOCUS

Listen for an opening eight-note **riff** that unifies and sectionalizes the work, and a twelve-bar blues progression.

FORM AT A GLANCE

Three large sections of twelve-bar blues choruses, each signaled by riff.

TIMED LISTENING GUIDE

Introduction

0:00 eight-note riff stated four times by the piano

Section One

0:06 A material in piano begins first twelve-bar blues progression

0:17 top of the twelve-bar harmonic progression

0:27 harmonic progression begins again, piano in upper range

0:37 last time through the twelve-bar progression in this section

Transition

0:48 riff introduces section two

Section Two

0:55 A material in piano

1:06 opening riff sets up extended drum solo

1:13 drum solo with piano interjections

1:24 drum solo continues through another chorus

Transition

1:35 riff sets up section three

Section Three

1:43 A material in piano

1:54 harmonic progression begins again

2:05 top of the harmonic progression again

2:17 top of the harmonic progression again

Transition

2:28 opening riff sets up closing material

Closing

2:35 last time through the twelve-bar harmonic progression

RIFF
a pattern that repeats

Louis to break from King Oliver's group, and from 1925 to 1927, the Armstrongs, along with Johnny Dodds on clarinet, Kid Ory on trombone, and Johnny St. Cyr on banjo, performed as the Chicago-based "Hot Five." That group later reconfigured as the "Hot Seven," and both ensembles recorded extensively in Chicago, due in large part to Lil's organizational work with record companies such as Okeh. Along with performing and doing managerial work, Lil also composed and arranged for the groups. The fast tempos and layered improvisation of the hot jazz style received significant attention due to the number of recordings released by the two ensembles. Accordingly, the Armstrongs also attained wide recognition.

After the Armstrong divorce, Lil spent her ensuing professional years in Chicago and New York, performing at the most established clubs and theatres in the country. She configured and led a number of her own groups, and was house pianist for Decca Records. Her extensive recording history also included work with such companies as Okeh, Columbia, and Paramount.[12] Along with her managerial skills, she was a composer with impressive talent who wrote over 150 works. Her place in jazz history is multi-faceted, including a significant influence on Louis Armstrong's career during his developmental years in Chicago.[13]

BEYOND THE KEYBOARD

Jazz stands today as a respected genre due to its musical complexity and virtuosic performance demands. In the 1920s, however, jazz performers and creators were marginalized in American society due to racial prejudice. Further, jazz developed in the illegal bars of the Prohibition era, amid alcohol sales, smoking, and police raids, connecting the genre to both disobedience and excitement.[14] On the pages of written history, the jazz scene of this era appears to be a male world. In reality, women played important roles, and for black women, it was race more than sex that limited their careers.

Chicago remained a center of jazz activity in the 1920s, but new developments also took place in New York, which had also been an important jazz site since the beginning of the Great Migration. Retaining the "hot" quality of improvisation, bands began to increase in size from ensembles of five or seven to groups of eleven or more. With the addition of personnel came a need to write more pre-arranged music. Improvisation still took place within the context of a **chart**, but pre-written segments assured a tight ensemble sound. The **swing** era that developed in the 1930s featured orchestral arrangements with **solo breaks**, rich harmonization, and increased timbral color. Like its musical ancestors, swing was related to dance, and this time the people who adopted the genre danced along. Dance marathons were supported with the music of big bands with leaders such as Duke Ellington

CHART
in jazz, the written score that contains the skeletal outline of the music; allows for individuality in performance, while providing basic musical material upon which to improvise

SWING
a style of jazz; characterized by the use of large bands, fast tempos, and written arrangements for ensemble playing

SOLO BREAK
in jazz, when a soloist takes over while the ensemble pauses

FOCUS TOPIC 13.1

Genre Focus: Jazz versus the Blues

The influence of the blues is evident in many aspects of jazz performance. The flexible vocal style of the blues singer was imitated by instrumentalists who slid, growled, and scooped their melodic lines. The crucial role of improvisation in the blues also remained a vital component of jazz, with a basic harmonic progression setting the backdrop for soloists. Call and response dialogue took place between vocalist and instrument, or instrument to instrument, again in blues-like fashion. Jazz was not just an instrumental version of the blues, however. Jazz-specific techniques also developed, including the use of **riffs**, extended solo breaks, and **scat singing**. Although vocal jazz certainly existed, the documented story is that of the instrumental world. This is so much the case that some people erroneously believe that jazz is solely an instrumental genre.

RIFF
a pattern that repeats

SCAT SINGING
in jazz, nonsense vocables used in an improvisatory manner

at the helm. Ellington and others performed for white audiences in venues where band members were not even allowed to enter through the front door. Most of the big-name bands that made the headlines in the white press were led by men, and the featured groups were racially segregated as well as gender segregated, except for a few specific roles for women.

Women in traditional histories were included in the jazz story, but it was almost always the vocalists who made the headlines. The so-called **"canary" roles** featured visually attractive women vocalists who soloed in front of the band. Jazz singers such as Billie Holiday (1915–1959) were often spotlighted in front of bands of men.[15] The singer was to be watched as much as heard, and job applications often required women to submit photographs. It was undeniable that physical appearance was a critical factor in employment consideration.

CANARY ROLE
in jazz, a female vocal soloist who is spotlighted in front of an ensemble

Holiday especially caught the imagination of the nation, and became the subject of plays, movies, books, and documentaries, many of which portrayed her vulnerability as much as her musicianship. Her physical beauty and smooth vocal style resulted in vivid descriptions of an artist who was labeled "smoldering," "sophisticated," and "dripping with sensuality."[16] Lesser recognized in the wider media was her significant musical impact on jazz musicians who emulated her style. Holiday's interpretative technique, which she said was a combination of Louis Armstrong's syncopation and Bessie Smith's feeling, resulted in a complex rhythmic delivery that was dubbed "dual-track time." Lagging behind the beat and harmonizing beyond the chords, her work impacted musicians as diverse as Lester Young and Sarah Vaughan.[17]

The trend to highlight jazz vocalists and ignore women instrumentalists continued into the twenty-first century in written materials and audio-visual documentaries. Vocalists such as Billie Holiday, Sarah Vaughan (1924–1990),

Figure 13.7
Billie Holiday.
Source: William Gottlieb Collection

Ethel Waters (1896–1977), and Ella Fitzgerald (1917–1996) were often included in these histories, while instrumentalists were largely absent. It was true that women who aspired to perform as drummers or horn players in swing bands found it almost impossible to gain employment in big-name gender-integrated ensembles. That did not mean, however, that they did not perform.

ALL-GIRL SWING BANDS

The black press of the swing era reveals some interesting alternative headlines to the often-told jazz story, and this version placed women behind the horns, not just in front of the microphone. The phenomenon of the women's swing band was largely missing in the white press until the First World War, but black publications such as the *Chicago Defender* featured extensive coverage of groups such as the Harlem Playgirls and Vi Burnside's Combo, among others. As noted in Chapter 1, the International Sweethearts of Rhythm were formed in 1937 and became one of the best-known gender-segregated ensembles in history. These groups shatter the myth that all-women bands were formed only to replace men who were called into military service.[18]

On December 7, 1941, President Franklin Delano Roosevelt announced the bombing of the American naval base in Pearl Harbor, Hawaii, and America was plunged into a costly war, both in terms of money and human life. Americans tried to hold on to their beloved swing bands during the war years, and swing flourished for several years after the war's outbreak. Hundreds of women's groups existed during this period, and black groups such as The Darlings of Rhythm and The Hip Chicks were joined by white groups such as The Melody Maids, and Dixie Sweethearts.

Like all-women groups in the orchestral and concert band world, the all-women jazz groups often created a visual sensation as they performed. Some of this was due to expectations from male managers, but sometimes groups embraced the sexy stage presence on their own accord. Band members wore long gowns and impractical high heeled shoes (that drummers sometimes stripped off after they got behind the drum set) and were expected to wear make-up and maintain perfect hairstyles. Some band leaders even required

Figure 13.8
One of the most famous "all-girl" groups of the 1930s was Ina Ray Hutton and her Melodears. Like many other female ensembles, Hutton's group was famous for its visual presentation during performances.

Source: Leonard Feather Collection. Photo used by permission of the University of Idaho

Figure 13.9
The attire worn by bassist Vivien Garry in this 1947 photo is typical of the dress code for women instrumentalists of the swing era.
Source: William P. Gottlieb Collection

the women to wear contact lenses.[19] White or black, women in the all-girl bands had to uphold a visual standard and maintain sexual appeal.

Despite the existence of hundreds of all-girl bands in the 1930s and 1940s, their stories were written out of jazz histories until the 1980s. Extensive studies resulted in four books written by women: works by D. Antoinette Handy, Sally Placksin, Linda Dahl, and Sherrie Tucker. When Tucker conducted her research, which relied extensively on interview data, she was surprised by several issues. First, she had to adjust her intended label for the ensembles. Women of the swing era preferred the term all-girl, a label long avoided by feminist scholars who decried the tendency to call women "girls" and men "men." The musicians interviewed preferred the term all-girl, however, and not in quotation marks. They explained that they were concerned that "it makes it look like we were all lesbians." Thus, Tucker was in for her second surprise. Women of the swing era were deeply concerned about the representation of their sexuality, and wanted to avoid any non-traditional references. To survive in public music performance in the 1940s, it was important to be perceived as straight, as bands could otherwise lose bookings.

Regardless of their sexual orientation, jazz women of this era were discriminated against because of their sex. Horn players and drummers were criticized for their lack of femininity and had to work hard to counteract the physical demands of performing on those instruments. Tucker was sensitive to the wishes of her interviewees, and did not elaborate on their feelings about the representation of non-traditional sexuality. "Regardless of sexual orientation," Tucker said, "all women who played in all-girl bands were at times viewed as sexually suspect, either as loose or as lesbian. This was an occupational hazard shared by the many women in other professions who held jobs associated with men."[20]

GENDER INTEGRATION IN TIME OF WAR

Although all-women groups dominated the women's jazz scene during the Second World War, there were women who performed in gender-integrated bands during that era. Pianist Mary Lou Williams (1910–1981) came to the attention of the wider public when she performed with Andy Kirk and his Clouds of Joy, a band that existed from 1930 to 1941. The Kirk band was Williams' long-time gig, and the orchestral style of the band was a perfect match for her hard-playing style, full harmonies, and powerful bass lines. Not only a stellar performer, Williams was a significant arranger and composer, producing arrangements for such artists as Benny Goodman, Duke Ellington, Tommy Dorsey, Louis Armstrong, Cab Calloway, and others. She always maintained that her sex was not a limiting factor in her work, and that she did not experience discrimination.[21]

Figure 13.10
Mary Lou Williams, c.1946.
Source: William P. Gottlieb Collection

Figure 13.11
Melba Liston at a trombone convention with Matthew Gee, Trummy Young, Henry Coker, Benny Powell, Al Gray, and Leonard Feather.

Source: Leonard Feather Collection. Photo used by permission of the University of Idaho

The reality for other women who performed in gender-integrated settings was that they faced significant harassment and discrimination. Trombonist Melba Liston (1926–1999) was one of the first women horn players to break into the big-name male bands. Liston likely landed her job in part because of her stellar arranging skills, an invaluable asset as groups with missing members traveled across the country in time of war. Despite her performance and arranging gifts, Liston experienced prejudice, enduring labels ranging from "bitch" to "mom." Unlike Williams, Liston admitted that the road was difficult. Still, she persevered throughout the war years and beyond, performing with Count Basie, Dizzy Gillespie, and John Coltrane, among others. Liston continued to compose and arrange throughout her life as well, and was inducted into the Pioneers Hall of Fame at the International Women's Brass Conference in 1993. Liston won over the men in the end, through skill and determination.[22]

ONE OF THE BOYS?

The ways in which women operated within gender-segregated jazz groups varied. Pianists Lil Hardin Armstrong and Mary Lou Williams admit that they emulated the hard-playing style of men. Armstrong worked in a music store and recalls Jelly Roll Morton walking in, sitting down, and rocking the piano so hard that Armstrong had goose pimples "sticking out all over." Morton then made a gesture as if to say, "Let that be a lesson to you," and Armstrong said that it *was* a lesson—she played as hard as she could from that day onward.[23] Mary Lou Williams also felt a debt of gratitude to men, and embraced the notion that she was not like other women:

> Now I feel I'm out of place . . . I know some very good women musicians but—I'm just out of place with them. They're just thinking this way, and I don't think that way . . . I have something that has been embedded in me through good, strong men . . . I was just like one of the boys.[24]

Electric and acoustic bassist Carline Ray (b. 1925), who started her long performance career with the International Sweethearts of Rhythm, had a different viewpoint about women's anomaly status in jazz. Said Ray:

> It was like, oh you play good for a girl, that was one thing, or, you play just like a man. These were the supreme compliments . . . My argument always is, you put a screen in front of a bunch of musicians, see if you can tell me what gender of person is playing, and really who cares, what difference does it make? It's the music that counts.[25]

For Ray, being compared to a man was not a compliment.

Trumpeter Clora Bryant (b. 1927), another woman who started her career in an all-women's band, admits that she entered gender-integrated groups by focusing on her music and having a lot of nerve:

> When I started going to the jam sessions . . . they all respected me because they knew that I was tunnel vision with my music . . . I was the only female in L. A. that went to the jam sessions, and sat in because I wanted to learn, and they let me. I had nerve—that was it, I had the nerve, and I was aggressive. I had my trumpet and I'd come in and they'd say, "Okay here comes Clora with her widdle trumpet" . . . Good, bad or indifferent, I was going to go up there and try.[26]

Bryant had a long career after the war years, and was highly regarded by Dizzy Gillespie, Quincy Jones, Duke Ellington, Count Basie, and Louis Armstrong, with whom she performed. She not only succeeded in the big band world but continued as a studio and ensemble performer throughout much of the twentieth century.

LISTENING EXPERIENCE 13.3

"Sweet Georgia Brown" (1957)
Clora Bryant
Playlist

LISTENING FOCUS

Listen to Bryant sing through the thirty-two-bar tune, which cycles through several key areas. Four improvised choruses follow the same pattern.

FORM AT A GLANCE

Five choruses of thirty-two-bar song form.

TIMED LISTENING GUIDE

Introduction

0:00 four-bar instrumental introduction

First Chorus (sung)

0:06 A section, eight bars

0:19 B section, eight bars

0:32 A section, eight bars

0:45 C section, eight bars, with descending harmonic "turnaround" in last four bars

Second Chorus (trumpet improvisation)

0:58 A section

1:10 B section

1:23 A section

1:35 C section with "turnaround"

Third Chorus (trumpet again)

1:48 A section

2:01 B section

2:13 A section

2:26 C section with "turnaround"

Fourth Chorus (saxophone improvisation)

2:39 A section

2:51 B section

3:03 A section

3:16 C section with "turnaround"

Fifth Chorus (piano improvisation)

3:28 A section

3:39 B section

3:51 A section

4:02 C section

Closing

4:14 voice closes

BEYOND THE WAR

The post-war period led to jazz developments that were less appealing to America's mainstream audience. By the late 1940s, rock and roll was just about to emerge, and the new jazz style, **bop**, featured intense harmonies, extended formats, and smaller ensembles. It was not dance music but rather was geared to an audience who understood the complexity of the chamber-style music.

BOP
jazz combo style of the 1950s with extended solos; sometimes called hard bop

Mary Lou Williams continued to be a prominent figure during the bop period, performing with bop forerunners such as Dizzy Gillespie, both in America and in Europe. She continued composing as well, writing works such as "Lonely Moments" and "Whistle Blues" for Benny Goodman, and "In the Land of Oo Bla Dee" for Dizzy Gillespie. In 1956, Williams converted to Catholicism, and spent time devoting herself to religious studies. Although she returned to the jazz performance scene in the later 1950s, she eventually turned to jazz-based religious composition, writing her famous *Mary Lou's Mass* in 1969. Again she inspired others, as composers such as Duke Ellington also explored religious composition.[27]

OTHER JAZZ VENUES

> *Jazz is a purely male concern.*[28]
>
> Peter Kunst, German Hot Club Director, in a 1956 article on women and jazz

Some American jazz women went to Europe after the war, as the European scene was generally considered less restrictive in terms of gender bias. European audiences had been enthralled with jazz since the 1920s, and "hot clubs" that featured jazz were established in France, for example, as early as 1932. Still, it was from a more restrictive environment that a woman named Jutta Hipp emerged into bop.

Perhaps little known to Americans during the war years, Germans were listening to American jazz on the radio. As they hid in shelters and listened covertly to the music, they felt a sense of freedom and release. Jutta Hipp (1925–2003), the leading jazz pianist of either gender in post-war Germany, was among the listeners. "I remember nights when I didn't go down to the safe cellar because we listened to records. We just had the feeling that you were not our enemies."[29] After the war, Hipp left Germany for the Bavarian Alps and worked on her performance skills. By the early 1950s, she was back in Germany and opened a performance in Frankfurt for Dizzy Gillespie. Soon she was performing regularly.

Women in Germany were banished from the jazz scene due to perceptions about the "overly sexual" women who were associated with the genre. Even women who danced to the style were considered sexual delinquents.[30] The restrictive environment did not stop Jutta Hipp. Jazz historian Leonard Feather explained the shock of walking into a jazz scene in post-war Germany and discovering her quintet. "As we entered a crowded cellar in Duisburg, music floated up to our ears that we could hardly believe was the work of five Germans."[31] Feather helped to arrange for a recording with Blue Note Records, one of the highest regarded jazz labels in America, and Hipp became the first white female artist to record for the label.

COMPOSER/ARRANGERS

Like Melba Liston and Mary Lou Williams, other women combined their performance skills with expertise in composing and arranging and left significant marks on jazz in the latter half of the twentieth century. A pioneer of band leadership and arranging in the **West Coast** style was Japanese-American Toshiko Akiyoshi (b. 1929). Akiyoshi's arranging skills in the compositionally based West Coast tradition have led to fourteen Grammy nominations and consistent praise. Akiyoshi was born in Manchuria and moved to Japan at the end of the Second World War. An accomplished pianist, she was discovered by jazz pianist and composer Oscar Peterson in 1952, and thereafter moved to the United States to begin studies at the Berklee School of Music in Boston. She moved to Los Angeles in 1972 with her husband, jazz saxophonist/flutist Lew Tabackin, and together they founded the Toshiko Akiyoshi Jazz Orchestra.

WEST COAST JAZZ
subgenre of cool jazz that featured arranged charts, smooth sounds, and less aggressive rhythms than bop

Figure 13.12
Toshiko Akiyoshi.

Source: Leonard Feather Collection. Photo used by permission of the University of Idaho

LISTENING EXPERIENCE 13.4

"Harlequin's Tear"
Toshiko Akiyoshi with the SWR Big Band
Playlist

LISTENING FOCUS

Akiyoshi's chart combines pre-written and improvised material. Listen for opening and closing pre-written segments that feature designated sections of the band, and two extended, improvised solos.

FORM AT A GLANCE

Pre-written material, extended tenor saxophone solo, extended trombone solo, pre-written material.

TIMED LISTENING GUIDE

0:00	rhythm section (piano, bass, drums) introduction
0:50	piano break leads into arranged full band segment
0:52	full band
1:03	pre-written saxophone section feature, accompanied with brass interjections
1:44	tenor saxophone solo break
1:46	extended tenor saxophone improvised solo, accompanied by rhythm section
2:40	solo continues with horn interjections
3:31	trombone solo break
3:33	extended trombone improvised solo, accompanied by rhythm section
4:26	solo continues with horn interjections
5:16	drum break sets up full band return
5:18	full band with pre-written material
5:28	pre-written brass section feature
5:43	pre-written sax section feature
6:03	drum sets up return to opening material
6:12	opening material returns in horns
6:18	pre-written sax section feature, leading to full band close (7:01)
7:19	applause and acknowledgement of soloists

The big band medium allowed Akiyoshi's compositional and arranging abilities to shine, and she and her group are considered innovative forces in late twentieth-century jazz. Along with creatively bringing out individual voices within the big band setting, Akiyoshi weaves Asian musical elements into her charts, as well as other unique colors and textures. Akiyoshi was the first woman to win *DownBeat*'s best arranger and composer award in jazz, and, at the time of writing, remains an active performer and arranger.[32]

Another performer/composer is Carla Bley (b. 1936), who is among the most creative minds in modern jazz. A keyboardist, saxophonist, composer, and band leader, Bley moved to New York in the 1950s and began to compose at the suggestion of her first husband, Paul Bley. By the 1960s she was associated with the experimental jazz movement in New York, was a prominent member of the Jazz Composer's Guild, and co-founded the Jazz Composer's Orchestra. She has won numerous awards, including a Guggenheim Fellowship for composition, many *DownBeat* "best arranger" awards, and multiple Grammy nominations.[33] Bley continues to arrange for ensembles of all sizes, and performs extensively with her second husband, jazz bassist Steve Swallow.

POSTMODERNISM
an aesthetic that reflects fragmentation, and rejects boundaries between high and low art

Considered one of the greatest jazz composer/arrangers of her time, Bley offers a **postmodern** blend that fuses jazz, rock, classical, and world music, including Indian ragas. For example, in the fourteen-and-a-half minute "Wolfgang Tango" from her *Fancy Chamber Music* album, she combines European-style chamber music elements with jazz, while she makes fun of "uppity" high-art Vienna with the reference to Wolfgang Amadeus Mozart in the title. Using jazz harmony throughout, Bley cleverly combines a European chamber music group with drum set and jazz bass, and additionally blends a Tango rhythm with a Viennese waltz. Typical of the post-modern tendency to use humor and irony to merge popular and "high art" genres, Bley pokes fun with segments that hang on clumsily too long, and uses rhythmic lilting.[34]

ALL-WOMEN'S ENSEMBLES IN THE TWENTY-FIRST CENTURY

Like the orchestral realm that was the subject of Chapter 10, jazz has been slowly changing territory in terms of gender roles. Despite the work of many key women, the deep roots of male dominion are still felt. The twenty-first century mindset that one *should not* discriminate sometimes makes discrimination even more covert, and this is strongly felt in a gigging world such as jazz, where performers get invitations to perform via social networking rather than via formal job announcements and auditions. One pianist mused, "Now it's all subtle, because it's not cool to be sexist or racist. It's all under the table."[35]

Figure 13.13
Sherrie Maricle and DIVA.
Source: Photo courtesy of DIVA

Sometimes sex-based discrimination is still overt. Sherrie Maricle, a drummer who co-founded the all-women ensemble DIVA in the early 1990s, was fired from a trio when the group was contracted to perform for a famous comedian who refused to work with women musicians.[36] Despite the achievements of artists such as Toshiko Akiyoshi, Carla Bley, and others, some women have preferred to return to gender-segregated groups because of such discrimination. Maricle, for example, has enjoyed a long history with DIVA, and the fifteen-member band not only performs extensively but additionally features charts arranged by group members. DIVA is joined by other groups such as Maiden Voyage and Straight Ahead, who selectively perform in segregation. Although there are many women in jazz who perceive segregation as equivalent to being ghettoized, some women believe that the benefits of segregation outweigh the negatives.[37]

SUMMARY

To the public, instrumental jazz has largely been a man's world, and women who ventured into it suffered not only discrimination about their performance ability, but also social discrimination. Performers who lived through the 1940s and 1950s once believed that deeply held sexist beliefs would never change. Although the 1990s saw a great expansion in the involvement of jazz women, women who sought employment still maintained that they had to be exceptionally skilled and extremely persistent. The informal gigging network remains very much alive.

There was a time when the known women of jazz could have been listed in a short paragraph. Today, attempting to list accomplished women would result in a woeful number of omissions. It is a sign of change that has come slowly and often painfully. As the stories of women in jazz increasingly come to light, the documentation of women's achievement is slowly changing as well.

QUESTIONS FOR CRITICAL THINKING AND DISCUSSION

1. Discuss the current gender balance in jazz ensembles familiar to you, including high school and collegiate groups. Are there still lingering perceptions about women who perform with these groups?
2. Make connections between the Western art music canon and the jazz world in terms of their use of written music. How might this have impacted early scholarly treatments of jazz?
3. Bring some recordings to class that you believe were musically inspired by jazz and discuss the jazz-based features.

IDEAS FOR FURTHER RESEARCH

1. Using the information in this chapter as a starting point, further investigate similarities and differences between jazz and blues. Additionally, identify gender perceptions that exist in both genres.
2. Listen to Mary Lou Williams' *Mary Lou's Mass* and identify jazz characteristics in the music.

CHAPTER 14

Music Technology in the Hands of Women

Technology has always driven musical change. From the moment in time when the first flute was created, a new timbre permanently entered the sonic environment. In the early nineteenth century, valves allowed brass instruments to become bearers of bold melodies rather than harmonic markers that were limited to a few pitches. By the end of the same century, Thomas Edison discovered that the indentation of sound waves on tin foil allowed him to store and reproduce both the spoken word and music. When Emile Berliner invented a flat disc system to store recorded data, "records" went into mass production.

In the twentieth century, electronic technology captured the imagination of musical creators, and as they used it to generate and manipulate sound waves, they created music that was unimaginable to the previous generation. Sounds that were considered eerie and unnatural in the 1920s evolved to become a part of an aural vocabulary that modern listeners take for granted, and electronically derived sound appeared everywhere. From the hum of power plants and appliances to the soundtracks of horror films, it was a whole new aural world.

FROM SOUND REPRODUCTION TO CREATION

Initial attempts to record music focused on faithful reproduction of live performance. Despite the best efforts of recording experts, however, speakers were small, and damage or debris on the record surface created pops and skipping. Early radio broadcasts were equally poor representations of reality. Performers worried that audiences would abandon live performance venues, and that recordings would be perceived as acoustical reality.

From the moment recording devices were created, however, innovative people looked beyond sound reproduction and began to utilize the new technology for composition. Recorded sound samples became building blocks for new creations, and over time, the recording studio challenged the stage as a site of artistic creation.

The extent to which we have embraced "produced" music since those early days is stunning. If you have ever been disappointed in a live concert performance because the artist did not "live up to" a recording, you understand this phenomenon. In a total reversal of earlier performance practice, the recording became the hallmark of desired sound. Woe to a performer who took a new tempo or deviated from the subtle bends and dips of a previously recorded melody! Audiences became increasingly critical of the human tendency to err as well, forgetting that performers were allowed multiple "takes" in the studio before sound engineers edited remaining flaws.

As the characteristic "sound" of a group increasingly was formulated in the hands of producers and engineers, the locus of artistic control shifted away from the performer. Initially, that control was firmly in the grasp of men. Pioneering work in electronic music technology took place in the 1940s and 1950s, an era when women were not encouraged to study topics such as physics, mathematics, and mechanics—the roots of music technology. In addition, expectations regarding societal gender roles created roadblocks for women who sought access to studios. In a field where the ability to operate and repair equipment was just as important as the ability to calculate an algorithm, lack of access created significant disadvantages for aspiring technicians who could not break into the system. In spite of the challenges, many women distinguished themselves in music technology, and this chapter also highlights a history of excellence that took place despite the struggles.

To acknowledge the importance of technology and to enhance understanding of this chapter, readers are encouraged to seek official websites maintained by many of the composers, performers, and technicians mentioned. Not only will this provide the most current information available, it will bring to life visual elements that are critical to multimedia work.

FROM THE LABORATORY TO *THE JETSONS*

The noise-filled, high-speed life of early twentieth-century cities was largely sparked by the rapid societal distribution of electricity. Electric lights allowed the population to stay up late at night, and electronically produced sounds permeated the air. People in the arts expressed the charged atmosphere in a movement known as **futurism**. For musicians, electronic instruments were the perfect means to express the new aesthetic. Not only did new-age instruments generate sounds that floated in a netherworld between music and noise, machines sometimes performed the music without human intervention.

FUTURISM
early twentieth-century aesthetic that embraced speed, noise, and technology

The twentieth century also marked the softening of a line that had been drawn between art and popular music. Popular music genres such as jazz were infused into art music works, and the musical sounds created by physicists and engineers in private and university music laboratories were often utilized in popular culture. The widespread use of the **theremin** provides a good example of this phenomenon.

THEREMIN
early electronic instrument controlled by the performer's proximity to antennae

The theremin was an electronic instrument created in 1927 by a Russian professor named Leon Termen (Westernized as Theremin). The instrument was "played" without direct human contact by altering a simple **sine wave** tone via body proximity and hand motion. As the performer altered frequency and volume by standing in front of the instrument and moving her hands, it appeared that sounds were being pulled out of the air. Clara Rockmore, a virtuoso theremin performer, worked with Termin to modify the machine to meet her performance demands. With her input, the machine was redesigned to increase timbre control and range, and its use expanded into the entertainment industry.[1] Not only did the theremin provide "other-worldly" sounds for horror movies and science fiction shows, it was used to create special effects for many radio and television themes, ranging from the 1930s radio show *The Green Hornet*, to the 1960s-era television show *The Jetsons*.

SINE WAVE
a continuous uniform wave with unchanging frequency (how often the wave recurs) and amplitude (vertical measurement); associated with a pure sound that contains no harmonics

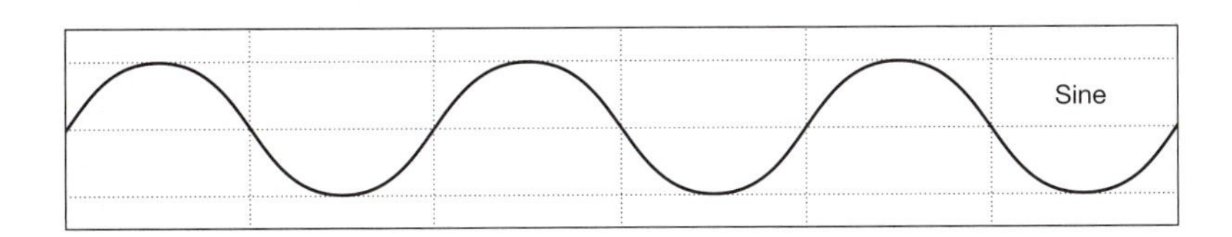

Figure 14.1
Note the uniform recurrence of the sine wave (the frequency), as well as its uniform height (the amplitude). Electronic instruments such as the theremin can be used to generate and modulate (alter) sine tones.

From the vantage point of readers who have always had home computer systems, portable synthesizers, and music software, it may be difficult to imagine the expertise needed to produce electronic music in the early years. **Electroacoustic** compositional activity often took place in university music or technology labs, where composers with extensive background in mathematics and physics worked in collaboration with engineers to develop new equipment. Early synthesizers could fill the space of a small room and were operated via manual patch cord connections. The composition process was informed by algorithmic calculation of recurrent sound wave patterns, and techniques such as **frequency modulation** and **signal filtering** were used to create and shape sound. Mathematical calculations also informed machine-realized rhythms of great complexity.

ELECTROACOUSTIC
general term that describes multi-faceted music genres, all of which use electronic technology to allow access to sound

FREQUENCY MODULATION
altering (modulating) a wave form by changing the frequency with which the wave recurs, resulting in timbral change

SIGNAL FILTERING
altering the frequency content of a sound signal to create desired effects

Like most scientific endeavors, collaboration and experimentation were hallmarks of early electroacoustic work, and women who lacked access to laboratories often were restricted in what they could accomplish. One pioneer who successfully entered the field was Bebe Barron (b. 1927), who collaborated with her husband Louis (1920–1989) in early electronic music experimentation. The Barrons' Manhattan apartment studio became a laboratory where they worked with tape-generated music, noise-producing circuits, and filters to create and manipulate electronic sound. It was the Barrons who brought outer space to life in MGM's 1956 movie *Forbidden Planet*, the first all-electronic movie score. Bebe Barron was a charter member of SEAMUS, the Society for Electroacoustic Music in the United States, and received its annual Lifetime Achievement Award in 1997 along with her ex-husband.[2]

TAPE TECHNOLOGY

The Barrons' manipulation of sound on tape was a development that took shape in Germany as early as 1935, when inventors expanded upon the discovery that sound could be recorded by encoding magnetic patterns on wire. Tape technology used the same magnetic principle, but it resulted in sound manipulation possibilities that were to impact art and popular music throughout the century. An encoded tape could be cut up, reordered, "spliced," run in reverse, or played at variable speeds.[3]

The French also challenged the line between music and noise with recorded technology. By the late 1940s, Pierre Schaeffer (1910–1995) led a movement in which everyday sounds were recorded, rearranged, mixed, and manipulated via tape splicing and playback methods. The movement was called **musique concrète** (real music), referring to the type of sound sources that provided the samples. Sounds such as dripping water or a passing train were recorded and used to create artistic works. Along with its applications in art music, sampling also was used frequently in the mass music market later in the century, notably beginning with 1960s rock, and later including other genres such as rap.

MUSIQUE CONCRÈTE
technique in which recordings of live sounds are used as compositional building blocks

AMERICAN INNOVATIONS

Post-war art music experimentation in America often took place in university music laboratories, and women who were involved in these centers were sometimes omitted from subsequent written histories despite important foundational work. One of the leading American laboratories was the Columbia Princeton Electronic Music Center (CPEMC), where Alice Shields and Pril Smiley collaborated with well-known composers Vladimir Ussachevsky (1911–1990), Otto Luening (1900–1996), and Milton Babbitt (b. 1916), beginning in the 1960s. Shields (b. 1943) had a Doctor of Musical Arts (DMA) from Columbia and served as associate director of the facility. Along with composing numerous works, she was also a studio instructor, even though she was not named as a faculty member. Pril Smiley (b. 1943) also wrote many works, developed curricula for the center, instructed classes, and helped test Buchla and Moog synthesizers. At the current facility, known as the Columbia Music Center, both Shields and Smiley stand in high regard and are proudly depicted in historical documentation. In the wider media, however, their work is lesser known, despite their critical contributions.[4]

PAULINE OLIVEROS (B. 1932)

> *Through the years I understood the Expanded Instrument System to mean "time machine" . . . present/past/future is occurring simultaneously.*[5]
>
> Pauline Oliveros, regarding her system for electronic sound processing environments

One of the leading figures in post-war electroacoustic music is Pauline Oliveros, who spent her early years composing in laboratories and universities on the West coast. Along with her innovations in meditative improvisation (readers may recall the excerpt from Oliveros' *Deep Listening* discussed in Chapter 1), Oliveros' groundbreaking theoretical and compositional work in electroacoustic music continues to impact the field.

Oliveros' experiments in conscious listening began in her youth. She was fascinated with electronic sound and liked to analyze the sound effects that were used on popular radio programs of the 1940s. She also listened intently

Figure 14.2
A 1951 Webster-Chicago wire recorder. The manipulation of recorded sound dramatically changed music composition after the Second World War.

Source: Photo by Gregory F. Maxwell, taken at *The History of Audio: The Engineering of Sound,* an exhibition of the San Francisco Airport Museums in SFO Airport. Used with permission

WHITE NOISE
the presence of all pitches sounding randomly from which a composer may select particular areas or band widths to hear; can be compared with the concept of white light

WIRE RECORDER
predecessor of the tape recorder, on which a magnetic code on a wire enables preservation of sound

COMBINATION TONE
an extraneous sound that can be heard when two (generally loud) musical tones are sounded together; the tone is not present when either of the original tones is sounded separately

to sounds that many people attempted to ignore, purposefully tuning her grandfather's wireless radio between stations to listen to **white noise**. When her mother gave her an early-model **wire recorder**, Oliveros manipulated the sounds she improvised and recorded by varying the playback speed. Listening to those early recordings, she heard "background" sounds that she had previously failed to notice, and her way of listening and creating profoundly expanded.[6]

Oliveros pushed the sonic envelope with acoustic instruments as well, and used her discoveries to inform later electronic applications. When she began taking accordion lessons, she delighted in the extraneous **combination tones** that arose from combining fundamental pitches on the instrument.[7] Although this physical phenomenon produces faint acoustic sounds, Oliveros discovered that amplification allowed access to unchartered sonic territory. When she later realized that she could electronically isolate combination tones apart from their fundamental pitches, she declared, "I felt like a witch capturing sounds from the nether realm."[8]

Oliveros' sonic imagination was rich as well, and her "mentally imaged" sounds were brought to reality via manipulation of sound and time. One of her primary systems for exploring the sound-time connection was tape delay. Using early reel-to-reel machines, Oliveros found that she could string tape from the supply reel of one machine to the take-up reel of another, and listen to acoustic sounds being transformed and layered. Tape delay yields amazing sonic results, with more complicated effects created by using additional machines. On a two-machine system, material being played on one machine is being recorded on the second machine, which in turn routes the tape back so that the first unit is playing back its own material. Thus the sound of the past becomes one with the present, with the initial taped source in essence playing back its own material, slightly delayed.[9] The time delay varies by distance between the machines. As the process continues, the texture becomes increasingly thick as layer upon layer of sound is added. The ongoing layering, as well as the reverberation caused by the delay, impacts timbre, texture, and intensity. The performer must control the sounds created by the increasing layers of material so that one sound does not completely obliterate the others. Extraneous acoustical sounds that are captured by the microphone during a performance also become incorporated in the recording.

Pauline Oliveros is particularly known for her expertise in controlling such sound environments, and her Expanded Instrument System (EIS) has been used by many composers to help them produce desirable results. Her system evolved from early explanations of reel-to-reel tape delay to digital methods, and eventually utilized computer software. In a 2007 address, she explained the capacity of computer-driven EIS at that point in its ongoing development:

> Acoustic input . . . can be processed with up to forty variable delays, modulated with fluctuating waveforms, layered and spatialized. Sounds may be diffused in four, six, or eight channels. More outputs could be programmed for sixteen, thirty-two, sixty-four, and beyond. Time delays range from milliseconds to one minute or more depending on CPU power.[10]

Oliveros' long career has included extensive foundational work at university music centers, including work as a founding co-director of the influential San Francisco Tape Music Center, beginning in 1961. Her compositional output is large and varied, and she continues to express social and feminist concerns via her compositions. In addition to an extensive number of electronic works, she has composed works for stage, instrumental ensembles, and voice.

> *(Bye Bye Butterfly) bids farewell not only to the music of the nineteenth century but also to the system of polite morality of that age and its attendant institutionalized oppression of the female sex.*[11]
>
> Pauline Oliveros

Bye Bye Butterfly

Oliveros' electronic works are a combination of improvisation and tightly controlled studio techniques that lead to profound aesthetic meaning. The importance of the aesthetic is clearly evident in *Bye Bye Butterfly*, where the central character of Giacomo Puccini's 1904 *Madame Butterfly* receives a new focus in the hands of Oliveros. In the original opera, a young, pregnant Japanese mother (Butterfly) is abandoned by her American G. I. husband when he leaves for America without her at war's end. He returns to Japan not only with a new wife but also with the intent of taking custody of Butterfly's son. In operatic characterization that depicts utter helplessness, Butterfly crumples in agony without a fight, and sings one of opera's most revered arias before she commits suicide.

Oliveros' work takes a short segment of the opera (played in real time on a phonograph) and uses electronic counterpoint to combine the operatic material with a high, narrow band of white noise. (Readers can listen to radio static to get a sense of multiple pitch levels.) Tape delay creates both reverberation and alteration of the recorded Butterfly material. Butterfly's singing is heard for several minutes, but it seems to be coming from another world, misshapen by frequency modulation, and increasingly challenged by a melodic line created of static. The intertwining sounds create an effect that is both beautiful and haunting. Butterfly's voice goes out of focus and disappears as the operatic material gives way to static.[12] Metaphorically, the composer is also saying good bye to an era and a genre that oppressed women.

LISTENING EXPERIENCE 14.1

Bye Bye Butterfly (1965)
Pauline Oliveros
Playlist

LISTENING FOCUS

This tone poem uses tape delay to intertwine a high, narrow band of white noise and a section of Puccini's *Madame Butterfly*. Oliveros used two Hewlett Packard oscillators to produce an electronic signal, two line amplifiers, a turntable playing a recording of Puccini's *Madame Butterfly*, and two tape recorders in a delay setup. She controlled and modulated the sound in real time.

FORM AT A GLANCE

A B A

TIMED LISTENING GUIDE

A Section

0:00	click of turntable evident, but opera recording not yet audible; electronic signal prevails
0:57	electronic signal modulated and melodically shaped by tape delay; listen for the return of this material in the B section as layers are added

B Section

3:15	turntable click (recorded at the beginning of the work) is now heard as a percussive sound due to layering
3:23	operatic music from phonograph audible, electronic signal on steady pitch
3:53	operatic vocal line and original chordal accompaniment recognizable, interwoven with lines of static; tape delay causes reverberation and modulation
4:30	static moves melodically against opera material
5:03	static melodically falls, then remains steady
5:35	static rises and falls against operatic material
6:08	vocal line fades; harmony from opera still audible
6:21	vocal segments waver in and out, 6:27 harmony still audible

A Section

6:37	operatic material no longer discernable; static rises and falls melodically
7:33	high steady pitch and lower band of sound audible
7:45	high steady pitch heard alone, then fades away[13]

COMPUTER MUSIC AND THE DIGITAL WORLD

Analog synthesis and tape manipulation were mainstays of electroacoustic composition throughout the early years of its development, but new technology always emerges. **Digital technology** and computers allowed complex mathematical analysis of waveform structures that resulted in increasingly sophisticated compositional techniques. **Spectrum analysis** is a technique in which a computer creates a model that is abstracted from a live sound. Not only does this allow better recreation of sounds for home-use synthesizers, but it also permits composers to analyze unique harmonic structures and to manipulate sound in original works. **Timbre** became a new focus of spectral composition.

ANALOG TECHNOLOGY
technology that takes an audio signal and translates it into electronic pulses

DIGITAL TECHNOLOGY
technology that breaks an audio signal into a binary code where the signal is represented by a series of 1s and 0s, transfers them to their destination, then reassembles them into their original format

SPECTRUM ANALYSIS
computer analysis of waveforms that allows electronic reproduction of acoustic sounds as well as creation of new sounds

TIMBRE
the characteristic quality of sound that distinguishes one voice or musical instrument from another; "tone color"

POST-SPECTRAL
compositional technique that goes beyond sound spectrum analysis, and reunites timbral and harmonic elements with other elements of music

Spectral and Post-Spectral Composition

Post-spectral composers use knowledge gained from spectral composition, placing it within a new framework that attempts to "reconcile" musical elements. One of the leading proponents of spectral and post-spectral composition is Finnish composer Kaija Saariaho. Born in 1952, she began her training at the Sibelius Academy in Helsinki, studying with Paavo Heininen. After hearing a performance of spectral music that she felt was a "revelation," she began taking courses in computer music, first in Freiburg, Germany and later at Paris' IRCAM (Institut de Recherche et de Coordination Acoustique-Musique). The IRCAM research institute remains her home, and she has been a leader in computer-assisted composition since the 1980s.

Saariaho's interest in spectrum analysis is artistically enriched by her concern for reaching audiences with music that goes beyond timbre exploration. To ensure that a composition makes structural sense, she diagrams a macro structure before she composes, sketching out a sense of direction for the transformation of sonic material over time. In addition, she mimics the harmonic idea of tension and release by contrasting two ends of a "sonic axis." On one end are pure sine waves (imagine the sound of a bird whistle), and on the other end is a "noisy, gritty" sound (imagine static, or a breathy voice). Saariaho's manipulation of timbral "tension and release" takes place throughout a work, but is also used to structure big-picture form.[14]

Post-spectral composers such as Saariaho also link electronic elements with live musicians, exploring amplification and on-site sound manipulation. The audience hears the live performers directly, while they simultaneously hear an electronically altered version of the live sound source.[15] In a sense, Saariaho's sonic axis applies here too, with acoustic instruments on one end of the spectrum opposite the electronic sources. The computer functions as an intermediary that blends and fuses the two elements.

Saariaho's aesthetic sense has led to great success in a field that sometimes is limited to an artistically elite audience. Internationally known, and busy with commissions, she has utilized a variety of genres, including song cycles, chamber music, orchestral works, and operas.[16]

Six Japanese Gardens

Six Japanese Gardens is a nineteen-minute work divided into six short parts, the second of which is included on the playlist. In its entirety, the work is a reflection on gardens that the composer saw in Kyoto while traveling in Japan during the summer of 1993. Saariaho was struck by similarities in music and architecture as she viewed the gardens, and noted that both forms select materials, let them grow, and prepare contrasting elements. She also equated the contrasting use of materials in the gardens, such as sand, stones, and moss, to timbral materials of music. Segments of the piece allow percussionists to select non-specified instruments within timbral categories of wood, stone, and metal. In keeping with her tendency to balance musical elements, the composer alternates "purely coloristic material" with rhythmic material.

LISTENING EXPERIENCE 14.2

"Garden of the Kinkaku-ji," Movement II from *Six Japanese Gardens* (1994)
Kaija Saariaho
Playlist

LISTENING FOCUS

Live percussion timbres are combined with pre-recorded ritual singing of Buddhist monks, and pre-recorded traditional Japanese instruments. Using a Macintosh computer and the Chant sound synthesis program, Saariaho produced "ready-mixed" segments to insert into the live performance. Saariaho allows the performer to select instruments within timbre groups; thus each performance of this work might vary.

TIMED LISTENING GUIDE

0:00	percussionist triggers pre-recorded segment of synthesized voices and metallic percussion
0:14	percussionist adds ostinato patterns using mallet percussion; ready-mixed segments continue simultaneously
1:11	live mallet part slows
1:14	live timpani roll

All six movements reflect on rhythmic transformation, starting from a simplistic introduction and moving into polyrhythmic and ostinato figures.[17]

To further expand upon the timbre of the percussion ensemble, electronics are added to the performance. While in Japan, Saariaho recorded nature sounds, the ritual singing of Buddhist monks, and traditional Japanese instruments from the Kunitachi College of Music collection in Tokyo. She then electronically produced the material in her home studio with a Macintosh computer using Chant, a sound synthesis program developed at IRCAM. During the live performance, a percussionist triggers the "ready-mixed" sections using a computer.[18]

LAURIE ANDERSON: CREATOR/PRODUCER/ TECHNICIAN

Laurie Anderson (b. 1947) is not easy to categorize, but she has consistently used technology to create a wide variety of works. She is also part of a newer generation of composers who challenge the demarcation between art and popular music. Anderson burst on to the popular music scene with the release of her 1981 single, "O Superman," a work that was higher art in its construction, yet gripping enough to capture a wide audience. Against a synthesized background, Anderson's electronically altered voice warns, "I've got a message . . . here come the planes," and begs a metaphorical "mom" to hold her in her "automatic arms, electronic arms, petrochemical arms, and military arms." Written during the Iran-Contra scandal, the work also resonated with audiences after the September 11, 2001 attacks on the World Trade Center in New York. Although "O Superman" was embraced mostly by the alternative/ underground market in America in the 1980s, it rose to number two on the charts in Britain.[19] This break connected her with the major label Warner Brothers, where she remained for many years.

Anderson is a multi-faceted artist, having earned degrees in art history and sculpture. Prior to her break with "O Superman," she was an artist and performer in New York's avant-garde art scene, working in theatres and galleries. Anderson's experimental side often reveals itself via a variety of musical/artistic "gadgets" of her own creation, including lights and speakers that she has placed inside of her mouth, and sensors that she has planted on her body to send signals to a drum machine. She has frequently experimented with voice distortion via microphones, making a chorus out of her voice, or rendering it gender neutral. (For a reflection on gender perceptions in electronic voices, see Focus Topic 14.1.) Anderson states that her work comes from "just playing around with equipment, seeing what it will do." She believes that the tools are the teachers, and suggests that hands-on education is essential.[20]

Anderson has continually experimented with multimedia throughout her career, combing music with movies, dance, special stage effects, and special lighting. Readers are encouraged to see excerpts on her website to better understand her work. In spite of her cross-over appeal, Anderson's art-pop is sometimes a bit too alternative for the masses. When she performed on *Late Night with David Letterman* in 1984, they cut to a commercial in the middle of her appearance.[21]

FOCUS TOPIC 14.1

Genre Focus: Gendered Voice Roles and Power Perceptions in Electronic Music

Although technology has changed the delivery method, composers have often portrayed gendered notions of power via use of the human voice in composition. In historical opera and film, women's voices were frequently used in weak, wordless roles such as sobbing and screaming, while male voices were usually favored in powerful text-driven functions. (Think of educational films with narration, and you'll probably hear a deep male voice in your head.) Hannah Bosma traced the evolution of this phenomenon into the realm of tape and computer-generated composition and surmised that many of the same notions were replicated in works that utilized electronic technology. Taped works often captured and manipulated samples of wordless female voices, symbolically holding them "captive" and helpless on tape. This is especially significant considering that male voices rarely were used in this manner in art music composition. Similarly, computer-generated music often features powerless/text-less "female" voices, with authoritative spoken-text roles assigned to male-sounding voices.

See Hannah Bosma, "Gender and Electroacoustics" and "Male and Female Voices in Computer Music." 20 August 2004, at www.hannahbosma.nl.

"Late Show"

One of Anderson's signature "gadgets" is her tape-bow violin, utilized in a work called "Late Show," from her 1986 *Home of the Brave* soundtrack album. Upon first hearing, the listener might wonder in which segment the violin is used. Anderson's modified instrument replaces the hair of the violin bow with pre-recorded audio tape, allowing her to control playback speed and direction by moving the bow.[22] In "Late Show" Anderson builds her work around a spoken sound sample recorded by William S. Burroughs, an author and spoken text performer. The recording also utilizes a minimalistic element, with a background figure that repeats underneath the fragmented sound sample. It is not until the very end of the piece that the recorded sentence is heard in its entirety.

LISTENING EXPERIENCE 14.3

"Late Show" (1986)
Laurie Anderson
Playlist

LISTENING FOCUS

This is a soundtrack from Anderson's 1986 film *Home of the Brave.* Listen for a MIDI audio sample of William S. Burroughs saying "Listen to my heart beat" manipulated via violin bow. The voice sample is layered over a continuous ostinato, which might be compared to a heartbeat.

TIMED LISTENING GUIDE

0:00	Introduction; 0:03 ostinato pattern appears; 0:14 new layer added; 0:20 another layer added
0:56	pre-recorded voice sample audible over ostinato; "listen"
1:09	ostinato layers continue without voice sample
1:38	pre-recorded sample reenters; "listen . . . to . . . . . . my . . ."; speed and pitch manipulated by violin bow
2:04	extended instrumental section, ostinato continues
3:49	pre-recorded sample over ostinato: "listen . . . to . . . my . . ."
4:12	pre-recorded sample complete statement: "listen to my heart beat"; ostinato sputters out

ONGOING ACCOMPLISHMENTS

As women gained access to higher education in the latter half of the twentieth century, the number of women in electroacoustic music exploded in such a manner that it is impossible to include a comprehensive list of composers in a textbook such as this. While a few pioneers will be named here, readers are encouraged to seek additional names via material suggested in the bibliography.[23] Along with composers Barbara Kolb and Thea Musgrave, highlighted in previous portions of the text, some notable women in the field include Jean Eichelberger Ivey (b. 1923), Ruth Anderson (b. 1928), Emma Lou Diemer (b. 1927), Annea Lockwood (b. 1939), Laurie Spiegel (b. 1945), and Elaine Barkin (b. 1932). Whether or not the prolific work of women in electroacoustic music will be incorporated into mainstream historical textbooks remains to be seen, but the amount and quality of their work marks an undeniable change in music history.

TECHNOLOGY AND POPULAR MUSIC

> *We are musicians in our own right. We're playing the console and the tape machines and the microphone.*[24]
>
> Susan Rogers, Producer and Sound Engineer

Women have seemingly cracked a barrier in electroacoustic art music, but women in popular music technology remain a significant minority. Even though the history of electronic popular music is relatively short, its foundation was firmly embedded with societal gender connotations that involved technology, particularly in rock performance and recording. (For information on gendered constructs regarding lyrical content and popular music, see Chapter 15.)

Les Paul's Gibson electric guitar began to dominate rock music shortly after it hit the mass market in the early 1950s and, shortly thereafter, acoustic basses were quickly replaced with electric units, notably the Fender bass. The electrification of guitars created a gender-based dividing line that still persists in rock performance. Acoustic guitars and their stringed ancestors had long been in the female sphere, but blaring amplification (and the gadgetry associated with amplifiers and mixers) quickly placed the public's perception of the electric version in the male domain. The role of lead guitarist in fronting the band, with its subsequent perception of power and control, has been especially difficult for women to transcend. If women played in gender-integrated rock bands at all, they usually found themselves on bass or rhythm guitar.

Guitars and amplifiers were only one segment of emerging rock technology, however. If electric guitars were considered too mechanical and powerful for women, imagine perceptions of women in the 1960s recording studio. Women's liberation was being verbally expressed during this decade, but in reality, there were many remaining roadblocks to equality. Sound equipment was loaded with knobs, wires, and cords, and manipulation of sound waves was a technical skill that required knowledge of the physical properties of sound. It was extremely difficult for women to prove that they were capable of managing the equipment, and aspiring sound engineers reported that even female artists often distrusted women behind the mixing board.

WALL OF SOUND
recorded tracks in which massed instrumental and vocal parts were heightened with echo

The significance of being blocked out of recording technology during this time period cannot be overstated, since much of the artistic creation of popular music shifted into the studio. Within a decade of rock's inception, the field moved away from attempts to faithfully reproduce the sounds of live performers toward studio production and special effects. From the insertion of electronic surf and seagulls in the Beach Boys' hits to the "**wall of sound**" that accompanied the girl groups, popular music language decidedly changed. The producer began to play the role of composer, piecing together the desired timbre, formal design, and construction of a finished product. In essence, it was in the producer's power to orchestrate and shape the trademark "sound" of a group. Increasingly, performers were placed in an artistically inferior position.[25]

SOUND ENGINEERING

The field of sound engineering has been particularly difficult for women to enter. With tremendous power and command, engineers in the studio alter sound after it has been captured, literally taking artistic control into their own hands. In live performance, engineers control sound in real time, using knobs and faders to ensure a desirable mix.[26] Replicating the hallmark "sound" of an artist or group is considered critical, and depends on the skill of the engineer. A group with a bass-driven sound needs to maintain that balance or risk disappointing the audience. Similarly, an imbalance of instruments over voices can obliterate lyrics for groups who care about having their message heard.

Because the engineer's job is so crucial to maintaining a characteristic sound, performers often have strong preferences regarding their sound mixers. Artists tend to pre-judge women engineers unless they walk into the studio with a proven record of excellence, and that necessitates hands-on experience. Accessing studios and equipment, however, has been a key limiting factor that has impacted women in the field. Like any area where control is at stake, access is often denied by those who are reluctant to relinquish power, and the route to the mixing board often begins with apprenticeships. As in many other music fields, women in technology often have had to find other gateways to enter the system.[27]

GAINING ACCESS

Many women worked their way into recording and production by learning from the side of the studio where they were accepted: as performers. Genya Ravan, of Britain's all-women rock band Goldie and the Gingerbreads, eventually began to produce punk acts, and Tina Weymouth took over production of Tom Tom Club, the group she led after she left Talking Heads. With that experience, she was able to work with other artists, co-producing several Ziggy Marley albums and mixing for other groups. Similarly, Salt 'n Pepa's Cheryl James (Salt) got tired of being told what to do and began to do her own production.[28]

Another avenue for women who wished to enter the production arena was to form their own labels. Cordell Jackson (1923–2004) was a widely respected pioneer who gained experience by founding Moon Records in Memphis, Tennessee in 1956. She was ridiculed frequently in the early years, but gained knowledge and esteem by avoiding the mainstream industry. Forty years after she established her label, she lamented that music production and technology was still "a man's world."[29] Another successful label executive is Sylvia Robinson (b. 1936), who established the Sugar Hill record label with her husband in 1979. It was on Sugar Hill that Robinson produced America's first Top-40 hip-hop single, "Rapper's Delight." Subsequently, she is widely credited for introducing hip-hop to mainstream America.[30]

The woman behind the sound for the majority of Laurie Anderson's early recordings was Grammy- and Oscar-nominated producer and sound mixer Roma Baran. Baran approached Anderson in the late 1970s, offering her technological services after she heard Anderson perform. Anderson reflects that Baran made critical suggestions that ultimately impacted her work,

Figure 14.3
Vivian Stoll (left) and Roma Baran (seated at the computer) in their studio.

Source: Photo courtesy of Roma Baran and Vivian Stoll

including the combination of singing and talking that Anderson utilizes, as well as her musically minimalist tendencies.[31] In 2010, another Anderson recording, co-produced by Baran, was released. Baran is not only a producer and engineer but also a performer and a lawyer. Along with Vivian Stoll, she owns and operates Roma Baran and Vivian Stoll Productions in New York. Stoll is a producer, audio engineer, and drummer who was formerly a staff engineer for National Public Radio, and a mastering engineer for world music label Lyrichord.[32]

Independent labels and **women's music festivals** also provided valuable experience for women who sought engineering and production work. Olivia Records, an independent label established by Judy Dlugacz in 1973, not only promoted women artists but also gave women a chance to produce and do live sound mixing. During the same era, the Michigan Womyn's Music Festival (in existence from 1975 to 1985) was a training ground for many of the female sound engineers who were active in the first decade of the twenty-first century. Every aspect of the festival was intended to empower women, from song lyrics to production and engineering. Women's festivals allowed women engineers to gain critical skills in an environment that was safe and encouraging. Engineer Boden Sandstrom recalls her sense of empowerment when she was asked to organize sound for five stages, and to mix on the main stage. "It was the first time I didn't have to fight . . . for recognition."[33]

WOMEN'S MUSIC FESTIVALS feminist music festivals in which all aspects are run by women, including performance, management, staging, and sound

> *It's difficult for an all-male staff to suddenly work with a woman who is not in a traditionally female role. Men are used to women acting as caretakers, note takers, studio managers, assistants . . . not as the ones making the technical decisions.*[34]
>
> Engineer and Producer Leslie Ann Jones

Although she began her technology career working with a gender-segregated band, Leslie Ann Jones quickly worked her way into gender-integrated studio settings. The daughter of entertainer Spike Jones and singer Helen Grayco, Jones launched her impressive career as an audio expert first by working as the road manager and sound mixer for Fanny, one of the early all-female rock bands. She went on to become the first female recording engineer to be hired at ABC Recording Studios in Los Angeles before she moved to the Automatt Studios in northern California. At the Automatt, she worked with such artists as Herbie Hancock, Bobby McFerrin, and Holly Near and began her film score mixing career, working on the movie *Apocalypse Now*. Jones was hired as a staff engineer for Capitol Studios in Hollywood in 1987, where she distinguished herself in the field of jazz recording, and since 1997 she has been Director of Music and Scoring at Skywalker Sound in California. At Skywalker, Jones has done extensive work on film and television score recording as well as video game scores. Her work has been heard on television programming on HBO,

Figure 14.4
Leslie Ann Jones.
Source: Photo courtesy of Leslie Ann Jones

PBS, and CBS, and she has served as live sound mixer for the Grammy Award ceremonies. Throughout her career, the Grammy-winning engineer has worked with an impressive array of performers, including Joan Baez, Carlos Santana, Rosemary Clooney, and the Kronos Quartet. In an interview with National Public Radio, Jones indicated that she specialized in jazz and classical scores because those genres were more "welcoming" to women than rock, which is especially subject to "typecasting."[35]

Women are slowly making strides in the popular music recording industry. In 1998, Trina Shoemaker became the first woman to win a Grammy in engineering for her work on Sheryl Crow's album, *The Globe Sessions*, and subsequently won a Grammy for best pop/contemporary gospel album with *All Things New*, by Steven Curtis Chapman.[36] Still, women continue to be a minority in the field, and while many have worked their way into second engineer positions due to perceptions about their managerial skills, lead engineer positions for women have been harder to attain.[37] In 1993, fewer than 2 percent of lead positions were held by women, and in 2010, women accounted for fewer than 5 percent of people in music technology.[38]

Not unlike the male-dominated fields of instrumental conducting and performance, there is a burden on women who enter music technology in terms of the potential impact on other women. Although men in technology are usually judged as individuals, a woman who does poorly can jeopardize the future of other women in the field.[39] It is a heavy burden to bear.

SUMMARY

As future generations look back, the twentieth century will be viewed as an era of life-changing technology. The impact of electronic technology has been immense on both art and popular music development, and history will show that many women initially found it difficult to gain access to studios, equipment, and hands-on experience in the field. In popular music in particular, women have had to work their way into the profession using a variety of alternative routes, including formation of their own labels and businesses. Standing so near this still-emerging history, we are aware that many women rose above the challenges to become leaders and innovators. What remains to be seen is how this portion of history will be documented for generations yet to come.

QUESTIONS FOR CRITICAL THINKING AND DISCUSSION

1. Think about your response to the art music works in this chapter, and discuss how you might have reacted if you lacked background information on each of them. Does education impact aesthetic response to a work?
2. Sometimes artistic forms that appear to be haphazard are actually strictly controlled. Along with the music discussed in this chapter, discuss how this works in other arts areas. What gives these works the illusion of spontaneity? At the same time, what are the artistic benefits of the "freer" elements of these works?
3. Consider concepts of gender and control in non-musical areas in society that replicate the topics covered in this chapter. For example, the vast majority of primary-grade teachers are women, but many school principals are men. How do you account for the continuation of this phenomenon?
4. Voice your opinion regarding "over-produced" popular music. Also discuss current artists who deviate from this type of production.

IDEAS FOR FURTHER RESEARCH

1. Using computer and video material that you frequently use, analyze gendered voice roles. Do you notice a continuation of male-dominated instructional "voices" and weaker roles for "female" electronic voices?
2. Futurism existed in many artistic forms, including literature, visual art, film, and architecture. Compare characteristics of musical futurism with one or two other artistic forms. Try to determine if there was gender domination in other arts areas at the turn of the twentieth century.
3. Because the topic of music and technology is historically new, we are aware of a blending of art and popular music. Research an older historical period and investigate the merging of art and popular music. Hypothesize about the role of historical documentation in creating a dividing line.

CHAPTER 15

A New Message

Taking Charge in the Mass Music Market

She's an eagle when she flies . . .
Written and sung by Dolly Parton

$1.29 was all it took to make The Go-Go's a household name in the United States. Like other **girl bands** that were successful in Europe in the late 1970s, the Los Angeles-based Go-Go's found the American market difficult to access, so signing with cutting-edge label I.R.S. was a significant break. The second break was seemingly smaller, but had huge repercussions. When the band's single "Our Lips are Sealed" was presented to I.R.S. executives, label bosses initially decided to price the song at $2.98, the label's usual UK-based pricing structure for singles. Barbara Bolan had another idea, however. Newly hired by I.R.S. in 1981 as a sales manager, Bolan had listened to material by The Go-Go's repeatedly and knew that this group could be "something big." She convinced label executives to price and market the song at $1.69 instead, the going rate for singles in the United States. It was a good decision for The Go-Go's, I.R.S., and Bolan.

GIRL BAND
rock band in which women play their own instruments; as opposed to a girl group that consists of singers

LISTENING EXPERIENCE 15.1

"We Got the Beat" (1981)
Performed by The Go-Go's, written by Charlotte Caffey
Playlist

"We Got the Beat" was a single from the number one album from The Go-Go's, *Beauty and the Beat* (1981). Along with performing their own instrumentals, the band members penned eight of the eleven singles on the album. Although girl bands had been accepted in Europe, the success of The Go-Go's in the American market was unprecedented.

Figures 15.1 and 15.2

In the 1970s and 1980s, Barbara Bolan frequently was the only woman in the room at conferences (other than Playboy Bunnies, as in this 1979 photo taken at a Warner-Elektra-Atlantic Records conference). In the second photo, Bolan is shown holding a framed photograph of The Go-Go's.

Sources: 15.1 Courtesy of Barbara Bolan; 15.2 Photo by Michelle Stocker, Copyright Wisconsin State Journal. Reprinted with permission

"Our Lips are Sealed" broke into the Top 40, and Bolan's next few months were spent eating, sleeping, and breathing The Go-Go's. Bolan accompanied the band on a tour bus, worked the record stores and radio stations, and reported on marketing progress during evening sound checks. The news kept getting better. As the women loaded the bus each night, they did so to the sound of their own voices on the airwaves. They had made a hit, and they were making history. The Go-Go's became the first all-female rock band to have a number one album in America.

In terms of career, Bolan "made it" too, in an industry that was predominantly run by men. After rising to the level of general manager at I.R.S., she moved on to Virgin Records America, and eventually became senior director of international marketing for industry giant Rhino Entertainment. Along the way she promoted such artists as Tina Turner, the Spice Girls, Lenny Kravitz, R.E.M., and David Bowie. Bolan's rise through the industry was not without its awkward moments. She was often the only woman in the room at convention gatherings, and for years was the only woman at weekly I.R.S. executive meetings. When she became pregnant shortly after the big break for The Go-Go's, Bolan was understandably worried about disclosing the news, as her pregnancy marked another significant first at I.R.S. Although the company responded favorably, her announcement sent a puzzled label executive in search of his father for advice about how to handle the situation.[1]

CULTURAL VALUES AND THE BOTTOM LINE

It would be easy to blame an overabundance of male music executives for blocking women's bands from the American rock scene, but that would be telling only part of the story. The bottom line for business is to make a profit, and the goal in marketing is to capture the imagination of consumers willing to pay for a product.[2] Rock's target consumer base was reluctant to accept women in genres that were loud, aggressive, and delivered by electronics, as discussed at length in Chapter 14.

The perception of power exuded by early rock was propelled by a simplistic three-chord harmonic progression that almost anyone could learn to play. Rock was more than music, however. It was a form of social rebellion that focused on sexuality, and in the 1950s, women were not supposed to be rebellious or aggressively sexual. Without a doubt, male rockers also were criticized by a generation that preferred Bing Crosby and Rosemary Clooney. Still, the profitability of rock recordings signaled a cultural genre shift, and with it, an acceptance of lyrics that boldly objectified women. Changing that mold was difficult for industry executives to imagine.

Worldwide revenues in the music industry topped sixty-six *billion* dollars in 2010, and a phenomenal number of people operate the inner workings of

Figure 15.3
Janis Joplin c.1960.
Source: © Tom Copi/Getty Images

the system. Industry employees include managers, legal analysts, financiers, talent scouts, marketers, producers, salespeople, and distributors. These positions constitute just some of the links in the music business chain that must align to connect a potential star to a mainstream audience. Breaking in is challenging for anyone, but particularly so for anyone perceived as a financial risk.

One of the pioneering women in rock who successfully broke the traditional mold was Janis Joplin (b. 1943). A woman of legend, her story is often told with the tragic spin of popular media. She sang her guts out on stage, expressing a raw sexuality that had previously been in the realm of men. Particularly inspired by blues singers such as Big Mama Thornton, Joplin's signature hit was a cover of Thornton's "Ball and Chain." Joplin's blues-inspired rock spoke to the depths of her audience, and her wailing, growling voice projected freedom and passion. She died of a heroin overdose at age twenty-seven, and it only added to her legacy. Her story lived on as people speculated about her death, convinced that it was connected to low self-esteem that she masked with an aggressive stage presence.[3]

Despite the many ways in which Joplin was an anomaly, she nonetheless operated somewhat within the bounds of societal expectation by remaining primarily a vocalist. The majority of women in rock who became commercially successful did so with the aid of a microphone, acoustic guitar, or piano. Women who delivered rock's message to the tune of their own electric guitars were considered the true outsiders of the rock world.

LEADER OF THE BAND, OWNER OF THE LABEL

Rock Messages Old and New

She does just what she's told . . . she's under my thumb.
Mick Jagger in "Under my Thumb"

A girl can do what she wants to do . . .
Joan Jett in "Bad Reputation"

Just as I.R.S. Records was marketing the second big single for The Go-Go's, "We Got the Beat," they ran into stiff competition from a hit called "I Love Rock and Roll." The artist was Joan Jett, and her "bad reputation" image was a double dose of lyrical content and electric guitar playing. Inspired by rock guitarist Suzi Quatro, Jett followed the international women's rock scene with interest, and began to project an image similar to Suzi's: black leather jacket, jewelry, shag haircut, and, of course, an amplified instrument. Jett went to her first guitar lesson expecting to rock. When the teacher gave her a weird look and began to teach her "On Top of Old Smokey," she knew she would have to go another route. She taught herself by playing along with Black Sabbath recordings and listening to Led Zeppelin.[4]

As a teen, Jett joined an all-girl band called The Runaways. (A 2010 movie about the group was co-produced by Jett.) The fifteen- and sixteen-year-old girls adopted a tough-girl look, performed hard rock, and partied like any other band in the market. Although the partying lifestyle was the norm for male groups, the American public was not ready to accept the image for young girls. The thrill of performing rock blended with the frustration of being ridiculed, musically dismissed, and socially isolated. The Runaway's American audience was 99 percent male and, to some extent, out to make fun of the group. Jett said, "That was kind of depressing. Why didn't women—our own gender—come out and support us?"[5]

There were few other girl bands with whom to connect and exchange frustrations, and the frustrations were many. Promotional interviews were often disastrous in terms of public relations. Band members entered interviews expecting to talk about music, but interviewers inevitably wanted to talk about sex. When the girls declined that angle, the interviewers called them "every name you can call a woman," said Jett. "How are you going to react when you're sixteen?"[6] The foul-mouthed response of the girls in the band resulted in making bad reputations even worse. It was not long before group members went in individual directions. Lead guitarist Lita Ford went on to a career in metal, singer/bassist Micki Steele became associated with The Bangles, and Jett had a huge career looming on the horizon. First, however, she had to forge her way into the marketplace by taking matters into her own hands.

Jett was despondent after The Runaways disbanded, but a connection with husband-wife managers Kenny and Meryl Laguna helped save her. Ignoring Kenny's initial advice that she should hire a male guitarist for her next set of demos, Jett retained the lead role and hired three men to back her, forming the group The Blackhearts. The group immediately experienced roadblocks. "Nobody wanted anything to do with us. They said Joan Jett from the Runaways has a bad reputation."[7]

INDIE
independent record label

When The Blackhearts sent out their initial set of demo recordings, they received twenty-three rejection letters, not only from major labels but also from **Indies**, who were known for taking on alternative and underground groups. It was not about the musical material. The tapes contained four eventual hits, including "I Love Rock and Roll," "Do You Want to Touch Me?" "Bad Reputation," and "Crimson and Clover." Still, Jett was told that there were "no good songs" in the batch. Whether it was prejudice or just poor judgment on the part of the record companies, Jett knew better.[8]

The Blackhearts made 5,000 copies of "Bad Reputation" and sold them out of the trunk of the Lagunas' car after concerts in New York. There was such a "buzz" that they printed and sold another 5,000. Before long, the band was shutting down freeways when they performed in Long Island. By forming the "Blackheart Records" label, Jett was able to bypass the discovery stage, and additionally retained the artistic creativity she desired. The next step was connecting to a company to manage distribution and sales, and Blackheart signed with a small company called Boardwalk. With increased market success, the Blackheart label moved to increasingly bigger companies, including Epic and Warner Brothers. The woman who had been told to hand over her guitar to a man is now listed among *Rolling Stone*'s Top 100 guitarists of all time.[9]

LISTENING EXPERIENCE 15.2

"I Love Rock and Roll" (1982)
Joan Jett and The Blackhearts
Playlist

"I Love Rock and Roll" was the number one single for seven weeks in 1982. Jett formed her own label, Blackheart Records, to propel her group past the difficult "discovery" stage. After "I Love Rock and Roll," her discovery days were history. Her message: women can rock, and can make money doing so.

Figure 15.4
Suzi Quatro's electric bass playing and wardrobe inspired female rockers who wanted to challenge conventional ideas about femininity in rock music.
Source: Photo courtesy of Suzi Quatro

EXPLOITATION AND MARKETING

Music executive Bettina Richards also understands the travails of breaking into the music industry, but from another angle. Before starting the Thrill Jockey label in 1992, Richards was hired to do A&R (artist and repertoire) research for "the majors." She started her own label because she was troubled by the "boy's club" mentality, and by the tendency to treat musicians as commodities. "They were no longer artists, they were product, and if something didn't fit, it was chucked."[10] Industry executive Barbara Bolan confirmed that she customized her sales techniques to the perspective of individual buyers. While some were musical and wished to discuss an artist's musicality, other buyers spoke only of "product," and simply wanted to receive an artist selection number.[11]

It is probably difficult for readers to imagine their favorite pop stars referenced by selection number. The seemingly glorious celebrity lifestyle is often deceptively difficult, however. The thrill of a multi-thousand dollar advance from a major label quickly dissipates when artists find that decision-making shifts behind someone else's desk. In addition, bands have to pay for manager and lawyer fees, studio time, and promotional costs. Many groups end up in debt. Further, the company owns permanent rights to the group, including copyright on recordings, sheet music, and artist photographs. In 2000 Courtney Love complained:

> When you look at the legal line on a CD, it says copyright 1976 Atlantic Records or copyright 1996 RCA Records. When you look at a book, though, it'll say something like copyright 1999 Susan Faludi, or David Foster Wallace. Authors own their books and license them to publishers. When the contract runs out, writers get their books back. But record companies own our copyrights forever.[12]

Marketing strategies also impact women artists who disagree with the types of sexual imagery used in promotion. Hard-rock artist Pat Benatar, for example, was repeatedly subjected to sexist marketing strategies that left her embarrassed and frustrated, including a shot for *Billboard* in which part of her shirt was airbrushed off. She retaliated with the only bit of control she had, by cutting her hair short.[13]

The Go-Go's drew criticism from feminist groups who, while they celebrated the group's success, decried publicity such as the August 1982 *Rolling Stone* cover image that had the women dressed in underwear alongside the caption, "Go-Go's Put Out." The contents of the article also made it clear where mainstream rock writers placed women in rock at that point in history: "They're simply comfortable being female . . . the Go-Go's are safe, wholesome and proudly commercial."[14]

Prior to The Go-Go's, and beneath the scenes of the wider music industry, other women had been refusing to submit to the kind of fame that drew praise from *Rolling Stone*. For these women, alternative genres and distribution methods became the means of expressing their own brand of musical rebellion.

GOING UNDERGROUND: TAKING OWNERSHIP OF THE MESSAGE

Conflicting Messages

I was born a woman I didn't have no say . . . because to be his woman no price is too great to pay.

Sandy Posey in "Born a Woman," 1966

In the coming age of feminine society, we'll regain our human dignity.

Yoko Ono in "Woman Power," 1973

The seeds of women's alternative music were sown in the 1960s, a period of cultural change that was marked by the Vietnam War, the Civil Rights movement, and discussions about equal rights for women. Despite the talk, however, media representations and social realities for women remained largely unchanged. Other than the studio-produced girl groups of the 1960s, the most visible female members of the popular music world were folksingers such as Joan Baez (b. 1941), Joni Mitchell (b. 1943), and Mercedes Sosa (1935–2009). The unadorned appearance and message-filled lyrics of these singers appealed to people who cared about issues such as peace, justice, and environmentalism. Although singer-songwriters and folksingers addressed socially controversial topics, their acoustic accompaniments and song-like delivery placed them in alignment with historical notions of women as singers rather than instrumentalists. As such, they achieved lasting fame more regularly than did women who favored hard rock and alternative styles.

LISTENING EXPERIENCE 15.3

"Solo Le Pido a Dios" ["I Only Ask of God"] from *30 Años* (1993)
Mercedes Sosa
Playlist

Mercedes Sosa, known as the "voice of the voiceless," conveyed a tireless message of compassion and empowerment on behalf of people in poverty. "I only ask of God . . . He won't let me be indifferent to the suffering."

Until the 1960s, the rebellion associated with rock had been focused on the male perspective, and women who addressed their own views found their voices silenced by the industry. To express their opinions, many elected to subvert the musical system. Along with the amateur punk movement that was formulating in the garage band scene, several avant-garde performers began to sound alternative messages.

To many Americans, Yoko Ono (b. 1933) was best known as "the wife of John Lennon." In the history of women's music, she was a fundamental voice who inspired others to address women's concerns in musical performance. Ono's arts background was diverse. She was a classically trained pianist who was familiar with the work of experimental composers Arnold Schoenberg (1874–1951) and John Cage (1912–1992), and also had extensive literary background. Ono combined her areas of expertise to create performance events that featured music, poetry, and readings. Her performances, delivered

Figure 15.5
Joni Mitchell in a 1979 jazz festival photograph.
Source: Leonard Feather Collection. Reprinted by permission of the University of Idaho

with harsh, screaming vocals, contained lyrics that addressed sexism and inequality. Although her work was considered noise by many, her choice of topics and her delivery style foreshadowed the wave of punk that was to come.[15]

Similarly, Patti Smith (b. 1946) combined rock, theatre, poetry, and visual art in the New York avant-garde arts world of the early 1970s. Along with her onstage look and raw-voiced presentations, she also lived the punk lifestyle offstage, defying the media and refusing to answer questions she did not like. Her album covers depicted an androgynous persona that was as unusual for women performers of that era as was her music. For women in rock, it was a bold new expression.[16]

PUNK ROCK
rock subgenre characterized by simple chords, loud volume, distortion, and strong anti-establishment messages

GARAGE BAND
amateur rock band named for the perceived site of their operations, the garage

MISOGYNY
a hatred of women or girls

By the mid-1970s, punk bands in the United Kingdom began to proclaim an anti-establishment message that ridiculed the rock star image, including the genre's extended guitar and drum solos, smoke screens, and use of technology. In America, **punk rock** was connected with the **garage band** movement that made similar statements against the rock music industry, and additionally decried the objectification of women.[17] Punk rockers returned to basic I IV V chord progressions rather than extended technical solos, purposefully distorted their guitars, and screamed angry messages that addressed discrimination, **misogyny** and liberal feminism.[18] Because punk culture condemned technique, amateurs were welcome, and that included women who had not previously played electric guitar.[19]

Distribution methods for punk also subverted the system, and included reproduction of inexpensive cassette tape recordings as well as hand- or typewritten **fanzines** (zines) that were published and reproduced on copy machines. Along with spreading the message of the music, the zines were used as teaching vehicles. Women who did not know about electric guitars or chord progressions often learned from the underground, via instructions and diagrams.

FANZINE
also referred to as zine; a publication created by supporters of a particular movement, often reproduced and distributed inexpensively

As the punk movement gained momentum, a number of women became involved in groups, several of which were gender-integrated. Britain's X-Ray Spex featured female front-person Marion Elliot (known as Poly Styrene), and that group was chronologically followed by The Au Pairs, as well as the all-female Raincoats. Female punk groups often addressed issues of rape and sexual abuse, as they simultaneously refused to allow the music industry (or rigid feminists of the era) to tell them how to dress, play their instruments, or move on stage. Art punk groups such as Talking Heads, with Tina Weymouth on bass, were far more likely to include women in gender-integrated bands than were mainstream groups. Talking Heads, and other groups like them, saw risk-taking as part of their art, and having a woman in the midst of the band was not considered an abnormality. Even in these groups, however, the role of lead guitar remained a "last bastion" of the male rock domain. Despite the skill of women such as Joni Mitchell, Joan Jett, and Liz Phair, the image of the male lead guitarist was difficult to change, and few new role models were evident in 1980s media such as MTV.[20]

Although women in punk were not widely embraced by the general public, they did their part to move women in rock beyond novelty status. By the 1980s, women were able to move into punk's offshoot genres. Soon thereafter, women entered the mainstream rock/pop market in force, often addressing topics that would have been considered commercial suicide just a decade earlier.

DIVERSE VOICES OF 1980s ROCK

Like many alternative styles, punk eventually was captured by the industry and evolved into studio-produced genres such as **New Wave** and **hard punk**. With the market success of New Wave groups such as The Go-Go's, women increasingly broke into the market. They performed in a wide array of styles and genres. Soloists such as Sara McLachlan stood in contrast to rock bands such as Heart, fronted by sisters Ann and Nancy Wilson, but both genres were commercially successful. Kate Bush exemplified a post-punk bohemian style that blended Irish folk with rock, and Pat Benatar favored the hard rock style.

NEW WAVE
spin-off punk genre that featured a more manufactured sound, but retained the simplicity of 1950s rock

HARD PUNK
spin-off punk genre that was more aggressive than original punk; also called hardcore

With four Grammy awards and eleven Top-40 singles, Benatar proved that women could capture the mainstream market while addressing topical issues such as abuse and bad relationships.[21]

By the mid-1980s, women were no longer novelties in rock. When Suzanne Vega's song "Luka" hit the Top 10 in 1987, it surprised industry executives who had not anticipated the song's success. In addressing the topic of child abuse, Vega completely removed herself from the historical roots of rock. It was a major turning point in rock history.[22] Female performers began to get more press, and articles with headlines about women as "best new artist" began to emerge. When it was clear that commercial success was possible, the major labels came on board. It was not long, however, before some women sought to break free of those labels again.

WOMEN, PRODUCTION, AND A NEW MESSAGE

As different as rap, country, rock, and pop sound musically, one thing the genres have in common is a historical tendency to objectify women. Lyrics about women taking orders, women being humiliated, and women being physically abused were prevalent in all commercial genres. The women of the lyrics had no choice but to remain silent, and when marketing turned to video, women's faces revealed that they *liked* being objectified and abused. The listening public was saturated with sexist messages that were delivered in a conscious-numbing manner, smoothed over by the benign delivery mode of music.

Stories of male producers who orchestrated this imagery are legendary. Although some producer tales have been exaggerated in the form of movies and other media, there is undeniable evidence that many women were dissatisfied with their lack of artistic control. In every genre from rock to country, performers complained about being subjected to offensive camera angles, undesirable dance instructions, and sexist marketing techniques. At worst, some women even had to sing lyrics that they found offensive. Women who wanted to control their own images and messages found that the best avenue was to produce their own work.

Rapping a New Message

. . . didn't know what hit her, didn't have time to ask.

Ice-T in "6 'n the Mornin"

You say I'm nothing without ya, but I'm nothing with ya, a man don't really love you if he hits ya.

Queen Latifah in "U.N.I.T.Y."

RAPPING ABOUT RAP

New York disc jockey Afrika Bambaataa is credited with developing the music that eventually became known as "**rap**." Bambaataa was an ex-gang member who believed that the arts could be used in a positive way to combat gang violence. In the 1970s, Bambaataa promoted such artistic expressions as break dancing, rapping, and graffiti drawing. Performances took place at parties, on playgrounds, and in the streets. "Hip-hop, you don't stop" was the frequent chant that led to a labeling of the genre, and by the mid-1970s, it had become dance music. DJs used turntables and a sound mixer to take musical segments and create a rhythmic layering above which they improvised verses. The MC, almost always a man, eventually took on the role of "rapping," so the DJ could focus on spinning records and mixing.

RAP
genre that features an MC who recites verses over a DJ accompaniment

A **hip-hop culture** developed around the music, and by the early 1980s, rap groups were touring and reaching out to a wider public. The early commercial rappers were almost all men, including M. C. Hammer, Ice-T, Dr. Dre, Ice Cube, Snoop Doggy Dogg, and L L cool J (Ladies Love Cool James).[23] Like much of 1970s and 1980s rock, commercial rap lyrics were sometimes overtly sexist and some were violently misogynist. The rap community divided, and subgenres emerged that espoused a variety of beliefs, ranging from gangsta rap to music that addressed societal inequity.[24]

HIP-HOP CULTURE
cultural movement that includes rap, break dancing, graffiti art, and urban fashion

Some of the first women to break into the commercial rap scene were artists who began to do their own production. Salt 'n' Pepa (Cheryl James, b. 1964, and Sandy Denton, b. 1969) became the first female rappers to hit the Top 40. With hits such as "Spinderella's Not a Fella" (referring to their

Figure 15.6
Queen Latifah, 2009.
Source: © Neilson Barnard/ Getty Images

female deejay) to "Tramp" (which turned the lyrical table by referring to promiscuous men), they tackled subject matter from a female perspective. They gained even more ground when they took control of their careers and began to write their own material, with Cheryl James working as producer.

Queen Latifah (Dana Owens, b. 1970) also moved into production, and was embraced by listeners who respected not only her performance ability but also her Afrocentric and socially conscious lyrics. Latifah used her talent to address the objectification of women, sometimes directly attacking the misogynist rap element. In "U.N.I.T.Y." (1993), she rapped, "Who you calling a bitch," while her "Latifah's had it Up 2 here" made it clear that women had taken enough abuse. Latifah has been reluctant to label herself a "feminist," preferring to align herself with male rappers who addressed social issues in non-violent ways. Like many black women before her, Latifah addressed male domination and abuse while remaining firm in her commitment to fight alongside black men for the liberation of all black people.[25] She upheld the positive elements of rap by making it clear that real women dislike objectification and violence.

LISTENING EXPERIENCE 15.4

"U.N.I.T.Y." (1993)
Queen Latifah
Playlist

Queen Latifah's message in U.N.I.T.Y. was clear: women's self-esteem is found within, and breaking away from an abusive situation is empowering. "You say I'm nothing without ya, but I'm nothing with ya, a man don't really love you if he hits ya."

WOMEN OF COUNTRY MUSIC: A NEW PERSPECTIVE

Country Messages Old and New

I got girls who cook, I got girls who clean, I got girls who do everything in between.

Hank Williams Jr., in "All my Rowdy Friends are Comin' over Tonight"

Just consider me gone.

Reba McEntire, in "Consider Me Gone"

Women in rap and rock were not the only performers taking matters into their own hands by the latter decades of the twentieth century. Although women in country music had been writing lyrics since the days of Maybelle Carter, their work was often unrecognized on paper, and their influence in business affairs had been limited. Those who aspired to create change had a good role model in Dolly Parton.

Born in a one-room cabin in Tennessee, Dolly Parton (b. 1946) was the fourth of twelve children. Her father was a sharecropper/moonshiner, while her mother did the work of the home and taught her children to sing despite their poverty. Dolly's songwriting skills were immediately apparent, and equally apparent was her courage in addressing women's issues in her song lyrics. From the topic of prostitution in "Mama Say a Prayer" to being pregnant and abandoned in "Down in Dover," she wrote songs that extolled the strength of women, including "Coat of Many Colors," written about an actual patchwork coat that her mother had made for her. More controversial were songs such as "The Bargain Store," in which she compared her body to used goods. Long associated with country star Porter Wagoner as a duet partner, Parton was also connected to his recording empire. Although Dolly was becoming one of the biggest female stars in the country industry by the mid-1970s, she was not making any money. The woman who grew up in a cabin without electricity and running water did not think that was fair, so she cut ties with Wagoner. Her courageous step resulted in a lawsuit, but freed her to create an empire.[26]

Not only did Dolly Parton make a fortune, she also opened new doors for the entire country music industry, men and women included.[27] Her "blond wig and big-eyelashes" image was intentional. "You'd be amazed at how expensive it is to make a wig look this cheap," she joked.[28] Her savvy carried over into the business side of the music industry as well. She has successfully engaged in such diverse activities as hosting a television show, building a theme park, and owning a movie production company. Even before the turn

LISTENING EXPERIENCE 15.5

"Coat of Many Colors" (1969)
Dolly Parton
Score excerpt available in *Contemporary Anthology of Music by Women*
Playlist

Dolly Parton frequently writes songs about strong women. In "Coat of Many Colors" she wrote of her own mother's positive spirit and ingenuity in the face of poverty. At the same time, she addressed the self-giving of all mothers who sacrifice for their children. "We had no money, but I was rich as I could be . . ."

of the twenty-first century, her monetary worth was reportedly two hundred million dollars. Her gift to the country music industry was an understanding of how to market to the masses.[29]

Reba McEntire's (b. 1955) entrance into country music was not unlike that of other women in the genre, but her business endeavors were groundbreaking. Reba was raised on a 7,000-acre ranch, where she lifted feed sacks and worked cattle. Her mother taught the kids to sing harmony in the back seat of a car as they drove between rodeo sites. Reba was discovered singing the national anthem at a rodeo, and after a successful demo session, she signed with Mercury Records in 1975.

Like Dolly Parton, McEntire became commercially successful but found that she was often out of money. She did not know anything about the music business when she arrived in Nashville, but it did not take her long to learn. After being awarded the County Music Association Female Vocalist of the Year three years in a row (1985–1987), she decided that she did not want to be "a puppet anymore" and began to manage her own affairs. She fired her manager and began to coproduce her albums. Eventually, she established a publishing firm, a booking agency, and a management company. Showing her marketing savvy, she was one of the first country artists to explore music video as an area of promotion, a medium that had been dominated by rock.

Not only did Reba build a dynasty for herself, she made it a point to help other women, engaging the services of women songwriters whenever possible, and singing material that addressed women's concerns. Since the 1990s, McEntire has been instrumental in helping other women make a break in the male-dominated country music industry. "Women still have to prove themselves four times as much as a man does," she claimed. The woman who entered the country music scene in blue jeans had taken matters into her own hands.[30]

MESSAGES VERSUS MANUFACTURING

In the 1990s, women found unprecedented market success. Not only was commercial achievement possible, it was probable, and women began dominating the Grammys. A wide range of female artists came into the public eye, including Alanis Morissette, Celine Dion, the Spice Girls, Tori Amos, and Lauryn Hill, as well as crossover artists such as Shania Twain and LeAnn Rimes. The decade also marked the establishment of Lilith Fair, an all-woman tour and traveling festival founded by Sarah McLachlan that ran from 1996 through 1999. With social consciousness as a theme, the festival raised over ten million dollars for charitable organizations for women.[31]

Just as women were finding widespread commercial success, trouble was looming for the music industry. Part of the fallout was a result of their own

LISTENING EXPERIENCE 15.6

"World on Fire" (2004)
Sarah McLachlan
Playlist

Which would you choose? $11,000 for video editing, or $11,000 to run a hospital for street children for one year?

Sarah McLachlan's low-cost video for "World on Fire" suggests how music video production expenditures could be used for basic necessities in third-world countries. In her words, "The more we take, the less we become . . ."

creation, as audiences rebelled against stale, merchandise-driven music that was manufactured in the studio. Some performers were so musically weak that pitch correcting software was needed to disguise their singing. Internet music sales created additional financial trouble for the industry when file downloading replaced the $16 compact disc with $.99 singles. Many music industry executives lost their jobs.[32]

> *We don't look at Mariah Carey as a dance-pop artist. We look at her as a franchise.*[33]
>
> Don Ienner, Columbia Records

Trouble for the industry impacted artists as well. Record companies merged into national and international conglomerates, and national radio mergers such as Clear Channel eliminated many locally owned and operated music stations. As a result, artist rosters were rapidly reduced.[34] Industry downsizing impacted women and men, as companies embraced the factory model of production, pouring financial resources into developing single raw "products" rather than multiple artists. The success of performers such as Mariah Carey brought huge relief to corporate investors. Not only was Carey's voice and stage persona marketable, she had the ability to cross into multiple markets. Not all financially successful performers have been as musically able as Carey, however. With stage and screen presence of utmost importance, many musically excellent groups remained untapped by the industry.[35]

HISTORY REPEATED? RIOT GRRRL AND REGGAETON

Although the electronic portion of rock/pop history is brief, it has already experienced the pendulum shifting found in every aspect of historical study.

Just as Classicism gave way to Romanticism, and times of war turn to times of peace, overproduced music and market-produced images of women resulted in a resurgence of punk-style sound and messages in the late 1990s. The name of the new rebellion was **Riot Grrrl**. Like the punk movement that preceded it, Riot Grrrl was a support group system and sociological movement as well as a genre. Along with art and film projects, Riot Grrrl groups returned to underground methods of distribution and communication, using internet-distributed fanzines. Groups often used private labels to avoid censors.[36] A "girlish" dress code was one way of lashing out against assimilation of male culture via dressing "tough," and topics such as self-abuse, incest, date rape, and lesbian relationships were addressed with "in your face" aggressiveness.[37] As Riot Grrrl groups exposed their bodies and threw themselves into mosh pits, they displayed violence in performance that reflected the fury they felt inside.[38]

RIOT GRRRL
feminist movement of the 1990s associated with third-wave feminism

Misogyny reemerged in the form of **reggaeton**, a multi-ethnic music that developed in Panama and gained momentum in Puerto Rico. Due to transnational record company mergers, reggaeton spread rapidly in international markets. Just as elements of rap expressed important sociological messages, reggaeton also was a source of ethnic identity that spoke against poverty and racism, this time on behalf of a multi-ethnic youth culture.[39] On the negative side, though, reggaeton was criticized for its connections to violent gang culture and persistent portrayals of female submission. Like most genres, reggaeton splintered into diverse subgenres that spoke to a variety of special interests. Women were in the minority in presenting alternative views, but performers such as Ivy Queen found strong commercial success.

REGGAETON
multi-ethnic music that developed in Panama and Puerto Rico in the 1990s; blends reggae with Latin dance styles

SUMMARY

The world of popular music is a rapidly changing entity, but some trends are nonetheless evident. Society has continued to uphold female singer-songwriters who deliver their messages with acoustic guitars, piano accompaniments, and discernable lyrics. At the same time, rock instrumentalists and hard-rock lyricists (unless they are male) often have had difficulty tapping into a mainstream industry that is concerned with commercial success. To practice their art, women have often turned to gender-segregated groups and alternative formats. When the industry inevitably grasps the musical success of their alternative world, it ironically destroys the original message by producing it to fit a wider market. New voices rebel again, and the cycle continues.

The commercialism of popular music has resulted in a consistent trend to market women in a manner that reaches the dominant culture. Since popular music artists are judged by commercial success and overall popularity, the burden on women to have a "look" has sometimes prevailed over the requirement that they are musically able. For that reason, marginal performers can attain notoriety, while stronger musicians sometimes remain in relative obscurity. This only serves to perpetuate stereotypes about women's musical ability.

In any age, popular music is a reflection of cultural values. Cultures that label "women engineers," "women presidents," and "women rock bands" are labeling men as normal by default. How strange it would be to encounter a history of "men in rock."[40]

On the positive side, women in popular music have always found a way to remain vocal and productive in spite of challenges and lack of recognition. As history continues, we can confidently predict that messages of importance to women will not be silenced.

QUESTIONS FOR CRITICAL THINKING AND DISCUSSION

1. Discuss today's music industry in terms of performers and marketing. Considering both male and female performers, how does the current situation compare with the historical account presented in this chapter?
2. Discuss the current status of protest music in America. Who is involved, and what messages are being conveyed? Are these artists working outside of the mainstream market by choice?
3. Using a sample of several different genres currently on the mainstream market, determine which musical features are common across genres. Then determine which musical elements give each genre its distinctive flavor. Is current studio production leading to a more generic mass music product?

IDEAS FOR FURTHER RESEARCH

1. With historically changing gender roles in mind, review the history of black social protest music and compare it with rap.
2. Compare and contrast the lyrical messages and musical quality of two current popular artists. Focus on one artist who does her own production and one who works with a producer. Do you notice any differences in their final products?

GUIDED RESEARCH PROJECT PART V

"WOMEN'S MUSIC" AND SEGREGATION

Debating the Pros and Cons

Part V presented information about three areas that were particularly reluctant to include women. Many times, women opted to operate in segregation to allow themselves opportunities to participate and gain valuable experience in these areas. Is segregation the best option? One way to broaden your perspective on this topic is to research the role of Women's Music Festivals and women-identified music. The culmination of your research will be an in-class debate.

Some preparatory work prior to the debate:

1. Begin with a quick internet search of current festivals labeled as "women's music festivals." What types of music are included, and who is hosting the current festivals?
2. Now look at the festival movement historically, investigating such festivals as the Michigan Womyn's Music Festival of the 1970s and 1980s as well as the historical underpinnings of Lilith Fair. What were the goals of such gatherings originally and how do they compare with today's versions of the same festivals?
3. With the guidance of your instructor, attempt to access opposing feminist viewpoints regarding women's music festivals. You may also wish to access non-feminist perspectives.
4. Attempt to define and understand the term "women-identified music."
5. Research Olivia Records, a label founded in the 1970s to promote women's music. What were the goals of this label? Did they succeed? Why or why not?

With the above material in hand, divide the class and have a debate regarding the role of women's music and women's music festivals in furthering the cause of women in music. Be prepared to take either side of the argument.

Glossary

absolute music music that does not seek to suggest a story or scene, but is concerned with formal construction; distinguished from program music

aesthetic experience emotional and sometimes physiological response elicited by an artistic work

affect predominant emotion of an artistic work

agrément French for "charm"; refers to an ornament in music, usually indicated by a written sign in the music

Akan ethnic group of West Africa

analog technology technology that takes an audio signal and translates it into electronic pulses

antebellum period period before the Civil War

antiphon type of chant sung before or after the recitation of a psalm in the Office; also associated with psalmody in the Mass

arch form a sectional musical structure in which music progresses toward a midpoint and then retraces its steps, usually symmetrically

aria lyric song for solo voice; also found in several large-scale genres, including opera and cantata

art song a song written by a trained composer to convey a specific artistic idea, as in projecting the mood and meaning of a poetic text

atonal lacking a tonal center, or "key"

avant-garde a French military term, meaning to be in advance of others; in music, refers to those who lead the way to the artistic future, even at the expense of risk

backbeat in popular music, a primary accent on the second and fourth beats of a four-beat measure

ballad in the blues and popular music tradition of the twentieth century, a smooth, lyrical song often about love; in the folk tradition, a song that tells a story of everyday life

barrelhouse-style piano blues style that combined rag-inspired melodies with boogie-woogie bass lines

basso continuo "continuous bass"; Baroque system in which a bass line is written out and an instrument fills in appropriate harmony

bitonal simultaneous use of two different keys

blackface theatrical make-up used in vaudeville and minstrel shows that portrayed racist stereotypes of black Americans

blues scale in Western terms, a major scale with flatted third, fifth, and seventh tones

boogie-woogie piano style that emerged in the 1930s; featured syncopated melody against driving, repeated bass figure

bop jazz combo style of the 1950s with extended solos; sometimes called hard bop

Brill Building office building on Broadway in New York that was a central focus of girl group music production in the late 1950s and early 1960s

Broadway New York theatre district associated with musical productions; also used in reference to the productions themselves

call and response a musical form where one (or more) musician performs a musical phrase or statement (the call), and another soloist or group answers with another phrase or statement (the response)

canary role in jazz, a female vocal soloist who is spotlighted in front of an ensemble

cantata based on the Italian "to sing"; sacred or secular vocal work with performance forces ranging from soloist, to chorus and orchestra

case study research method that focuses on collection and presentation of detailed information about a particular person or small group; research using this technique is not intended for generalization

castrato castrated male singer who sings in the soprano or alto range

chamber music music for performance by a small group, usually with one performer to a part, as in a string quartet; originally for small audiences

chance music in which random procedures (such as coin tossing) determine the outcome of a work

chanson French secular song

chant a monophonic, liturgical song; sometimes referred to as "Gregorian" chant or plainsong

character piece quasi-programmatic piece for piano that emerged in the nineteenth century that suggested a mood or feeling via title or overall aesthetic; tended to be fairly simple in structure

chart in jazz, the written score that contains the skeletal outline of the music; allows for individuality in performance, while providing basic musical material upon which to improvise

chord three or more pitches sounding simultaneously

classic blues blues that emerged in urban centers in the 1920s; often accompanied by piano and drums

collective improvisation the simultaneous layering of individual solo lines to create complex polyrhythms

combination tone an extraneous sound that can be heard when two (generally loud) musical tones are sounded together; the tone is not present when either of the original tones is sounded separately

concerto delle donne "group of ladies"; professional female court singers

consonance combination of tones that creates a sense of stability or calm

coon song late nineteenth-century popular song that presented a stereotyped view of black Americans; often performed by white singers in blackface

courtesan female court attendant who is educated or trained as a performer in multiple artistic and intellectual areas

courtly love "fin' amors" in Occitan; refined, unattainable love for one who is admired from a distance; associated with troubadour song

cover recording made by an artist that replicates the recording of a previous artist

cultural displacement the separating of people from their native culture

Dalcroze eurhythmics an approach to music education based on movement and dance

digital technology technology that breaks an audio signal into a binary code where the signal is represented by a series of 1s and 0s, transfers them to their destination, then reassembles them into their original format

dissonance combination of tones that sounds unstable; sometimes considered harsh, or in need of resolution

dissonant counterpoint a compositional method in which two or more dissonant melodic lines are simultaneously combined

Doctrine of Ethos ancient Greek belief that upheld music's power to impact the soul of the listener

Doctrine of the Affections Baroque doctrine in which music was believed to elicit specific emotional responses such as sadness, anger, or joy

dodecaphonic a type of composition based on the manipulation of a row or series of twelve chromatic pitches that are contained within an octave; often called twelve-tone technique

Edo period Japanese historical period from 1603 to 1868; associated with the development of many lasting Japanese artistic genres

electroacoustic general term that describes multi-faceted music genres, all of which use electronic technology to allow access to sound

ethnomusicology field of study that uses sociological and musicological research methods to study the world's music

experimental music a twentieth-century term associated with music that explores new and unusual sounds and compositional techniques

extra-musical musical work that contains non-musical references such as a story or program

fanzine also referred to as zine; a publication created by supporters of a particular movement, often reproduced and distributed inexpensively

field cry/field holler improvised monophonic song with flexible pitch and rhythm, sung by workers in the fields

fieldwork research situation in which a participant-observer is immersed in the culture being studied

form the way in which segments are structured in a unified whole; a "blueprint" for the structure of the piece

frequency modulation altering (modulating) a wave form by changing the frequency with which the wave recurs, resulting in timbral change

futurism early twentieth-century aesthetic that embraced speed, noise, and technology

gamelan percussion-dominated ensemble prevalent in several regions in Indonesia

garage band amateur rock band named for the perceived site of their operations, the garage

gaze the sexual objectification of a body by an empowered viewer

geisha courtesan of the Japanese tradition associated with performance of traditional Japanese art forms such as song and dance

genre a classification or style; in music, could refer to any number of popular or art music styles such as rock, pop, songs, symphonies, opera, etc.

girl band rock band in which women play their own instruments; as opposed to a girl group that consists of singers

girl group a small ensemble of female vocalists who sing popular music

gospel black religious music that emerged in urban centers during the early decades of the twentieth century

Great Migration massive movement of Southern African-Americans to Northern cities in the first decades of the twentieth century

griot West African musician-historian

hard punk spin-off punk genre that was more aggressive than original punk; also called hardcore

harmony two or more pitches sounding simultaneously

heterophonic texture in which a melody is performed by two or more parts simultaneously, but with variation; for example, one part may be more ornamented than the other

hip-hop culture cultural movement that includes rap, break dancing, graffiti art, and urban fashion

homophonic musical texture in which multiple lines move together rhythmically

humanism philosophy that emerged in the Renaissance in which ancient Greek and Roman culture inspired the study of human knowledge

improvise to compose, or simultaneously compose and perform, on the spur of the moment

Indie independent record label

Jim Crow laws named for a minstrel character, these laws sanctioned the denial of equal rights for black Americans, including racial segregation in public facilities

juba slave dance adapted from African tradition; included rhythmic patting and supple body movements

Kabuki theatre dance theatre of Japan that emerged in the Edo period; women were banned from this form of theatre

kolisha "the voice of woman"; a belief in Orthodox Judaism that women must not sing in the presence of men due to the potential to distract men in prayer

kouta Japanese "short song" of one to three minutes' duration, often with erotic, poetic text that is filled with metaphor; associated with the geisha tradition

large-scale work in music, refers to genres that require large numbers of performers (such as symphonies and opera); also refers to genres that are of significant length

leitmotiv German for "lead motive:" a musical idea that represents a person, event, or idea in a dramatic work

libretto the written story of an opera

lied German for song; in formal music study, usually refers to German art song

life-cycle rituals community events that celebrate important rites of passage such as birth, puberty, marriage, and death

liturgy ritual for public worship; usually has a prescribed format

madrigal Italian secular vocal genre that utilizes poetic texts; stylistic traits and number of voice parts change by historical period

male gaze the sexual objectification of the female body by an empowered viewer

mariachi Latin American ensemble originally from Mexico; traditionally features a variety of guitars as well as two or more of each of the following: violins, vihuela, guitarron, trumpets

Mass Roman church liturgy; also a musical genre or setting for certain parts of this liturgy

matrilineal tracing ancestral descent through the maternal line

melisma a succession of multiple pitches sung on a single syllable

melody a sequence of single tones, usually unified in a system such as a key or mode; the "tune" of a work

minimalism artistic movement that used small elements of repeated material that evolved slowly over time; emerged in the 1960s

misogyny a hatred of women or girls

modal music that is based on modes (sequences of whole and half steps) other than major or minor

monody style that features a vocal soloist with an instrumental accompaniment

monophonic music having a single melody without accompaniment or harmonizing parts, as in chant

morality play allegorical drama in which the characters personify abstractions, such as vice, virtue, and charity

motive a short rhythmic or melodic idea that recurs in a work

Motown record company originally based in Detroit, Michigan; named for the city's nickname, the "motor city"

musica reservata music reserved for an elite, invited audience; often featured virtuoso performers; term used in the sixteenth and seventeenth centuries

musical a theatrical production that includes singing and dancing; utilizes a plot

musique concrète technique in which recordings of live sounds are used as compositional building blocks

neoclassicism style that emerged in the early decades of the twentieth century, and bowed to Classical style characteristics such as form-driven structure, transparent texture, tonality, and lack of extra-musical program

New Wave spin-off punk genre that featured a more manufactured sound, but retained the simplicity of 1950s rock

octave notes spaced eight tones apart; in Western music, this results in renaming the pitch "at the octave," for example, C-C

Office liturgy of eight prayer services in which psalms, readings, and prayers are recited or sung at specified hours

okomfo/akomfu priest or priestess in the Akan tribal religion

opera a dramatic work that is entirely sung

Ordinary (of the Mass) Mass texts that remain the same on most days of the year; musical settings may change

ostinato a short musical pattern that persistently repeats

palindrome a row of letters or numbers that can be read the same way in either direction; in music, refers to a row of notes or rhythms

parlor song simple popular song performed by amateurs to the accompaniment of piano, parlor organ, or small stringed instrument

pentatonic a five-tone melodic system

phrase a short, distinct part or passage; a musical "sentence"

polyphonic musical texture in which two or more independent melodic lines sound simultaneously

polytonal utilizes more than one key at once

postmodernism an aesthetic that reflects fragmentation, rejects boundaries between high and low art, and is not opposed to embracing the past; *modernism* rejects the old in favor of the new

post-spectral compositional technique that goes beyond sound spectrum analysis, and reunites timbral and harmonic elements with other elements of music

prima prattica "first practice"; referencing sixteenth-century text setting in which the music sometimes overshadows the text; sometimes associated with polyphony

primary source artifact that provides first-hand accounts of historical events or subjects; letters, diaries, and original music manuscripts are examples

program music instrumental work that tells a story or suggests a non-musical idea; may actually be associated with a written program, but sometimes only includes a suggestive title

Proper (of the Mass) Mass texts that change according to specific days of the church calendar

punk rock rock subgenre characterized by simple chords, loud volume, distortion, and strong anti-establishment messages

quarter-tone interval half the size of a half-step; the half-step is traditionally recognized as the smallest interval in Western music, thus the quarter-tone can be perceived as dissonant or even "out of tune" by people accustomed to Western tonal music

race record music industry term for recordings of black artists that were primarily marketed to black consumers

ragtime musical style from the turn of the twentieth century that featured a syncopated melody against a steady bass

rap genre that features an MC who recites verses over a DJ accompaniment

recitative technique found in opera, oratorio, and cantata in which the text is sung in a speech-like manner, as opposed to the lyrical aria style

reggaeton multi-ethnic music that developed in Panama and Puerto Rico in the 1990s; blends reggae with Latin dance styles

responsory a verse or set of verses used in the Office; often performed with soloist alternating with group

review in staged musical productions, a variety show with music, but no plot

rhythm the time-oriented organization of silence and sound

riff a pattern that repeats

Riot Grrrl feminist movement of the 1990s associated with third-wave feminism

ritornello a short musical passage that returns throughout a work in the manner of a refrain

rondo musical form in which the opening section (A) recurs between contrasting segments; some sample rondo forms include A B A C A B A and A B A C A

rural blues blues that originated in the rural South; accompanied with acoustic guitar or simple stringed instrument such as a diddley-bow

sacred madrigal solo vocal work with a sacred text

salon a regular gathering of distinguished guests; in music, often references a meeting of literary or artistic people in a home

sanctified church an umbrella term for a number of black Baptist and Pentecostal churches

scat singing in jazz, nonsense vocables used in an improvisatory manner

schola cantorum "singing school"; church-sponsored school for the teaching of ecclesiastical chant

scriptoria a writing room used for copying manuscripts, writing, and studying, usually in a convent or monastery; associated with the preservation of musical manuscripts

seconda prattica "second practice"; referencing seventeenth-century text setting in which textual clarity takes precedence over music; associated with the monodic style

secondary source document that has been interpreted by someone other than the direct source; in music, a newspaper review of a concert or a textbook are examples

serialism an atonal compositional method that systematically orders musical elements according to a fixed series

shamisen a plucked, three-stringed instrument of Japan; associated with the geisha

shul a synagogue

signal filtering altering the frequency content of a sound signal to create desired effects

sine wave a continuous uniform wave with unchanging frequency (how often the wave recurs) and amplitude (vertical measurement); associated with a pure sound that contains no harmonics

siren half-human, half-animal female who tempts men via song

solo break in jazz, when a soloist takes over while the ensemble pauses

sonata genre for one or two solo instruments; features multiple movements

sonata form frequently found in the first movement of a sonata or symphony; usually consists of an exposition with contrasting segments, followed by a development of the exposition, and a recapitulation which returns to the original key or tonality

song musical work that is sung and has lyrics

song demonstrator person who performed sheet music for customers who were considering a purchase

soul gospel-influenced popular style that peaked in the 1960s

spectrum analysis computer analysis of waveforms that allows electronic reproduction of acoustic sounds as well as creation of new sounds

spiritual religious music of black Americans that originated in time of slavery

strophic form form in which each poetic verse is set to the same music

swing a jazz style characterized by the use of large bands, fast tempos, and written arrangements for ensemble playing

Symbolism a late nineteenth-century aesthetic popular in France and elsewhere, which embraced the musical sensuousness of sound and text; typical themes were mysticism and otherworldliness

symphony extended work for orchestra, usually with multiple movements

syncopate to accent a note that falls between main beats

syncretism the blending and merging of two or more distinct cultures into a distinctive new culture

tempo the speed at which a work is performed

theme and variation form segmented musical form in which an original theme is first utilized, and subsequent segments of the work vary the original theme via manipulation of musical elements such as rhythm and harmony

theremin early electronic instrument controlled by the performer's proximity to antennae

third-culture kid child whose parents reside outside of their passport country for extended periods of time

through-composed works in which new music is used for each section, as opposed to forms in which segments recur

timbre the characteristic quality of sound that distinguishes one voice or musical instrument from another; "tone color"

Tin Pan Alley popular music style associated with the sheet music industry between 1880 and 1950; also a physical location of the publishing firms in New York

tonal related to major and minor scalar systems, as opposed to modal systems; in actual practice, a tonal musical work will be organized around a given note or key

tritone a dissonant interval of an augmented fourth

trobairitz female poet-composer of southern France in the twelfth and thirteenth centuries

troubadour poet-composer of southern France in the twelfth and thirteenth centuries

ululation a wavering, trilling vocal sound

utilitarian stressing usefulness over aesthetic value

vamp a repeating musical accompaniment common in jazz, gospel, soul, and musical theatre; usually outlines a single harmony or harmonic progression over which a soloist improvises

vernacular "of the people"; as opposed to work of the educated elite

virtuoso performer who possesses astounding technical skills

wall of sound recorded tracks in which massed instrumental and vocal parts were heightened with echo

West Coast jazz subgenre of cool jazz that featured arranged charts, smooth sounds, and less aggressive rhythms than bop

white noise the presence of all pitches sounding randomly from which a composer may select particular areas or band widths to hear; can be compared with the concept of white light

wire recorder predecessor of the tape recorder, on which a magnetic code on a wire enables preservation of sound

women's music festivals feminist music festivals in which all aspects are run by women, including performance, management, staging, and sound

word painting in texted works, using musical gestures or elements to reflect movement and emotion in the text

Notes

1 REFLECTIONS ON "DEEP LISTENING"

1. Boulanger, 1944.
2. Brunner, 2006.
3. Oliveros, 2005, quoted in Brunner, 2006, 716.
4. Oliveros, 1994.
5. Titon, 2002.
6. Huey, 2009.
7. For a full analysis see Citron, 2004: 134. The author also acknowledges Citron's translation of the German text.
8. Closson, 1930.
9. Dunbar, 1998.
10. Smith, 1953, 41.
11. For a historical example of aesthetic education language of this type, see Reimer, 1970.
12. As cited in Hayes and Williams 2007, 123.
13. Marshall, 1992.
14. Placksin, interview from *Jazz Profiles*. This website also features interviews of women who performed with the bands. Placksin has written extensively on the subject of women's big bands.
15. Amott and Matthaei, 1999, 131–142.
16. Tucker, 2001.
17. Ibid.
18. Ibid.
19. Hayes and Williams, 2007, 122.

2 MEDIEVAL LITURGICAL ROOTS AND THE DOCUMENTATION OF THE WESTERN CANON

1. Monson, 2004, 119. Monson's research provides excellent information about the musical activities of cloistered nuns in Italian convents, and particularly explores how convent music was accessed by listeners outside of the convent walls. Although church officials attempted to curtail the musical activity that inadvertently reached the public, it proved difficult to control the musical inner workings of the convent.
2. Shapiro, 1994. Shapiro discusses this phenomenon outside of musical settings in "Ecriture Judaique: Where are the Jews in the Western Discourse?"

3 Heskes, 1992.
4 Ibid.
5 For more information, see, for example, Koskoff, 1987a.
6 *Catholic Encyclopedia*. The English version of this resource was created between 1905 and 1914, and was originally contained in fifteen volumes. It represents the conservative voice of the church, and provides extensive historical information that can be very helpful in understanding the perceived role of women in the church.
7 Monson, 2004, 120.
8 It should be noted that early notation was quite imprecise, containing only general reference to pitch direction. As such, it served as a memory aid in what remained essentially an aural tradition. As notation developed, however, it became possible to notate rhythms and accurate melodic movement. Western music increasingly leaned toward written musical notation as a means of preservation.
9 Although the church predominantly preserved sacred works, secular works were also copied.
10 Monson, 2004, 120.
11 An anchoress was a woman who took an extreme vow of seclusion and usually lived in a cell that was physically anchored to a church. As such, the woman was not removed from the world, but was "anchored" in the church. It was this type of setting that Hildegard encountered when she first entered religious life and studied with Jutta.
12 See for example Zubicaray, 1996, and Edwards, 2001b.
13 Edwards, 2001b, 46.
14 Grant, 1980, 7.
15 Edwards, 2001b, 47.
16 As cited in Neuls-Bates, 1982, 18–19.
17 Larsen, 1995.
18 Ibid.
19 Killam, 1993, 230.
20 Campbell, 1997.
21 Lukomsky, 1998, 5. This article features an extensive interview with the composer, translated from Russian by Lukomsky.
22 Ibid.
23 Ibid.
24 Cusick, 1998a. Cusick cites the work of Joan Scott in Scott, 1986, 1053–1075.
25 Cusick, 1998a.
26 Spiegel, 2008. Previously published in *EAR* Magazine 6, no. 3 (April–May 1981).

3 WOMEN IN WORLD MUSIC

1 Stone, 2008.
2 Ibid.
3 Titon, 2008.
4 One such nationalized test is the Educational Testing Services Praxis exam. Many states use this test as part of the teacher licensure process.
5 Apple, 1988.
6 Titon, 2008. The first edition of the Titon text taught research methodology and ethnomusicological pedagogy as well as content.

7 Scholars also study gender issues in textbook photography at a deeper level, critically examining how men and women are portrayed and labeled, and to what extent the photography represents written content. See, for example, the work of Koza, 1991 and 1992, and Regueiro, 2000.
8 Stone, 2008.
9 Ibid., 147.
10 Koskoff, 1987b. Also, Bakan, 2007.
11 Weinbaum, 1995.
12 Jones, 2001, 424–425.
13 Brown, 2009. Interview data from Kwesi Brown that follows in this chapter will not be cited separately.
14 Wallach, 2009. Interview data from Michelle Wallach that follows in this chapter will not be cited separately.
15 Some of the names of people described in interview data in this chapter are pseudonyms.
16 O'Hagin and Harnish, 2006, 56.
17 Weinbaum, 1995.
18 Vergara, 2009. Interview data from Lucy Vergara that follows in this chapter will not be cited separately. Pseudonyms are used.
19 Boyea, 1999, 31.
20 Rüütel, 2004, 295.
21 Ittzés, 2004.
22 Stokes, 1994.
23 Allsup, 2003.
24 Mogaka, Wendy, 2009. Interview data from Wendy Mogaka that follows in this chapter will not be cited separately. Readers may wish to compare Kemunto Mogaka's birth song experience to a Nigerian study that details the connection between the birth song and women's maternal destiny. See Okereke, 1994, 19.
25 Mogaka, John, 2009. Interview data from John Mogaka that follows in this chapter will not be cited separately.
26 For more information on the mother's role in children's language acquisition, see Longhi, 2009. This study examines cultural connections between linguistic and musical rhythms.

4 THE RENAISSANCE AND BEYOND

1 Newcomb, 1986.
2 Feldman and Gordon, 2006, 10. Also, Hadlock, 2008.
3 Hadlock, 2008.
4 Downer, 2006, 225.
5 Ibid., 224–225.
6 Hahn, 2004, 323.
7 Matsugu, 2006, 244.
8 As cited in Matsugu, 2006, 246.
9 Matsugu, 2006, 244.
10 Ibid.
11 Downer, 2006.
12 Titon, 2005.
13 Post, 1994, 44.
14 Foreman, 2002.

15 Matsugu, 2006. Also Screech, 2006.
16 Downer, 2006, 238.
17 Ibid.
18 As cited in Arden, 1994, 3–4.
19 Aubry, 1969.
20 Some musicians, known as jongleurs, did move from castle to castle, singing the songs written by the troubadours. See Aubry, 1969.
21 Bogin, 1980, 9.
22 Bogin, 1980.
23 Ibid. This book provides extensive detail regarding the vida and historical facts.
24 See Aubrey, 1996 for a more thorough discussion of formal design.
25 Kisby, 2001.
26 Ibid., as cited on 45.
27 LaMay, 2005, 366.
28 Brown, 1986.
29 LaMay, 2005, 369.
30 Pescerelli, 2004, 44.
31 LaMay, 2005, 397.
32 Brown, 1986.
33 Pescerelli, 1979.
34 LaMay, 2005, 384.
35 Feldman and Gordon, 2006, 190.
36 As cited in Brown, 1986, 95.
37 Post, 1994, 45.

5 BAROQUE KEYBOARD AND VOCAL GENRES

1 Sadie, 1987.
2 Cusick, 2009.
3 Jackson, 2001.
4 Sadie, 1987.
5 Cusick, 2009.
6 Ibid., 11–12.
7 Ibid.
8 Bowers, 1987, 123–124.
9 Cusick, 1998b.
10 Translation by Cusick, 2009, 122.
11 Cusick, 2009, 41.
12 Ibid.
13 Cusick, 2004. The Medici production was based on Ariosto's *Orlando furioso*, an Italian Romantic epic from 1532.
14 Cusick 2009, 201–207.
15 Rosand, 2007.
16 Ibid.
17 Ibid., 172.
18 Ibid.
19 Jackson, 2001, 102–106. Strozzi appeared in Walther's German *Lexikon*, and Charles Burney and John Hawkins both included her in their English compilations as well. Her work has been compared qualitatively to that of Giacomo Carissimi and Marc' Antonio Cesti, both of whom received far greater coverage in twentieth-century secondary resources.

20 Rosand, 2004.
21 Mardinly, 2002.
22 Rosand, 1987.
23 Burkholder, Grout, and Palisca, 2010.
24 As cited in Jackson, 2001. Jackson cites the source as the *Mercure gallant*, July 1677.
25 Sadie, 1987, 191.
26 Jackson, 2001, 120.
27 Erickson, 2004.

6 ROMANTIC-ERA PERFORMER/COMPOSERS

1 Craig, 1991, 154.
2 Ibid.
3 Plantamura, 1988.
4 As cited in Kimber, 2004, 44.
5 Interested readers may wish to access biographical dictionaries such as the highly regarded *Oxford Dictionary* to discover how Hensel is portrayed.
6 Kupferberg, 1972. Kupferberg theorizes that Moses Mendelssohn probably paved the way for Reform Judaism.
7 Kimber, 2004, 44–45.
8 As cited in Kimber, 2004, 42.
9 As cited in Kimber, 2004, 49–51.
10 Several musicologists provide evidence that Fanny Hensel co-wrote some of the *Songs without Words*. Interested readers might access works by Marcia Citron and Herbert Kupferberg, for example. There were eight sets of six pieces each in this collection, published between 1830 and 1845. Publishers sometimes added programmatic titles such as "Spinner's Song," and the "Bee's Wedding."
11 As cited in Kimber, 2004, 51. Songs under Felix's name that were actually by Fanny Hensel: *The Homespell, Italy,* and *Suleika and Hatem* from Opus 8, and *Sleepless, Forsaken*, and *The Nun,* from Opus 9.
12 Reich, 2004, 24. J. S. Bach was not always a revered composer in the Western canon. Historical sources credit Felix Mendelssohn with the Bach revival largely because of public response to his performance of Bach's *St. Matthew Passion* in 1829 in Berlin. Organizations such as the Bach Gesellschaft later went on to promote Bach's work. Meanwhile, Fanny Hensel's widely attended weekly salon events continuously featured and promoted the works of J. S. Bach, Gluck, and other composers then considered conservative.
13 As cited in Kimber, 2004, 43.
14 Neuls-Bates, 1996, 146 and 148–149.
15 Kimber, 2004, 45.
16 Plantamura, 1988. The quoted statement is also quite similar to statements made in highly respected musical dictionaries and reference materials.
17 Neuls-Bates, 1996, 149.
18 As cited in Reich, 2004, 29.
19 As cited in Reich, 2004, 28. From a letter dated July, 1846.
20 Kimber, 2004, 51.
21 Neuls-Bates, 1996, 148.
22 Neuls-Bates, 1996, 149.
23 As cited in Reich, 2004, 29.

24 25 August 1829, in Elvers, 1990, 96.
25 Reich, 2001.
26 Reich believes that Brahms had an artistic relationship with Clara Schumann, but that the relationship was not sexual.
27 Reich notes that Liszt admired Clara, but that Clara found Liszt's music wild, "hellish," and sloppy. She was the conservative Romantic, and he represented the less-conservative side.
28 Reich writes extensively about Clara Schumann's collaboration with these composers.
29 Reich, 2001.
30 Ibid., 29.
31 Ibid., 57.
32 Ibid., 41.
33 Ibid., 33.
34 Ibid., 68.
35 See Reich for translations of Clara's diary entries discussing her concern about the impact of subsequent pregnancies on her performance career.
36 Reich, 2001, 159.
37 Ibid., 276–277.
38 For an art song that better displays Schumann's virtuosic piano abilities, see *Er ist gekommen durch Sturm und Regen* in the Briscoe anthology (Briscoe, 2004a).
39 Reich, 2001, 299, citing a September 1838 review from the *Allgemeiner Musikalischer Anzeiger.*
40 The first movement score and recording are available in the Briscoe anthology (Briscoe, 2004a).
41 Reich, 2001.

7 AMERICAN POPULAR MUSIC: 1895–1945

1 Cook, 1999.
2 Ammer, 2001.
3 Ammer, 2001, 38–41. Urso spoke at the 1893 World's Fair in Chicago regarding this topic.
4 *New York Times*, 1874.
5 Neuls-Bates, 1987, 330.
6 Block, 2001, 203–204.
7 One of Sousa's most famous piccolo soloists was Meredith Wilson, a male soloist who became famous for writing the musical *The Music Man.* He was with the band from 1921 to 1923.
8 *New York Times*, June 8, 1905.
9 Handy, 1998, 204.
10 Handy, 1998. Handy lists dozens of ensembles and wind and percussion soloists, names gathered from a variety of primary source materials, photographs, and newspapers.
11 Bowers and Tick, 1987, 341.
12 Block, 2001, 211.
13 Ammer, 2001.
14 Epstein, 2006, 48.
15 Riis, 1989.
16 Riis, 2006.

17 Handy, 1998.
18 Riis, 2006 and Handy, 1998.
19 Ammer, 2001.
20 Bowers and Tick, 1987, 331.
21 Kingman, 1998.
22 Hairston, 2008, 65.
23 Cook, 1999.
24 Ibid.
25 George-Warren, 1997.
26 Ibid.

8 EMPOWERED VOICES IN THE PUBLIC EYE

1 Davis, 1986. Literary devices common in Black preaching include repetition of words and short phrases, use of metaphor and figurative language, solicitation of audience participation, and manipulation of vocal sound via vocal timbre, volume, and pitch. Davis also notes the use of specific physical motion, including hand gestures and facial expression, as important to text delivery. The author acknowledges finding this article in Deborah Smith Pollard's research, cited in the bibliography (Pollard, 2007). Pollard notes the use of the tradition in the work of gospel announcers.
2 Collins, 2008.
3 Ibid.
4 duCille, 1993. duCille provides perspective regarding a tendency to view the blues with "rose colored glasses," and compares the musical tradition to the literary tradition.
5 Kubik, 1999.
6 Jackson, 2004.
7 Burnim, 2006.
8 Reagon, 2001.
9 Ibid.
10 Ibid.
11 For details on the complication of compiling statistics regarding the Southern Diaspora, including data on people who returned to the South, see Gregory, 2005.
12 Jackson, 2004.
13 Ibid., 17–18.
14 Ibid., 11.
15 Ibid., 31.
16 Richardson, 1997, 33.
17 Reed, 2003.
18 Jackson, 2004, 70.
19 Ibid.
20 Starr and Waterman, 2006.
21 Jackson, 2004.
22 Ibid., 40.
23 Ibid., 102.
24 Wald, 2005.
25 Jackson, 2004.
26 Richardson, 1997, 30.
27 Carlin, 2005.

28 Mammy images dated from the Civil War period and depicted black women as obese domestic servants who contentedly served white families and did not appear to have any family life of their own. The image appeared on numerous items, including ashtrays, toys, detergent, and maple syrup bottles. The Jezebel image stereotyped the black woman as a "devilish" temptress, a stereotype that predates slavery.
29 Kernodle, 2004.
30 See Davis, 1999 for detailed information on the compositional work of classic blues singers.
31 Bohanon, 2001.
32 Harrison, 2006, 516.
33 Tribbett, 1996.
34 Tribbett, 1998.
35 John, 1993.
36 Ibid., 88–91.
37 See for example Davis, 1999 and Carby, 1999, 351. Carby also writes on nineteenth-century narrative and spirituality.
38 Referenced in Tribbett, 1998.
39 Johnson, 2007.
40 Hughes, 1943. The author acknowledges first finding portions of this article in Maria Johnson's work, cited in the bibliography.
41 Farley, 2003,198.
42 Burnim, 2006, 525.
43 Echols, 1997, 38. For more evidence that Brown was considered a champion of performer's rights, see her obituary in the *New York Times*, November 18, 2006.
44 Maultsby, 2006, 272.

9 VISUAL MEDIA AND THE MARKETING OF WOMEN PERFORMERS

1 Cusick, 1999.
2 McClary, 1991, 138.
3 Cusick, 1999.
4 Ibid.
5 As cited in Rohlfing, 1996, 96.
6 Cyrus, 2003.
7 Ibid.
8 Ibid.
9 As cited in Cyrus, 2003.
10 Cyrus, 2003.
11 As cited in Cyrus, 2003, 189.
12 As cited in Cyrus, 2003, 188–189.
13 As cited in Cyrus, 2003, 187.
14 Cyrus, 2003.
15 Gaines, 1997, 107.
16 Rohlfing, 1996.
17 Ibid.
18 Ibid.
19 Gaines, 1997.
20 Jhally, 2007. Numerous other studies noted similar imagery.

21 Online discussions of the game indicate that many men play this game with their sons. Gamers advise one another that you can get more points in the game by beating and robbing the woman. For example, "when ur done beat her down to get your money back," posted in 2008.
22 As cited in Berry, 1994, 188.
23 Whitely, 2000.
24 McClary, 1991.
25 Roberts, 1996.
26 Lister, 2001.
27 Bell, Lawton, and Dittmar, 2007. This is just one of many studies that link music videos to low self-esteem in adolescent girls.
28 Kosman, 2004.
29 As cited in Browning, 2006.

10 GENDER INTEGRATION IN TWENTIETH-CENTURY INSTRUMENTAL ENSEMBLES

1 Ammer, 2001, 253.
2 McClary, 1991, 53.
3 Doubleday, Killick, and Nooshin, 2008, 7.
4 Ibid., 21. Doubleday, Killick, and Nooshin cite Judith Tick.
5 *NPR's Jazz Profiles*, no date. The NPR website contains recorded interviews.
6 Doubleday, Killick, and Nooshin, 2008 and Koskoff, 1987b.
7 Cook and Tsou, 1994.
8 Koskoff, 1987b.
9 Ibid., 242.
10 Ammer, 2001, 33–34.
11 Ibid.
12 Ibid., 251.
13 Ibid., 251.
14 Ibid., 132.
15 As cited in Ammer, 2001, 250.
16 As cited in Goldin and Rouse, 2000.
17 Ammer, 2001.
18 Goldin and Rouse, 2000.
19 Bruenger, 1992, 17.
20 Ibid., 17.
21 Ibid.
22 Magliocco, 1992.
23 International Alliance for Women in Music, 2010. The organization cites the source of the quote as an Austrian weekly, dated February 24, 2003.
24 Burgermeister, 2003. Burgermeister also cites Vienna Conservatory teacher Henrietta Bruckner as saying that women needed to be "150 percent as good as men" to get into the Vienna Philharmonic.
25 Neuls-Bates, 1987.
26 Collins, 1974. The film was re-released in DVD format in 2003.
27 Ammer, 2001, 128–129.
28 Kendall, 1976.
29 Rosenstiel, 1982, 292.
30 Hillis, 1998.
31 Neuls-Bates, 1987.

32 Lofaro, 2005. To read more, see www.time.com/time/magazine/article/0,9171,1086150,00.html#ixzz0hzImvYM8.
33 Ibid.
34 League of American Orchestras, 2009.
35 NBA, 2010.
36 For example, see Bruenger, 1992.

11 TWENTIETH-CENTURY LARGE-SCALE WORKS

1 Waleson, 1990.
2 DeLorenzo, 1992.
3 As cited in Kendall, 1976, 18.
4 As cited in Block, 1999, 103.
5 Along with Beach, the other Second New England School composers were: John Knowles Paine (1839–1906), Arthur Foote (1853–1937), George Chadwick (1854–1931), Edward MacDowell (1861–1908), George Whiting (1861–1944), and Horatio Parker (1863–1919). The ascendance of America in music education and composition was strongly impacted by Beach and her contemporaries.
6 Composer Edward MacDowell and pianist Marian MacDowell founded the colony in 1907, shortly before Edward's death in 1908. Amy Beach and others contributed financially.
7 Block, 1999.
8 Block, 2004.
9 Ibid.
10 When she died, Beach left the rights to her music to the MacDowell Colony. The Beaches had no children.
11 Beach began notating bird calls as a child, having first had a transcription published in a scientific journal by an ornithologist when she was only eleven years old. Her own compositions reflected her continued fascination with birdsong, including the song "The Hermit Thrush at Morn" (1922), along with other works for piano and voice. "The Hermit Thrush at Morn" is available in Block, 1990.
12 Block, 1999.
13 As cited in Hacquard, 2000.
14 Ibid.
15 Gelfand, 1999.
16 Potter, 2004.
17 Brown, 2008: xxxv.
18 Brown, 2008.
19 Ibid.
20 Ibid.
21 Ibid.
22 Ibid.
23 Brown, 2008.
24 Edwards, 2001a.
25 Brown, 1990 indicates that government funding led to an outpouring of artistic works by black artists, poets, and musicians to the extent that the period was sometimes called the Chicago Renaissance.
26 DeLorenzo, 1992.

27 Ibid.
28 Edwards, 2001a.
29 Twentieth-century German composer Arnold Schoenberg is credited with creating the term "developing variation." He used the term to analyze the work of Johannes Brahms, and others.
30 For detailed analyses, see Schnepel, 1989 and also Gunn, 1993.
31 As cited in Edwards, 2001a, 334.
32 Chen is her family name, Yi is her personal name. In the Chinese tradition, the family name is given first.
33 Edwards, 2001a.
34 Pilchak, 2006.
35 www.presser.com/Composers/info.cfm?Name=CHENYI.
36 Moh Wei Chen indicates that the woodblock is commonly used to suggest the mental pondering of characters in Chinese opera (Chen, 1997).
37 Ibid. For an extensive analysis, including Chen Yi's use of tri-tones and harmonic structure, see Moh Wei Chen's dissertation, listed in the bibliography.
38 Chen, 1997.
39 Chen, 1996.
40 Roma, 2001.
41 Roma, 2006.
42 Briscoe, 2004b: 60–62.
43 Tick, 1987, 325.

12 OLD GENRES, NEW SOUNDS

1 Roma, 2001. Also, Briscoe, 1997.
2 BBC Interview with Lutyens, no date.
3 Roma, 2006.
4 Briscoe, 1997.
5 Roma, 2001.
6 Briscoe, 1997, 180.
7 BBC Interview with Lutyens, no date.
8 Pinsonneault, 2010.
9 Tick, 1997.
10 Ibid.
11 Seeger, 1933.
12 Ammer, 2001.
13 Brodie, 2009.
14 Tower, no date.
15 As cited in Edwards, 2001a, 325.
16 Ammer, 2001.
17 Lochhead, 2005.
18 Edwards, 2001a.
19 Miller, 2004, 31.
20 Ibid.
21 Ran, 1994.
22 Duckworth, 1989.
23 Briscoe, 1997.
24 Marranca, 1992.

13 INSTRUMENTAL TO JAZZ

1 As cited in Ammer, 2001, 137.
2 Southern, 1997. For more on women's roles in handing the juba from one generation to the next, see Reagon, 2001.
3 Southern 1997. Also Hasse, 1985.
4 Morath, 1985.
5 Harer, 2006.
6 Ibid.
7 Ibid.
8 Morath, 1985.
9 Southern, 1997.
10 Tucker, 2006, 532.
11 Handy, 1998.
12 Ibid., 230–233.
13 Ibid., 230–233. Handy cites an article in *Melody Maker*, September 4, 1971.
14 Gourse, 1995. The sale of alcohol was illegal from 1919 until 1933. Speakeasies (illegal bars) picked up the business, and jazz maturated inside of them.
15 Monson, 2006, 154.
16 Holiday is frequently referenced in this manner. Interested readers might want to try an internet search to confirm the labeling of the singer today.
17 Huang and Huang, 1994.
18 Tucker, 2001.
19 Ibid.
20 Ibid.
21 Southern, 1997. Also, Briscoe, 1997.
22 Gourse, 1995, 20.
23 *NPR's Jazz Profiles*, no date.
24 Ibid.
25 Ibid.
26 Ibid.
27 Briscoe, 1997.
28 Schlicht, 2008, 299.
29 Ibid.
30 Ibid.
31 Ibid., 297.
32 Gourse, 1995. See also Akiyoshi, no date.
33 Ammer, 2001.
34 Alper, 2000.
35 Gourse, 1995, 9.
36 Ibid.
37 Ammer, 2001, 138.

14 MUSIC TECHNOLOGY IN THE HANDS OF WOMEN

1 Termen's grandniece, Lydia Kavina, also became known worldwide as a leading performer on the instrument. See www.lydiakavina.com.
2 Hinkle-Turner, 2006.
3 Ibid.
4 Ibid.
5 Oliveros, no date.

6 Van Gunden, 1983, 50. See also http://paulineoliveros.us.
7 Van Gunden, 1983, 4.
8 As cited in Van Gunden, 1983, 58.
9 Ibid. See also http://deeplistening.org.
10 http://deeplistening.org.
11 http://sfsound.org, website for 2010 tape music festival.
12 Van Gunden, 1983.
13 Ibid., 56–57. Adapted from a more complex analysis by Heidi Van Gunden. Readers with musical background are encouraged to seek this resource.
14 Saariaho biography on www.chesternovello.com. See also Pousset, 2000.
15 Emmerson, 1998.
16 Pendle and Zierolf, 2001, 278.
17 Moisala, 2009, and www.chesternovello.com.
18 Moisala, 2009.
19 Gaar, 1997, 441.
20 Odintz, 1997, 215.
21 Ammer, 2001.
22 Ibid., 243.
23 For example, see Hinkle-Turner, 2006.
24 Odintz, 1997, 212.
25 Moorefield, 2005.
26 Sandstrom, 2000.
27 Ibid.
28 Odintz, 1997, 211.
29 Ibid., 212.
30 www.npr.org/programs/atc/features/2003/apr/producers/index.html.
31 Odintz, 1997.
32 www.baranstoll.com.
33 Sandstrom, 2000, 295.
34 Odintz, 1997, 213.
35 www.npr.org/programs/atc/features/2003/apr/producers/index.html.
36 http://trinashoemaker.com.
37 Odintz, 1997.
38 This statistic was cited by the Women's Audio Mission, a San Francisco based, non-profit organization that provides hands-on technical training for women.
39 Odintz, 1997.

15 A NEW MESSAGE

1 Bolan, 2010. Also, Burns, 2009.
2 Bolan, 2010.
3 Sutton, 1997, 157.
4 Juno and Vale, 1996.
5 Ibid.
6 Ibid. Also Gaar, 2002.
7 Juno and Vale, 1996.
8 www.nylonmag.com/?section=article&parid=4469. Also Gaar, 2002.
9 Juno and Vale, 1996.
10 Juno and Vale, 1996, 183.
11 Bolan, 2010.
12 Love, 2000.

13 Gaar, 2002, 280.
14 As cited in Gaar, 2002, 274.
15 Gaar, 2002.
16 Gaar, 2002, also Frost, 1997.
17 Coulombee, 1999, 264.
18 Frost, 1997, 269.
19 Gaar, 2002.
20 Arnold and Dahl, 1997, 436.
21 Gaar, 2002.
22 Ibid.
23 Southern, 1997.
24 Ibid., 601–603.
25 Berry, 1994. Berry cites Mary Ellison's article "Lyrical Protest: Black Music's Struggle against Discrimination," 1989.
26 Bufwack and Oermann, 1993.
27 Ibid.
28 Briscoe, 1997.
29 Briscoe, 1997. Also, Bufwack and Oermann, 1993.
30 Bufwack and Oermann, 1993.
31 Garofalo, 2008.
32 Ibid.
33 Ibid., 425.
34 Ibid.
35 Ibid.
36 Barkin and Harnessley, 1999, 257.
37 Whitely, 2000.
38 Coulombee, 1999.
39 Samponara, 2009.
40 Gaar, 2002.

Bibliography

Akiyoshi, Toshiko. "Performer Roster Biography, Berkeley Agency." At www.berkeley agency.com/html/toshiko.html (accessed February 15, 2010).

Allsup, Randall Everett. "Transformational Education and Critical Music Pedagogy: Examining the Link between Culture and Learning." *Music Education Research* 5, no. 1 (March 1, 2003): 5.

Alper, Garth. "Making Sense out of Postmodern Music." *Popular Music and Society* 24, no. 4 (January 1, 2000): 1.

Ammer, Christine. *Unsung: A History of Women in American Music*. Portland, OR: Amadeus Press, 2001.

Amott, Teresa L. and Julie A. Matthaei. *Race, Gender and Work: A Multicultural Economic History of Women in the United States*. Cambridge, MA: South End Press, 1999.

Arden, Heather. "Time Zones of the Heart." In *The Cultural Milieu of the Troubadours and Trouvères*, edited by Nancy Van Deusen. Ottawa, Canada: Institute of Mediæval Music, 1994.

Arnold, Gina and Shawn Dahl. "Chicks with Picks." In *Trouble Girls: The Rolling Stone Book of Women in Rock*, edited by Barbara O'Dair. New York: Random House, 1997.

Aubrey, Elizabeth. *The Music of the Troubadours*. Bloomington, IN: Indiana University Press, 1996.

Aubry, Pierre. *Trouvères and Troubadours. A Popular Treatise*. New York: Cooper Square, 1969.

Austern, Linda Phyllis. "Music and the English Renaissance Controversy over Women." In *Cecilia Reclaimed: Feminist Perspectives on Gender and Music*, edited by Susan Cook and Judy S. Tsou. Urbana and Chicago, IL: University of Illinois Press, 1994.

Babiracki, Carol M. "The Illusion of India's 'Public' Dancers." In *Women's Voices Across Musical Worlds*, edited by Jane A. Bernstein. Boston, MA: Northeastern University, 2004.

Bakan, Michael. *World Music: Traditions and Transformations*. New York: McGraw-Hill, 2007: 346.

Bammer, Angelika, ed. *Displacements: Cultural Identities in Question*. Bloomington, IN: Indiana University Press, 1994.

Barkin, Elaine and Lydia Hamessley, eds. *Audible Traces: Gender, Identity, and Music*. Zürich, Switzerland: Carciofoli, 1999.

BBC. "Interview with Elisabeth Lutyens." No date. At www.bbc.co.uk/bbcfour/audiointerviews/profilepages/lutyense1.shtml.

Bell, Beth T., Rebecca Lawton, and Helga Dittmar. "The Impact of Thin Models in Music Videos on Adolescent Girls' Body Dissatisfaction." *Body Image* 4, no. 2 (June 2007).

Berry, Venise T. "Feminine or Masculine: The Conflicting Nature of Female Images in Rap Music." In *Cecelia Reclaimed: Feminist Perspectives on Gender and Music*, edited by Susan C. Cook and Judy S. Tsou. Chicago, IL: University of Illinois Press, 1994: 183–201.

"Best of the Century." *Time*, December 31, 1999. At www.time.com/time/magazine/article/0,9171,993039,00.html (accessed January 28, 2010).

Block, Adrienne Fried. "Amy Beach." In *New Historical Anthology of Music by Women*, edited by James R. Briscoe. Bloomington, IN: Indiana University Press, 2004.

Block, Adrienne Fried. *Amy Beach, Passionate Victorian: The Life and Work of the American Composer, 1867–1944*. New York: Oxford University Press, 1999.

Block, Adrienne Fried. "Dvorak, Beach and American Music." In *A Celebration of American Music: Words and Music in Honor of H. Wiley Hitchcock*, edited by Richard Crawford, R. Allen Lott, and Carol J. Oja. Ann Arbor, MI: University of Michigan Press, 1990.

Block, Adrienne Fried, assisted by Nancy Stewart. "Women in American Music, 1800–1918." In *Women in Music: A History*, 2nd ed., edited by Karin Pendle. Bloomington, IN: Indiana University Press, 2001.

Bogin, Meg. *The Women Troubadours*, New York: W. W. Norton, 1980.

Bohanon, Margaret Ann. "'Wild Women Don't Have the Blues': African-American Women Blues Singers and Working Class Resistance." Ann Arbor, MI: University Microfilms International (MI), 2001. *RILM Abstracts of Music Literature*, EBSCO*host* at www.ebsco.com (accessed February 9, 2010).

Bolan, Barbara. Interview with Julie Dunbar, April 20, 2010.

Bosma, Hannah. "Gender and Electroacoustics" and "Male and Female Voices in Computer Music." August 20, 2004. At www.hannahbosma.nl.

Boulanger, Nadia. Class lecture notes taken by Genevieve Pinion. Nadia Boulanger papers, 1942–1944, Sinsinawa, WI: Sinsinawa Mound Archives.

Bowers, Jane. "The Emergence of Women Composers in Italy, 1566–1700." In *Women Making Music*, edited by Judith Tick and Jane Bowers. Urbana, IL: Illinois University Press, 1987: 116–167.

Bowers, Jane and Judith Tick, eds. *Women Making Music*. Chicago, IL: University of Illinois Press, 1987.

Boyea, Andrea. "Encountering Complexity: Native Musics in the Curriculum." *Philosophy of Music Education Review* 7, no. 1 (March 1, 1999): 31.

Briscoe, James R., ed. *Contemporary Anthology of Music by Women*. Bloomington, IN: Indiana University Press, 1997.

Briscoe, James R., ed. *New Historical Anthology of Music by Women*. Bloomington, IN: Indiana University Press, 2004a.

Briscoe, James R. "Thea Musgrave." In *New Historical Anthology of Music by Women*, edited by James R. Briscoe. Bloomington, IN: Indiana University Press, 2004b: 60–62.

Brodie, Susan. "Two Composers Turn 70: Celebrating Tower and Zwilich." *Music in Concert* (January/February 2009).

Brooks, Jeanice. "Chivalric Romance, Courtly Love and Courtly Song: Female Vocality and Feminine Desire in the World of Amadis de Gaule." In *Musical Voices of Early Modern Women: Many-Headed Melodies*, edited by Thomasin LaMay. Aldershot: Ashgate, 2005.

Brown, Howard Mayer. "Women Singers and Women's Songs in Fifteenth-Century Italy." In *Women Making Music: The Western Art Tradition, 1150–1950,* edited by Jane Bowers and Judith Tick. Urbana, IL: University of Illinois Press, 1986.

Brown, Kwesi. Interview with Julie Dunbar, November 18, 2009.

Brown, Linda Rae. *Florence Price Symphonies Nos. 1 and 3,* edited score collection, Madison, WI: AR editions, 2008.

Brown, Linda Rae. "William Grant Still, Florence Price, and William Dawson: Echoes of the Harlem Renaissance." 1990. *RILM Abstracts of Music Literature,* EBSCO*host* at www.ebsco.com (accessed June 14, 2010).

Browning, David. "Deborah Voigt: Off the Scales." *CBS News* (January 29, 2006). At www.cbsnews.com/stories/2006/01/27/60minutes/main1245332.shtml (accessed May 2, 2008).

Bruenger, David. "Women At Work: Trombonists in North American Orchestras and Universities." *ITA Journal* 20, no. 2 (April 1992).

Brunner, Lance W. "Review of *Deep Listening: A Composer's Sound Practice.*" Notes: Quarterly *Journal of the Music Library Association* 62, no. 3 (2006): 716.

Bufwack, Mary A. and Robert K. Oermann. *Finding Her Voice: The Saga of Women in Country Music.* New York: Crown, 1993.

Burgermeister, Jane. "First Woman Takes Bow at Vienna Philharmonic." *The Guardian,* January 10, 2003. At http://guardian.co.uk/world/2003/jan/10/gender.arts.

Burkholder, J. Peter, Donald Grout, and Claude V. Palisca. *A History of Western Music,* 8th ed. New York: W. W. Norton and Company, 2010.

Burnim, Mellonee V. *Women in African American Music—Gospel in African American Music, an Introduction,* edited by Mellonee V. Burnim and Portia K. Maultsby. New York: Routledge, 2006.

Burns, Jane. "Rock and Roll Refuge: Music Industry Veteran Wants to Save Community Television." *The Capital Times,* June 24, 2009.

Cai, Camilla. "Fanny Hensel's 'Songs for Pianoforte' of 1836–37: Stylistic Interaction with Felix Mendelssohn." *Journal of Musicological Research* 14, no. 1–2 (January 1, 1994): 55.

Campbell, Karen. "A Russian Composer's Path to Freedom." *Christian Science Monitor* (August 27, 1997).

Carby, Hazel. "It Jus Be's Dat Way Sometimes: The Sexual Politics of Women's Blues." In *Keeping Time: Readings in Jazz History,* edited by Robert Walser. New York: Oxford University Press, 1999.

Carlin, Richard. "Mahalia Jackson." In *Encyclopedia of American Gospel Music,* edited by W. K. McNeil. New York: Routledge, 2005.

Catholic Encyclopedia. At http://newadvent.org.

Chen Yi. *The Music of Chen Yi* CD-ROM liner notes. NA 090 CD. San Francisco, CA: New Albion Records, 1996.

Chen, Moh Wei. "Myths from Afar: Chinese Myths Cantata by Chen Yi." Doctoral Dissertation, University of Southern California, 1997.

Citron, Marcia J. "Fanny Mendelssohn Hensel." In *New Historical Anthology of Music by Women,* edited by James R. Briscoe. Bloomington, IN: Indiana University Press, 2004: 134.

Closson, Hermann. "The Case against 'Gebrauchsmusik.'" *Modern Music* 7 (February–March 1930): 18.

Coldwell, Maria. "Jougleresses and Trobaraitz: Secular Musicians in Medieval France." In *Women Making Music: The Western Art Tradition, 1150–1950,* edited by Jane Bowers and Judith Tick. Urbana, IL: University of Illinois Press, 1986.

Collins, Judy. *Antonia: A Portrait of the Woman*. Directed by Jill Godmilow and produced by Judy Collins. Geneon Studio, 1974.

Collins, Patricia Hill. *Black Feminist Thought: Knowledge, Consciousness, and the Politics of Empowerment*. New York: Routledge, 2008.

Cook, Susan. "Watching Our Step: Embodying Research, Telling Stories." In *Audible Traces*, edited by Elaine Barkin and Lydia Hamessley. Zurich and Los Angeles: Carciofoli Verlagshaus, 1999: 177.

Cook, Susan and Judy S. Tsou. *Cecilia Reclaimed: Feminist Perspectives on Gender and Music*. Urbana and Chicago, IL: University of Illinois Press, 1994.

Coulombee, Renee T. "The Insatiable Banshee, Voracious Vocalizing . . . Riot Grrrl . . . and the Blues." In *Audible Traces: Gender, Identity, and Music*, edited by Elaine Barkin and Lydia Hamessley. Zürich, Switzerland: Carciofoli, 1999.

Craig, Gordon. *The Germans*. New York: Penguin Books, 1991: 154.

Cusick, Suzanne G. "Feminist Theory, Music Theory, and the Mind/Body Problem." In *Music/Ideology: Resisting the Aesthetic*, edited by Adam Krims and Henry Klumpenhouwer. Amsterdam: G+B Arts International, 1998a.

Cusick, Suzanne G. "Feminist Theory, Music Theory, and the Mind/Body Problem." *Perspectives of New Music* 32, no. 1 (January 1, 1994): 8.

Cusick, Suzanne. "Francesca Caccini." In *New Historical Anthology of Music by Women*, edited by James R. Briscoe. Bloomington, IN: Indiana University Press, 2004: 48–50.

Cusick, Suzanne. *Francesca Caccini at the Medici Court*. Chicago, IL: University of Chicago Press, 2009.

Cusick, Suzanne. "On Musical Performances of Gender and Sex." In *Audible Traces: Gender, Identity, and Music*, edited by Elaine Barkin and Lydia Hamessley, 25. Zürich, Switzerland: Carciofolo Verlagshaus, 1999.

Cusick, Suzanne G. "'Who is this Woman . . . ?' Self-Presentation, Imitations, Virginis, and Compositional Voice in Francesca Caccini's Primo Libro of 1618." *Il Saggiatore Musicale: Rivista Semestrale de Musicologia* 5, no. 1 (January 1, 1998b): 5.

Cyrus, Cynthia J. "Selling an Image: Girl Groups of the 1960s." In *Popular Music* Vol. 22/2. Cambridge: Cambridge University Press, 2003: 173.

Davis, Angela. *Blues Legacies and Black Feminism: Gertrude "Ma" Rainey, Bessie Smith, and Billie Holiday*. New York: Vintage Books, 1999.

Davis, Gerald L. *I Got the Word in Me and I Can Sing It, You Know: A Study of the Performed African American Sermon*. Philadelphia, PA: University of Pennsylvania Press, 1986.

DeLorenzo, Lisa C. "An Interview with Ellen Taaffe Zwilich." *Music Educators Journal* 78 (1992): 46–47.

Doubleday, Veronica, Andrew P. Killick, and Laudan Nooshin. "Sounds of Power: Musical Instruments and Gender." *Ethnomusicology Forum*, XVII/1 (June 2008): 3.

Downer, Lesley. "The City Geisha and their Role in Modern Japan: Anomaly or Artistes?" In *The Courtesan's Arts: Cross-Cultural Perspectives*, edited by Martha Feldman and Bonnie Gordon. New York: Oxford University Press, 2006.

Drinker, Sophie Lewis Hutchinson. *Music and Women: The Story of Women in Their Relation to Music*. Washington, DC: Zenger, 1975 (1st ed. 1948).

duCille, Ann. "Blue Notes on Black Sexuality: Sex and the Texts of the Twenties and Thirties." In *American Sexual Politics: Sex Gender and Race Since the Civil War*, edited by John C. Fout and Maura Shaw Tantillo. Chicago, IL: University of Chicago Press, 1993.

Duckworth, William. "Talking Music: Conversations with Five Generations of American Experimental Composers." Unpublished interview transcription, 1989.

Dunbar, Julie. "Art Music on the Radio, 1927–37." *Bulletin of Historical Research in Music Education* 19, no. 3 (1998).

Echols, Alice. "Smooth Sass and Raw Power: R&B's Ruth Brown and Etta James." In *Trouble Girls: The Rolling Stone Book of Women in Rock*, edited by Barbara O'Dair. New York: Random House, 1997.

Edwards, J. Michele. "North America Since 1920," In *Women and Music, a History*, edited by Karin Pendle, 2nd ed. Bloomington, IN: Indiana University Press, 2001a.

Edwards, J. Michele. "Women in Music to ca. 1450." In *Women and Music: A History*, edited by Karin Pendle. Bloomington, IN: Indiana University Press, 2001b: 26.

Elvers, Rudolf, ed. *Felix Mendelssohn: A Life in Letters*. trans. Craig Tomlinson. New York: Froom International Pub., 1990: 96.

Emmerson, Simon. "Acoustic/Electroacoustic: The Relationship with Instruments." *Journal of New Music Research* 27, no. 1–2 (June 1, 1998): 146.

Epstein, Dena. "Secular Folk Music." In *African American Music, An Introduction*, edited by Mellonee V. Burnim and Portia K. Maultsby. New York: Routledge, 2006: 35.

Erickson, Susan. "Elisabeth-Claude Jacquet de la Guerre." In *New Historical Anthology of Music by Women*, edited by James R. Briscoe. Bloomington, IN: University of Indiana Press, 2004: 80–82.

Farley, Christopher John. "Memphis Minnie and the Cutting Contest." In *Martin Scorsese Presents the Blues: A Musical Journey*, edited by Peter Guralnick, Robert Santelli, Holly George-Warren, and Christopher John Farley. New York: Amistad, 2003.

Farrah, Scott David. "Signifyin(g): A Semiotic Analysis of Symphonic Works by William Grant Still, William Levi Dawson, and Florence B. Price." 2007. *RILM Abstracts of Music Literature*, EBSCO*host* at www.ebsco.com (accessed March 14, 2010).

Feldman, Martha and Bonnie Gordon, eds. *The Courtesan's Arts: Cross-Cultural Perspectives*. New York: Oxford University Press, 2006.

Foreman, Kelly Marie. *The Role of Music in the Lives and Identities of Japanese Geisha*. Ann Arbor, MI: University Microfilms International, 2002.

Frost, Deborah. "Patti Smith." In *Trouble Girls: The Rolling Stone Book of Women in Rock*, edited by Barbara O'Dair. New York: Random House, 1997.

Gaar, Gillian G. "Laurie Anderson." In *Trouble Girls: The Rolling Stone Book of Women in Rock*, edited by Barbara O'Dair. New York: Random House, 1997.

Gaar, Gillian G. *She's a Rebel: The History of Women in Rock and Roll*. New York: Seal, 2002.

Gaines, Donna. "Girl Groups: A Ballad of Codependency." In *Trouble Girls: The Rolling Stone Book of Women in Rock*, edited by Barbara O'Dair. New York: Random House, 1997: 103.

Garofalo, Reebee. *Rockin' Out: Popular Music in the USA*. Upper Saddle River, NJ: Pearson Prentice Hall, 2008.

Gelfand, Janelle Magnuson. "Germaine Tailleferre (1892–1983): Piano and Chamber Works." 1999. *RILM Abstracts of Music Literature*, EBSCO*host* at www.ebsco.com (accessed March 1, 2010.)

George-Warren, Holly. "Hillbilly Fillies: The Trailblazers of C&W." In *Trouble Girls: The Rolling Stone Book of Women in Rock*, edited by Barbara O'Dair. New York: Random House, 1997: 43.

Goldin, Claudia, and Cecilia Rouse. "Orchestrating Impartiality: The Impact of 'Blind' Auditions on Female Musicians." *American Economic Review* 90, no. 4 (2000): 715–741.

Gourse, Leslie. *Madame Jazz*. New York: Oxford University Press, 1995.

Grant, Barbara L. "An Interview with the Sybil of the Rhine: Hildegard von Bingen (1098–1179)." *Heresies* 3, no. 2 (Summer 1980): 7.

Gregory, James N. *The Southern Diaspora*. Chapel Hill, NC: University of North Carolina Press, 2005.

Griffiths, Paul. *Modern Music and After*. Oxford: Oxford University Press, 1995.

Gunn, Nancy. "Organicism, Motivic Development, and Formal Design in Ellen Taaffe Zwilich's *Symphony No. 1*." 1993. *RILM Abstracts of Music Literature*, EBSCO *host* at www.ebsco.com (accessed June 14, 2010).

Hacquard, Georges. *Germaine Tailleferre Musique pour Piano, Harpe, Chant*, CD-ROM liner notes. CD 7341. Nuova Era Internazionale, 2000.

Hadlock, Heather. "Review of The Courtesan's Arts: Cross-Cultural Perspectives." The *Journal of the American Musicological Society* 61, no. 3 (2008): 633–645.

Hahn, Tomie. "Shifting Selves: Embodied Metaphors in Nihon Buyo." In *Women's Voices Across Musical Worlds*, edited by Jane A. Bernstein. Boston, MA: Northeastern University Press, 2004: 213.

Hairston, Monica. "Gender, Jazz and the Popular Front." In *Big Ears: Listening for Gender in Jazz Studies*, edited by Nichole T. Rustin and Sherrie Tucker. Durham, NC: Duke University Press, 2008.

Handy, D. Antoinette. *Black Women in American Bands and Orchestras*, 2nd ed. Lanham, MD: Scarecrow Press, 1998.

Harer, Ingeborg. "Ragtime." In *African American Music, An Introduction*. Edited by Mellonee V. Burnim and Portia K. Maultsby. New York: Routledge, 2006.

Harrison, Daphne Duvall. "Blues." In *African American Music, An Introduction*, edited by Mellonee V. Burnim and Portia K. Maultsby. New York: Routledge, 2006.

Hasse, John Edward. *Ragtime: Its History, Composers, and Music*. Florence, KY: Schirmer Books (Cengage Learning), 1985.

Hayes, Eileen M. and Linda F. Williams, eds. *Black Women and Music, More Than the Blues*. Urbana, IL: University of Illinois Press, 2007: 123.

Heskes, Irene. "Miriam's Sisters: Jewish Women and Liturgical Music." *Notes: Quarterly Journal of the Music Library Association* 48, no. 4 (June 1, 1992): 1193.

Hillis, Margaret. "Obituary." *New York Times*, February 6, 1998.

Hinkle-Turner, Elizabeth. *Women Composers and Music Technology in the United States: Crossing the Line*. Aldershot: Ashgate, 2006.

Huang, Hao and Rachel V. Huang. "Billie Holiday and Tempo Rubato: Understanding Rhythmic Expressivity." *Annual Review of Jazz Studies* 7 (January 1, 1994): 181.

Huey, Steve. "Toni Braxton biography." *Billboard*. At www.billboard.com/#artist/toni-braxton/bio/30331 (accessed June 10, 2009).

Hughes, Langston. "Music at Year's End." *Chicago Defender*, January 9, 1943.

International Alliance for Women in Music. Website. At www.iawm.org/vpowatch (accessed March 7, 2010).

Ittzés, Mihály. "Zoltán Kodály: 1882–1967." *International Journal of Music Education* 22, no. 2 (August 1, 2004): 131.

Jackson, Barbara Garvey. "Musical Women of the Seventeenth and Eighteenth Centuries." In *Women and Music, a History*, edited by Karin Pendle, 2nd ed. Bloomington, IN: Indiana University Press, 2001.

Jackson, Jerma. *Singing in My Soul: Black Gospel Music in a Secular Age*. Chapel Hill, NC: University of North Carolina Press, 2004.

Jhally, Sut. *Dreamworlds 3: Desire, Sex and Power in Music Video*. Video. Northampton, MA: Media Education Foundation, 2007.

John, Lawrence. *Nothing but the Blues*. New York: Abbeville Press, 1993.

Johnson, Maria V. "Black Women Electric Guitarists and Authenticity in the Blues." In *Black Women and Music: More than the Blues*, edited by Eileen M. Hayes and Linda F. Williams. Urbana, IL: University of Illinois Press, 2007.

Jones, L. JaFron. "Women in Music around the Mediterranean." In *Women in Music: A History*, edited by Karin Pendle, 2nd ed. Bloomington, IN: Indiana University Press, 2001.

Juno, Andrea and V. Vale, eds. *Angry Women in Rock*. New York: Juno Books, 1996.

Keener, Shawn Marie. "Virtue, Illusion, Venezianità: Vocal Bravura and the Early Cortigiana Onesta." In *Musical Voices of Early Modern Women: Many-Headed Melodies*, edited by Thomasin LaMay. Aldershot: Ashgate, 2005.

Kendall, Alan. *The Tender Tyrant, Nadia Boulanger: A Life Devoted to Music: A Biography*. London: MacDonald and Jane's, 1976.

Kernodle, Tammy L. "The Blues as the Black Woman's Lament." In *Women's Voices Across Musical Worlds*, edited by Jane A. Bernstein. Boston, MA: Northeastern University Press, 2004.

Killam, Rosemary N. "Women Working: An Alternative to Gans." *Perspectives in New Music* 31, no. 2 (June 1, 1993): 230.

Kimber, Marian Wilson. "Felix and Fanny: Gender, Biography, and History." In *The Cambridge Companion to Mendelssohn*, edited by Peter Mercer-Taylor. Cambridge: Cambridge University Press, 2004: 44.

Kingman, Daniel. *American Music: A Panorama*. New York: Schirmer books, 1998.

Kisby, Fiona. "Urban History, Musicology and Cities and Towns in Renaissance Europe." In *Music and Musicians in Renaissance Cities and Towns*, edited by Fiona Kisby. Cambridge: Cambridge University Press, 2001.

Koskoff, Ellen. "The Sound of a Woman's Voice: Gender and Music in a New York Hasidic Community." In *Women and Music in Cross-Cultural Perspective*. edited by Ellen Koskoff. Westport, CT: Greenwood, 1987a.

Koskoff, Ellen, ed. *Women and Music in Cross-Cultural Perspective*. Westport, CT: Greenwood, 1987b.

Kosman, Joshua. "She Can Sing, But How's She Look? Deborah Voigt's Firing Shows How Opera's Becoming Like Hollywood." *San Francisco Chronicle*, March 15, 2004.

Koza, Julia. "Music and the Feminine Sphere: Images of Women as Musicians in Godey's Lady's Book, 1830–1877." *The Musical Quarterly* 75, no. 2 (June 1, 1991): 103.

Koza, Julia. "Picture This: Sex Equity in Textbook Illustrations." *Music Educators Journal* 78, no. 7 (March 1, 1992): 28.

Kubik, Gerhard. *Africa and the Blues*. Jackson, MS: University Press of Mississippi, 1999.

Kupferberg, Herbert. *The Mendelssohns*. New York: W. H. Allen, 1972.

LaMay, Thomasin. "Composing from the Throat: Maddalena Casulana's Primo Libro de Madrigal, 1568." In *Musical Voices of Early Modern Women: Many-Headed Melodies*, edited by Thomasin LaMay. Burlington, VT and Aldershot: Ashgate, 2005.

Lamb, Roberta. "Composing and Teaching as Dissonant Counterpoint." In *Ruth Crawford Seeger's Worlds: Innovation and Tradition in Twentieth-Century American Music*, edited by Ray Allen and Ellie M. Hisama. Rochester, NY: University of Rochester Press, 2007.

Larsen, Libby. *Missa Gaia*, CD-ROM liner notes. New York: Koch International Classics, 1995.

League of American Orchestras. "Seminar for Women Conductors." 64th National Conference Announcement and Agenda. At www.americanorchestras.org/conference_2009/women_conductors.html (accessed March 11, 2010).

Lister, Linda. "Divafication: The Deification of Modern Female Pop Stars." *Popular Music and Society*, 25, no. 3–4 (January 1, 2001): 1.

Lochhead, Judith. "Texture and Timbre in Barbara Kolb's Millefoglie for Chamber Orchestra and Computer-Generated Tape." 2005. *RILM Abstracts of Music Literature*, EBSCO*host* at www.ebsco.com (accessed June 14, 2010).

Lofaro, Lina. "A Symphony of Her Own." *Time*, July 25, 2005.

Longhi, Elena. "'Songese': Maternal Structuring of Musical Interaction with Infants." *Psychology of Music* 37, no. 2 (April 1, 2009): 195.

Love, Courtney. Transcript of speech to Digital Hollywood online entertainment conference, given in New York on May 16, 2000.

Lukomsky, Vera. "Sofia Gubaidulina: 'My Desire is Always to Rebel, to Swim Against the Stream!'" *Perspectives of New Music* 36, no. 1 (January 1, 1998): 5.

Magliocco, Huga. "A Special Endurance." *ITA Journal*, 20, no. 2 (1992): 22.

Mardinly, Susan J. "Barbara Strozzi: From Madrigal to Cantata." *Journal of Singing: The Official Journal of the National Association of Teachers of Singing* 58, no. 5 (May 1, 2002): 375.

Marranca, Bonnie. "Meredith Monk's Atlas of Sound: New Opera and the American Performance Tradition." *Performing Arts Journal* 14, no. 1 (January 1992).

Marshall, Penny, dir. *A League of Their Own* DVD. Columbia Pictures Corporation, 1992.

Matsugu, Miho. "In the Service of the Nation: Geisha and Kawabata Yasunari's Snow Country." In *The Courtesan's Arts: Cross-Cultural Perspectives*, edited by Martha Feldman and Bonnie Gordon. New York: Oxford University Press, 2006.

Maultsby, Portia K. "Soul." In *African American Music, an Introduction*, edited by Mellonee V. Burnim and Portia K. Maultsby. New York: Routledge, 2006.

McClary, Susan. *Feminine Endings: Music, Gender, and Sexuality*. Minneapolis, MN: University of Minnesota Press, 1991.

Miller, Malcolm. "Between Two Cultures: A Conversation with Shulamit Ran." *Tempo: A Quarterly Review of Modern Music* 58, no. 227 (January 1, 2004): 15.

Mogaka, John, 2009. Interview with Julie Dunbar, November 24, 2009.

Mogaka, Wendy. Interview with Julie Dunbar, November 24, 2009.

Moisala, Pirkko. *Kaija Saariaho*. Urbana, IL: University of Illinois Press, 2009.

Monson, Craig A. "Putting Bolognese Nun Musicians in Their Place." In *Women's Voices Across Musical Worlds*, edited by Jane A. Bernstein. Boston, MA: Northeastern University, 2004: 119.

Monson, Ingrid. "Jazz." In *African American Music, An Introduction*. Edited by Mellonee V. Burnim and Portia K. Maultsby. New York: Routledge, 2006.

Moorefield, Virgil. *The Producer as Composer: Shaping the Sounds of Popular Music*. Cambridge, MA: MIT Press, 2005.

Morath, Max. "May Aufderheide and the Ragtime Women." In *Ragtime: Its History, Composers, and Music*, edited by John Edward Hasse. New York: Schirmer Books, 1985.

NBA (National Band Association). Website. At www.nationalbandassociation.org (accessed February 11, 2010).

Neuls-Bates, Carol, ed. *Women in Music: An Anthology of Source Readings from the Middle Ages to the Present*. New York: Harper and Row, 1982: 18–19.

Neuls-Bates, Carol, ed. *Women in Music: An Anthology of Source Readings from the Middle Ages to the Present*, revised ed. Boston, MA: Northeastern University Press, 1996: 146 and 148–149.

Neuls-Bates, Carol. "Women's Orchestras in the United States, 1925–45." In *Women Making Music*, edited by Jane Bowers and Judith Tick. Chicago, IL: University of Illinois Press, 1987.

New York Times. "A Singer to Wed." *New York Times*, June 8, 1905.

New York Times. "Viennese Ladies' Orchestra." *New York Times*, July 27, 1874.

Newcomb, Anthony. "Courtesans, Muses, or Musicians? Professional Women Musicians in Sixteenth-Century Italy." In *Women Making Music: The Western Art Tradition, 1150–1950*, edited by Jane Bowers and Judith Tick. Urbana, IL: University of Illinois Press, 1986.

NPR's Jazz profiles. Women in Jazz. No date. At www.npr.org/programs/jazzprofiles/archive/women_1.html (accessed February 1, 2010).

Odintz, Andrea. "Technophilia: Women at the Control Board." In *Trouble Girls: The Rolling Stone Book of Women in Rock*, edited by Barbara O'Dair. New York: Random House, 1997.

O'Hagin, Isabel Barbara and David Harnish. "Music as Cultural Identity: A Case Study of Latino Musicians Negotiating Tradition and Innovation in Northwest Ohio." *International Journal of Music Education* 24, no. 1 (April 1, 2006): 56.

Okereke, Grace. "The Birth Song as a Medium for Communicating Woman's Maternal Destiny in the Traditional Community." *Research in African Literatures* 25, no. 3 (September 1, 1994): 19.

Oliveros, Pauline. *Deep Listening* (no date). At www.deeplistening.org/site/content/expandedmusicalinstruments.

Oliveros, Pauline. *Deep Listening: A Composer's Sound Practice*. Bloomington, IN: iUniverse, Inc., 2005.

Oliveros, Pauline. *Deep Listening* CD-ROM liner notes. Elizaville, NY: New Albion Records, 1994.

Oliveros, Pauline and Panaiotis. "Expanded Instrument System." 1992 *Proceedings of the International Computer Music Conference*. San Jose: International Computer Music Association, 1992.

Pendle, Karin and Robert Zierolf. "Composers of Modern Europe, Israel, Australia, and New Zealand." In *Women and Music, a History*, edited by Karin Pendle, 2nd ed. Bloomington, IN: Indiana University Press, 2001.

Pescerelli, Beatrice. *I madrigali di Maddalena Casulana*. Firenze: Leo S. Olschki, 1979: 27.

Pescerelli, Beatrice with James Briscoe. "Maddalena Casulana." In *New Historical Anthology of Music by Women*, edited by James Briscoe. Bloomington, IN: Indiana University Press, 2004.

Pilchak, Angela, ed. "Yi, Chen." *Contemporary Musicians*. Vol. 51. Gale Cengage, 2005. eNotes.com. 2006. At www.enotes.com/contemporary-musicians/yi-chen-biography (accessed June 14, 2010).

Pinsonneault, Albert. "Elisabeth Lutyens' Magnificat." Unpublished paper, 2010.

Placksin, Sally. Interview from *Jazz Profiles, Women in Jazz*. National Public Radio. At www.npr.org/programs/jazzprofiles/archive/women_1.html.

Plantamura, Carol. *Women Composers*. Santa Barbara, CA: Bellerophon Books, 1988.

Pollard, Deborah Smith. "That Text, That Timbre: Introducing Gospel Announcer Edna Tatum." In *Black Women and Music: More than the Blues*, edited by Eileen M. Hayes and Linda F. Williams. Urbana, IL: University of Illinois Press, 2007.

Post, Jennifer C. "Erasing the Boundaries Between Public and Private in Women's Performance Traditions." In *Cecilia Reclaimed: Feminist Perspectives on Gender and Music*, edited by Susan Cook and Judy S. Tsou. Urbańa and Chicago, IL: University of Illinois Press, 1994.

Post, Jennifer C. "Professional Women in Indian Music: The Death of the Courtesan Tradition." In *Women and Music in Cross-Cultural Perspective*, edited by Ellen Koskoff. Westport, CT: Greenwood, 1987.

Potter, Caroline. "Germaine Tailleferre." In *New Historical Anthology of Music by Women*, edited by James R. Briscoe. Bloomington, IN: Indiana University Press, 2004.

Pousset, Damien. "The Works of Kaija Saariaho, Philippe Hurel and Marc-André Dalbavie: Stile Concertato, Stile Concitato, Stile Rappresentativo." *Contemporary Music Review* 19, no. 3 (January 1, 2000): 67.

Predota, Georg A. "Towards a Reconsideration of the Romanesca: Francesca Caccini's Primo Libro delle Musiche and Contemporary Monodic Settings in the First Quarter of the Seventeenth Century." *Recercare: Rivista per lo Studio e la Practica della Musica Antica* 5 (January 1, 1993): 87.

Prizer, William F. "Renaissance Women as Patrons of Music: The North-Italian Courts." In *Rediscovering the Muses: Women's Musical Traditions*, edited by Kimberly Marshall. Boston, MA: Northeastern University, 1993.

Quin, Carol Lynelle. "Fanny Mendelssohn Hensel: Her Contributions to Nineteenth-century Musical Life." 1981. *RILM Abstracts of Music Literature*, EBSCO*host* at www.ebsco.com (accessed June 14, 2010).

Ran, Shulamit. "Performance Notes, *Mirage* Score." King of Prussia, PA: Theodore Presser, 1994.

Raney, Carolyn. "Francesca Caccini, Musician to the Medici, and her Primo Libro (1618)." *RILM Abstracts of Music Literature* (1971), EBSCO*host* at www.ebsco.com (accessed March 4, 2010).

Reagon, Bernice Johnson. *If You Don't Go, Don't Hinder Me*. Lincoln, NE: University of Nebraska Press, 2001.

Reed, Roxanne Regina. "Preaching and Piety: The Politics of Women's Voice in African-American Gospel Music with Special Attention to Gospel Music Pioneer Lucie E. Campbell." *RILM Abstracts of Music Literature* (2003), EBSCO*host* at www.ebsco.com (accessed February 9, 2010).

Regueiro, Patricia. "An Analysis of Gender in a Spanish Music Textbook." *Music Education Research* 2, no. 1 (March 1, 2000): 57.

Reich, Nancy. *Clara Schumann: The Artist and the Woman*. Ithaca, NY: Cornell University Press, 2001.

Reich, Nancy. "Fanny Hensel and the Mendelssohn Family." In *Women's Voices Across Musical Worlds*, edited by Jane Bernstein. Boston, MA: Northeastern University Press, 2004: 24.

Reimer, Bennett. *A Philosophy of Music Education*. Englewood Cliffs, NJ: Prentice-Hall, 1970.

Richardson, Susan. "Heavenly Creatures: the Great Gospel Singers." In *Trouble Girls: The Rolling Stone Book of Women in Rock*, edited by Barbara O'Dair. New York: Random House, 1997.

Riis, Thomas L. *Just Before Jazz: Black Musical Theatre in New York, 1890 to 1915*. Washington, DC: Smithsonian Institution Press, 1989.

Riis, Thomas L. "Musical Theatre." In *African American Music, An Introduction*, edited by Mellonee V. Burnim and Portia K. Maultsby. New York: Routledge, 2006: 185.

Roberts, Robin. *Ladies First: Women in Music Videos*. Jackson, MS: University Press of Mississippi, 1996.

Rohlfing, Mary E. "'Don't Say Nothin' Bad About My Baby': A Reevaluation of Women's Roles in the Brill Building Era of Early Rock 'n Roll." *Critical Studies in Mass Communication*, 13, no 2 (June 1996): 93.

Roma, Catherine. *The Choral Music of Twentieth-Century Women Composers: Elisabeth Lutyens, Elizabeth Maconchy, and Thea Musgrave*. Lanham, MD, Toronto and Oxford: Scarecrow Press, 2006.

Roma, Catherine. "Contemporary British Composers." In *Women and Music, a History*, edited by Karin Pendle, 2nd ed. Bloomington, IN: Indiana University Press, 2001.

Rosand, Ellen. "Barbara Strozzi." In *New Historical Anthology of Music by Women*, edited by James R. Briscoe. Bloomington, IN: Indiana University Press, 2004: 60–62.

Rosand, Ellen. *Opera in Seventeenth-Century Venice: The Creation of a Genre*. Berkeley, CA: University of California Press, 2007.

Rosand, Ellen. "The Voice of Barbara Strozzi." In *Women Making Music*, edited by Judith Tick and Jane Bowers. Urbana, IL: Illinois University Press, 1987: 168–190.

Rosenstiel, Léonie. *Nadia Boulanger, A Life in Music*. New York: W.W. Norton, 1982.

Rüütel, Ingrid. "Traditional Music in Estonia Today." *Fontes Artis Musicae* 51, no. 3–4 (July 1, 2004): 295.

Sadie, Julie Anne. "Musiciennes of the Ancien Régime." In *Women Making Music*, edited by Judith Tick and Jane Bowers. Urbana, IL: Illinois University Press, 1987: 191–223.

Samponaro, Philip. "Oye Mi Canto (Listen to My Song): The History and Politics of Reggaetón." *Popular Music and Society* 32, no. 4 (October 1, 2009): 489.

Sandstrom, Boden. "Women Mix Engineers and the Power of Sound." In *Music and Gender*, edited by Beverly Diamond and Moisala Pirkko. Urbana, IL: University of Illinois Press, 2000.

Schlicht, Ursel. "Better a Jazz Album than Lipstick: The 1956 Jazz Podium Series Reveals Images of Jazz and Gender in Post-War Germany." In *Big Ears: Listening for Gender in Jazz Studies*, edited by Nichole T. Rustin and Sherrie Tucker. Durham, NC: Duke University Press, 2008.

Schnepel, Julie. "Ellen Taaffe Zwilich's Symphony No. 1: Developing Variation in the 1980s." *Indiana Theory Review* 10 (March 1, 1989).

Scott, Joan. "Gender: A Useful Category of Historical Analysis." In *American Historical Review* 91, no. 5 (December 1986): 1053–1075.

Screech, Timon. "Going to the Courtesans: Transit to the Pleasure District of Edo, Japan." In *The Courtesan's Arts: Cross-Cultural Perspectives*, edited by Martha Feldman and Bonnie Gordon. New York: Oxford University Press, 2006.

Seeger, Charles. "Ruth Seeger." In *American Composers on American Music: A Symposium*, edited by Henry Cowell. New York: Frederick Ungar Publishing Company, 1933.

Shapiro, Susan E. "Ecriture Judaique: Where are the Jews in the Western Discourse?" In *Displacements*, edited by Angelika Bammer. Bloomington, IN: Indiana University Press, 1994.

Smith, Julia. *Aaron Copland*. New York: E. P. Dutton & Co., 1953.

Southern, Eileen. *The Music of Black Americans: A History*. New York: W. W. Norton, 1997.

Spiegel, Laurie. "Comments on Common Complaints," *Retiary*, at www.retiary.org/ls/writings/ear_women_article.html (accessed September 11, 2008).

Starr, Larry and Christopher Waterman. *American Popular Music from Minstrelsy to the MP3*. 2nd ed. New York: Oxford University Press, 2006.

Stokes, Martin, ed. *Ethnicity, Identity and Music: The Musical Construction of Place*. Oxford: Berg, 1994.

Stone, Ruth M. *Theory for Ethnomusicology*. Upper Saddle River, NJ: Pearson-Prentice-Hall, 2008.

Straus, Joseph. *The Music of Ruth Crawford Seeger*. Cambridge: Cambridge University Press, 1995.

Sutton, Terri. "Janis Joplin." In *Trouble Girls: The Rolling Stone Book of Women in Rock*, edited by Barbara O'Dair. New York: Random House, 1997.

Swartly, Ariel. "Little Mamas, Wild Women, and Balls of Fire: The Blues." In *Trouble Girls: The Rolling Stone Book of Women in Rock*, edited by Barbara O'Dair. New York: Random House, 1997.

Taylor, Jeffrey. "With Lovie and Lil: Rediscovering Two Chicago Pianists of the 1920s." In *Big Ears: Listening for Gender in Jazz Studies*, edited by Nichole T. Rustin and Sherrie Tucker. Durham, NC: Duke University Press, 2008.

Tick, Judith. "Dissonant Counterpoint Revisited: The First Movement of Ruth Crawford's *String Quartet* 1931." In *A Celebration of American Music: Words and Music in Honor of H. Wiley Hitchcock*, edited by Richard Crawford, R. Allen Lott, and Carol J. Oja. Ann Arbor, MI: University of Michigan Press, 1990.

Tick, Judith. "Passed Away is the Piano Girl: Changes in American Musical Life, 1870–1900." In *Women Making Music*, edited by Jane Bowers and Judith Tick. Chicago, IL: University of Illinois Press, 1987.

Tick, Judith. *Ruth Crawford Seeger: A Composer's Search for American Music*. New York: Oxford University Press, 1997.

Tick, Judith. "Writing the Music of Ruth Crawford into Mainstream Music History." In *Ruth Crawford Seeger's Worlds: Innovation and Tradition in Twentieth-Century American Music*, edited by Ray Allen and Ellie M. Hisama. Rochester, NY: University of Rochester Press, 2007.

Titon, Jeff Todd, ed. *Worlds of Music: An Introduction to the Music of the World's Peoples*, 2nd ed., shorter version. New York: Schirmer Books, 2005.

Titon, Jeff Todd, ed. *Worlds of Music: An Introduction to the Music of the World's Peoples*, 4th ed. New York: Schirmer Books, 2002.

Titon, Jeff Todd, ed. *Worlds of Music: An Introduction to Music of the World's Peoples*, 5th ed. New York: Schirmer Books, 2008.

Tower, Joan. Biography notes. No date. At www.schirmer.com/default.aspx?TabId=2419&State_2872=2&ComposerId_2872=1605 (accessed August 18, 2010).

Tribbett, Marcus Charles. "'Everybody Wants to Buy My Kitty': Resistance and the Articulation of the Sexual Subject of the Blues in Memphis Minnie." *Arkansas Review: A Journal of Delta Studies* 29, no. 1 (April 1, 1998): 42.

Tribbett, Marcus Charles. "Lyrical Struggles: Hegemony and Resistance in English Broadside Ballads and African-American Blues." *RILM Abstracts of Music Literature* (1996), EBSCO*host* at www.ebsco.com (accessed February 9, 2010).

Tucker, Sherrie "Jazz." In *African American Music, An Introduction*. Edited by Mellonee V. Burnim and Portia K. Maultsby. New York: Routledge, 2006.

Tucker, Sherrie. *Swing Shift: "All-girl" Bands of the 1940s*. Durham, NC: Duke University Press, 2001.

Van Gunden, Heidi. *The Music of Pauline Oliveros*. Metuchen, NJ: Scarecrow Press, 1983.

Vergara, Lucy, 2009. Interview with Julie Dunbar, September 7, 2009.
Wald, Gayle F. "Have a Little Talk: Listening to the B-side of History." *Popular Music* 24, no. 3 (2005): 323.
Waleson, Heidi. "Women Composers Find Things Easier—Sort of." *New York Times*, January 28, 1990.
Wallach, Michelle. Interview with Julie Dunbar, November 11, 2009.
Weinbaum, Batya. "Matriarchal Music Making." In *Sounding Off: Music as Subversion/Resistance/Revolution*, edited by Ron Sakolsky and Fred Wei-han Ho. Brooklyn, NY: Autonomedia, 1995.
Whitely, Sheila. *Women in Popular Music: Sexuality, Identity and Subjectivity*. New York: Routledge, 2000.
Zubicaray, Helen de. "On Hildegard's Perception of Pitch in Her Chants." *Sonus: A Journal of Investigations into Global Musical Possibilities* 16, no. 2 (March 1, 1996): 1.

WEBSITES

www.baranstoll.com
www.chesternovello.com
www.deeplistening.org/site/
www.laurieanderson.com
www.npr.org/programs/atc/features/2003/apr/producers/index.html
www.paulineoliveros.us
www.petals.org/Saariaho
www.sfsound.org/tape.html
www.skysound.com
www.trinashoemaker.com
www.womensaudiomission.org

Index

Note: Page numbers in italics refer to illustrations; entries in italics refer to illustrations, films, and musical examples.